Critical and Dialectical Phenomenology

Selected Studies in Phenomenology
and Existential Philosophy 12

Board of Editors

Critical and Dialectical Phenomenology

Edited by
Donn Welton
and
Hugh J. Silverman

State University of New York Press

Published by
State University of New York Press, Albany

For information, address State University of New York Press,
State University Plaza, Albany, N.Y., 12245

Library of Congress Cataloging in Publication Data

Critical and dialectical phenomenology.

  (Selected studies in phenomenology and existential philosophy ;   12)
  Includes index.
  1. Phenomenology.   I. Welton, Donn.   II. Silverman,
Hugh J.   III. Series.
B829.5.C74   1987   121   86-30922
ISBN 0-88706-474-4
ISBN 0-88706-475-2 (pbk.)

10   9   8   7   6   5   4   3   2   1

Contents

Acknowledgements   ix

Introduction   Donn Welton   xi

I. For a Transcendental Semiotics

   1. Linguistic Meaning and Intentionality   2
                  Karl-Otto Apel

II. Hermeneutics and Critical Theory

   2. From Hermeneutics and Critical Theory
      to Communicative Action and
      Post-Structuralism   54
             David M. Rasmussen

   3. Hermeneutics and Critical Theory   64
             George Schrader

   4. Enlightenment as Political   76
             Dick Howard

III. Phenomenology and Dialectics

   5. Phenomenology and the Problem of Action   90
             Jacques Taminiaux

   6. Hegel and Husserl:
      Transcendental Phenomenology
      and the Revolution Yet Awaited   103
             Merold Westphal

7. From Immediacy to Mediation:
   The Emergence of
   Dialectical Phenomenology   136
                           James L. Marsh

IV. **Knowledge and Critique**

8. Heidegger and Peirce:
   Toward New Epistemic Foundations   152
   Patrick L. Bourgeois and Sandra B. Rosenthal

9. Shifting Paradigms:
   Sartre on Critique, Language and
   the Role of the Intellectual   166
                           Thomas Busch

10. Merleau-Ponty and the
    Problem of Knowledge   176
                           Henry Pietersma

V. **Hermeneutics of Persons and Places**

11. Place:
    A Certain Absence   204
                           Joseph C. Flay

12. I and Mine   216
                    Bernard P. Dauenhauer

13. Individuation, Mimetic Engulfment
    and Self-Deception   230
                           Bruce Wilshire

VI. **Critique of Cognitive Psychology**

14. Information Processing and the
    Phenomenology of Thinking   250
                    Christopher A. Aanstoos

15. Merleau-Ponty and the Cognitive Psychology
    of Perception   265
                           Frederick J. Wertz

16. The Structure of Consciousness of
    the Child:
    Merleau-Ponty and Piaget   285
                           Richard Rojcewicz

Contributors   297

Index of Proper Names   299

Acknowledgements

A very special note of thanks to Stephen Michelman for his assistance in the editing of both the collected essays and the introductory paper. His consistency and insights were most appreciated. Sharon Meagher, James Hatley, and Robert Parigi also labored hard on editing authors' copy. Gratitude is due, finally, to Anderson Weekes for long hours of proofreading of the main text and to Mary Bruno for help with the Introduction.

Introduction

The essays in this volume were given as papers at the 1984 and 1985 meetings of the Society for Phenomenology and Existential Philosophy. They represent not only some of the most recent work in continental philosophy in North America and Europe but also certain important transformations of the phenomenological method itself. In this introductory essay let me invite the reader to envision these essays along these lines.

I. Transcendental Semiotics

No thinker on the continent today has contributed more to securing the epistemology underlying Critical Theory[1] than K.-O. Apel. His monumental two-volume work *Transformation der Philosophie*[2] along with his work on the logic of social scientific explanations[3] and the philosophy of C. S. Peirce[4] places him at the very forefront of thinkers concerned with questions of intentionality, meaning, truth, and method. The essay opening this volume gives us an overview of both his approach and his method. To be sure, this paper is but a torso and each section leaves much unsaid. Still, it is the most recent statement of his system and it provides a valuable roadmap that connects the various areas in which he has labored in other essays and books.

Apel's paper is an effort to root a theory of meaning in a three-dimensional semiotics which accords to the pragmatic or interpretative framework the same transcendental status envisioned for the syntactic and semantic frameworks. He provides a third alternative to the approaches of formalistic semantics and the theory of intentional consciousness. Apel shows that there are constitutive pragmatic conditions obtaining not only for the relationship between sign and interpreter or speaker, a point recognized even by Carnap and Morris, but also for the semantic relationship between sign and reference. In particular, the difference between *designatum* (roughly, semantic referent) and *denotatum* (roughly, object in space and time) cannot be clarified just by looking at the representative dimension of a semiotic system but must include a pragmatic or "intentional chain" that ties sign and referent. The mistake of a theory of consciousness, however, is its failure to move beyond monological conditions of constitution to intersubjective conditions of communication. Apel's theory is pragmatic in that action and interaction is accorded primacy over acts. It is transcendental in that it attempts to isolate necessary conditions not only of meaning but of validity, not only by the way we know things but of the way facts are.

II. Hermeneutics and Critical Theory

While Apel is occupied by the confrontation with analytic and pragmatic philosophies of language, it is an engagement with and transcending of hermeneutics that shape the epistemological side of Jürgen Habermas's work. David Rasmussen traces Habermas' development from this starting point into his most recent theory of communicative action.[5] Habermas argues that Gadamer's hermeneutic falls into a kind of relativistic idealism: idealism because the theory of meaning and language has no point of reference (such as production or interaction) beyond itself; relativism because the very universality of its reflection provides us only with a way of understanding or, at best, appropriating diversity, not submitting it to questions of validity. It is Rasmussen's conviction that the theory of communicative action puts Habermas in an especially strong position to argue the efficacy of critical reason in the face of both contemporary hermeneutics and the most recent post-modern attempts to subvert it. We might view these concerns of Habermas as a prolegomena to a theory of democracy, for politics as theory and politics as action become impossible without the legitimacy of critical discourse.

The essay by George Schrader gives us pause, however. He argues that closure to the debate between hermeneutics and critical theory cannot be drawn as quickly as Habermas suggests. The crucial question is whether hermeneutical reflection, as Gadamer employs it, can include the moment of critique so central to Critical Theory. Schrader argues not only that it can but that hermeneutic reflection shows us the illusion of precisely that kind of reflection required by Critical Theory, one that breaks out of the hermeneutical circle. When Habermas presses for an explanatory theory to complement interpretation or understanding, Schrader boldly suggests, he in fact resurrects the Enlightenment ideal of theory without prejudice and makes the mistake of privileging transcendental analysis over "social deliberation."

The suspicion that Schrader introduces at the level of epistemology is analogous to a suspicion that Dick Howard entertains in the context of political theory itself.[6] With the loss of traditional Marxist grounds justifying a theory of political action – the emancipatory praxis of the working class, the necessary movement of history – a Marxist theory of politics loses its necessity. Critical Theory was an attempt to recover that necessity, yet it failed to bridge the gap between the ideal and the real because it identified civil society with capitalist economy and thus treated it only as an irreal reality to be overturned. In addition, it requires theory to tie discourse to actual, historical ensembles and thus is caught in a "discourse of particularity." What Howard goes on to suggest is that a recovery of the "objective" or real foundation for political thought requires that Critical Theory rediscover the political and that its method be complemented by hermeneutics, for it is only the latter that can secure universality for the theory.

III. Phenomenology and Dialectics

The problem of politics just discussed provokes further reflections on the phenomenological method itself. It could be argued that, more than any other issue, the problem of action in a situation of social alienation moved phenomenology beyond its contemplative to its interpretative and dialectical mode.

The piece by Jacques Taminiaux,[7] one of the most important philosophers in Belgium today, shows that the story is not quite so simple. For when phenomenology first approached the problem of action it overwhelmed it, viewing it only in terms that the method itself allowed, terms that actually inscribed ancient distinctions running as far back as the Greeks. Thus, the accounts of action given by such thinkers as Husserl, the early Heidegger, and even the Sartre of the *Critique of Dialectical Reason*[8] must be critically revised if phenomenology is to arrive at a genuine understanding of action. Drawing on the writings of Hannah Arendt, Taminiaux's analysis of active life emphasizes the difference between activities of labor, work and action, and suggests that the world of action and interaction cannot be accurately conceptualized using the traditional distinctions that informed most earlier phenomenological accounts.

The term "dialectics," of course, turns us back to Hegel. The opposition that Merold Westphal traces between Hegel and Husserl is one of the most fruitful studies in this volume.[9] While there are several points of agreement between the two – most importantly their rejection of the method of introspection and the development of a theory of intentionality – they differ strongly over the question of philosophical method.

Husserl is a foundationalist, which means that for him philosophical method, at its best, proports to bring us before certain privileged insights or givens, which themselves serve to legitimate philosophical claims. With his emphasis on immediacy and certainty, at least for what Husserl calls his Cartesian Way, method is attended to only so that it can then properly efface itself before that which it brings to presence. As theory, it attempts to give us those "rules" which regulate the various fields open to description. But in no way is its method actually *constitutive* of such fields.

Hegel's holism reverses the direction of Husserl's procedure, not only because it privileges mediacy over immediacy – what is most immediate is most thin, most abstract, and most in need of the labor of dialectical inclusion – but because truth is a function of the coherence and development of the entire system. There are no freestanding parts, elements or levels that could be sustained apart from the whole. Thus, there are no foundations upon which the edifice of knowledge could be erected.

No doubt we realize today that Hegel's quest for absolute knowledge, that vision of the whole which secures the truth of each part, is a dream without fulfillment. But this loss has had great significance; once our century removed totality from dialectics, it created the space of interpretation. Dialectics, for our time, has become a procedure of supplementation.

In the hands of James Marsh this structural contrast between Husserl and Hegel configures the actual development of the phenomenological movement itself, from Husserl to Habermas. The initial stage of descriptive phenomenology (Scheler, Husserl, early Heidegger, early Merleau-Ponty and early Sartre) took a hermeneutical turn (late Heidegger, Gadamer, Ricoeur), which was then enhanced and transformed by a critical discussion of the psychological (Ricoeur) and of the social unconscious (Critical

Theory). Marsh's essay, more than any other, attunes us to the resources of phenomenology, for it helps us see the continuity between phenomenology and the approaches of hermeneutics and Critical Theory.

IV. Knowledge and Critique

In many respects Thomas Busch finds in Sartre that same turn from a classical to a more dialectical and critical phenomenology that is at least adumbrated by all of the authors in this volume. As Sartre expanded his thought beyond the limits of *Being and Nothingness*,[10] it was no longer the possibility of lucid insight and unfettered freedom but, in the *Critique of Dialectical Reason*, the problem of ambiguity and conditioned existence that increasingly drew his attention. The latter work overcomes the dyadic opposition between the in-itself and the for-itself as consciousness itself is subordinated to praxis and thus is thrown toward that otherness and ambiguity inherent in all forms of action. At the level of method dialectical thought displaces intuition: what in his earlier work could be captured by evidential insight escapes, he realizes, the gaze of the eye. It must be approached obliquely and described in such a way that its movement beyond itself is primary.

One essay that breaks new ground historically is the piece by Patrick Bourgeois and Sandra Rosenthal comparing Heidegger and Peirce. The bridge between these two thinkers is built by looking at their interpretations of Kant.

The temporalization of the categories, what Kant calls schemata, provides an ontological tie, Heidegger suggests, between pure concepts of understanding and the world of experience. Because the categories are transcendental, schemata are, first, "transcendental determinations of time." Yet time is not itself a pure concept, but a pure form of intuition and thus the schemata also form "the horizon of transcendence," of the world as it is present in and for genuine knowledge. The decisive addition (for the authors's purposes) that Heidegger introduces is his interpretation of the schema as scheme-image. At first this surprises us, for Kant expressly contrasts the scheme to the image (*Bild*) and argues that schemata are not pictures or images of the object to which they are related.[11] But Bourgeois and Rosenthal seem to have empirical concepts in view and are speaking about a first-order schematization special to sensible experience. The scheme-image is the representation of the object precisely under the aspect delineated by the empirical concept. Not only does this notion, much like Husserl's concept of types, enable us to capture the Gestalt features of objects, it also allows for an introduction of a theory of existential time much more basic than Kant's elaboration of time through the notion of number.[12]

Because the ontological analysis just proposed necessarily encompasses the being of the knower, there are specific epistemological issues entailed by Heidegger's analysis. Considering them turns us to the thought of Peirce who, more than Heidegger, ties the analysis of schemata to a theory of "vital intentionality."

Peirce argues that imagery, what Heidegger calls the image-scheme, makes possible the application of concepts to experience. At the same time schemata are a condition for the emergence of meaningful experience. Yet, as in Heidegger, significant changes in the Kantian landscape are also found. In place of the notion of productive imagination, which Kant set in contrast to understanding, Peirce changes both by combining them in his concept of habit. The priority of the pragmatic, or what Heidegger calls the ready-to-hand, means that the level of experience as analyzed by Kant in terms of its conditions is a *derived* level; it rests upon more fundamental structures that are essentially open and changing as a result of human action and interaction. Accordingly, Peirce sets no number to the categories nor fixed limits to understanding and this has the effect of making all concepts into what Kant would have called empirical concepts. To put it another way, the movement from sensuous experience to conceptual articulation to transcendental concepts proceeds across a single continuum rather than across different domains. In fact, I think it fair to say that Peirce, as does Heidegger, displaces Kant's emphasis upon concepts and conditions by a theory of meaning and relational contexts – one which incorporates not only the logical but also the affective and teleological dimensions of experience.

If we want to draw out the implications of these ideas for epistemological theory per se, however, we must turn to the essay by Henry Pietersma. Merleau-Ponty's own conception of intentionality is sufficiently close to what we have just sketched to see his work on the theory of truth as compatible with Peirce. One of Pietersma's most suggestive ideas is that the new view of intentionality proposed by thinkers such as Heidegger, Peirce and Merleau-Ponty – the view that all objects of experience are contextual and that such objects and our cognitive involvement with them form a unitary matrix – brings with it a redefinition of the task and scope of epistemology. The older Cartesian problem of general doubt no longer makes sense because such doubt is impossible to formulate without already assuming precisely that perceptual faith in the world that it attempts to dissolve. In place of this Merleau-Ponty deals with the problem of specific doubt, the problem of appraising individual claims and theories, and what we might call the problem of emergent truths, the problem of tracing the sense-history of certain prevailing conceptions.

Pietersma praises several important features of Merleau-Ponty's theory of truth. He applauds its stress on the way presence to a subjet is always nested in a kind of intersubjective view of the object, on a relativity which is really a necessary relationality of cognitive claims, on the non-identity of object-perceived and object-perceived-as-reflected-upon, and, finally, on his treatment of Kantian type categories as second-order ideas that provide logical but not existential conditions of the experienced world. It is also true that Merleau-Ponty rejects the notion of a pure thinker, a subject whose own transparency ultimately requires us to treat things as ideas. In its place we find a theory of the obscure subject, one whose lack of lucidity, paradoxically, accounts for the visibility of things as things. Yet Merleau-Ponty, Pietersma suggests, does introduce an underlying coherence between subject and object through his notion of flesh. And this may entail that the bounds of what is true are kept within what can be rendered evident. In short, Pietersma asks whether Merleau-Ponty, like some idealists of the past century, is not left with a problem of accounting for error.

V. Hermeneutics of Persons and Places

Interpreting the person phenomenologically requires, first of all, envisioning the condition of our situatedness, that peculiar convergence of space and time that we call place. Joseph Flay[13] works with a very productive contrast between objective places, those relative to each other and given in a matrix of space/time coordinates, and primordial place, that which is not within the objective matrix, functioning as a necessary condition or, better, clearing for objective place. Heidegger calls this the place of *Da-sein* and, as in our use of indexicals, it forms that constant here-now which I am and which allows the contrasts between here and there, now and then, this and that to have specific references.

In Flay's hands this contrast is used not only to designate the ambiguous place of persons, caught as they are in two different kinds of place, but also to lend some credibility to the metaphysical notion of presence. In the case of objective place, since we have places that are only and always relative to each other, what is absent can be defined in terms of presence, i.e., as what is not present relative to what is. But in the case of primordial place we are dealing with an absolute presence lacking any internal differentiation between presence and absence precisely because it is not relative and because the place where I am is never absent. And yet, by one of those inversions philosophy tends to misconstrue, this primordial presence is also a primordial absence for, as the place in which all relative absence and presence is found, it can never be made present.

Over the past five decades increasingly complex explanatory theories – whether sociobiology, artificial intelligence, or the structuralism of Levi-Strauss and Althusser – have in effect removed from "mind," as Descartes understood this term, those traits thought to set it in opposition to "body." The nucleus of traits, necessary for establishing a difference between mind and the physical world while it preserved an identity between body and nature, has been subjected to detailed scrutiny. Yet the very effort to understand the mind helped to introduce a new model of rationalization. Interestingly enough, the rationalization process itself with its attempt to construct nomological models provides a "grammar" to various theories of mind that lies deeper than our usual contrasts between materialistic, computational and structuralist models. Since this grammar applies equally well to the analysis of the body, the uniqueness of mind and, thereby, the distinctness of persons seems to dissolve.

What is most suggestive about Bernard Dauernahauer's essay "I and Mine"[14] is his attempt to define a notion of the person that rejects such a rationalization of the problem. He does so by arguing for a notion of the person that accepts the *logical* possibility that we could supply both necessary and sufficient conditions for all human phenomena, but that stresses the idea that the *material* or causal intervention of human agents in history is such that a different course of action, a novel solution, a new direction could have also occurred. It is a notion of person that thinks of history as moved from within.

The dramatic unity of the self argued for in Dauenhauer's paper finds rich description in Bruce Wilshire's analysis of the notion of individuation. In some respects Wilshire takes the objective place of the self established by Dauenhauer and fills it with a dynamic life.[15] He does so by inviting us to incorporate the first-person point of view into our theory in such a way that we do not return to the solidarity of a Cartesian *ego-cogito* but rather uncover a self in need of being discovered and, thus, a self with possible degrees of individuation.

Finding Schelling much more suggestive than Hegel on this issue, Wilshire attempts to overturn the tacit ego-centricism animating most theories of personal identity. His novel notion of "mimetic engulfment," – a situation, neither voluntary nor involuntary, where one literally incorporates the gestures, roles or even life-styles of another – is used to explore the range of self-deception. He argues that the clarity and degree of individuation of the self decreases as engulfment increases. Suggestively, Wilshire thinks of this interplay between engulfment and self-deception not as a "problem" that can be cured but an inescapable structural feature of communial life, a constant challenge to the project of achieving individuality.

VI. Critique of Cognitive Psychology

One of the genuine strengths of continental philosophy is the way it views direct engagement with other disciplines as internal to the very process of philosophizing itself. The final three essays demonstrate this by looking at certain aspects of cognitive psychology.

Much of the work in the interface between continental philosophy and psychology has focused on psychoanalysis and has effected a hermeneutical reinterpretation at the level of method in order to explore fundamental features not only of psychic life, but also of the culture at large. Paul Ricoeur's book on Freud[16] and the work of Jacques Lacan[17] set the stage for ongoing research at this crossroads.[18] Yet at the same time, following the lead of Maurice Merleau-Ponty in his *Phenomenology of Perception*,[19] there have been a number of psychologists and philosophers working at the interface of phenomenology and recent experimental psychology.[20] The three papers concluding this volume were written by researchers indebted to Merleau-Ponty and to the valuable work in this country of Amedeo Giorgi.[21] They deal with issues and problems central to contemporary cognitive psychology by taking critical distance to recent experimental work and then providing fresh insight into the matter at hand.

Even the most enthusiastic researchers in cognitive psychology quickly recognized major difficulties in applying an information processing model to such cognitive skills as perception and imagination. What Christopher Aanstoos boldly suggests, however, is that thinking, an activity considered to be most susceptible to such modeling, exhibits a number of traits that are not computational and thus cannot be understood as cases of processing discrete bits or elements according to predetermined rules. Thinking, for the most part, is task-oriented and concerned as much with relations *implied* in any given situation as with focal objects or items. It is not hard to tell why current information processing models are blind to this phenomena: the reduction of information to binary choices between equally weighted, explicit alternatives allows no place for what is not explicit and what is not isolatable by binary parsing. It seems that though the cybernetic branch of cognitive psychology sets itself in opposition to behaviorism, the objectivistic and mechanistic fashion in which it views information processing betrays a deeper alliance. As Aanstoos argues, there has not been a genuine paradigm change.

Cybernetic modeling is not the only branch of current experimental psychology, as Frederick Wertz goes on to show. There are any number of researchers, especially in perception theory, who have overcome the limits of an information processing approach and who offer a much broader understanding of cognitive psychology than is provided by a cybernetic model. What Wertz suggests is that these research programs operate with ideas and models quite close to those offered by Merleau-Ponty. Like Merleau-Ponty, Ulrich Neisser strikes a third alternative between the strong realism of J. J. Gibson and the constructivism of most information processing models. He introduces a notion about which we have already heard much, that of *schema*: something "internal" to the perceiver and responsible for guiding the process of perception but not for composing its content. Yet in spite of other striking similarities − taking ordinary objects in their "ecological" context as a starting point, the transcendent nature of perception, the primacy of wholes (meaning) over parts (elements) − the concept of schema also shows their most significant point of divergence. Neisser's characterization of schemata is itself an ambiguous discourse, caught between physicalism and mentalism. Merleau-Ponty theoretically displaces a notion like Neisser's through his theory of the incarnate subject and thus proposes a notion of schema which integrates the perceiver into the perceptual practices of the body, while it distinguishes between the corporeal level and the higher order of representation or conception.

Not only does the phenomenological theory proposed by Merleau-Ponty set itself in contrast to Neisser's broad version of cognitive psychology, it also undertakes a critique of Piaget's version as well. Richard Rojcewicz, using an untranslated text of Merleau-Ponty's, shows how Piaget's theory of the thought and perceptual world of the child is intellectualist. Piaget's analysis of the child's world suffers from the retrospective fallacy of reading essentially adult and theoretical contrasts back into the experience of the child, while his theory of child perception assumes that the schemata of perception are superimposed upon uninterpreted data or elements making up the perceptual object. In Merleau-Ponty's account, the child's thought functions anterior to contrast of material and ideal, physical and psychical. In the case of perception there are no elements except as moments of a whole, organized by structures that are more than the mere combinatory features of the data. In defending Merleau-Ponty against Piaget's counterreply, Rojcewicz argues that phenomenology is not first-person, introspective analysis but, in its reflective concern with the way things are, is both "objective" (capable of being confirmed) and concrete (concerned with phenomena intersubjectively available).

Conclusion

The emergence of new fields of empirical research, the concern with the possibility of political theory, and the confrontation of a theory of intentionality with our contemporary appreciation of the depth of language are some of the factors that have moved phenomenology beyond its first formulations in the early work of Husserl and Heidegger. As the essays in this volume show, phenomenology becomes critical when it discovers that a simple, reflective apprehension of "the things themselves" is not possible and that analysis involves a "dismantling" of what would otherwise remain buried, an interrogation of what would otherwise not speak. Furthermore, it becomes dialectical when the process of thinking requires us to think historically and to realize that what something is, as well as what it is not, lies both within and beyond the conflict of interpretations.

Donn Welton
SUNY at Stony Brook

Notes

1. For a general introduction to Critical Theory see David Held, *Introduction to Critical Theory: Horkheimer to Habermas* (Berkeley: University of California Press, 1980). An assessment of Critical Theory that figures very much in current discussions is Albrecht Wellmer, *Kritische Gesellschaftstheorie und Positivismus* (Frankfurt am Main: Suhrkamp, 1969); *Critical Theory of Society*, trans. by John Cumming (New York: Seabury Press, 1974). On the philosophy of language envisioned by Critical Theory see *Sprachpragmatik und Philosophie*, ed. by K.-O. Apel (Frankfurt am Main: Suhrkamp, 1976).

2. Karl-Otto Apel, *Transformation der Philosophie*, Vol. 1: *Sprachanalytik, Semiotik, Hermeneutik*; Vol. 2: *Das Apriori der Kommunikationsgemeinschaft* (Frankfurt am Main: Suhrkamp, 1973); *Towards a Transformation of Philosophy*, trans. by Glyn Adey and David Frisky (Boston: Routledge & Kegan Paul, 1980).

3. *Die Erklären-Verstehen Kontroverse in Transcendental-Pragmatischer Sicht* (Frankfurt am Main: Suhrkamp, 1979); *Understanding and Explanation: A Transcendental-Pragmatic Perspective*, trans. by Georgia Warnke (Cambridge: MIT Press, 1984).

4. *Der Denkweg von Charles S. Peirce* (Frankfurt am Main: Suhrkamp, 1975).

5. Jürgen Habermas, *Theorie des kommunikativen Handlens*, Vol. 1: *Handlungsrationalität und gesellschaftliche Rationalisierung*; Vol. 2: *Zur Kritik der funktionalistischen Vernunft* (Frankfurt am Main: Suhrkamp, 1981); *The Theory of Communicative Action*, Vol. 1: *Reason and the Rationalization of Society*, trans. Thomas McCarthy (Boston: Beacon Press, 1984). See also *Vorstudien und Ergänzungen zur Theorie der kommunikativen Handelns* (Frankfurt am Main: Suhrkamp, 1984).

6. A fuller discussion of his ideas is found in Dick Howard, *From Marx to Kant* (SUNY Press, 1985).

7. Some of the ideas in this essay echo his earlier work *La Nostalgie de la Grèce à l'aube de l'idéalisme allemand* (The Hague: Martinus Nijhoff, 1967). Two other books by him are *Le regard et l'excédent* (The Hague: Martinus Nijhoff, 1977) and *Dialectic and Difference: Finitude in Modern Thought*, trans. James Decker and Robert Crease (Atlantic Highlands, New Jersey: Humanities Press, 1985).

8. Jean Paul Sartre, *Critique de la raison dialectique* (Paris: Gallimard, 1960); *Critique of Dialectical Reason*, trans. by A. Sheridan-Smith (London: NLB, 1976).

9. For his interpretation of Hegel see his *History and Truth in Hegel's Phenomenology* (Atlantic Highlands, New Jersey: Humanities Press, 1979).

10. Jean Paul Sartre, *L'Etre et le neànt: Essai d'ontologie phénoménologique* (Paris: Gallimard, 1943); *Being and Nothingness*, trans. by Hazel Barnes (New York: Philosophical Library, 1956).

11. Immanuel Kant, *Kritik der reinen Vernunft*, ed. by Raymund Schmidt (Hamburg: Felix Meiner, 1956), A140/B179ff.

12. *Kritik der reinen Vernunft*, A143/B182.

13. For his analysis of Hegel see his *Hegel's Quest for Certainty* (Albany: SUNY Press, 1984).

14. This essay pursues a different set of issues than his earlier book *Silence: The Phenomenon and its Ontological Significance* (Bloomington: Indiana University Press, 1980).

15. For further analysis see his *Role Playing and Identity* (Bloomington: Indiana University Press, 1982).

16. *Freud and Philosophy* (New Haven: Yale University Press, 1970).

17. One of the only pieces to appear in English translation is *The Four Fundamental Concepts of Psycho-Analysis*, trans. by Alan Sheridan (New York: W. W. Norton, 1978), which is Vol. 11 of *Le Seminaire du Jacques Lacan* (éditions du Seuil).

18. See most recently Julia Kristeva, *Soleil noir; dépression et mélaucholie* (Paris: Gallimard, 1987).

19. *Phénoménologie de la Perception* (Paris: Gallimard, 1945); *Phenomenology of Perception*, trans. by Colin Smith (New York: Routledge & Keegan Paul, 1962).

20. See, for example, Patrick Heelan, *Space-Perception and the Philosophy of Science* (Berkeley: University of California Press, 1983) and, most recently, Edward Casey *Remembering: A Phenomenological Study* (Bloomington: Indiana University Press, 1987).

21. A statement of his program can be found in Amedeo Giorgi, *Psychology as a Human Science: A Phenomenologically Based Approach* (New York: Harper and Row, 1970).

Part I.
For a
Transcendental Semiotics

1. Linguistic Meaning and Intentionality: The Compatibility of the "Linguistic Turn" and the "Pragmatic Turn" of Meaning-Theory within the Framework of a Transcendental Semiotics

Karl-Otto Apel

Exposition

From the somewhat complicated subtitle of my paper it becomes obvious that there are some presuppositions of my whole project that need to be clarified in advance — presuppositions concerning facts as well as concerning terms: for example, the terms "linguistic turn," "pragmatic turn," and especially the somewhat esoteric term "transcendental semiotics." The best way for me to clarify, at least initially and approximately, those presuppositions is to tell a story about the prehistory of the present stage of the philosophy of language and semiotics from my subjective perspective. This might reveal and expose to some extent my own pre-notions and prejudices in the matter; and thereby provide better preconditions for mutual understanding — at least at the beginning — than would be by abstract definitions and apparently self-sufficient (unconditional) arguments.

I shall try to develop my argument within the context of my story which will gradually become a systematic account of the problems.

The frame of my background-story may be marked by the following scheme of three stages:

I. The *linguistic* turn in philosophy and the abstractive fallacy of *transcendental semanticism*

II. The *pragmatic* turn as the overcoming of the abstractive fallacy of transcendental semanticism and hence as the completion of the linguistic turn as *transcendental-pragmatic* turn within the framework of a transcendental semiotics

III. The overturning of the *pragmatic* turn by reducing meaning to *pre-linguistic intentions* and the possibility of its refutation.

Let me then start out with a very rough and short reconstruction of the first stage.

I. The Linguistic Turn in Philosophy and the Abstractive Fallacy of Transcendental Semanticism

The first part or stage of my story may be represented by the *Tractatus Logico-Philosophicus* of the early Wittgenstein and also, in a slightly different sense, by the constructive *logical semantics* of Carnap and Tarski. In Wittgenstein's *Tractatus* the *linguistic* turn of First Philosophy becomes obvious as a *transcendental-semantic* turn, so to speak. As such, it is marked first by the rigorous and thoroughgoing substitution of *linguistic* concepts in the place of the *mentalistic* concepts of modern philosophy from Descartes to Husserl, such as consciousness, judgment, thought, or intentionality. A good example of this substitution is sentence 4: "Der Gedanke ist der sinnvolle Satz." ("The thought is the meaningful sentence.")

This first mark of the *linguistic turn* is supplemented by a second one which definitively determines the transcendental-semantic character of Wittgenstein's linguistic turn. What I mean is the replacement, so to speak, of Kant's "supreme principle of synthetic judgements" (for example, that "the conditions of the possibility of experience are the conditions of the possibility of the objects of experience") by an equivalent postulate with regard to the *transcendental-logical conditions of pure language* as being the *conditions of the possibility of facts as elements of a describable world*. This transcendentalist interpretation of the *Tractatus*, which was thoroughly carried through by Eric Stenius,[1] is sometimes called into question, but, in my opinion, it is sufficiently confirmed by Wittgenstein himself, e.g., in the following dictum from *Vermischte Bemerkungen*:

> Die Grenze der Sprache zeigt sich in der Unmöglichkeit, die Tat-sache zu beschreiben, die einem Satz entspricht . . . , ohne eben den Satz zu wiederholen. (Wir haben es hier mit der Kantischen Lösung des Problems der Philosophie zu tun.)
>
> The limit of language shows itself by the impossibility of describing the fact that corresponds to a sentence . . . without repeating precisely that sentence. (We are dealing here with the Kantian solution to the problem of philosophy.)[2]

I would like to nail down the point of this statement by calling it the principle of the onto-semantic autonomy and methodological non-transcendability of language; and I want to make clear from the beginning that, in a certain sense still to be clarified, I consider this principle an irreversible standard of this century's philosophy and a criterion by which at least part of the meaning of the so-called linguistic turn is defined.

However, on Wittgenstein's account in the *Tractatus* the meaning of linguistic sentences about facts is not only intranscendable – at least in an intersubjectively valid form – by a *pre-linguistic intuition* of facts in themselves but even less so by a *meta-linguistic reflection* (i.e., reflection upon the representative function of language by language); for, on Wittgenstein's account, there is no self-referential use of language. Hence, Wittgenstein's own metalinguistic sentences about the relationship between the structure of language and the structure of the world are denounced and renounced as "nonsensical" at the end of the *Tractatus*, as is well known.[3]

This paradoxical overstatement of the transcendental character and function of the structure of sentences implies among other things that there is no I or subject of meaning-intentions or interpretations that could provide a transcendental status not only to the logical struc-ture of language but also to the reflective use of language (or to reflective conventions about the use of language). Instead, there is only a *transcendental I* that – like an "extensionless point" – is absorbed, so to speak, by the logical form of language, such that the "limits of language are the limits of my world" and "solipsism coincides with pure realism."[4]

In my opinion, this version of linguistic transcendentalism has at best a degree of plausibility on the following presuppositions:

1. there should be only one pure language or at least only one logical deep structure of all possible languages, that prescribes

the ontological structure of the describable world once and for all, so to speak, so that there would not be any need for a reflective communication about language or for conventions about the logical grammar of language;

2. the whole language should consist of propositional sentences which have only one function, namely that of a representation of states of affairs so that there are no self-expressive and communicative functions of language that could serve as a basis for a reflective communication about language and thus even for reflective conventions about its use;

3. the reference of signs to real objects (within the context of the representation of existing states of affairs by propositions) should be guaranteed somehow by the structure of language (say, by the depicting function of elementary sentences as protocols of facts).

The first part of these presuppositions – that is the idea of one pure language or at least one logical deep structure of all possible languages – was given up already by R. Carnap; it was replaced, according to the "principle of tolerance", by a pluralism of possible syntactico-semantical frameworks which took over, so to speak, the quasi-transcendental function of prescribing the structure of scientific descriptions and explanations of the world of experience.[5]

Now, even if Carnap's "principle of tolerance" with regard to the logical form of language might not be completely justifiable, in any event it became clear in this context that Wittgenstein's principle of the intranscendability of the syntactico-semantical form of language *has* to be transcended in a sense by the principle of metalinguistic reflection upon language, and that means, finally, reflective communication by language not only about (conventions about) the logical form of artificial languages that are to be constructed, but also about the use of the non-formalizable language that is presupposed by the construction of artificial languages as the ultimate pragmatic metalanguage, so to speak.

This methodological problem-situation already demonstrates that the quasi-transcendental conception of syntactico-semantical frameworks, which leads from Wittgenstein's *Tractatus* to the logical semantics of Carnap and Tarski, suffers from an abstractive fallacy; in other words, it has to be supplemented by the conception of a (transcendental) pragmatics that could deal with the subjective-intersubjective conditions of the possibility of reflective communication by language about language. Carnap however, as is well known, did not recognize these problems as those of a theoretical philosophy but precluded reflection upon them by declaring all so-called "external questions" about the constitution of "semantical frameworks" to be purely "practical questions."[6]

In close connection with this aspect of the abstractive fallacy of logical semantics stands another one also inherited from Wittgenstein's *Tractatus*: that of *reference* to the *real*, or in Carnap's terminology, that of *verification*. For it quickly became clear that this problem transcended the scope of Tarski's explication of the concept of truth for abstract, constructed semantical systems. Should there not also be a problem of a transcendental-pragmatic explication of a criteriologically relevant concept of truth that could serve as a basis for the methodology of *verification*?[7] Carnap sees here, however, not a further problem of theoretical philosophy, but only a problem of *empirical pragmatics*, i.e., of an empirical (behavioristic) psychology of the scientific behavior of verification.

At this point Charles W. Morris intervened in the development with his "Foundations of the Theory of Signs"[8] where he proposed a three-dimensional semiotics consisting of "syntactics," "semantics" and "pragmatics." Thereby, Morris, in a sense, brought to bear on the issue Charles S. Peirce's conception of a semiotics that is based on the triadic or three place relation of the sign-function or semiosis; namely, the relation between the sign itself, its real referent, and its user or interpreter. But, on a closer look into the matter, this claim of Morris's turns out to be thoroughly misleading. For the pragmatic dimension, by which Morris actually supplements Carnap's logical syntactics and semantics, is not allowed to take over the same quasi-transcendental status as the syntactico-semantic framework has in Carnap's account. That is to say: the intentional or interpretative use of the framework is not reflectively integrated, so to speak, into the quasi-transcendental function of the syntactico-semantical framework, but is conceived only as a possible object of empirical science, i.e., as a possible object of the semantic sign reference which already presupposes the syntactico-semantical framework and its actual interpretation (see Figure I).

The reason for this depotentiation of the pragmatic dimension of semiosis, or respectively, semiotics is to be found in the dogma of post-Russellian or post-Tarskian logical semantics that there could not be such a thing as a linguistic self-reference of the sign-function or semiosis, for example, of the meaning-intentions or the meaning-interpretations of the human subjects of semiosis as subjects. As a consequence, Morris and Carnap (who eventually accepted Morris's proposals) could only conceive of pragmatics as a matter of empirical behavioristics or, beyond that, at best as a matter of a constructive-

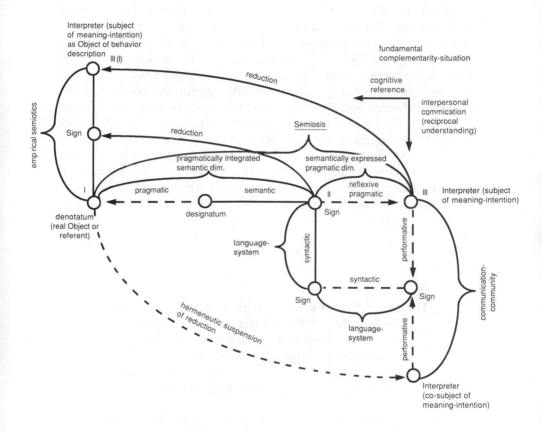

reduction of the PEIRCEan scheme of semiosis within the frame of Logical Empirism and Behaviorsim (CARNAP and MORRIS)

transcendental-pragmatic supplementation (integration) of the scheme of semiosis within the frame of Transcendental Semiotic

FIGURE I. Syntactico-semantical Framework

formal pragmatics, that is, of a metalinguistic constructing of a syntactico-semantical framework for an empirical description of the use of language.[9]

But it seems clear that such a program of pragmatics cannot deal *reflectively* with the pragmatic dimension of the constitution — say by explicit conventions — of syntactico-semantical frameworks for empirical descriptions of the world. Hence it cannot deal with the quasi-transcendental functions of the pragmatic dimension of semiosis. Nor can it complete the linguistic turn of First Philosophy by showing that the whole triadic function of semiosis in Peirce's sense is the transcendental semiotic condition of the possibility of our having intersubjectively valid knowledge about the world. On the contrary, Morris's and Carnap's introduction of the pragmatic dimension of semiosis reconfirmed the abstrative fallacy of the semanticist stage of the linguistic turn (see figure I).[10]

In what follows, I will try to illustrate in an affirmative way the difference between the Morris/Carnap conception of pragmatics and my own idea of a transcendental pragmatics within the framework of a transcendental semiotics. I thereby come to deal with the second part of my story.

II. The Pragmatic Turn of Meaning-Theory as the Overcoming of the Abstractive Fallacy of Transcendental Semanticism and as the Completion of the Linguistic Turn as Transcendental-Pragmatic Turn within the Framework of Transcendental Semiotics

On the condition of the triadic or three place relation structure of the sign-function or semiosis, there are two aspects or directions for a necessary overcoming of the abstractive fallacy of semanticism: one with regard to the so-called semantic dimension of sign-reference and one with regard to the so-called pragmatic dimension of sign-use. The reason for this double aspect to the problem lies in the fact that even the semantic dimension of reference poses a problem of *pragmatics*, as has to be shown. Let us then first consider the so-called semantic dimension of sign-reference (see Figure I, left side of the scheme).

II. 1. The Integration of Semantics and (Transcendental) Pragmatics with regard to the Semantic Dimension of Sign-reference

Contrary to Morris's suggestion in the *Foundations*,[11] it has to be pointed out that the problem of identifying the real *denotatum*, which may or may not correspond to a *designatum* in the world of space and time, is not *only* a matter of the semantic dimension of a syntactico-semantical system. This is easy to recognize if one considers the fact that an abstract semantical system of language may contain *designata* that cannot at all be identified as *denotata*, as, e.g., unicorns or hell or Santa Claus. Hence identifying a denotatum is a matter not only of the semantic but also of the pragmatic dimension of semiosis. There has to be a sign-*interpreter* (see Figure I, right side of the triadic scheme of semiosis) in order to identify the *real denotatum* of a sign (Figure I, left side of the triadic scheme of semiosis).

But even Morris's pragmatics, i.e. his account of "sign-mediated behavior,"[12] cannot show what identifying the referent of a proper name (or identifying an individual referent of a general name) really is. For he can at best describe an external causal chain of behavior that is supposed to connect the original object of denotation with the "organism" that uses the name (see Figure I, left side, "empirical semiotics"). But, as J. Searle has recently shown once more in a brilliant discussion of the "causal theory of reference,"[13] an external description of the causal chain of behavior can never ensure that the meaning-intention of the user of a name correctly *refers* to its denotatum. In the case of a so-called historical causal chain between the original baptism of a thing and the actual use of the proper name, the intentional content of the name may very well have changed at a certain stage of the chain, notwithstanding the continuous causal connection of verbal behavior. This happened with many proper names – as, e.g., with the name "Madagaskar" which before Marco Polo referred to some part of continental Africa – and, with many general names whose etymological meaning is different from their actual meaning.

Thus it becomes clear that a pragmatics of identifying denotata must simultaneously be an account of causal *and* intentional chains. It must be able, in principle, to trace the use of a name down to a situation where the meaning of the name – be it a proper name or a general name – can be ostensively introduced, or reintroduced, in such a way that the user can intentionally and reflectively identify an existing and hence also causally effective referent. This is precisely the way Peirce has explained the function of identifying real denotata with the aid of indexical signs.[14] One should think that identification of real referents as denotata of signs is a case of the complete integration of all three dimensions of the triadic sign-function or semiosis. For, in the situation of identifying a denotatum as an instance of a general name, the meaning-intention of the sign-user must not only coincide with the perception of the existing and causally effective referent but also fit in with the syntactico-semantical framework of a language. Thus identifying a denotatum is a case of an encounter with the real world that is at the same time *mediated by language* and language-constitutive. Therefore, it may serve as a paradigm-case for understanding what may be called the *pragmatic completion* of the linguistic turn in philosophy within the framework of transcendental semiotics.

Thus far my semiotic account of the problems of sign-reference has been very roughly sketched. It passed over many intricate problems and, in order to suggest the possibility of a transcendental-semiotic integration of pragmatics and semantics, it neglected intentionally the differences between certain cases of identifying denotata: thus for example the difference between a subsumptive identifying of an exemplar of a well-known species and, on the other hand, introducing a new general name in order to be able to subsume a hitherto unknown phenomenon under this heading; or the difference between these procedures and identifying the referent of a proper name.

In what follows I will discuss these problems a bit more thoroughly from the point of view of the following question: Is it really true that in all these cases a complete integration of the semantic and the pragmatic dimension of language comes about? That is to say, may one still claim, according to the linguistic turn, that mediation by language is a nontranscendable condition of the possibility of our identifying something as something and thus of our intersubjective knowledge of the world?

One could conceive of objections to this claim as coming from two perspectives. On the one hand, one could think that identifying the real denotatum is a matter of the mental intentionality of a subject of perception that is independent from, or goes beyond, the meaning of the signs of a language-system. Thus the problem of identifying would lead us back to a mentalistic philosophy of intentionality, say in the sense of Brentano's philosophical psychology or of Husserlian phenomenology. This seems indeed to be the opinion that underlies certain tendencies of a new philosophy of intentionality. On the other hand, one could rather argue that intentionality and linguistic meaning in the sense of intensionality belong together, whereas reference to the real denotatum would lead us beyond both of these notions — say towards grasping the real essence or nature of things which causally determines the meaning of signs qua extensionality of names. This latter contention seems to make up the point of the post-Wittgensteinian realistic semantics of Saul Kripke and Hilary Putnam.[15] This conception could also be considered incompatible with the linguistic turn of philosophy, or so it appears.

In view of these diverging trends of the present theory of meaning qua reference, I shall try to show two things. First, there are indeed different empirical affinities, and hence priorities, of the three ways of understanding meaning, namely extensionality, intensionality and intentionality, with regard to the problem of reference. But, notwithstanding these differences, there is also an internal relationship between the three concepts of meaning, such that we cannot, in the last resort, separate them from one another. In other words, although the theory of reference leads beyond semanticism (in the Carnapian sense and in a narrow sense of linguistic meaning or usage) it does not lead beyond the transcendental-semiotic postulate of an integration of the semantics and pragmatics of language. I shall try to show this in a triangular discussion, so to speak, with regard to the relations between the three concepts of meaning.

II. 1.1.

To begin with, I want to argue that it is not possible to separate the notion of referential intentionality, say in the perceptual identifying of something *as* something, from the notion of public meaning qua intensionality of proper or general names. This holds in my opinion, although it is often possible and necessary to ascertain a difference between the factual intentionality of perceptual reference and the conventional meaning qua intensionality of those words in the light of which the identification of the referent is possible. In this context the factual intentionality may both fall short of the public meaning qua intension or even transcend it in grasping the real essence of things. What does this mean?

From a logician's point of view Frege was right to make an abstractive distinction between *Sinn* and *Bedeutung* — or, for that matter, intensionality and extensionality — of names, on the one hand, and the psychologically relevant concept of meaning-intentions (e.g. "ideas" in the sense of John Locke), on the other hand. He thereby was able to separate methodically between ideal, "timeless" and "intersubjectively valid" meanings, to be dealt with in the formalizable context of logical truth transfer and particular, subjective mental states, to be dealt with in empirical psychology. If one were to argue that, after all, different people can be in the same psychological state – say by grasping the same intersubjectively valid meaning – Frege could answer that this is just a postulate from the point of view of the logical semantics of *Sinn*. Indeed, a psycho-linguist would never find empirically the *same* state of mind in two different people, or even in the same human being at different time but only (at best) sufficiently similar states of intending the same public meaning; the latter being, so to speak, the regulative principle of their thought and the necessary institutional fiction of their possible communication by language. That is to say, public meanings of sign-types of language, to be explicated as intensions, are indeed the ideal standards or paradigms of meaning-identity, and hence of intersubjective (sometimes called "objective") validity of meaning. Platonism, always recurrent among mathematicians and logicians, is just an ontological hypostatization of the abstractive notion of public meaning or intensionality.

From an epistemological point of view, however, the abstractive separation between public meaning-intensions and subjective meaning-intentions has to be suspended, notwithstanding Frege's verdict against psychologism. The reason for this postulate is that a logical semantics of a Fregean or Carnapian type would loose its meaningful function if we did not suppose that the ideal, intersubjectively valid meanings of language-signs can be grasped, in principle, by every human being qua subject of meaning-intentions. Otherwise we could not understand that different people can agree, in principle, on the intersubjective validity of an argument. Furthermore, it must even be possible for every subject of meaning-intention to contribute by his or her meaning-intentions to the public meaning-intensions. Otherwise we could not understand that human experience can constitute the content of public meaning-intensions of language-signs; for it is only the human subject of meaning-intentions that may realize the reference dimension of public meanings by identifying real *denotata*, as we know already. In short, suspending the abstractive separation between public meaning-intensions and subjective meaning-intentions turns out to be an implication of what we have postulated before under the label of an integration of abstract semantics by pragmatics.

However, after what we have said about the difference, in principle, between ideal, timeless meaning-intensions and empirical concepts of mental states, it must also be clear that the *subject* who grasps ideal meaning-intensions by meaning-intentions cannot be a possible *object* of empirical psychology (or another discipline of empirical pragmatics). In other words, in order to reconcile traditional Platonism of intersubjectively valid meaning-intensions with a philosophy of meaning-intentions, one needs to reintroduce the Kantian idea of a "transcendental subject." (Every human being must be able in principle, so to speak, to take over the role of the transcendental subject of cognition and meaning-intentionality.) This is what Husserl clearly understood, as opposed to the present revivers of so-called "philosophical psychology" (who sometimes even dream of reducing intentions to something in the brain).

But Husserl, in accordance with the tradition of mentalistic transcendentalism prior to the linguistic turn, went so far as to suppose that a transcendental ego-consciousness that would survive the "bracketing" of the world (including language and communication with other subjects) could *constitute*, in principle, all timeless meanings by its intentionality. In contradiction to this methodological solipsism, it has to be pointed out that the single subject of intentionality, even for his or her self-understanding as "I," has to presuppose public, intensional meanings that must be always already carried by language-signs. The subject of intentionality can at best claim to share public meanings by sign-interpretation or to contribute to the publicly sharable meanings of language by his or her meaning-intentions. The transcendental subject-function of the single subject of intentionality lies precisely in his or her proposing those meaning-claims (e.g., in the context of argumentative discourse) whose intersubjective validity may be confirmed by an indefinite community of sign-interpretation. Therefore, the indefinite community of sign-interpretation, in accordance with certain suggestions of Charles Peirce and Josiah Royce, is the definite transcendental subject of meaning-intentions (and hence virtually of intersubjectively valid knowledge).[16]

The point of this *semiotic transformation of transcendentalism* lies in its account of the empirical facts. Thus it is in accordance with the fact that in modern societies the meaning-intentions of the single subjects of sign-interpretation, or of cognition in the light of sign-interpretation, will usually – i.e., in the case of laymen – fall short of the public meanings that are valid in the language community; whereas sometimes – in the case of creative experts – they will even transcend them in addressing, so to speak, the indefinite community of sign-interpretation. Both facts are possible because intentionality, in contrast to public meaning qua intensionality, is needed for realizing pragmatically the semantic dimension of sign-reference by identifying real denotata. In order to illustrate this point further, let us now consider the relationship between intensionality and extensionality.

II. 1.2.

The classical doctrine with respect to this problem says that the ideal intension of a name determines its possible extension, and this should hold quite independent of the factual intentions of human beings. Again, this tenet appears to me to be correct as a logician's argument against any version of psychologism. And in this sense one could be inclined to say that "meanings," i.e. intensions and extensions of terms, "are not in the head," to use Putnam's phrase.[17] Putnam, however, does not use this slogan in order to defend the classical tenet of logical semantics against psychologism but rather in order to question the classical position as a psychologistic one from an epistemological and ontological point of view. For him extensions of terms may be different from intensions and intentions (both of them being taken as mental states and thus as "something in the head"); in this case extensions have priority over both intensions and intentions, since the latter two express only subjective states of knowledge, so to speak, whereas the extensions virtually represent the real essence of things.[18]

Now, in the face of this challenge, a first thought might be that, nonetheless, there must be after all some *internal* relationship between the extensions and the intensions and intentions. For how should it otherwise be possible to speak meaningfully about extensions as meanings that are "not in the head." If the extensions were not determined at least by possible intensions, they could not be conceived as extensions of terms or names; and if they were completely different from our possible meaning-intentions, which may function in our perceptual identifications of real denotata, then we could not know anything about them and could not even *mean* them.

I think indeed that at least on the level of *possible* intentions, intensions and extensions, an internal relationship between the three concepts of meaning must be realizable. But we have already seen that this type of relationship does not spare us from considering, and accounting for, important differences between the factual realizations of the three dimensions of meaning. Now, with regard to Kripke's and Putnam's point, this problem may be illustrated by a case in which we do not succeed in subsuming a given material — let us say, some extraterrestrial stuff — under the head of a general concept. How should we identify the strange stuff as the subject of a sentence by which we could state the very impossibility of its determination with the aid of a possible intension of a term? If it were true that given things, i.e., individuals and supposed exemplars of natural kinds, could only be identified with the aid of possible intensions of terms – as it indeed was the assumption of Leibniz and, in a sense, of Hegel – then we would need to know *everything* about the strange thing – i.e., its complete intensional definition – in order only to say that we don't know anything about it. For, in order to say this, we would need to identify the thing with the aid of our conceptual knowledge about it.

It was this paradoxical situation, which was exposed by New-Hegelians like Bradley and Royce, that provoked Charles Peirce to his explication of the semiotic and epistemological function of indexical signs – like "this," "there," "here," "now," "then," "I," "you," etc. – in the context of identifying real objects of perceptions as subjects of any further determination with the aid of general concepts.[19] And it was one of the main points in Kripke's and Putnam's realistic semantics, I suggest, to connect this indexical function of identifying with the function of names (i.e., proper names and general names of natural kinds).

That is to say, Kripke and Putnam tried to detach the determination of the extension of names from the intensions or conceptual contents of names by instead connecting it with the indexical function that a name takes on by the "original baptism" of an individual – say "Aristotle" – or an exemplar of a natural kind – say "gold" or "water" or "fish." In the case of identifying individuals by proper names, the determination of the extension by baptism would comprise everything that is identical with this (indexically identified) individual in every possible world. And this would detach the extension of the proper name from any definite description that could constitute its intension on the basis of the fates of the baptized individual in some possible world. In the case of a natural kind, the determination of the extension by baptism would comprise everything that is identical in its real essence with this (indexically identified) stuff in every possible world. This determination would detach the extension of the general name – say of "water" or "gold" – from any available conceptual content that could constitute the intension of the term. In both cases, the name or term whose extension is indexically defined would be a "rigid designator," because its extension would be independent from the different and changing conceptual contents that constitute the intensions of proper or general names, i.e., it would be identical in every possible world.

Now, against these proposals of indexical determinations or definitions of the extensions of names or terms, the following objections could be directed in the name of the postulate of the internal relationship between all three concepts of meaning. First, it may be said that with *only* the aid of *indexical* words, i.e., without any support by intensional determination, it is not possible, on Aristotle's and Peirce's account, to identify an individual or an exemplar of a natural kind. Indeed, an individual entity that is baptized in such a way that its name could only be defined indexically by the word "this (there)" (Aristotle's *tode ti*) or, for that matter, even a supposed natural kind that is baptized in such a way that the extension of its name could only be defined by the phrase "everything that is identical in its essence with *this*": such a thing would be a good example for an unknowable *Ding an sich*. Now, this interpretation is obviously not in accordance with Kripke's or Putnam's intention to rehabilitate an epistemological and ontological realism and even essentialism with the aid of a new semantics. Indeed, this method would also not fit in with Peirce's idea of ensuring – by indexical definition – that something encountered as real, but unknown thus far, may be progressively determined conceptually as the subject of a sentence. What then would be the right method in order to make use of a semantics of the indexical definition of names?

The first requirement of the method would be to make sure that the indexical definition that is connected with the "original baptism" can be remembered and transferred by communication. For, as we have pointed out before in accordance with Searle, the "original baptism" and the communicative transfer of the name must not be confused with a causal reaction and its transfer, which could be the object of an external description of a "causal chain" of behavior. (Thus far the talk of a "causal theory of meaning" is at least misleading.) Now, in order to provide for the fact that the causal transfer goes along with its control by an intentional transfer of meaning, we need a formulation of the indexical definition connected with the original baptism that goes beyond the above report about the encounter with the *Ding an sich*. How could it read? In order, e.g., to refer by baptism to an *individual* in such a way that the indexical definition can be remembered and transferred by communication, it would at least be necessary to determine the extension of the attached proper name by a phrase something like this: "the child that was baptized at the time t at place p by person p'". Now this is a definite description that provides a Fregean *Sinn* that at least initiates the *intensional* determination of the *extension* of the proper name by further definite descriptions. In the case of the "original baptism" of some (supposed) exemplar of a natural kind that cannot yet be subsumed under the heading of a general concept – say by the name "baboo" – it would not even suffice to provide a definite description like: "the material that was baptized at time *t* and place *p* by person *p*." For this would not provide a sufficient determination of the extension of a supposed natural kind by indexical identification of its real essence. In order to achieve this, one either has to complement the indexical definition of "baboo" by some picture (say by a photograph) or to provide some description of the phenomenal qualities (and relations of qualities) that point to the structure of the given material, such that one could arrive at a definition somewhat like:

> "baboo" means everything that is identical *in its structure* with that material that was baptized at time *t* and place *p* by person *p*; and the structure of "baboo" may be described by the following list of phenomenal qualities: . . . ."

But if this proposal is relevant, then it would appear as if the intended detachment of the indexical definition of the extension of the name from its intension has already been proved impossible. This verdict, however, would be precipitous in a sense. For what has been shown thus far is only that there must be an *internal* relationship between the indexical definition of the *possible* extension and the definition of the *possible* intension of the name. But this does not prevent us from providing a definition of the extension of a name that, by its indexical dimension, is partly independent from our present concepts (i.e., from the factual intensions of the words of our language) and thus open to a further intensional determination, e.g., by the progress of science.

In this sense it may indeed be claimed that pragmatically the extension of all proper names (especially as they are used in history) is not defined definitively by definite descriptions (not even by a cluster of them!) but also by the open dimension of the indexical definition of proper names as "rigid designators." And it seems to be clear that only this type of (pragmatical and semantical) definition ensures the possibility of progress in historical research – say about the real biography of Plato or Aristotle.

(This interpretation would not exclude that our definition of the meaning of "Plato" and "Aristotle" by a cluster of definite descriptions could provide a *necessary* condition for our use of these proper names. The reason for this restriction of the scope of the indexical definition of the proper names as rigid designators would lie in the fact that historical persons have attracted our cognitive interest not just by their being born and baptized, but by their having continued their *real* existence not in a possible world, but in our factual world of history.)

Similarly it may be claimed that pragmatically the extension of all general names of natural kinds (especially as they are used in natural science) is not defined definitively by the factual intensions (i.e. the conceptual content) of our terms but also by the open dimension of the indexical definition of the general names or terms as "rigid designators." And again only this type of (pragmatical and semantical) definition ensures the possibility of scientific progress.

In order to illustrate this latter point, I will briefly discuss Putnam's theory of a "linguistic division of labor," which is a very important empirical illustration for the possibility and necessity of an overcoming of the methodological solipsism of traditional epistemology.[20] The point of Putnam's theory may be summarized in the following way: at least in modern societies which are characterized by a differentiated social division of labor there must prevail a corresponding linguistic division of labor. This means that for almost every part of the first-hand knowledge of things by experience, and hence for the corresponding knowledge about the extensions of general names, there are experts who by far outrun the laymen. These experts therefore really determine the public meaning of words.

Now this theory is rather ambiguous with regard to our problem of the factual relationship between extensions or intensions as determinations of linguistic meanings. For, in one sense, the theory is in accordance with the classical assumption that the extensions of terms are determined by their intensions. The experts, it may be claimed, are just marking out the public standards about the intensions upon which the extensions are logically dependent; and thereby they may even determine, in a sense, the *use* of words by the laymen although these have no first hand knowledge about the extensions of most terms. (This interpretation is indeed supported linguistically by the structuralist theory of "fields" of meanings or "word-contents." For this theory may explain to a certain extent how laymen as competent native speakers may in a certain sense correctly use words about which they have neither an adequate knowledge concerning the intensions nor the extensions. This holds good, e.g., with regard to my own use of the word "gold" or "hemlock," and even of words like "elms" and "beeches.") In brief, the common use of a language just provides, so to speak, a pragmatic proliferation of the collective knowledge about intensions of words and thereby enables laymen to dispose in a sense of the knowledge of the experts.

Still, there is another interpretation of the theory possible in light of the realistic semantics of Kripke and Putnam. The experts, it may be said, are not only competent for the factual standard determination of the intensions of terms and thereby for the public use of language, but they are also in charge of those (partly) indexical definitions of the extensions of terms as rigid designators that keep the dimension of intensional meaning of terms open to further determination; and they will usually even be a little bit ahead of the collective, standard determination of intensions by their "tacit knowledge" by experience with respect to those extensions of terms that are not yet covered by the collective, standard intensions. Thus far it may indeed be claimed that, in as far as scientific progress is determining the use of modern languages, there is a factual priority of the exploration of the extensions of words over the fixation of their intensions.

Again, this statement does not, of course, refute our general claim that there is an internal relationship between possible ideal extensions and intensions of terms and that on the level of this relationship the logical postulate of the determination of extensions by intensions must hold. But this claim must not be confused with the claim (suggested by abstract logical semantics of constructed language systems) that the extension of the words of a living language may be determined once and for all by the well-defined intensions of the terms of a semantical system. For a constructed semantical system simply cannot keep up with the pragmatic difference between the factual intensions and the factual extensions of the words of a living language, which has to keep up with the growth of human experience and especially with the progress of science. This shows only that the pragmatic difference between intensions and extensions requires a pragmatic completion of the linguistic turn of philosophy in order to overcome the abstractive fallacy of logical semantics in the Carnapian sense, as we have suggested previously.

Now the pragmatic difference between extensions and intensions of the words of a living language must obviously be realized by acts of identifying real *denotata* of words, and that means: by *referential intentionality*. This fact leads us to the last problem of our triangular discussion of the relationship between the three paradigm concepts of meaning: what about the *internal* and *factual* relationship between Kripke's and Putnam's indexical definition of the extensions of names and the concept of referential intentionality?

II. 1.3.

After what we have said about the role of intentionality in the context of indexical identifying, it seems to be clear that not only the *possi-*

ble but even the *factual* intentionality of our indexical references must be able to keep up with the determination of meaning as extension. For it is just by the intentional content of our indexical definitions that we can open up a dimension of extensional meaning that transcends the factual intensions of our terms. At first sight, this point appears to make up the twist of Searle's recent argument against Putnam's contention that "meanings are not in the head."[21] And I would indeed agree that the intentional content of an indexical definition must reach precisely as far as the extension of a term that is defined by the indexical definition, since otherwise it could not determine the empirical conditions of its satisfaction. Thus far it may be claimed that meaning is "in the head." (But *this* meaning of the metaphorical phrase can only be justified if we at this point presuppose a transcendental-epistemological, and not an empirical-psychological, concept of intentional-meaning. The metaphysical paradigm or pre-figuration of what I called a transcendental conception would be Aristotle's or Thomas Aquinas' dictum *"anima quodammodo omnia."* It seems clear that Putnam did not have this conception in mind when he thought of "meanings in the head." He rather thought of contents of the mind in an empirical-psychological sense; and thus far he is right in claiming that "meanings are not in the head."

But Searle does not only claim to be right with regard to the equation of the meaning of "intentional content" and of "indexical definition" but also with regard to the equation of "intentional content" and (factual) intension and thus thinks it possible to defend the traditional thesis that the intension determines the extension on this presupposition. Thus far his argument against Putnam may be summarized as follows:

Premise (Searle along with Putnam): Two people, say Jones on Earth and his *Doppelgänger,* twin Jones on twin Earth, have *type-identical mental states* in saying: "I have a headache;" but the *extension* of "I" in their verbalized thoughts is different, because it is determined by *indexical definition.*

Conclusion (Searle against Putnam): In both cases the *intension* determines the *extension* since the *intentional contents* (that means the *self-referential concepts* Jones and Twin Jones have of themselves) are also different.

It seems clear to me that Searle would be right in arguing this way *against* Putnam, if, and only if, it were possible to equate the different situation-bound indexical meanings of "I" in the two different utterances of Jones and Twin Jones, respectively, with two different general concepts, and hence — in the case of our example — with two different *intensions* of the same sign-type. Searle is seduced into making these assumptions by considering the indexical, self-referential self-conceptions of Jones and Twin Jones — which are indeed different according to the different intentional contents of their verbalized thoughts — as different *concepts* and hence intensions of the term "I". But this seems to be semiotically untenable since it in fact obscures the fruitful and indispensable distinction between *general concepts* or *intensions of terms* whose meaning must not be situation-bound, and indexical definitions. It thereby obscures the good point in Putnam's distinction between the indexical definition of the extension of a term from a situation-bound point of view and the conceptual contents or intensions of terms.

But things are indeed different with regard to the intentional content of the utterance of an indexical definition. This content, which must only be partly indexical, in order not to be cognitively blind may also be called *intensional*. Thus far Searle may be entitled to argue, "first, that if by 'intension' we mean intentional content then the *intension of an utterance of an indexical expression* [my emphasis] precisely does determine extension; and, second, that in perceptual cases two people can be in type-identical mental states . . . and their intentional contents can still be different; they can have different conditions of satisfaction."[22]

This point is, however, in accordance with the claim of the realistic semantics that it is possible to transcend the intensional scope of our concepts (i.e., of the factual intensions of our terms or words) by indexical definition of the extensions of terms as rigid designators. This becomes clear from Searle's interpretation of Putnam's example concerning the meaning of "water" on Earth and on twin Earth, which according to Putnam is supposed to be *intensionally* identical but *extensionally* different. It reads:

> The indexical definition given by Jones on earth of "water" is defined indexically as whatever is identical in structure with the stuff causing *this* visual experience, whatever that structure is. And the analysis for twin Jones on twin Earth is: "water" is defined indexically as whatever is identical in structure with the stuff causing *this* visual experience, whatever that structure is. Thus, in each case we have type-identical experiences but in fact in each case something different is meant. That is, in each case the conditions of satisfaction established by the mental content (in the head) is different because of the self-referentiality of perceptual experiences.[23]

Still, this example is paradoxical precisely from the point of view of Searle's concept of "intentional content." For it obviously supposes that Jones and twin Jones may actually *mean* different things although they *know* nothing about this difference. If we universalize this supposition, we arrive at the conclusion, suggested previously, that the indexical definition of the extension of the real (i.e., its definition in the vein of Kripke's and Putnam's causal or realistic theory of meaning) amounts to a definition of the unknowable *Ding an sich*. For we would arrive at a situation where people *could not know* anything about that which they *must* define purely indexically: for example, the extension of the general name of the *real*, which could read: "whatever is identical in essence with that which is causing (Kant says "affecting") *this* (i.e., *my* present) experience (e.g., of resistance), whatever that structure is." According to Charles Peirce such a (purely indexical) *definition* is nonsensical because it cannot show, in principle, how the meaning of "identical in essense with . . . this . . ." could be *conceptually interpreted*. Thus it reduces the meaning of the *real* — or of whatever is encountered and baptized as real — to the limit case of a bumping (of the will of the I) against something in the night (the resistance of the non-I).

Now, this is obviously not supposed to be the meaning of Putnam's or Searle's example. But it has to be noticed that Searle's insertion of the phrase "in structure" (instead of "in essence") in the indexical definition and his emphasis on the "self-referentiality" of "perceptual experiences" does not change the paradoxical situation. On the contrary, the paradoxicality of the example rests precisely on the suggestion that Jones and twin Jones are considered to have the *same experiences*, as far as their knowledge reaches, but different indexical (even self-referential) *intentions*.

This shows that the given example demolishes the good sense of both Kripke's and Putnam's realistic semantics and Searle's theory of intentionality. In order to avoid an abstractive fallacy and make visible the good point of both theories, it is necessary to consider the example not as a *paradigm case* but as a *limit case* within the historical context of the development of human knowledge and of the meaning-content of human languages. The given example must not be universalized as such but considered from the point of view of those people who *already know* (say, by a better theory of water than that of Jones and twin Jones) that Jones and twin Jones in fact referred to different natural kinds (say, different species of water or water and something else).

But, in order to conceive of the possibility of such a development of knowledge and of language, the example of the limit case is misleading, since it cannot show, in principle, how the fact that Jones and twin Jones were referring (on Searle's account, even somehow *intentionally*) to different materials can be discovered and thus how the supposition of the semantic theories can be verified. This becomes clear if we imagine the case where Jones detects — say as a member of a scientific expedition — that the "water" on twin Earth is something quite different from "water" on Earth. This would possibly be an occasion for an "original baptism" in Kripke's sense.

As I suggested previously, in such a case the indexical definition of the extension of the name must not only contain phrases like "identical in structure" and "causing this visual experience, whatever that structure is", but it must be supplemented by a picture or a description of the structure of the visual (or, for that matter, non-visual, but sensual) experience, say by a list of the qualities (and relations of qualities) that appear to make up the structure of the causally effective entity that is pointed to by "this".

It has to be noticed that such a supplementation of the indexical definition of the extension of the name would not mean that the discoverer could already provide a conceptual definition by which he could subsume the phenomenon under the head of some class. But he would indeed make his indexical definition of the extension *epistemologically* relevant. For he would provide a *meaning* to the intentional content of his definition of the name that is neither purely indexical (and hence cognitively blind) nor completely conceptual (and hence not open for the still unknown real extension of the name through the rigid designator). But if this characterization of the role of the representation of the phenomenal (qualitatively given) structure is relevant, then the whole dichotomy of indexical definition and conceptual definition (in the sense of a possible subsumption) does not suffice in order to deal adequately with the problem of the intension of the intentional content of a baptism-protocol. It does not sufficiently explain how we can introduce into the scientific discourse a newly discovered object of experience as subject of further determination. The theories thus far discussed do not yet suffice, it appears, to explain semiotically and epistemologically the pragmatic difference and the possible continuum of meaning between *extensions, intensions* and *intentions*.

In what follows I shall therefore try to review the whole triangular discussion in terms of a transcendental semiotics that draws heavily on some basic conceptions of Charles Peirce. Before entering into this discussion of the problem of reference, I want to recall our leading question as to whether it may be shown that the identification of real referents as *denotata* of our signs amounts to showing that the linguistic turn of philosophy may be completed by a *pragmatic* turn, i.e., by a pragmatic integration of the semantic dimension of sign-reference (see Figure I, left side).

II. 1.4.

In order to introduce the tools of a Peircean semiotics into the discussion of our problem, let us come back to our example of the "original baptism" of a piece of extraterrestrial material by the name "baboo." As I pointed out previously, the baptism cannot be done by just pronouncing the name "baboo" as a physical reaction to the causal affection by the strange stuff, but it has to provide something like a *baptism-protocol*; that is, a little story about the procedure of identifying the referent of "baboo" which makes it possible to remember and to communicate the new name in such a way that its referent can be intentionally re-identified as that which was intentionally identified as cause of his experience by the first discoverer. In a Wittgensteinian vein one could say: the "original baptism" must be performed according to a public rule of identifying that can be followed in a sense by the first discoverer as well as by all potential re-identifiers. Thus far I would claim that the procedure of identifying within the context of the "original baptism" is already a step beyond the privacy of a pre-linguistic procedure of ascertaining evidence for just one consciousness, in the sense of methodological solipsism (from Descartes and Locke through Husserl). It is already the entrance into the range and realm of a public language-game (Wittgenstein) and of the indefinite community of sign-interpretation (Peirce).

But it has to be noticed that the rule of the language game of "original baptism" in the sense of Kripke precludes the possibility that the meaning of the name "baboo" might be explained in terms of some *factual use* of language. Since the meaning of "baboo" is that of a rigid designator whose extension is the same in any possible world, it must transcend, in a sense, the range of any language-game that is centered around the rules of a factual use of language. But this, it seems to me, is an essential feature of every explication of meaning on the level of the scientific (or philosophic) language-game, a feature that is only made visible in a special way by the case of introducing a new and partly open meaning by the procedure of "original baptism." In principle, no explication of the meaning of a scientific term — say of "heavy" or "simultaneous" on the level of physics, or of "justice" or, for that matter, "meaning" on the level of philosophy — can be reached by just describing a given use of language. Rather we need an experiment of thought by which we could imagine how the term that is to be explicated *could* or *had to be* interpreted and hence used on the ground of all conceivable experiences or, for that matter, practical consequences. This point of Peirce's "pragmatic maxim" constitutes the difference and the superiority of a normative transcendental-pragmatic approach to meaning-explication over a Wittgensteinian *pragmatics of language-use*, not to speak of Morris's behavioristic pragmatics.[24]

Let us then try to give a Peircean account of the procedure of identifying that goes along with the discovery and original baptism of what is called "baboo." The discoverer, I suggest, might say to his companion (or, if this is not possible, to himself) something like this:

"This thing *over there* — under the big tree in the foreground — looks *so and so* (to be specified by describing the perceptible qualities and relations of qualities that make up the phenomenal structure). On the basis of these perceptible qualities, I don't know how to determine *what* it is (i.e., under which general concept it could be subsumed). That is, I find it impossible *at present* to provide a conceptual subsumption of the given stuff on the basis of an *abductive inference* of the form: '"This there is so and so; what is so and so might be an exemplar of A; therefore this there might be an exemplar of A'. Hence, in order to provide for the possibility of a later determination on the basis of a reidentification, I will give it a name: I *hereby* baptize the given stuff by the name "baboo." I thereby define the extension of "baboo" as *being everything that is the same as this over there* which *now* causes my present experience by presenting the following phenomenal structure (to be specified by a picture or by a list of phenomenal qualities)."

The semiotically interesting feature of this account of an original baptism, and that which goes beyond our former accounts, lies in its recourse to two classes of non-conceptual signs (in Peirce's terminology: "indices" and "icons") whose function is connected in our baptism-protocol in some way with the function of signs of general concepts (i.e., "symbols" in Peirce's terminology). Thus all three classes of signs together will constitute, so to speak, the *intension* (in Searle's sense) of the "intentional content" of our protocol. Let us illustrate that in more detail.

The use of linguistic indices (or rather quasi-indices, as has still to be shown) like "this" is needed in order to testify to the *existence* of the given stuff and its *causally affecting* the sign user and, at the same time, *being intentionally identified* by him. The use of further linguistic indices like "over there" and "now" or "at present" concretizes the situation-reference of the protocol by indicating the space-time-relation of the phenomena to the sign-user and vice versa. Finally, linguistic indices like "I" and "hereby" (and possibly "you" for addressing a companion) indicate the performance of the speech-act of baptizing as part of an explicitly or implicitly communicative situation that may serve as point of departure for a further process of communication about the object of the original baptism.

Thus far the recourse to *indices* reconfirms our prior analysis of the "original baptism" as utterance of an "indexical definition." But, in our example, the function of the *linguistic indices* is supported and supplemented by the function of icons (e.g., photographs) or what could be called linguistic quasi-icons in the sense of a Peircean semiotics. This function obviously makes up the new feature of our Peircean account, which is not easy to explicate. Linguistic icons are used in the descriptive parts of our protocol; and they function, so to speak, *inside of the conceptual predicators* by which the discoverer is describing the given qualities (and relations of qualities) that make up the phenomenal structure of the material that is to be baptized.

This function of linguistic icons belongs to the indexical definition of "baboo" in so far as the qualities that make up the phenomenal structure are not described as pure phenomena of relation-free "suchness" (i.e., of "Firstness" in the sense of Peirce's theory of categories). That is to say, the phenomena are not described as merely *possible* qualities, but as qualities *given for* the consciousness of the discoverer whose attention is drawn to them by the function of the indices. (The function of the indices corresponds to Peirce's category "Secondness," which expresses a dyadic or two place-relation, e.g., the *encounter* between the *I* and the *Non-I*).

But the function of the linguistic icons belongs also together with that of the conceptual predicators, inside of which they are functioning as quasi-icons in describing the qualities of the given phenomena. By this quasi-iconic function the conceptual predicators of the description are, so to speak, recharged with a meaning-evidence that they can only acquire in the situation of perception, but lose as abstract conceptual predicators. This means that the quasi-iconic function of predicators in the context of description (e.g., of perceptual judgments) does not so much serve to *subsume* a given phenomenon under the head of a general concept or class but rather, in advance of that abstractive logical operation, to *grasp and present* the given quality (or perceptible structure) of the referent. Therefore linguistic icons

cannot function in the context of abstract – true or false – propositions about facts but only inside of perceptual judgments about what
is actually given with "phenomenological" of "phaneroscopic" evidence
– as in our example of the carefully described qualities of the strange
stuff that cannot be subsumed under the head of some concept or
class (as yet).

It is this function of the linguistic icons that obviously makes it
possible to support and supplement the indexical definition of the
extension of "baboo" by a description that is not yet a conceptual subsumption but makes the indexical definition cognitively (and hence
epistemologically) relevant by preparing, so to speak, for a later conceptual subsumption. Thus far this element of our semiotic account
goes beyond the purely indexical account of the definition that
belongs to the original baptism, but it is obviously in good accordance
with Kripke's and Putnam's approach as well as with Searle's conception of the "intension" of the "intentional content" of the "utterance of
the indexical definition." It covers indeed both the causal and the
intentional aspect of referential identifying, and it especially supports
the Kripkean claim that by baptism the real essence of individuals and
of natural kinds is somehow grasped by and integrated into the names
through rigid designators – in contraposition to the nominalistic
claim that all description with the aid of general concepts amounts
merely to a linguistic arrangement of terms in the service of pragmatic
purposes.

This point of convergence of our semiotic approach with that of
essentialistic realism is certainly in agreement with the general spirit
of Peirce's emphatic anti-nominalism. But in the face of this fact the
crucial question of our present approach arises in a new and acute version: the question whether this semiotic approach must not rather
represent a contraposition to the linguistic turn of contemporary
philosophy. This has in fact been claimed for Kripke's and Putnam's
realistic theory of reference; and if this approach may be integrated
into and, so to speak, *"aufgehoben"* in a Peircean semiotics, then the
question arises of how the latter may be interpreted as a pragmatic
completion of the linguistic turn, even in the sense of a transcendental
semiotics.

My answer to this question would be: a transcendental semiotics
based on the Peircean transformation of Kant's "transcendental logic"[25]
provides a third way beyond and out of the traditional alternative of
nominalism and essentialistic realism or, for that matter, of common-
sense realism and transcendental criticism. It does so especially by a
conception of semiotics that is capable of going beyond, and mediating

between, the semanticist version of the linguistic turn, which is based only on the function of conceptual symbols (if not on the notion of abstract syntactico-semantical frameworks), and, on the other hand, the position of pre-linguistic ontology and transcendental philosophy (including Kantianism and Husserlian phenomenology). I can suggest this point in the present context only with regard to the problem of reference or, respectively, of the triangular discussion of the three concepts of meaning.

Thus far I have wanted to suggest — along with Peirce — that the function of linguistic indices and icons, transcends any possible function of conceptual signs by fixing or tightening the language to causally effective real objects of perception and to their structural qualities. This function of the non-conceptual sign-types of language, which is bound up with the context of the perceptual situation, may indeed account semiotically for the indispensable *evidence*-basis of human cognition: i.e., in Peircean terms, the *dyadic* relation ("Secondness") of the *I*'s clash with the causal affections of the *non-I* and the monadic (relation-free) suchness of the given phenomena ("Firstness"). Thus far Peircean semiotics refutes the precipitate contention (of logical semantics and semanticist philosophy of science, including even Popperianism) that *evidence* may be reduced to just a *psychological feeling*, and hence amounts to nothing for epistemology in the face of the fact that all intersubjectively valid results of perception are impregnated with linguistic interpretation or, for that matter, by theories. Peircean semiotics indeed saves vis-à-vis modern semanticism the truth-core of a Husserlian phenomenology of evidence and especially of the Aristotelian claim that perceptual judgments are incorrigible in a sense, i.e., with regard to given qualities in the sense of *secondness* and *firstness*. (Peirce offers also an evolutionist explanation of this property of perceptual judgments: they function as boundaries [borders] and vehicles of transition between, on the one hand, natural processes of sign information, not to be influenced by man, and, on the other hand, processes of sign-interpretation that make up the subject or topic of the normative semiotic logic of science.[26])

On the other hand, however, Peircean semiotics also provides crucial arguments for the transcendental-pragmatic completion of the linguistic turn. For, in contradiction to Husserl's pre-linguistic version of phenomenology, Peircean semiotics holds that *evidence* of given phenomena in the sense of "Firstness" and "Secondness" is not (yet) the same as (intersubjectively valid) knowledge, as long as it is abstractively separated from the symbolic interpretation which has to complete our cognition in the sense of the category of *Thirdness*, i.e., of the conceptual mediation of the intuitively given phenomena with understanding or reason. (Here Peircean semiotics amounts to a critical reconstruction of the epistemological development from Kant to Hegel.) Correspondingly, Peircean semiotics cannot agree either with a pre-linguistic version of real essence ontology or naturalistic causal theory of reference. For it must insist on the fact that even indexical and iconical signs, in so far as they function within the context of the "original baptism" (i.e., of indexical definition and, beyond that, of a structural description of the phenomenon), are linguistic signs, after all. This means that their function is interwoven with that of conceptual signs (i.e., symbols) in a twofold way.

First, it has to be noticed that the whole text of our baptism-protocol, i.e., the text of our indexical definition and, moreover, the text of the accompanying structural description, must combine the function of all three classes of signs, i.e., *indices, icons* and *symbols* in the Peircean terminology, in order to constitute the intension of the intentional content of that protocol.

Secondly, it is time now to make clear what it means to say that the linguistic indices and, respectively, icons are only quasi-indices and quasi-icons. In a sense one could say that in both cases they function only inside conceptual signs (i.e., symbols). Thus linguistic indices like "this," "that," "here," "there," "now," "then," "I," "you," etc., do not function like "indices" outside of language, say smoke as an index of fire or the pulse as an index of blood-pressure. They include rather an element of *conceptual thirdness*, which determines the type of their *situation-bound secondness*. Thus the meaning of "this," in contradistinction to "that," is somehow determined by the *conceptual* distinction between "thisness" and "thatness" which is not situation-bound. The same holds with regard to "here," in contradistinction to "there," etc. Nonetheless, Hegel was of course semiotically wrong when he acknowledged only this conceptual part, and thereby denied the situation-bound indexical part, of the meaning of these linguistic indices in his chapter on *sinnliche Gewissheit* ("sensuous certainty") in the *Phänomenologie des Geistes*. Even his antagonist Ludwig Feuerbach, who insisted on the evidence of intuition, overlooked − like Hegel − the fact that there are linguistic signs, different from conceptual symbols, whose function is precisely to introduce and integrate the situation-bound evidence of intuition into the conceptual meaning of language.

Still, Hegel's talk of the "indetermined immediate" which, on his account, is denoted by the indexical signs, would be correct if it were not the case that indexical signs are capable, within the context of the actual situation, to direct our attention (and intention) to *given qualities* (i.e., "Firstness"), and, possibly to qualities of hitherto unknown phenomena. This leads us to the other systematic-semiotical connection of sign-functions that was recognized by Peirce: that of a quasi-iconical grasping and presenting of qualities (in the sense of "Firstness") inside the conceptual meaning of predicators (i.e., "Thirdness").

As has already been suggested, it is the internal connection between all three types of linguistic signs that opens living language to an enrichment of meaning by human experience, especially by the progress of the sciences. In this context, it has to be emphasized that the integration of iconical meaning into the conceptual intensions of predicators within the context of the intensions of baptism-protocols remains semantically effective beyond that stage. It operates as a *normative* steering function towards reaching the ideal "logical interpretant" throughout the indefinite process of sign-interpretation that has to be postulated on Peirce's account of meaning expliction. Thus, one might conceive of the entire history of the word "heavy" from its introduction by an ostensive definition of the underlying quality through its further determination by Newton's and finally Einstein's theory of gravitation. The later stages of such a process are not merely determined by conceptual interpretation but also by new situational confrontations (e.g., of the experiential consequences of theories) with the phenomena and, hence, by new occasions for an integration of all three sign-functions.

On considering this semiotical theory of an integration of the conceptual and non-conceptual sign-functions, it becomes clear that this approach, which leads beyond abstract semanticism and saves phenomenological evidence, does not abandon the linguistic turn but rather completes it. It does so by means of a pragmatic integration of the semantic reference of linguistic signs that may be called *transcendental-pragmatic* for the following reasons.

First, the Wittgensteinian point of a transcendental semantics, which I have introduced as a criterion for the linguistic turn, has not been abandoned but, indeed, only widened (expanded) by the paradigm of a baptism-protocol. This becomes clear if we consider only the intentional content of the original baptism which may be expressed by a ceremonial speech-act of the first discoverer that sounds like this: "I hereby baptize the material over there by the name 'baboo' defining the extension of this name as comprising everything that is the same as this over there which now causes my present experiences by presenting the following phenomenal structure . . . ."

We are here no longer — as in Wittgenstein's dictum — only concerned with a propositional sentence that describes a fact, but rather with an expanded performative sentence that reflectively describes and thereby also performs the speech-act of identifying, baptizing and defining the given name. Thus, not only an objectively given state of affairs (a Wittgensteinian "fact") is described, but also an historical situation and a human response to it. Nevertheless, the transcendental point of the Wittgensteinian statement is preserved. For it is not possible, in principle, for the performer of the original baptism, who thereby has to provide the initial stage of an interpretation process, to go somehow beyond the limits of his language-game. In order to achieve the same identification, baptism and definition, he has to repeat the same performative sentence.

Secondly, as I have intimated previously, the rule and the range of the language game of the original baptism are somehow continued throughout the further interpretation process, notwithstanding the possible progress in meaning-determination, in order to ensure the possibility of an intentional re-identification. Now, if we universalize this point with regard to identifying and interpreting what is called the *real*, we must recognize that there is no possibility, at any stage of the process, to go beyond the limit of the pertinent language-game. Just by pragmatically integrating the phenomenological dimensions of intentional reference into the semantical dimensions of sign-reference, the transcendental-pragmatic point of the linguistic turn has been strengthened and shown to be nontranscendable. This may be clarified further by seeking the transcendental subject of the entire achievement of identification and interpretation.

The transcendental subject is obviously no longer the transcendental consciousness of the I in the sense of traditional mentalism and methodological solipsism; although the transcendental consciousness of the I still retains the function of ascertaining evidence together with the function of intentionality and also of the "synthesis of apperception" in the sense of Kant. However, the transcendental subject in the sense of transcendental semiotics must not be defined with respect to the evidence of experience and meaning-intentionality but rather with respect to the possible intersubjective validity of meaning-interpretation and hence of possible knowledge. It has to be capable, in principle, of functioning as subject of an ultimate consensus about sign-interpretation and thus about all conceivable truth criteria — i.e., as evidence of *correspondence* between intentions and given phenomena, *coherence* of sentences or theories, *pragmatic fruitfulness* of assumptions or strategies, etc.[27] In brief, it can only be the indefinite, ideal *community of sign-interpretation*, which on the level of argumentative discourse could arrive at the "final opinion" about the *real*, as we must postulate by a "regulative idea," whatever the facts about the future might be. Considered as referent with regard to this subject of sign-interpretation, the *real* must no longer be defined as the unknowable *Ding an sich* but rather – with Peirce – as the indefinitely *knowable* that can never be factually known definitely. This definition provides the point of an *"Aufhebung"* of common sense realism into transcendental semiotics; for the point of the former – that the real is independent from anybody's thought about it – is very much compatible with the point of the latter: that the real as identifiable and conceivable must be the object of sign-interpretation. This position may also be called a *meaning-critical realism.*[28]

II. 2. The Integration of Semantics and Transcendental Pragmatics with regard to the Pragmatic Dimension of Sign-Use.

Up to now I have considered primarily the problem of overcoming the abstractive fallacy of semanticism with regard to Morris's semantic dimension of sign-reference, i.e., of identifying real referents as *denotata* of signs (see left side of Figure I). Since, however, this problem turned out to be one of a (transcendental) pragmatic integration of semantics, I became concerned with Morris's *pragmatic* dimension of semiosis, i.e., with the use of signs by an interpreter (as a member of a community of interpretation) and in this context with self-referential intentionality (e.g., of the ceremonial speech-act of "original baptism"). In what follows, I shall consider primarily the problem of overcoming the abstractive fallacy of semanticism with regard to Morris's pragmatic dimension of semiosis, i.e., with primary regard to intentionality and its expression by speech-acts as communicative acts (see right side of Figure I).

With regard to the dimension of sign-reference, the abstractive fallacy of semanticism came about especially by overlooking the problem of a pragmatical integration of semantics, e.g., of dealing with the problems of intentional identifying of real referents and with the pragmatic difference between (factual) extensions and (factual) intensions of linguistic terms. With regard to the dimension of sign-*use*, the abstractive fallacy of semanticism comes about rather by overlooking the possible semantical integration of pragmatics, i.e., the linguistic aspect of the meaning-intentionality of speech-acts.

In order to understand this point, we have to remember that the original distinction of the semiotic dimensions in Morris's "Foundations of the Theory of Signs" was conceived primarily as a supplementation of Carnap's conception of abstract syntactico-semantical frameworks of constructed languages. Now, on these conditions, there is no need for a linguistic semantics of the pragmatic use of language, since a Carnapian semantical system allows only for propositional sentences whose function is merely that of a representation of states of affairs. But things are quite different with natural languages which serve not only the purpose of representation but also that of expressing the pragmatic functions by non-propositional sentences.

A good abstractive distinction between the different functions of natural language was offered by Karl Bühler in his *Sprachtheorie*.[29] He distinguished between the representation-function of propositions and, on the other hand, the functions of *self-expression* and of communicative *appeal*. But even Bühler was not prepared to account for the latter two functions as those of linguistic "symbols" but only as functions of "symptoms" and "signals." Accordingly, he and Karl Popper, who follows him, consider the two pragmatic functions as the "lower functions" of language which man has in common with the animals, in contradistinction to the representation-function of propositions as carriers of possible truth.[30] Thus far Bühler's and Popper's account is still in accordance with Carnap's abstract semanticism, since it conceives of the function of self-expression and appeal not as possible intentional and symbolically expressed dimensions of linguistic meaning (to be taken into account e.g., in a theory of argumentation) but as merely pragmatical functions to be dealt with only in empirical psychology and social science.

A decisive breakthrough towards reflecting the non-propositional but nonetheless symbolical and hence pragmatical *and* semantical functions of natural language was achieved by J. L. Austin's discovery of the "performative" phrases as linguistic expressions of "illocuitionary acts."[31] This holds especially with regard to his insight that the linguistic expression of the "illocutionary force" of speech-acts by performatives is not only a matter of institutionalized, ceremonial formulas – like those of baptizing or wedding – but is a possibility, in principle, of making explicit the potential pragmatic force of every sentence whose utterance would constitute a speech-act – even of a constative sentence, since it expresses not only a proposition but also the potential force of a constative, or assertive *act*. Why is this detection of the function of the performatives a decisive breakthrough that goes beyond Bühler's and Popper's understanding of the non-representative functions of language?

The point I have in mind was brought out partly by Strawson, partly by Searle, and partly by Habermas. I will explicate in turn and

I will at times go somewhat beyond the presumable self-understanding of the authors.

Peter Strawson brought together Austin's theory of "speech-acts" and Paul Grice's theory of "intentions."[32] In doing so he tried to understand Austin's distinction between "illocutionary" and "perlocutionary" acts as indicating different kinds of intentions, such that the former are expressions of genuine meaning-intentions by public language-signs, whereas the latter are a kind of covertly strategical act whose intentions cannot be made public by conventional signs of language in order to fulfil their purposes.

Already in Strawson's conceiving of illocutionary acts as expressions of meaning-intentions, it becomes clear that the non-representational functions of speech — i.e. self-expression and appeal in terms of Bühler's theory — are not just functions of "symptoms" and "signals," as is the case with animal behavior (or, with humans, in the case of non-intentional expressions of psychical states or interpersonal relations that are studied in psychology and especially in psycho-pathology). In contradistinction to these subconscious functions, the non-representational functions of speech, e.g. of performatives, obviously may symbolically express self-referential meaning-intentions and thereby become the medium of a public expression of self-reflection and responsibility with regard to interests and social claims — even with regard to the truth-claim in *statements* that is connected with the representational function of propositions. For this truth-claim may be explicitly expressed by the performative sentence "I hereby affirm . . . ."

Furthermore, with Strawson's distinction between *illocutionary* acts and (covertly strategical) *perlocutionary* acts, it becomes clear that the genuine meaning-intentions, which may be expressed by performatives, i.e., by non-propositional types of sentences, are different from those intentions that cannot at all be expressed by the public medium of language, namely those of strategical intentions, e.g., of suggesting a certain image of the speaker.

Both of these Strawsonian points were made once more by John Searle in his book *Speech Acts*. It is clear in this book that genuine meaning-intentions, which are to be understood as direct intentions of illocutionary acts, must also be capable of being linguistically expressed by explicitly performative sentences. Searle made this point with his "principle of expressibility," which states that "whatever can be meant can be said," with the following qualifications: " . . . even in cases where it is in fact impossible to say exactly what I mean it is in principle possible to come to be able to say exactly what I mean. I can in principle if not in fact increase my knowledge of the language, or more radically, if the existing language or existing languages are not adequate to the task, if they simply lack the resources for saying what I mean, I can in principle at least enrich the language by introducing new terms or other devices into it."[33] This qualifiction is supplemented by the other: that "the principle of expressibility does not imply that it is always possible to find or invent a form of expression that will produce all the effects in the hearer that one means to produce; for example, literary or poetic effects, emotions, beliefs, and so on."[34]

These qualifications seem to imply something like this: corresponding to what I have called the *pragmatic difference* between the fixed intension of terms and their possible extension as names of real referents, there is also a *pragmatic difference* between the conventional linguistic rules for expressing illocutionary acts and the meaning-intentions one may wish to express by speech acts. But, as in the case of the triangular discussion, we must also in this case take into account something like an *internal* relation between possible meaning-intentions, and possible conventional linguistic meanings. This means that, in both cases, one may suppose that a living language is *open*, in principle, to a public expression by conventional sign-types of those meaning-intentions that cannot be actually expressed in such a way as yet.

In my opinion, these qualifications of the principle of expressibility are still to be supplemented by the following clause (which allows for a compensation, so to speak, of the pragmatic difference by the communicative competence of the speaker): Within the situational context, it is always possible to express genuine meaning-intentions by non-conventional signs, e.g., by suggesting non-literal, occasional meanings of conventional linguistic signs or by the use of para- or extra-linguistic *ad hoc* signs. But also in these cases the possibility of sharing a public meaning, at least by the speaker and the hearer, is dependent on the presupposition of the conventional meaning of sign-types of language by the occasional meanings of the *ad hoc* signs; thus, e.g., on the presupposition of the literal meaning of words by their metaphorical meaning. Beyond this it is dependent on the fact that sharable meanings of *ad hoc* signs are based on successful *ad hoc* conventions about the use of the *ad hoc* signs, so to speak.[35] (I need not speak in this context of non-linguistic sign-types − as e.g., those of signal-languages whose meanings are parasitic on those of conventional linguistic sign-types − or of the use of signs by animals whose valid understanding as meaningful for us humans is always dependent on a *reconstruction* in the light of our understanding of conventional linguistic meanings.) In brief: insofar as the occasional meanings of *ad hoc* signs may be understood as public or intersubjectively valid meanings, they are in fact both dependent on conventional linguistic meanings and also virtually supplement those meanings by *ad hoc* conventions about public meanings.

On the condition of these qualifications, I think, Searle's "principle of expressibility" is valid; for it provides, indeed, the only criterion for a demarcation between genuine meaning-intentions, which may be expressed, in principle, by illocutionary acts, and strategical pseudo-meaning-intentions, i.e. direct-intentions of perlocutionary effects which cannot be expressed by illocutionary acts and hence cannot become publicly sharable meanings at all. On the condition of the "principle of expressibility," direct intentions of perlocutionary effects, and, in this sense, attempts at "perlocutionary acts," can indeed only be understood as intentions of purposive rational actions that incidentally use language-signs as means or instruments for suggesting certain conclusions to the hearer − conclusions that cannot be expressed publicly, in principle.

In accordance with the preceding, Searle's "principle of expressibility" provides a crucial argument for the *pragmatic completion of the linguistic turn in philosophy* in the sense of my contention. For it shows, as Searle puts it himself, that

> there are . . . not two irreducibly distinct semantic studies, one a study of the meaning of sentences and one a study of the performances of speech acts. For just as it is part of our notion of the meaning of a sentence that a literal utterance of that sentence with that meaning in a certain context would be the performance of a particular speech act, so it is a part of our notion of a speech act that there is a *possible* [my emphasis] sentence (or sentences) the utterance of which in a certain context would in virtue of its (or their) meaning constitute a performance of that speech act.[36]

It is an implication of this position that genuine meaning-intentions must be capable, in principle, of being articulated *publicly* (i.e., as meaning-claims whose intersubjective validity can be redeemed in principle by the indefinite community of interpretation). This would not be possible if there were no constitutive rules of "the" language, realized conventionally by some special language (i.e., "*langue*"), by which the meaning intentions can be articulated publicly. Every special language, so to speak, is an *institution* for articulating meaning-intentions publicly, and since every special language is open to articulating any *possible* meaning-intention, it is, so to speak, a quasi-transcendental institution providing – in a still contingent, historical form – the conditions of the possibility of intersubjectively valid meanings.

This is, of course, a re-statement of the point of the linguistic turn in philosophy; and from this re-statement it follows already that (intersubjectively valid) meanings cannot be reduced to pre-linguistic intentions, just because they are necessary public articulations of genuine meaning-intentions which of course are, from an empirical-genetical point of view, the origins of meaning. The point has to be defended against those attempts at reducing meaning to pre-linguistic intentions that have become fashionable again in recent years in a revived "philosophical psychology" or "philosophy of mind." In this context the linguistic turn has to be defended, as has yet to be shown, against the psychologistic turn of John Searle himself in his last work, *Intentionality*.

This brings me to the third part of my story.

III. The Overturning of the Pragmatic Turn by Reducing Meaning to Pre-Linguistic Intentions and the Possibility of its Refutation.

III. 1. Remarks on Gricean "Intentionalist Semantics."

One strand of the new *psychologistic turn* is represented by Paul Grice's "intentionalist" theory of meaning and the long series of attempted improvements and elaborations of this approach which, via S. R. Schiffer and J. Bennett, leads to an integration of D. Lewis's theory of "conventions" and thus to a strategical game theory of perlocutionary interaction.[37]

It is this strand of communication theory that may in the first place be characterized by calling it an "overturning of the *pragmatic* turn of meaning-theory." For the leading strategy here is, from the beginning, to play down, so to speak, the linguistic institution of publicly sharable "timeless" (Grice) meanings by reducing meanings to the intentions of purposive-rational actions of single actors. These actors, it is supposed, try to realize – just by the instrument of language – some perlocutionary effect, i.e., some response in or by the hearer that lies beyond the illocutionary effect of just understanding the publicly sharable meaning of a speech act (say, some overt reaction or only some mental disposition − a belief or an emotion − of the hearer). The conventions of interaction and communication − and in this context even the meaning-conventions and hence finally the intersubjectively valid "timeless" meanings − are to come about by the strategical game, i.e., by the rules of strategical reciprocity, of the intertwined purposive-rational actions of single actors.

This strategy of an intentionalist meaning theory can be refuted as incompatible with the genuine meaning-intentions of human speakers. In order to show this, one need not deny that in almost every human communication, covertly strategical actions − such as, e.g., suggestions of certain conclusions and emotional attitudes by rhetorical or other means and especially such a thing as "image-cultivation" − are in play. But, as Strawson has already shown, the intentions of those directly perlocutionary intentions may be sharply distinguished from the non-strategical meaning-intentions that underlie illocutionary acts. These latter intentions may be called *"verständigungsorientiert"* (approximately: "oriented toward understandable and acceptable validity-claims") in contradistinction to those that are simply *"erfolgsorientiert"* (approximately: "oriented toward one's perlocutionary intentions"), to speak along with Habermas.[38] It is important to notice, in this context, that those speech-acts that are *erfolgsorientiert* and hence use language only as an instrument − as, e.g., acts of suggesting a certain "image" of the speaker − must nonetheless appear to be *verständigandsorientiert* at the surface, in order to reach their covertly strategical purposes. In short, direct perlocutionary acts must be *parasitic upon* the possibility and pretended actuality of illocutionary acts. In order not to misunderstand this point, however, I think two comments are needed.

First, it has to be granted that our *illocutionary* acts are usually *erfolgsorientiert*, in a sense, and thus are means for reaching a perlocutionary effect in the hearer. Thus, e.g., informative statements wish to bring about some belief in the hearer; orders wish to be obeyed and hence to bring about some reaction, and even arguments are to convince the opponent and hence to bring about a conviction in his mind. But *these* perlocutionary intentions are not those of *direct* perlocutionary (i.e., covertly strategical) acts in the sense of Strawson. For their intended perlocutionary effects depend upon being first *understood* − on the level of a publicly sharable meaning-claim − and then, on the basis of this understanding, being judged and eventually accepted by the hearer with regard to their further validity-claims. Thus an informative statement is to be *accepted as true* before it is allowed to produce a belief; an order is to be accepted as legitimate before being obeyed; a condolence is to be accepted as sincere prior to its bringing about some feeling of consolation; and an argument is to be accepted as valid or sound before a conviction is acquired. (This was obviously Socrates's and Plato's point against the persuasive rhetorics.)

I am here following Habermas's claim concerning the four *universal* "validity-claims" ("meaning-claim," "truth-claim," "sincerity-claim," normative "rightness-claim") that are bound up with the illocutionary acts and make up the "binding force" of human speech, by which a "communicative coordination" of human actions – in contradistinction to a strategical coordination – may be reached. But I do not consider it useful to change – along with Habermas – the usual terminology and have the terms "illocutionary act" and "illocutionary effect" cover not only the "uptake" (Austin) or understanding of the speech-act but also its being accepted on the ground of its "binding force".[39] We simply cannot say, "I hereby convince you." Therefore, the act of *convincing* cannot be an illocutionary act, although it surely cannot be a direct perlocutionary act (i.e., a covertly strategical act) in Strawson's sense either. We should rather allow for a terminological distinction between three things:

(1) perlocutionary effects that are brought about accidently;

(2) perlocutionary effects that are brought about by a covertly strategical use of language;

(3) perlocutionary effects that are brought about by the binding force (of the validity claims) of our speech.

A second comment may be needed with regard to the relationship between Strawson's distinction of acts or intentions and the Gricean type of "intentionalist semantics." As a matter of fact, Strawson tried to improve on Grice's approach, in order to make it compatible with his distinction.[40] This tendency has been continued by offering further improvements of the so called "Gricean mechanism." This means: the speaker-hearer-reciprocity of intentionality and knowledge was to be reflected in advance by the self-referential meaning-intention of the speaker to such an extent that a *deception* of the hearer by a covertly strategical perlocutionary act would be excluded. Yet it can be shown that this is impossible, in principle, as long as there is an *asymmetry* between the perlocutionary intention of the speaker and the possible knowledge of the hearer about the speaker's intention.[41] This asymmetry, however, is a necessary implication of the Gricean approach. It can only be prevented if (and when) the speaker gives up using language *only* as an instrument, in order to reach some perlocutionary effect – be it even the effect of becoming totally transparent in his intentions for the hearer.

In order to realize a genuine *meaning*-intention, i.e., to express a meaning that is symmetrically intelligible for the speaker and the hearer, the speaker has to restrict his intention to that of an illocutionary act whose effect is a publicly sharable meaning. And in order to achieve this, he has to make his own and the hearer's understanding of his meaning-intention depend on the conventional meanings of language. For only conventional meanings of language provide the conditions of the possibility of intersubjectively valid meanings as we have already pointed out. Since this situation holds for us today – a situation that is a transcendental condition of our arguments – it seems to me to be completely irrelevant, in this context, to take recourse to the psychological, historical or even evolutionist priority of pre-linguistic meaning-intentions which – as may perhaps be claimed – are not yet underlying the distinction between illocutionary and direct perlocutionary (i.e., covertly strategical) acts. However language may have come about genetically, for us it is the condition of the possibility of *sharable* meanings.

Let us now consider the psychologistic turn of meaning-theory as it is represented by Searle's recent work, *Intentionality*.

III. 2. Remarks on Searle's Intentionalist Semantics

The strategy of argument in Searle's latest book seems to be rather different from that of the Griceans, although it appears that also for Searle the difference between genuine meaning-intentions expressed by illocutionary acts and the intentions of direct perlocutionary acts[42] has now lost its significance. This must be the case, it seems to me, since Searle now has abandoned altogether his former account of meaning-intentions in terms of communicative intentions.[43] This means that he no longer molds his concept of meaning according to the performative-propositional double structure of illocutionary acts or explicit sentences that express those acts. (This was Habermas's understanding of Searle's meaning-theory in *Speech Acts*.[44]) Instead, Searle now turns back to a pre-communicative and pre-linguistic paradigm of meaning in the sense of representation.[45] He summarizes his present position as follows:

> Communicating is a matter of producing certain effects on one's hearers [here obviously illocutionary *and* perlocutionary effects are

taken together!], but one can intend to represent something without caring at all about the effects on one's hearers. One can make a statement without intending to produce conviction or belief in one's hearers or without intending to get them to believe that the speaker believes what he says or indeed *without even intending to get them to understand it at all* [my emphasis].[46]

In the last sentence Searle's abandonment of his former ("illocutionary") concept of meaning is clearly formulated. And this means: his abandonment of the pragmatic completion of the linguistic turn by the theory of speech-acts.

The deeper reason for this turn is that he now thinks that "intentional states of the mind," as "beliefs," "desires," and "intentions" in the narrower sense of "intentionality," are more fundamental with regard to meaning than the linguistic meaning-conventions that rule the possible expressions of the meaning-intentions.[47] What arguments could be proposed in favor of these assumptions? Among the reasons for Searle's attempt at grounding the philosophy of language by a philosophy of the mind there are especially the following.

One reason is the quasi-Husserlian point that linguistic expressions as physical entities would not carry meaning at all if they were not *animated*, so to speak, by our pre-linguistic intentions and thus made the expressions of meaning.[48] Another important argument says that the "conditions of satisfaction" that are connected with illocutionary acts – as e.g., with statements, orders or promises – are *primarily* "conditions of satisfaction" with regard to the "intentional states" of the mind. "Thus, for example, my statement will be true if and only if the expressed belief is correct, my order will be obeyed if and only if the expressed wish or desire is fulfilled, and my promise will be kept if and only if my expressed intention is carried out."[49]

Now, in trying to deal with these arguments, I will, of course, not deny that intentionality is a necessary precondition or ingredient of speech, i.e., of the use of language, or, in other words, that a satisfactory philosophy of language must at the same time be an adequate philosophy of mind. For *this* contention belongs to the very point of my thesis that the abstractive fallacy of the semanticist stage of the linguistic turn has to be overcome by the pragmatic completion of the linguistic turn.

I think that a particular merit of the speech act theory lies precisely in the fact that the self-referentiality of the mind, which was made the foundation of critical philosophy in modern times but was tabooed by logical semanticism since Frege and Russell, has been rediscovered and rehabilitated in a sense by Austin's detection of the performatives. This is even further confirmed by Searle's analysis of the "self-referentiality of indexical propositions" where he shows that and how the utterance of an indexical expression can have a "completing Fregean sense," because it expresses an "intentional content" that indicates relations that the object he is referring to has to the utterance itself.[50] This pragmatic completion of "sense" was overlooked by Frege and his semanticist followers because they had a purely symbolical-conceptionalist idea of "sense," in Peirce's terms.

What then should be said in defending the linguistic turn against the psychologistic turn of the latest Searle?

In general I would argue that Searle is now sinning against the spirit of his own "principle of expressibility," because he *only* considers the dependence of illocutionary acts, and hence sentences, on intentional states of the mind (and the intentions to express them), but does *not* consider the inverse dependence of the meaning of intentional states on that of their possible expressions by illocutionary acts, and hence on explicit linguistic sentences. Let me try to show this in more detail with regard to his two arguments quoted before.

In the first quasi-Husserlian argument, Searle is overlooking or disregarding − along with the whole pre-linguistic turn philosophy − that one may not conceive of *physical* entities as linguistic entities without presupposing already a structure − e.g., of relevant oppositions of sounds − that corresponds to a linguistic meaning-structure. This reflects the complementary prejudice that the intentional states of the mind could have the status of articulated meaning-intentions without already presupposing a structure of meaning-differences that is conventionally and thus publicly fixed to the linguistically relevant structures of physical entities, as e.g., sounds as phonemes. So it looks as if a solitary person, or mind, could *animate* the purely physical entities of language with publicly valid meaning-intentions.

Searle illustrates this conception of the relationship between pre-linguistic meaning intentions and linguistic − or other possible − expressions of them by the following example:

> It sometimes happens to me in a foreign country . . . that I attempt to communicate with people who share no common language with me . . . .
> In such a situation I mean something by my gestures, whereas in another situation, by making the very same gestures, I might not mean anything.[51]

Searle seems to overlook completely in this story that those of his gestures which are animated by meaning-intentions are by no means a functional equivalent of linguistic entities, since their meanings are parasitic upon those linguistic meanings which Searle and his communication-partners presupposed, even when they did not share a common language with each other but only with their compatriots, in forming their meaning intentions. Instead Searle offers the following one-sided account of the relationship between intentionality and linguistic meaning:

> Since linguistic meaning is a form of derived Intentionality, its possibilities and limitations are set by the possibilities and limitations of Intentionality. The main function which language derives from Intentionality is, obviously, its capacity to represent. Entities which are not intrinsically Intentional can be made Intentional by, so to speak, intentionally decreeing them to be so. . . . New language games are expressions of pre-existant form of Intentionality.[52]

This time-honored common sense idea of the relation of mind and language[53] has been refuted most thoroughly, I think, by F. de Saussure. He has shown at least this much: language is the realm of *mutual differentiation* of "signifiants" and "signifiés," i.e., of physically based sign-vehicles and mentally based meanings, such that there arc no pre-linguistic entities that could already claim the status of inter-subjectively valid meanings. Saussure made this point clear in passages such as the following:

> Without language, thought is a vague, uncharted nebula. There are no pre-existing ideas, and nothing is distinct before the appearance of language.
> Against the floating realm of thought would sounds by themselves yield predelimited entities? No more so than ideas. Phonic substance is neither more fixed nor more rigid than thought; it is not a mold into which thought must of necessity fit but a plastic substance divided in turn into distinct parts to furnish the signifiers needed by thought . . . .
> . . . Neither are thoughts given material form nor are sounds transformed into mental entities; the somewhat mysterious fact is rather that "thought-sound" implies division, and that language works out its units while taking shape between two shapeless masses.[54]

Moreover, even Searle himself, in his *Speech Acts*, gave an important hint to the indispensability of the conventional rules of language for the constitution of publicly valid meanings. What I mean is his distinction between "constitutive rules," which are the conditions of the possibility of all "institutional facts" of human culture, including special languages, and "regulative rules" which, as, e.g., rules of technical skill, may refer immediately to natural activities, as e.g., eating or running. If the conventional rules of language could be dispensed with in constituting ("institutional facts" of) meanings, then we could dispense with "constitutive rules" in favor of resorting to the "regulative rules" for purposive-rational actions. This is precisely the strategy of those representatives of an "intentionalist" meaning theory who try to explain the public validity of "timeless meanings" of language by recourse to pre-linguistic purposes of human actors within the frame of strategical interaction. But these followers of the early Grice and of the economic theory of strategical games cannot explain the difference between illocutionary acts that constitute public meanings and those direct perlocutionary acts that are parasitic on the public meanings conveyed by illocutionary acts.

The question of the constitution of the public validity of meanings brings me to answer the second argument of the latest Searle. At first sight, it seems to be a very strong argument to say that the conditions of satisfaction of illocutionary acts, as statements, orders or promises, are primarily those of intentional states of the mind, as beliefs, wishes, or purposive intentions. But on a closer look, one sees that this argument is one-sided or ambiguous. The ambiguity of the argument rests on the concept of "conditions of satisfaction." This concept suggests a parallelism and a one-sided dependence relation between illocutionary acts and intentional states, whereas, there is a parallelism and a difference and a mutual dependence between them.

To suggest this point provisionally with regard to one of Searle's examples: it is of course true that "my statement will be *true* if and only if the expressed belief is *correct*" (my emphasis). But I would like to supplement this truism with the following claim: If the *correctness* of my belief is to mean as much as *intersubjective validity* which is to be examined and reconfirmed publicly, then also the following proposition holds: My *belief may be correct* if and only if my corresponding *statement* my be proven to be *true*, i.e., *intersubjectively valid*. For, otherwise, proving the *correctness* of my belief may mean just as much as providing representational evidence, just for myself, of the fact that a certain uninterpreted and possibly uninterpretable phenomenon that I suppose to exist is in fact given. This would in a sense provide a condition of satisfaction for *my belief*, but, nevertheless, it does not yet satisfy the *truth-claim of a statement*.

In order to elucidate this somewhat complicated contention, I will introduce at this point some tenets of J. Habermas's "universal" or "formal pragmatics"[55] Habermas received and elaborated precisely those points of Searle's early speech act theory that have been disregarded or dropped by the later Searle. Thus from the "principle of express-ibility," Habermas derived the conclusion that speech acts as well as explicit sentences of human language have a partly *performative* and partly *propositional* "double structure." From this he further concluded that, in virtue of the "double structure," sentences can make explicit the universal *validity-claims*, i.e., claims of public or intersubjective validity, that constitute the "binding force," and hence are necessarily connected with communicative acts of speech. Those validity-claims are:

1. the *truth-claim* which refers to the propositional part of a state-ment (or possibly to its existential presuppositions);

2. the *veracity-* or *sincerity-claim* which refers to the intentional state of the mind that is expressed by a speech act;

3. the *normative rightness-claim* which refers to a communicative act as part of a social action, and, I would emphasize, as a precondition for these three validity-claims;

4. the *meaning-claim* which refers to the intended effect of an *illo-cutionary act* (in contradistinction, e.g., to the strategically intended purpose of *direct perlocutionary acts*).

I am emphasizing this last point because it is only the sharing of the public meaning claimed by illocutionary acts that makes it possi-ble for the other three validity-claims of speech acts to be satisfied or redeemed, if it becomes necessary.

At first sight, one could think that this conception of satisfying or redeeming validity-claims should aim at something very similar to the later Searle's conception of satisfying the "conditions of satisfaction" of illocutionary acts and, more fundamentally, of "intentional states of the mind." However, precisely at this point an important difference becomes visible, a difference between a position that follows the strategy of a pragmatic completion of the linguistic turn and a position that falls back behind the linguistic turn of philosophy in favor of a version of psychologism and methodological solipsism. Let us con-sider this more closely.

As I already intimated, redeeming the truth-claim of a statement may be something quite different from proving the correctness of a belief, if the latter is not made dependent on the redeemability of the truth-claim of a statement. The reason for the difference is the follow-ing. A correctness-claim of a belief that could be satisfied indepen-dently from understanding the truth-claim of a statement and thus be considered "more fundamental" than the latter can only rest on the representational evidence of a perception, say, the perception that there is a state of affairs like this (see Figure II). Now, on Peirce's semiotic account, which I would follow, such evidence is that of an iconical representation of phaneroscopic Firstness. And this is not even a sufficient condition for grounding the truth-claim of a perceptual judgment. It is only a necessary condition for an "abductive inference" that necessarily includes a language-mediated interpretation. The abductive inference would have the form:

> This there looks so and so;
> what looks so and so should be a case of *p*;
> hence, this there should be a case of *p*.

The result of such an *interpretation* may then be formulated by the statement, "The cat is on the mat."

FIGURE II

But this result of the *interpretation* is by no means a matter of course philosophically, as Searle himself makes clear in his chapter on the "background" of the understanding of meaning, which is also determined by our linguistic competence.[56] There may indeed be other interpretations of our picture – e.g., those that are based on a different apprehension (conception) of the animal or the base it rests on, or even the situation that is referred to by the "on." (This situation, e.g., might be interpreted with the aid of a Newtonian or Einsteinian gravitation theory.) In any case, it is only the result of the *interpretation*, formulated by a statement, that can be made the object of a truth-claim and of its satisfaction. Of course, in real life a belief will usually be already the result of a linguistic interpretation, but to this extent it is dependent on the conditions of satisfaction of the truth-claim of a statement, and not the other way around, *quod erat demonstrandum*.

The difference and the mutual dependence between the conditions of satisfaction of intentional states and those of public validity-claims of speech acts becomes even more clear in the case of *orders* and the underlying *wishes* or *desires*. For in this case, the specific validity-claim of an order and its difference from the meaning of a private wish or desire does not even become visible on Searle's account. In fact, it cannot be satisfied or redeemed just by satisfying the underlying wish or desire, as Searle suggests; for, as a normative rightness-claim, the validity-claim of an order has to be *acknowledged* and, if necessary, *legitimated*, whereas the wish or desire as an intentional state of the mind may only be fulfilled (potentially, perhaps) as a consequence of acknowledging the validity-claim of an order. Thus it becomes clear that the public meaning of a speech act, in contradistinction to the intentional state of the mind that is said to determine the satisfaction conditions of a speech act, must imply a reason for the hearer's understanding and accepting the message. In the case of a statement the immediate reason is provided by its *truth-claim*; in the case of an order by its *rightness-claim*; but in the case of a simple *imperative*, the reason for obeying, which is suggested by the speech act, need not be the legitimacy of a validity-claim. It may rather be provided in this case by the *power* that is behind the imperative or, for that matter, by the sanctions to be expected in case of not obeying.[57]

Thus far it might even appear, as if there were only a difference, and no mutual dependence at all, between the satisfaction conditions of wishes and orders, and hence of "intentional states," on the one hand, and those of speech acts, on the other. But one should rather say – along with Habermas[58] – that recognizing the conditions of the satisfaction of intentional states in Searle's sense is just *one* component of the conditions of the acceptability of speech acts, since the latter must convey a binding force that is based on reasons beyond the satisfaction conditions of intentional states.

Thus far one has to grant that the illocutionary act of an order must, indeed, presuppose some sort of a *wish* or *desire*, which has to be fulfilled, even if, e.g., a military order may sometimes not be the expression of the *private* wish or desire of the speaker. On the other hand, however, one must also realize that a wish or desire, in order to be fulfilled, in many cases has to be expressed by a speech act that has some "binding force," e.g., by an order or demand or a question. Beyond this, even the meaning of the most intimate wishes or desires, which may be fulfilled by good fortune, must be *interpreted* in light of language in order to be the *meaning* of some *specific* intentional state.

This brings us back to the public meaning-claim of illocutionary acts which is indeed the most fundamental thing from the point of view of the linguistic turn of philosophy. For it is simply not possible to go behind this claim if we want to have a common basis for arguing. And *arguing* is the intranscendable basis for a philosophy after the linguistic turn, if this turn is conceived of as a transcendental-semiotic turn.

If my preceding critique of Searle's main arguments for his intentionalistic turn is justified, then it obviously cannot be true that one can make a *statement* without intending to get some hearer to understand it.[59] For, if one makes a *statement*, one must commit oneself to those universal validity-claims that are connected with speech, i.e., with its public meaning-claim. The case of a monological judgment – say, a perceptual judgment on some given state of affairs – may easily be explained as a case of the "voiceless dialogue of the soul with itself" (Plato). And it seems clear that – after the linguistic turn – this "voiceless dialogue" can only be understood as an internalization of the normal public dialogue by speech. Otherwise we could not understand that even a monological perceptual judgment participates in a public world-interpretation.

To summarize my critique of the intentionalist move of the later Searle, I am inclined to say the following: By resorting to pre-linguistic and pre-communicative representing of intentional states, Searle seems to fall back on what I have called the "methodological solipsism" of the philosophy of mind or consciousness from Descartes to Husserl. It is interesting to compare this result of Searle's "intentionalism" with the result of the other version of "intentionalism" which starts out from P. Grice and, via Schiffer, Lewis and J. Bennett, leads to a type of communication theory that integrates a theory of conventions by a strategical game theory of perlocutionary interaction. In a sense, this movement is a contraposition to Searle's *mentalism*, since it does not reduce meaning to a pre-communicative state of the mind but rather to a trans-communicative purpose of instrumental actions. But with regard to the linguistic turn of philosophy it ultimately has the same effect. For in both cases the pragmatic turn toward the meaning-intentions of the human use of signs or language has been overturned in such a way that it becomes incompatible with the philosophical achievements of the linguistic turn. This means that in both cases the functions of the transcendental institution of language, i.e., the function of constituting intersubjectively valid meanings by illocutionary acts, has been overlooked. (To say this with regard to Searle is a bit odd, since without his early work on speech acts I would not have reached my present view of the pragmatic completion of the linguistic turn.)

The most characteristic symptom of a complete loss of the transcendental point of the linguistic turn is the tendency in the later Searle as in other representatives of "philosophical psychology" to go even beyond "intentional states of the mind" and ground the theory of meaning on a theory of the "brain."[60] There is of course nothing to say against a theory of the relations between language, the mind, and the brain. Therefore, I do not wish to argue against Searle's particular account of this topic.[61] But the question is how to understand the talk about something being "more basic (or fundamental) than something else." There is no doubt that language and meaning "come very late" in the biological-evolutionist "order of priority." And there is no doubt either that the development of the *brain* is a biological condition of the possibility of the *mind* and to that extent of *language*. But the point of the linguistic turn was a *transcendental* one, as I tried to show from the beginning by recourse to Wittgenstein. That is to say, it was a new answer – different from that of Kant – to the question of the conditions of the possibility of the intersubjective validity of what we can mean. Now, it seems clear to me that from this point of view a theory of the brain cannot compete seriously with the transcendental claim of modern philosophy of language (just as before it could not compete seriously with the transcendental claim of a philosophy of the mind or consciousness.) For a theory of the brain cannot, of course, answer the question concerning the conditions of the possibility for our validity-claims in talking about the brain.

The aim of this paper was to show that the transcendental function of First Philosophy[62] cannot be fulfilled by a purely semanticist version of the linguistic turn either. It can be fulfilled by a transcendental-pragmatic completion of the linguistic turn within the framework of a transcendental semiotics.

Notes

1. E. Stenius, *Wittgenstein's 'Tractatus'* (Oxford: Basil Blackwell, 1964).

2. L. Wittgenstein, *Vermischte Bemerkungen* (Frankfurt a.M.: Suhrkamp, 1977), p. 27. Author's translation.

3. L. Wittgenstein, *Tractatus Logico-Philosophicus*, trans. D. F. Pears and B. F. McGuinness (London: Routledge and Kegan Paul, 1969), see 6.54, 7.

4. Ibid, see 5.64ff., 5.62ff.

5. See R. Carnap, "Empiricism, Semantics, and Ontology," in Linsky, ed., *Semantics and the Philosophy of Language* (Urbana: University of Illinois Press, 1952).

6. See Ibid.

7. See K.-O. Apel, "C.S. Peirce and Post-Tarskian Truth," in Freeman, ed., *The Relevance of Charles Peirce* (La Salle, Ill.: The Hegeler Institute, 1983).

8. C. Morris, "Foundations of the Theory of Signs," *International Encyclopedia of Unified Science* 1 (1938).

9. See R. Carnap, "On Some Concepts of Pragmatics," *Philosophical Studies* 6 (1955): 85–91; R. Martin, *Toward a Systematic Pragmatics* (Amsterdam: North-Holland Pub. Co., 1959).

10. I am here intentionally prefering the epistemologically and ontologically relevant explication of the triadic structure of *semiosis* to the immanent semiotic one which is based on the relation of the sign to its "immediate object" and its "interpretant," leaving aside the relations of the sign-function to the real object and the real subject of sign-mediated cognition. See K.-O. Apel, "Transcendental Semiotics and the Paradigms of First Philosophy" in *Philosophic Exchange* 2 (1978): 3–24 and "C. S. Peirce and Post-Tarskian Truth."

11. C. Morris, "Foundations of the Theory of Signs," p. 81.

12. See Ibid., and also C. Morris, *Signs, Language, and Behavior* (New York: Braziller, 1946).

13. J. R. Searle, *Intentionality* (New York: Cambridge University Press, 1983), chap. 9.

14. See J. J. Fitzgerald, *Peirce's Theory of Signs as Foundation for Pragmatism* (The Hague: Mouton, 1966), chap. 3; K.-O. Apel, *Towards a Transformation of Philosophy* (London: Routledge and Kegan, 1980), chap. 3; K.-O. Apel, *Charles S. Peirce. From Pragmatism to Pragmaticism* (Amherst: University of Mass. Press, 1981); K.-O. Apel, "C. S. Peirce and Post-Tarskian Truth," p. 189ff.

15. S. Kripke, *Naming and Necessity* (Oxford: Basil Blackwell, 1980); H. Putnam, *Mind, Language, and Reality*, 3 vols. (New York: Cambridge University Press, 1975–1983), 2: chap. 12.

16. See K.-O. Apel, *Towards a Transformation of Philosophy*, chaps. 4, 5; "Peirce and Post-Tarskian Truth."

17. H. Putnam, *Mind, Language, and Reality*, 2: pp. 223ff.

18. Ibid., 2: chap. 12.

19. See K.-O. Apel, in Charles S. Peirce: *From Pragmatism to Pragmaticism*, p. 137ff.

20. H. Putnam, *Mind, Language, and Reality*, 2: p. 227; cf. J. Leilich, *Die Autonomie der Sprache* (Munich: Profil-Verlag, 1983).

21. J. Searle, *Intentionality*, esp. pp. 205ff.

22. Ibid., p. 207.

23. Ibid., p. 208.

24. See K.-O. Apel, "Charles W. Morris und das Programm einer pragmatisch integrierten Semiotik," introduction to C. W. Morris, *Zeichen, Sprache, und Verhalten* (Düsseldorf: Schwann, 1973), pp. 9–66; K.-O. Apel, *Towards a Transformation of Philosophy*, chap. 4; and K.-O. Apel, *From Pragmatism to Pragmaticism, passim*.

25. See K.-O. Apel, *Towards a Transformation of Philosophy*, chap. 3; "Peirce and Post-Tarskian Truth."

26. See K.-O. Apel, *From Pragmatism to Pragmaticism*, p. 166.

27. See K.-O. Apel, *Peirce and Post-Tarskian Truth*.

28. See K.-O. Apel, *Towards a Transformation of Philosophy*, chap. 3; *From Pragmatism to Pragmaticism*, p. 25ff.

29. K. Bühler, *Sprachtheorie* (Jena: G. Fischer, 1934), sec. 2.

30. See K. Popper, *Objective Knowledge: An Evolutionary Approach* (Oxford: Clarendon Press, 1972), pp. 134, 293n., 295; also K.-O. Apel, "Zwei-paradigmatische Antworten auf die Frage nach der Logos-Auszeichnung der menschlichen Sprache," in Lützeler, ed., Kulturwissenschaften (Bonn: Bouvier, 1980), pp. 13–68.

31. J. L. Austin, *How to Do Things with Words* (New York: Oxford University Press, 1962).

32. See P. Grice, "Meaning," *The Philosophical Review* 66 (1957): 377–88; "Utterer's Meaning and Intentions," *The Philosophical Review* 78 (1969): 144–77.

33. J. Searle, *Speech Acts* (New York: Cambridge University Press, 1969), pp. 19–20.

34. Ibid, p. 20.

35. See K.-O. Apel, "Intentions, Conventions, and Reference to Things: Dimensions of Understanding Meaning in Hermeneutics and in Analytic Philosophy of Language," in Parret and Bouveresse, eds., *Meaning and Understanding* (Berlin: W. de Gruyter, 1981), pp. 103ff.

36. J. Searle, *Speech Acts*, p. 17.

37. See P. Grice, "Meaning," and "Utterer's Meaning and Intentions;" S.R. Schiffer, *Meaning* (New York: Oxford University Press, 1972); J. Bennet, *Linguistic Behavior* (New York: Cambridge University Press, 1969); D. Lewis, *Convention* (New York: Cambridge University Press, 1969).

38. J. Habermas, *The Theory of Communicative Action*, 2 vols., trans. T. McCarthy (Boston: Beacon Press, 1984, 1987), 1: chap. 3.

39. Ibid., pp. 290ff.

40. See P. Strawson, "Intention and Convention in Speech Acts," *Philosophical Review* 73 (1964): 439ff.

41. See K.-O. Apel, "Intentions, Conventions, and Reference to Things," pp. 93ff.; and "Lässt Sizh ethische Vernunft von strategischer Zweckrationalität unterscheiden?" in *Archivo di Filosofia*, 51, 1–3 (1983): 385ff.

42. See J. Searle, *Speech Acts*, pp. 43ff.; and *Intentionality*, p. 161.

43. See J. Searle, *Intentionality*, p. 166.

44. See J. Habermas, *Communication and the Evolution of Society*, trans. T. McCarthy (Boston: Beacon Press, 1979), chap. 1, pp. 41ff.; and *Communicative Action*, 1: chap. 3.

45. See J. Searle, *Intentionality*, pp. 164ff.

46. Ibid., p. 165.

47. Ibid., pp. 160ff.

48. Ibid., pp. 161–62, 176ff.

49. Ibid., p. 11.

50. Ibid., pp. 220ff.

51. Ibid., p. 162.

52. Ibid., p. 175.

53. See K.-O. Apel, "Transformation du Philosophie," Frankfurt a.M.: Suhrkamp, 1973, vol. II, 330ff.

54. F. de Saussure, *Course in General Linguistics*, trans. W. Baskin, eds. C. Bally and A. Sechehaye (New York: Philosophical Library, 1959), p. 112.

55. See Habermas, *Communication and the Evolution of Society*, chap. 1; and *Communicative Action*, 1, chap. 3.

56. See J. Searle, *Intentionality*, chap. 5.

57. See Habermas, *Communicative Action*, 1: pp. 299ff.

58. Ibid.

59. See J. Searle, *Intentionality*, p. 165.

60. Ibid., pp. 160ff.

61. Ibid., chap. 10.

62. See K.-O. Apel, "Transcendental Semiotics and the Paradigms of First Philosophy."

Part II.
Hermeneutics and
Critical Theory

2. From Hermeneutics and Critical Theory to Communicative Action and Post-Structuralism

David M. Rasmussen

The theses for debate which I will propose in the following essay are ones which may be derived from a reading of Habermas's recent work on the theory of communicative action and the theory of modernity. Philosophical debates have ways of appearing and disappearing in the course of time. Whether philosophical history is composed either of sharp breaks and radical ruptures or gentle transitions which retrieve the remnants of the recent past in each new emerging form is a matter of debate. In the discussion that follows I shall claim that the controversy which preoccupied continental thought in the sixties has re-emerged in a different form today. To be sure, "hermeneutics and critical theory." One could characterize the shape of the debate, the parameters of which could be designated precisely just mentioned, that the debate which shaped the controversy between hermeneutics and critical theory has moved to a new center. This very movement suggests two types of reflection on the topic "hermeneutics and critical theory." One could characterize the shape of the debate, the parameters of which could be designated precisely because they are past. Here one could paint one's grey on grey. The second course of action would be more speculative, namely, to try to designate the path which the philosophical spirit has chosen. To me the latter course appears more challenging perhaps because the outlines of the new controversy are not yet clear. In this sense the following theses are tentative indeed. Equally, they are intended as theses for debate.

1. The debate between hermeneutics and critical theory is largely over.

If one were to define the debate between hermeneutics and critical theory as a debate which had its origin in Germany during the sixties focusing on relativism vs. universalism, tradition vs. enlightenment, it can be argued that that debate has been more or less absorbed by the ongoing development of philosophy. In order to suggest the kind of discussion that dominated that debate it is only necessary to refer to Gadamer's famous essay, "On the Scope and Function of Hermeneutical Reflection," where he summarizes Habermas's position in the following manner:

> Habermas asserts that although the Hegelian procedure of reflection is not presented in my analysis as fulfilled in an absolute consciousness, nevertheless my "idealism of linguisticality" (as he calls it) exhausts itself in mere hermeneutical appropriation, development and "cultural transmission," and thus displays a sorry powerlessness in the view of the concrete whole of societal relationships. This larger whole, says Habermas, is obviously animated not only by language but by work and action; therefore, hermeneutical reflection must pass into criticism of ideology.[1]

Gadamer quite rightly recapitulates Haberman's position on critical theory here by suggesting that fundamental to the critique of hermeneutics is the distinction between traditional and critical theory as critique of ideology. In brief, the position of hermeneutics vis-à-vis Habermas's critique is that it is a-critical, animated only by language and not by labor and interaction. The latter categories are ones that became fundamental to Habermas's position through his reinterpretation of the early Hegel. The conclusion is that hermeneutics as a philosophical methodology is either non-social or, at best, impotent when confronted with social and institutional forms.

Characteristically, Gadamer does not take this criticism, which to his credit he has rightly summarized, lying down. Granted, hermeneutics may have its weaknesses, but then so does Habermas's version of critical theory.

> Habermas's critique culminates in questioning the immanentism of transcendental philosophy with respect to its historical conditions, conditions upon which he himself is dependent. Now this is indeed a central problem. Anyone who takes seriously the finitude of human existence and constructs no "consciousness as such" or "intellectus arche-

typus" or "transcendental ego," to which everything can be traced back will not be able to escape the question of how his own thinking as transcendental is empirically possible. But within the hermeneutical dimension that I have developed I do not see this difficulty arising.[2]

At issue here is the general critique of transcendentalism to which the early Habermas and Karl-Otto Apel were more or less subject. How is thinking as transcendental, empirically possible? That is the question which Gadamer's hermeneutics, grounded as it is in Heidegger's critique of Husserl, poses to Habermas. Hermeneutics can account for the historical conditions upon which philosophical analysis is grounded without having to construct a foundation for reflection outside those conditions. Of course Habermas replied that without those transcendental conditions (quasi-transcendental was said to be more appropriate) a hermeneutical position could not be critical and at the same time know the basis of its criticism.

The argument went further. Habermas claimed that hermeneutics, precisely because it lacked a foundation, was relativistic. Gadamer claimed that critical theory was essentially objectivistic, based on an enlightenment form of scienticism which has come under suspicion after Husserl's and especially after Heidegger's critique of technology. Indeed, this form of statement of the so-called debate has remained popular until recently. Richard Bernstein's *Beyond Objectivism and Relativism*, continues this argument.[3]

Looking back on this debate from the point of view of the current discussions on modernity and post-modernity, certainly the aspect of the debate that remains most interesting is the hermeneutical emphasis on both the retrieval of traditional forms of understanding, and the attempt to rehabilitate pre-enlightenment forms of thought. These attempts are still juxtaposed to those of critical theory, which finds its point of departure in the very abolition of tradition begun in the enlightenment and post-enlightenment periods. There is something very Nietzschean in this hermeneutic attempt to return to the origins of culture. The status of the enlightenment and its project of the rehabilitation of reason still hangs in the balance.

2. One line of critical theory has been transformed into the theory of communicative action.

For anyone who has read Habermas's post-1980 writings[4] the assumption contained in this thesis is rather commonplace. Habermas from the very beginning (Horkheimer, after all, refused his *Habilitationsschrift*) took an independent line from the so-called Frankfurt school even though he was a full-fledged student and co-worker (assistant to Adorno). However, as the discourse of continental philosophy has changed in the ensuing years since the late fifties and early sixties so have the assumptions which were essential to Critical Theory. Fundamental to that transformation is the development of the philosophy of language, linguistics, semiotics, etc. Habermas, along with Karl-Otto Apel, was aware of that transformation, which he tried to incorporate into his own approach to a critical philosophy. Hence the sub-proposition which supports the above thesis is the following: *Whereas Horkheimer and Adorno tried to locate their understanding of the dialectic of enlightenment in a distinction between traditional and critical theory, that distinction has been eclipsed by the distinction between the philosophy of consciousness and the philosophy of language.*

The theory of communicative action conceived under the rubrics of the philosophy of language attempts to locate critique in a more comprehensive understanding of rationality than that of the older Critical Theory. Habermas would have us perceive the process of rationalization under the limited perspective of the philosophy of consciousness which generated the idea of instrumental rationality as only an alternative mechanism of integration which is something less than communicative action. In various ways, Marx, Weber, Lukács, Horkheimer and Adorno, trapped within the philosophy-of-consciousness, were unable to perceive the essential conflict between mechanisms of integration. Limited by the subject-centered philosophy-of-consciousness model is that the relationship of the subject to the world is conceived instrumentally and not semantically. The way out of this paralysis of a philosophy of consciousness is to perceive the resolution of the problem at the level of a semantics of interaction, where the mechanism of integration is not instrumental control but rather intersubjectively reached modes of understanding conceived at the level of communication. The very reality that this option was not the chosen one provides the critical thesis, namely, that the fact that the new structures of knowledge were not institutionalized communicatively reflects the presence of certain system variables which tend to overwhelm and break down the cultural value system while effecting a deterioration of the *Lebenswelt*. In other words, the theory of communicative action conceived under the rubrics of the philosophy of language attempts to locate critique in a more comprehensive understanding of rationality than the older critical theory had.

Of course, Habermas's interpretation of the dilemma of critical theory is precisely that, an interpretation. Yet this interpretation assumes that the critique of instrumental reason which was fundamental to the efforts of Horkheimer and Adorno turned upon itself. They affirmed Weber's thesis that instrumental rationality was the predominant form of rationality in the modern period. Alas, they relinquished half of the original proposition implicit in the dialectic of enlightenment as Hegel had established it. Initially, the assumption was that reason had a certain reconciliatory power which would enable it to regenerate itself. In its pessimism Critical Theory denied this assumption. *Critique as self-referential undermined the business of critique itself.* The position drifted between instrumental reason and mimesis.

One could go on with this analysis. Certainly the thesis that reason is regenerative and reconciliatory is not flawless. There are those who would want to defend Horkheimer and Adorno on the basis of a kind of post-Weimar Republic realism, as opposed to what might be called by some a "semiotic realism" advanced by the theory of communicative action. However, I wish for the moment to leave the case where it is, in order to consider some of the consequences of the theses above.

3. Hermeneutics has been transformed into either the interpretation of discourses or the rehabilitation of phronesis.

Following Nietzsche's insight into the relativity of interpretation and Heidegger's use of that insight to focus on both the origins of Western philosophical thought and on original philosophical questioning, discursive orientations to philosophy have more or less given up traditional attempts to rehabilitate reason.

The status of the enlightenment is at issue here. If one could say that it was Hegel's thesis that the enlightenment was ambiguous, i.e., that the general assumptions with regard to science, art, religion and culture were subject to rational critique, and yet that reason was capable of generating its own foundations, then the dialectic of the enlightenment is in some sense the process of reason attempting to generate its own foundations. However, following Nietzsche and Heidegger, hermeneutics gives up on the dialectic of enlightenment. Of course, this comes as no surprise. Hermeneutics does not find its impetus in the "modern" attempt to regenerate reason. Instead, the enterprise is more humble. Following Nietzsche's and Heidegger's attempts to get behind Western thought by illuminating its origins, hermeneutics abandons any attempt to sustain the claims of enlightenment and modernity. Bearing this in mind, one kind of hermeneutics, following Gadamer, attempts to find in *phronesis* the kind of model for the rehabilitation of reason that the enlightenment lacked. Yet another form, following the more radical inclinations of Nietzsche, has transformed the program of hermeneutics into either the hermeneutics of suspicion or the total abandonment of the hermeneutic program. Foucault's focus on the discourses of power and Derrida's concentration on reading would support this assumption.

4. The theory of communicative action focuses on the discursive adjudication of validity claims.

The general sub-proposition which follows from this thesis is the following: *the theory of communicative action which has as its result the establishment of a framework for the discursive evaluation of validity claims attempts through an argument developed through speech-act theory to establish a basis for the intersubjective appropriation of utterances, to be distinguished from subject-object reflection, resulting in both the generation of and the evaluation of normative statements as well as statements of truth.*

Central to this set of claims which establishes the foundation for the theory of communicative action is a kind of argument for argument. Some arguments are better than others. On this, it is assumed, we would all agree. Reason enables us to make the necessary distinctions. Reason which pays attention to linguistic usage in argumentation can make judgments about validity claims.

The theory of communicative action depends in the first instance upon meaning and validity. The theory assumes the necessity of acknowledging the other in order to establish the meaning of an utterance and thereby examine its validity. Hence one could say that the "original mode" of linguistic usage is associated with orientation to "reaching an understanding," while instrumental usage of language is "parasitic."[5] Relying on Austin's distinction between illocutionary and perlocutionary discourse, Habermas identifies communicative action with illocutionary discourse. "I have called the type of interaction in which all participants harmonize their individual plans of action with one another, and thus their illocutionary aims *without reservation* 'communicative action.'"6 Perlocutionary utterances, on the contrary, are intent solely on producing a certain reaction in the hearer by the speaker. These latter can be defined as instrumental or strategic discourse. Communicative action will be concerned with the establishment of validity claims which can be tested in the context of interaction.

The second sub-proposition which supports the above thesis is the following: *through an immanent critique of the theoretical tradition elements can be established for a theory of rationalization and differentiation and a theory of evolution which will enable both the establishment of a normal theory and a critical foundation resulting in the discursive evaluation of validity claims.*

George Herbert Mead's theory of the social constitution of the self provides the model, after considerable revision and reconstruction, for the consensual building of individual identity. As society moves from a traditional model it is argued that there exists an inherent tendency to constitute the self on the basis of consensually mediated forms of social interaction. Durkheim provides the correlative view with regard to society. His concept of organic solidarity and the transition in accordance with the division of labor in this view becomes a theory of social evolution through consensual derivation of normatively regulated action. It is a case of transition from a society based on tradition to a society based on consensus.

As one can see, then, the theory of evolution leads to the development of a consensual model. One thinks of Hegel's remark that to him who looks at the world rationally the world looks rationally back. There is an unmitigated tendency in Habermas's work to see the consensual model in almost everything.

If the idea of evolution provides one side of the theory, the idea of differentiation provides the other. Initially, from the perspective of the evolution of society, system and life-world were conceived as one. As society evolves the social system progressively differentiates itself, i.e., the steering mechanism including state and economy separates itself from the life-world. As society develops, the levels of complexity increasingly can be reflected in the rationalization of the life-world, but not necessarily so. One has a choice of mechanisms for the mediation of new levels of complexity which enter into the system. Either they can be effectively brought into the life-world through communication, i.e., the democratic, praxiological way, or other media can be chosen, namely, money and power. If the latter path is chosen, the result will be effective deterioration of the life-world which will lead as a consequence to the state of affairs addressed by the critical thesis, namely, the potential *colonization of the life-world.*

5. A theory of communicative action takes its point of departure from a theory of modernity.

There are two sub-propositions that follow from this thesis: first, *an immanent critique of the sociological tradition in modern thought indicates that an instrumental reading of the emergence of modernity was too narrow.*

From Habermas's point of view Weber's concept of *Zweckrationalität* was too narrow to account for the development of rationality in the West. Weber thought that the purposive rational action triumphed over all other forms of rationality and rationalization leading him to view modernity and post-modernity not as the development of a new world of freedom but as an "iron cage." Habermas not only points to the limitations of this thesis – it did not account sufficiently for the actual differentiation of reason in the modern period – but he also tries to show how it affected the best of critical theory. Lukács, Horkheimer and Adorno found that the Weber thesis enabled them to get beyond Marx's attempt to derive a cultural analysis from his reading of political economy. While the first (Lukács) was able to see reification where *Zweckrationalität* had once been, the others (Horkheimer and Adorno) chose instrumental reason to specify the same dilemma. Yet, and this is Habermas's point, none was spared the Weberian irony. They too were to end up sharing Weber's "iron cage," Lukács reaching back to a reconstructed Hegelianism, Horkheimer and Adorno constructing a critical theory without a critical rational foundation.

The choice of Weber's theory of modernity as a central focus for discussion is a serious one for Habermas. Although Weber's solutions receive their apt criticism, the set of problems he chooses allows Habermas to interface a sociological with a philosophical program as did Weber himself. Briefly, Weber's famous theory of rational action, which Habermas conceives as too narrow because it is locked within the framework of a philosophy of consciousness, is replaced by the theory of communicative action. The theory of rationality and rationalization is conceived as too limited because it is not adequately differentiated to account for the complexity of modernity resulting in the "dead end" of reason referred to a moment ago. Finally, Weber's theory of evolution is perceived as too narrow, restricted by its dependence upon traditional forms of interaction which erode in the course of time.

Secondly, *an immanent critique of the philosophical claims to post-modernity finds in the very rejection of the problematic of modernity traces of that dilemma.*

This is the fundamental claim of Habermas's recent *Der philoso-phische Diskurs der Moderne,*[7] namely, that the very departure from modernity that the post-Nietzscheans have claimed for themselves bears the trace of modernity within it. This amounts to the claim that it is impossible to get around the fundamental claims of the enlighten-ment. Hence, one cannot avoid the dialectic of enlightenment. If that is true one cannot dismiss the claims of critical reason suggesting that philosophy must again return to adjudicate on questions of truth and validity. And this leads to a final summary thesis:

6. The debate between hermeneutics and critical theory has re-emerged twenty years later as the debate between the theory of communicative action and post-structuralism.

The general assumption implicit in this thesis may be stated in a sub-proposition: *A reading of Nietzsche, Heidegger, Bataille, Foucault and Derrida suggests that all share an attempt to avoid the dilemmas of moder-nity by attempting to get behind it.*

The conclusion to be drawn from this sub-proposition is that the giving up of the problematic of modernity results in the abandonment of the standards for rationality. The very attempt to abandon the dilemma of modernity is subject to its curse.

Although it would require a much longer discussion to demonstrate the thesis and sub-proposition from the point of view of the theory of communicative action, two examples may suffice. First, from the sociological perspective, the dilemma of *Zweckrationalität* forced Weber to abandon all standards of rationality resulting in the curious dilemma of the opacity of the modern situation. A study of Weber presents us with a vision of modernity turning against itself. This view of modernity then makes it impossible to make judgments about questions of validity and truth.

The second example may be seen in a study of the work of Foucault. From the point of view of the theory of communicative action the peculiar paradox resulting from a reading of Foucault is that the unity underlying the various discourses studied is given in the notion of power, a notion which is not given in the discourses themselves. One might anticipate the criticism:

1. power is a transcendental-empirical assumption;
2. power is only one form of medium whereby rationalization occurred in the modern epoch;
3. as a criterion power bears the trace of modernity by getting behind it.

This brief discussion allows us to anticipate at least one direction in which the communicative action/post-structuralism debate will move. Certainly, the reply, from the point of view of post-structuralism, will be that it is impossible to return to the forms of enlightenment reason which raised the question of the standards of reason. Propositions derived from a philosophy of language need not necessarily be derived from the enlightenment.

To summarize briefly, I have attempted to show how the formative elements of one debate which occupied Western continental philosophy for a certain time have led to another. The historical outlines are traceable. Whether the new debate will be as fruitful as the old is yet to be seen. Certainly, the new debate provides a challenge which may involve some of us for some time to come.

Notes

1. H.-G. Gadamer, *The Scope of Hermeneutical Reflection* (Berkeley: The University of California Press, 1976), p. 29.

2. Ibid., p. 36.

3. R. Bernstein, *Beyond Objectivism and Relativism* (Philadelphia: The University of Pennsylvania Press, 1983).

4. The principal work to which I will refer is J. Habermas, *Theorie des kommunikativen Handelns*, vol. 1 and 2 (Frankfurt am Main: Suhrkamp Verlag 1981); in English, *The Theory of Communicative Action*, vol. 1 and 2, trans. T. McCarthy (Boston: Beacon Press, 1984, 1987).

5. Ibid., 1:388; English, 1:288.

6. Ibid., 1:395; English, 1:294.

7. J. Habermas, *Der philosophische Diskurs der Moderne* (Frankfurt am Main: Suhrkamp Verlag 1985).

3. Hermeneutics and Critical Theory

George Schrader

The charge has been made by Habermas and others that philosophical hermeneutics cannot provide a critical social theory and, *a fortiori*, a critique of ideology. Habermas has claimed that hermeneutics must be supplemented by explanatory theory modeled after Marx or Freud. More recently he has taken a more Kantian turn, insisting upon the necessity of a priori conditions of communicative action. The latter claim is somewhat closer to hermeneutics in that communicative action must provide access to the norms which make it possible. But this turn towards transcendental conditions, as with Kant, invokes explanatory theory. In this paper I would like to consider whether the charge against Gadamer is sound and, particularly, whether the alleged deficiency could be made good by recourse to explanatory theory. Time does not permit an extended consideration of Gadamer's hermeneutical theory, but we can, at least, take note of his response to the criticism.

Gadamer not only acknowledges the legitimacy and importance of a critique of idealogy, but is prepared to embrace it as a "kind of hermeneutical reflection." "Ideological criticism represents only a particular form of hermeneutical reflection, one that seeks to dispel a certain class of prejudices through Critique."[1] If ideology critique is only a particular form of hermeneutical reflection, then there can be no conflict between Gadamerian hermeneutics and critical theory. Gadamer's responses, if successful, is something of a *tour de force*.

What, then, is this particular form of hermeneutical reflection which constitutes criticism? Gadamer's answer is swift and direct; it is precisely that reflection which "makes us aware of the illusion of reflection. . . . Hermeneutical theory which does that seems to me to come closer to the real ideal of knowledge, because it also makes us aware of the illusions of reflection."[2] This is a *tour de force* because, if Gadamer's depiction of this illusion is convincing, then his critics have already fallen prey to it. Gadamer's reply to this criticism is thus less defensive than it first appears. Not only the critique of ideology can be construed in hermeneutical terms, but any attempt to escape the hermeneutical circle by appeal to explanatory theory runs the risks of *dogmatism* and *ideology*. Therefore, it is not only a question of the possible critical potential of hermeneutics, but of the possible dogmatism of the challenge presented by the critical theorist. Since this is a crucial issue in evaluating Habermas' ideology critique, Gadamer's concept of the "illusion of reflection" is worth a closer look.

The illusion is that reflection can be free of bias, especially when pointing to bias in other quarters. "A critical consciousness that points to all sorts of prejudices and dependency, but one that considers itself absolutely free of prejudice and independent, necessarily remains ensnared in illusions."[3] In *Truth and Method*, Gadamer refers to this as "the delusion of enlightenment." There is no process of enlightenment, discipline, or purification by virtue of which the critical thinker can escape all bias, since to escape bias would amount to an escape from one's situation in the world. The import of Gadamer's claim is that in any interpretation the conditions of discourse must be included in the conversation. Or, to put it somewhat differently, no level of transcendental or a priori conditions of discourse can be exempted from the negotiations which are invariably involved in communication. Even the concepts of truth, rationality, and objectivity are not exempted from the necessity of achieving mutually acceptable understanding. Thus, from Gadamer's point of view, hermeneutics is so far from failing to provide a genuinely critical principle that, on the contrary, it supplies what may well be our only alternative to dogmatism and ideology. As will become clear in the course of my remarks, my sympathy on this point is with Gadamer. Hermeneutics surely can be developed along critical lines, particularly if one construes bias to include interpretations of the world and concrete forms of existence. To overcome bias would then require not only a change of world-views, but also a change of the world. Even though Gadamer's predilection is to stress interpretation over situation, he has left the door open for a semiotics of the concrete world. So understood, hermeneutics should not be unfriendly to the inclusion of

Freud and Marx in its stable of authors. Paul Ricoeur has in fact expressly included them in his version of hermeneutics.

The possibility that a critical social theory might be developed along hermeneutical lines should come as no great surprise to Habermas's readers. He has no quarrel with Gadamer or with hermeneutics as providing proper guidelines for approaching social theory. He departs from Gadamer only on the question of *completeness*. Habermas's aim has been to complete and supplement hermeneutics rather than to replace it. Even the use of Freudian and Marxist theory presupposes a hermeneutical understanding as the point of departure and the point of return. Habermas acknowledges his close affinity to hermeneutics in referring to his own theory as a critical or "depth hermeneutics." The personal and social knots which require Freudian and Marxist theory for their unraveling have been intentionally constituted. Moreover, once the knots have been loosened or untied, the situation can be handed back to the hermeneutics of everyday life.[4] Gadamer and Habermas agree in their respective critiques of positivistic social science which separates the inquirer from the object of his or her study and, in that sense, fails to be self-reflective. As Habermas puts it, "every natural language is its own meta-language."[5] Even when hermeneutical understanding is temporarily suspended for the sake of causal analysis, it is solely for the purpose of dissolving opaque elements in experience. Habermas's assumption is that the opacity is only provisional and, once dissolved or disentangled, can be reabsorbed into the meaning structures of everyday existence. Thus explanatory theory, at least initially, was not conceived as a substitute for hermeneutical exploration. (This is less obviously the case with Habermas's more recent appeal to normative conditions of communicative action.) Habermas could be said to avoid the "illusion of reflection" in his use of Freud and Marx in so far as he has regarded this excursus as a purely heuristic procedure. But if it is heuristic, it cannot be necessary, and the challenge to Gadamer is not serious.

Gadamer's hermeneutics, as Habermas interprets it, presupposes the *transparency* of intentional meaning to those who are party to the conversation. The meaning of any experiential situation is thus in principle available to the participants in any discourse. Although Gadamer recognizes that there is often what he terms an "excess of meaning," with accompanying anonymous intentions, even these meanings enter into a homogenous world of undertanding. This entails that, in principle, everything can be mediated by language and reflection. And it is on this point that Habermas and Gadamer disagree. Habermas insists that there are *opacities* which are not amenable to hermeneutical interpretation, and are stubbornly resistant to attempts to understand them. In his turn to Freud, Habermas came to regard repressed contents as systematically unavailable to us because they have been "desymbolized."[6] But this does not mean that they have not been intentionally constituted. On the contrary, the work of psychoanalysis is to return these "desymbolized" events to their appropriate place within the symbolic system. The fact that the analyst makes use of causal theory for purposes of analysis does not mean that the events in question have been causally generated. As we will see, this split between intentional and causal perspectives poses questions about the good faith of the practitioner and the suitability of psychoanalysis as a model for social critique.

From Habermas's point of view, a hermeneutical consciousness is not genuinely critical if it does not recognize its limits, namely, that there are incomprehensible expressions and incomprehensible actions which are inaccessible to hermeneutical interpretation:

> This specific incomprehensibility cannot be overcome by the exercise, however skillful, of one's naturally acquired communicative competence; its stubbornness can be regarded as an indication that it cannot be explained by sole reference to the structure of everyday communication that hermeneutical philosophy has brought to light.[7]

Hermeneutics is helpless when confronted with "systematically distorted expressions. . . . Incomprehensibility is here the result of a defective organization of speech itself."[8] In the case of systematically distorted communication, the participants themselves cannot recognize what is going on.

> . . . This is the case in the pseudo-communication in which the participants cannot recognize a breakdown in their communication; only an external observer notices that they misunderstand one another.[9]

We are presumably confronted in these instances with systematic distortions which derive from a source beyond experience, beyond the intentional structures of everyday life. Because the distortions are "systematic," the analysis of them must also be systematic. It is at this point that we are required to forego hermeneutical interpretation for the sake of causal analysis. The task is to "beat a path through to the pathologically blocked meaning-content."[10]

It is important not to misunderstand Habermas's appeal to casual explanation. Although for strategic purposes we must treat the unconscious as a repository of desymbolized meaning no longer accessible to consciousness, we need not interpret it as a transcending nature behind the experienced events. Such an appeal to nature as a thing in itself would be useless for explanatory purposes. At this point we are treading a narrow line between fact and fiction. We must regard the human psyche as if some elements of behaviour were being determined by natural causes, the very existence of which can only be surmised. But the device is necessary only to fill a silence, a gap in our experience. The fact that the desymbolized event was initially symbolized and that it can be incorporated into the original symbolic structure, suggests that there is *in fact* no transcending causal agency. That is why the appeal to causal theory can only be *heuristic*. The fact that it is only heuristic raises the question whether our plight was ever so desperate as we had thought. Must we really put our experience altogether aside to fill the gaps in communication? It is far from obvious that "depth hermeneutics" requires a leap beyond the data or radical transcendence of the text to be analyzed. There is even a question whether Freud characteristically proceeded in that fashion. Might the text be multi-layered with levels of meaning which, in Heidegger's sense, both conceal and reveal other levels? Might the rifts in communication and the "disrelationships within relationships"[11] point us toward the desymbolized meanings? In our leap beyond the data, we proceed "as if" there were entities beyond experience that causally determine the events to which we are witness. By mixing these totally different modes of experience, the one immanent and accessible and the other transcendent and beyond reach, we are expected to overcome the barriers to understanding. We need not remain permanently schizoid since we are promised an ultimate triumph of intentional meaning-structures. But we must be constantly on our guard that supposition does not topple over the edge into belief.

Taking Freud's interpretation of dreams as his paradigm, Habermas sketches a theory of systematically distorted speech. Distorted communication is characterized by the fact that it employs deviant rules. The assumption is that public rules provide us with rational norms and, hence, can serve as our standard for assessing deviance and distortion. This is not quite the same argument as the one we have just been considering with respect to inaccessible contents of the unconscious. And yet they are related, since both arguments claim that some types of events cannot be directly understood. The difference is that the appeal to public rules assumes a norm of rationality for appraising the deviant. In the latter case it is an appeal to conceptually formulable rules rather than to natural causes. The fact that a "deformed language game" involves rigidity and compulsion indicates that "semiotic content of a symbol has lost its specifically linguistic situational independence."[12]

It is more than a little surprising that here Habermas should appeal to public norms as his criterion of the deviant. What is surprising, of course, is not the mere fact of an appeal to public norms, but rather the assumption that they must be valid. It is surprising in view of Habermas's unhappiness about Gadamer's reliance upon consensus as the hallmark of truth. It is interesting that Habermas uses a political metaphor in speaking of contents which have been "excommunicated" or "banished" from the public domain. These banished contents are taken to be irrational and invalid in that they deviate from the norm. But what if the public rules were pathological and the private deviation from them the last vestige of the sane? There might then be a barrier between the linguistically competent "I," the intersubjectively competent speaker, and the private "I" who dwells in an inner exile somewhat like Malamud's "Tinker." Validity and invalidity would seem to depend here upon what is sanctioned and what is *banished*. How would we ever determine what subjects had been illegitimately banished and what public rules were fundamentally unjust? There is a concealed appeal here to social control which does not rule out the possibility of terror. It does not provide us with a satisfactory basis for social critique and certainly does not provide us with a standard for judging the adequancy of consensus. The reply to this charge is quite obvious, namely, to insist that communication has its own instrinsic norms. That is, indeed, the way in which Habermas has moved in some of his later writings. The reply is unsatisfactory, because it falls prey to Gadamer's "illusion of reflection," or what Sartre termed "the spirit of seriousness."

Quite apart from desymbolized contents there are questions about the way in which a subject can understand him or herself. Although the tendency to assume that we should be transparently available to our own reflecting consciousness is deeply entrenched, it may well be suspect. If, as Hegel had argued persuasively in his critique of the Cartesian *cogito*, we are a subject only through the mediation of other subjects, we should not expect to understand ourselves solely through our own individual efforts. It would, in the latter instance, not be at all strange to involve third parties in the endeavour. It is quite possible that we are sometimes confronted not simply with distorted communication, but a systematically distorted world. Motivating Habermas's recourse to Freud is his conviction that what is really going on in these systemically distorted segments of behaviour is inaccessible to any of the participants. Since none of the parties involved can possibly know what is going on, a neutral third party must be introduced, namely, the psychoanalyst. The analyst comes onto the scene in the first instance as an observer who must develop a dictionary and a grammar of the private languages involved and, eventually, reconstruct the repressed events which have given rise to distorted behaviour. But in the second instance, he must serve as a causally interacting *participant* in a drama in which he is both the primary actor and the director. In his dual role as observer/agent, the analyst holds theory and practice together. If he were not agent as well as observer he would hardly serve as a plausible model for social critique.

Although the analyst is a subject basically like his client, his subjectivity is suspended for the sake of treatment. And yet he must vibrate to the same experiences as his client. Freud once remarked that the analyst's unconscious must resonate with his patient's unconscious.[13] Habermas pays little or no attention to this important side of the analyst's role. He may be more comfortable in viewing the analyst as a theoretician who *explains* and predicts rather than *intervenes* and *interacts*. But the analyst does intervene and interact; transference and countertransference are at the core of psychoanalytic treatment. The analyst places him or herself in the exceedingly demanding position of being directly involved with the patient while standing completely at a distance from all involvement. As agent, it is incumbent upon him or her both to implement and validate the theories he or she employs. The analyst is concerned with the causality of blocked experience, as well as with his or her own causal interaction with the patient/subject.

Freudian analysis, as Habermas interprets it, does not permit analyst and patient to engage in hermeneutic discourse as a means of finding an interpretation on which they both can agree. They cannot interact normally either at the level of everyday discourse or at the level of theory. For them to discuss the fine points of psychoanalytical theory, or Habermas's interpretation of it, would, in Gadamer's phrase, "spoil the game" they are playing. Indeed, the client is not even supposed to know what the game is. The analyst is, then, interpreter/theorist as well as catalytic agent. However imposing the theory, psychoanalysis is not a purely intellectual affair. Among other things the patient needs to fall in love with the analyst and work through the experience of it (the transference neurosis). It is interesting here that a perfectly normal everyday experience is turned into something abnormal and even bizarre for the sake of enlightenment and transformation. Love is regarded as the liberating power to be awakened and redirected during analysis. But this serves to introduce a new involvement and a new set of experiences for both patient and analyst. The successful interpretation in which it is hoped that the analysis will culminate relies heavily on the relationship which develops between the two subjects. It could even be looked upon as a working out and working through of something like the master/bondsman relationship to which Hegel alludes in his discussion of self-certainty.

In so far as the analyst conceals from the patient the theory he is using and even the game he is playing, he or she manifests a certain "bad faith," even if a necessary one. The analyst pretends to deal directly with the patient, but in fact he or she objectifies him/her in order to understand him/her. The patient, on the other hand, never needs to understand the analyst. When they get to such a point, the analysis must end as it does with the seduction of Cordelia in the *Diary of the Seducer*.[14] It might be uncharitable, but not necessarily inexact, to characterize psychoanalysis as a program of systematic deception. Curious, then, that systematic distortion should be cured by appeal to systematic deception. What happens to fidelity and truth on this path to enlightenment and cure? I have no desire here to be harsh with psychoanalytic theory or practice, though these are considerations which have been and must be raised. My concern is rather with the claim, which I regard as very dubious, that Freudian psychoanalysis can serve as a model for critical social theory and the critique of ideology.

A further difficulty with psychoanalysis as a model for social critique is that it tends to assume that the false-consciousness of the individual, if we may call it that, is rooted in self-deception. In other words, the neurotic person is deemed to be his or her own oppressor. Thus nothing in the world need be changed save the patient's self-relation and, even there, more his or her self-interpretation than his or her life. But if we are not doctrinaire Cartesians, we must at least consider the possibility that there may be social conditions at work, conditions which must be changed for the sake of good health. There seems to have been a question for Freud whether his patients were reporting fantasies or real-life experiences, and whether it makes a difference. To divorce fantasies from life experiences leaves us with a very tenuous tie to reality. How are we to know that a delusional system is not generated and sustained by the social environment? And what if psychoanalysis itself was a part of the same system, playing essentially the same game as other participants in that social world? The question is virtually inescapable: might psychoanalysis serve an *ideological* purpose, namely, to direct our attention away from social reality and toward the subjective consciousness of individuals? Psychoanalysis might well play a similar role to that of these existentialists whom Sartre accused of being "ideologists of subjectivity." Nietzsche, I think, anticipated the advent of psychoanalysis in his portrayal of the ascetic priest. It is by no means compellingly evident that psychoanalysis is part of the *cure* rather than the *sickness* of modern society. If it were to be appropriated for the sake of social critique and social change, it would have to be considerably altered and reoriented. Habermas has given us no hints as to how that might be accomplished.

Habermas has not dealt with the politics of psychoanalysis, the fact that it takes as its paradigm a non-reciprocal relationship based on authority and power. Psychoanalysis relies upon a medical prototype, one of the more hierarchically structured institutions in Western culture. If there are systematic distortions or peculiarities, reflected in the institutionalized practices of medicine, including psychoanalysis, they are not likely to be scrutinized by a theory and practice that assumes their validity. Gadamer has rejected the claim that this model can have universal import. In so far as the analyst attempts to universalize his/her practice, Gadamer dismisses him/her as a "spoilsport." The role of authority is a problem for any social theory, in this case for Habermas no less than for Gadamer. No theory can be genuinely critical which fails to include its fundamental postulates of method within the sphere of discussion.

Habermas is not unmindful of the questions that have just been raised concering power and authority. Nor does he deny that they are genuine issues. But he prefers to approach them obliquely by reference to a theory of communicative competence, a topic to which he has devoted much time and attention in recent years.

It is a typically Kantian line of argument to claim that we can ascertain the a priori conditions of experience and employ them normatively whether in science or in ethics. The specified conditions are taken to be necessary in that without them the experience in question would not be possible. Thus, in Habermas's case, unless certain conditions are met, there could be no speech-act, and *a fortiori* no distorted speech, since the latter requires the norm no less than normal speech. This is a tricky sort of argument to bring off since one must avoid begging the question by simply defining an experience in terms of alleged conditions. Thus we might take a case of lying and attempt to show it is parasitic upon a non-lying or truthful communication which it distorts. Truth telling does not presuppose lying in the same way. But where that actually gets us is a bit hard to say. Lying and telling the truth are certainly ways of communicating, but it is by no means self-evident that communication aims to reveal more than to conceal and even to dissemble. In modern society a honest man is almost suspect, lacking credibility. In any case, communication covers a large territory and exhibits many forms. It can be no easy task to ascertain its essence, and to do so would require us to freeze it. It is significant that in the context of his discussion of "Psychoanalysis and Social Theory,"[15] Habermas saw fit to address a diatribe at Nietzsche. Habermas clearly saw that Nietzsche's challenge to the traditional concept of truth radically called into question his own appeal to objective norms. A passage is worth quoting:

> From this Nietzsche draws the conclusion that the theory of knowledge now has to be replaced by a doctrine of perspectives based on the affects. . . . Nevertheless, it is easy to see that Nietzsche would never have arrived at perspectivism if from the very beginning he had not rejected epistemology as impossible.[16]

Habermas is perfectly correct about Nietzsche. Nietzsche's denial of epistemology and, by implication, of non-perspectival truth subverts all claims to transcendental truth.

Habermas's strategy is to separate power from truth for the sake of validity claims. But that separation sets up the possibility of enforcing claims to truth on the grounds of validity. Or, put differently, the appeal to truth and validity is of little value for the critique of ideology if it smacks of power and privilege. Habermas, like Kant before him, believes in an autonomous reason which is independent of particular exemplifications. As a transcendental principle, the idea of reason is beyond the fray and outside the communicative situation. The conditions of experience are not in experience, as Kant likes to remind us. Like truth, reason is a presupposition of, rather than an issue for, the communicative situation. Still, Habermas has been sufficiently influenced by Hegel not to be comfortable in appealing to transcendent truth conditions which can be ascertained independently of experience. Thus he avoids, in so far as is possible, an appeal to rational a priori standards immune to critical scrutiny in the light of continuing experience. His answer to Gadamer depends upon his adaptation of Kant's transcendental a priori to a self-correcting reflection on experience. His theory of communicative competence represents one of the more interesting interpretations of Kant that we have seen in a long time. If successful, it would validate the essential transcendental claims of Kantian philosophy and absolve it of the charge of dogmatism.

To put it succinctly, Habermas's strategy is to permit discussion and negotiation of the *penultimate* conditions of communication while holding the *ultimate* conditions aloof. Claims to a priority and necessity are thus kept to an absolute minimum. It is not perfectly clear just how far Habermas is prepared to go in allowing the negotiation of a priori principles. One thing is clear, however, namely that in so far as they are negotiable, there is no significant difference between his theory and Gadamer's philosophical hermeneutics. If we do not expose such principles to deliberation, we objectify them and grant them a gratuitous validity which renders them immune to historical change. In spite of his attempt to weaken the Kantian a priori, Habermas does not go so far as to bring the ultimate conditions of communicative action into the arena of discussion. And, by the same token, it is not clear that he is prepared to subject the discourse about the conditions of discourse to political struggle. It seems that at the last level of analysis Habermas may, in turning back to Kant, have turned away from Hegel and Marx and, in the process, turned away from history. Can we legitimately distinguish between those norms which are arrived at through historical struggle and a "rational consensus" which is self-validating? If not, ideology critique ultimately falls prey to dogmatism and the "illusion of reflection." Not only that, but the claim to trans-empirical standards itself takes on an ideological flavour by masking the fact that the validity of such standards must be backed by power and authority.

Habermas criticizes Gadamer for relying too heavily upon consensus for the validation of truth claims. Yet, as we have seen, Habermas must rely upon the same consensus if he is to avoid dogmatism. Habermas's theory seems to suffer from the opposite failing, namely, that it obviates the need for consent so far as the ultimate conditions of discourse are concerned. And this means that, as with Kant, transcendental analysis takes precedence over social deliberation. Tacit appeal must be made to something like a transcendental ego that is formally identical in all rational agents. Formal identity displaces empirically based agreement. It is for these reasons that, in my judgment, Gadamer's hermeneutics provides a more satisfactory basis for critical theory than Habermas's ideology critique.

Notes

1. Hans-Georg Gadamer, *Philosophical Hermeneutics*, trans. and ed. David E. Linge (Berkeley: University of California Press, 1976), pp. 92, 93.

2. Ibid, p. 93.

3. Ibid.

4. Jürgen Habermas, *Knowledge and Human Interests*, trans. Jeremy J. Shapiro (Boston: Beacon Press, 1971), p. 233.

5. Jürgen Habermas, "The Hermeneutic Claim to Universality," in *Contemporary Hermeneutics: Hermeneutics as Method, Philosophy, and Critique*, ed. Josef Bleicher (London: Routledge & Kegan Paul, 1980), p. 192.

6. Habermas, *Knowledge and Human Interests*, pp. 219ff.

7. Habermas, "The Hermeneutic Claim to Universality," p. 190.

8. Ibid, p. 191.

9. Ibid.

10. Ibid., p. 189.

11. This is an expression which Søren Kierkegaard uses effectively in characterizing despair in his *Sickness Unto Death*, trans. and ed. Howard V. Hong and Edna H. Hong (Princeton, NJ: Princeton University Press, 1980), vol. 1, A.

12. Habermas, "The Hermeneutic Claim to Universality," p. 192.

13. Cf. George Dowell Downing III, "Freud's Concept of the Unconscious Mind" (Ph. D. dissertation, Yale University, 1969).

14. Søren Kierkegaard, *Either/Or*, with a Foreward by Howard A. Johnson, trans. David F. Swenson and Lillian Marvin Swenson (Princeton, NJ: Princeton University Press, 1959), vol. 1.

15. Habermas, *Knowledge and Human Interests*, pp. 290ff.

16. Ibid., p. 298.

4. Enlightenment as Political

Dick Howard

The Problem: Founding Politics

In a letter printed as an appendix to Richard Bernstein's *Beyond Objectivism and Relativism*, Gadamer describes the central difference between himself and Habermas as political. Obviously, "political" here does not refer to *Weltanschauungen* or party politics; it refers, rather, to different conceptions of the practical role of philosophy. As Gadamer describes it, Bernstein and Habermas deny that truly modern societies share the common *Ethos* or community of normative consciousness which founded Aristotle's transition from the *Ethics* to the *Politics*. Modern conditions demand instead the move from practical philosophy to social science. Gadamer rejects the *"hubris"* of this claim; he insists that social solidarities do exist, and that we are not living in a society "constituted only by social engineers or tyrants."[1] "Plato," he continues, "saw this very well: there is no city so corrupted that it does not realize something of the true city." This "something" shared by the community founds that *phronesis* which is the philosophically adequate form of practice.[2] The question is how to found the demonstration of its presence or absence.

Bernstein's book is a remarkable effort to draw together the disparate threads of contemporary philosophy around the structure of a modernity which he epitomizes as the "Cartesian Anxiety." The reader familiar with the "Critical Theory" elaborated by the first generation of the Frankfurt School will recognize in Bernstein's study the attempt to ground *immanently* the distinction between Critical and Traditional Theory which Max Horkheimer brought to a head in his 1937 article of the same title. Although Horkheimer's method differs from Bernstein's, their "political" goals are the same: in Bernstein's words, without sharing "Marx's theoretical certainty or revolutionary self-confidence," nonetheless to "dedicate ourselves to the practical task of furthering the type of solidarity, participation and mutual recognition" which will *in fact* "move us beyond objectivism and relativism."[3] Unfortunately, neither Horkheimer nor Bernstein succeed in founding this political imperative *as philosophical*.

It would be wrong to oppose critical to hermeneutic theory as if the former were resolutely "modern" while the latter's appeal to authority or "prejudice" is an irrational, external, and ultimately traditional foundation. Gadamer's reply to such criticism refers explicitly to Horkheimer and Adorno's *Dialectic of Enlightenment* as well as to Lukács's *History and Class Consciousness*.[4] He attempts to show the specifically historical character of a philosophically founded hermeneutics that goes beyond the naivetiés of 19th century historicism. "Truly historical thinking must think simultaneously its own historicity . . . . The true historical object is no object; it is . . . a relation in which the actuality of history as well as the actuality of historical understanding are co-present. An adequate hermeneutics would have to demonstrate the actuality of history in understanding itself."[5] This immanence of historical understanding and the historically given object refuses to appeal to external norms to explain either the genesis or the validity of hermeneutic knowledge. This leaves the philosopher confronted with the need to found his arguments.[6] The difficulty is that it refutes the claim that hermeneutics is premodern at the cost of making explicit a theoretical dilemma which the definition of hermeneutics as "ontology" tends to obscure. Gadamer's hermeneutics, like the politics of Critical Theory, must be founded philosophically.

From the point of view of political theory, Gadamer's description of an "adequate *(sachgemessene)* hermeneutics" recalls Hegel's insistence that true history can only be the history of states.[7] Critical theory and hermeneutics share an origin in German Idealism. Kant's critical theory was built on an ambiguous premise, expressed in the very title of the *Critique of Pure Reason*. Kant never explained the ambiguous genitive: is it reason criticizing, but under what warrant? Is reason being criticized, but by whom or what? Or is it the claim to purity that is at issue? But why then admit practical reason? Kant's *Critique* can claim either to show the conditions of the possibility of experience or the conditions of the possibility of knowledge — or, as Hegel noted, it can do both, becoming an ontology. But then, asks

Hegel in the *Logic*, with what must philosophy begin? This implies that the question of foundations and the question of beginnings imply one another. The result apparently excludes political practice.[8] At the end of the *Philosophy of Right*, Hegel's state is dissolved into the flow of History, which is "the Court of the Last Judgment." Exit Hegel – enter Marx.

The Critical Theory of the 1930s was simply a code name for Marxism. Horkheimer's Inaugural Lecture as director of the Frankfurt Institut für Sozialforschung in 1931, "The Present Situation of Social Philosophy and the Tasks of an Institute for Social Research," explains the birth of social philosophy from German Idealism without mentioning Marx. Yet, his definition of the "tasks" of social research is perfectly orthodox.[9] Marx did not worry about beginnings or foundations. His doctoral dissertation accepted the Hegelian realization of philosophy as philosophy; the next task was to "make worldly" that realized philosophy. Two years later Marx found the locus or beginning of realized philosophy in civil society, in the essay "On the Jewish Question," and then its agent and foundation in the proletariat in "Toward a Critique of Hegel's *Philosophy of Right*." Nearly a century later fascism's seizure of power and the Russian experience made it difficult to accept either the locus or the agent postulated by Marx. Without Marxism's foundational guarantee – whether as a proletarian praxis or a logic of historical or economic necessity articulated in civil society – Critical Theory is in the same position as modern hermeneutics. It retains from Marxism a theory of the immanence of crisis in capitalist society, but its political choices cannot be justified either by material or by theoretical necessity. The result is the tendency to conflate empirical research with metaphysical claims in the vain effort to conjure forth a new "revolutionary subject" in the guise of a new working class, a rainbow coalition of the oppressed, or perhaps the Third World or the Periphery. Each of these efforts must fail, and for theoretical reasons. The crisis is in theory "always-already" there, but the practical political solution is nowhere guaranteed. Critical Theory is no better off than Gadamer's assumed *phronesis* based on an undemonstrable but taken-for-granted communal solidarity.

The Politics of Theory

In their foundational essays of the 1930's,[10] Horkheimer and Marcuse seek to explain not only the "conditions of the possibility" of their critical theory, but also the conditions of its necessity. This philosophical demand for objective foundation as well as subjective beginning means that the "hermeneutic" quest for understanding is incorporated along with the "revolutionary" concern that "the point is not to understand . . . but to change" the world. This double imperative makes explicit the sense in which, philosophically, Marx goes beyond the ontological tradition of transcendental philosophy's *quid juris*. Although Horkheimer is aware of this philosophical demand, he is unable to satisfy it. For example, his second contribution moves toward an almost pathetic conclusion: "But when its concepts which are rooted in social movements today seem vain because nothing stands behind them but their enemies in pursuit, the truth will nevertheless emerge — for the goal of a rational society, which today appears to exist only in the imagination, is of necessity in every human."[11] The only ground for this faith in the human power to resist is sociological. Horkheimer speaks of an "existential judgment" based on the difference between stable feudalism's categorical and modernizing capitalism's hypothetical or disjunctive judgments. This attempt to found necessity in external material conditions is one of the often stressed criteria that define a theory as "traditional". It is correlative to the other major criterion of traditional theory, its "Cartesian" subjectivism.[12] A better case can be made . . . hermeneutically!

Whereas Horkheimer spoke of social theory, Marcuse begins his argument from the imbrication of philosophy with the very definition of humanity. "Philosophy wanted to discover the ultimate and most general grounds of Being. Under the name of reason it conceived the idea of an authentic Being in which all significant antitheses (of subject and object, essence and appearance, thought and being) were reconciled. Connected with this idea was the conviction that what exists is not immediately and already rational but must rather be brought to reason. Reason must represent the highest potentiality of man and of existence. Both go together."[13] While this "idealism" designates philosophy's inherently critical nature, it does not make philosophy itself into social, let alone political theory. The realization of Reason is not the task of philosophy itself. Marxism expected the proletariat to perform that task which would eliminate (or *aufheben*) philosophy. When this expectation was falsified, the nature of philosophy as critical is reaffirmed. This grounds the subjective possibility of philosophical critique; its objective necessity remains to be demonstrated.

Critical philosophy without the proletariat must develop a specific technique which combines demystifying criticism with positive critique. Marcuse wrote "The Concept of Essence" because "so much of men's real struggles and desires went into the metaphysical quest for an ultimate unity, truth and universality of Being" that analysis of such concepts reveals concretely the "phantasy" and "desire" for "material happiness" that animate mankind. Thus, for example, Marcuse asks why Descartes accompanies his mechanistic philosophy, analytic geometry, and treatise on machines with a philosophy based on the *ego cogito*. Marcuse does not interpret this as the "original sin" of modern philosophy's abstract subjectivism and dualism. Descartes was seeking to preserve a domain of human freedom and autonomy in the face of the mechanical-rational external world. The famous admonition to conquer one's self rather than fortune is not the abandonment of freedom, but the paradoxical attempt to preserve it. Similarly, what Marcuse analyzes as the "affirmative character of culture" is not just an escape from hard reality. Culture contains that Stendhalian *"promesse de bonheur"* which preserves the real-dream and existential phantasy of freedom even when material conditions do not allow its realization. The aim of this critical philosophy is to provide a "hermeneutic" demonstration of Horkheimer's phantasy and "existential judgment" by showing how philosophy's imbrication in the human world makes it a material force.

The difficulty with this solution is that, like the proletariat or Hegel's Spirit, it remains within the confines of a "philosophy of the subject." There is no demonstration of the necessary *receptivity* of the external world to the deliverance of the "existential judgment" and phantasy, just as Kant can be accused of incompleteness in the Transcendental Deduction of the first *Critique* because he does not show why the sensible manifold should be *in fact* receptive to the imposition of the categories of the Understanding.[14] Hegel's assumption of the rationality of the actual at least attempted to satisfy this imperative. Marx's *Capital*, or the logic of "alienation," provided the concrete demonstration of what Hegel and Kant could only postulate. The next move was suggested by Lukács's 1923 *History and Class Consciousness*. The logic of alienation, or the commodity logic with which Marx introduces the "fetish" character of capitalism explain what Lukács described as "second nature." But Lukács could still appeal to the class-conscious proletariat. Critical Theory tries to transform Marx's "Critique of Political Economy" into a "Critique of Instrumental Reason." "False consciousness" expresses the structure of the modern world within which the apparently autonomous and affirmative subject becomes either the analytic *Verstand*, which Sartre describes as a "passive activity" whose social relations are those of powerless "seriality,"[15] or the passive receptive subject hiding its dependence in the illusory affirmative culture which substitutes dreams for happiness. The analysis of the modern world as shaped by instrumental reason claims to overcome the dualism that vitiates a philosophy of the subject; because philosophy and social reality have the same structure, critical theory claims both subjective and objective necessity.

The Missing Theory of the Political

The Critique of Instrumental Reason is based on a significant paradox. As philosophy, Critical Theory was able to explain the conditions of its own possibility. It was unable, however, to demonstrate its necessity. The attempt to resolve this difficulty by showing the receptivity of the world to the deliverances of theory demanded the transition to critical theory as social theory, followed by the analysis of modern society as dominated by the principle of instrumental reason. Leaving aside the immanent difficulties in this proposal,[16] it fails for the symmetrically inverse reason: it is unable to explain the conditions of the possibility of that Critical Philosophy from which the entire quest began! The practical consequences of this circle of paradoxes emerged starkly in Herbert Marcuse's *One Dimensional Man*: Marcuse was left with recourse to notions like a qualitative physics, the revolt of the outsider, or the Great Refusal. The move to the critique of instrumental reason was too powerful; it destroyed the question from which it emerged.[17]

Marcuse's radical posture was the result of his violation of one of the cardinal premises of Critical Theory. If one-dimensional society were the *totality*, there would be no place from which that totality could be criticized, and no fulcrum from which it could be moved. As with Adorno's aphorism, "the whole is the untrue," this assumes the validity of the theory of instrumental reason; its difficulties suggest problems for that theory. The quest for an Archimedean point makes an illicit assumption. It introduces an externality, something or somewhere freed from the spell of instrumental or one-dimensional reason. This reintroduces the philosophy of the subject. It neglects the concept of totality which founded Lukács's attempt to transcend the theoretical and practical consequences of reification. Lukács's Hegelian Marxism, however, assumed that the proletariat as the subject-object of history represents the modern totality.

Marcuse recognizes that the standpoint of totality has to be reintroduced. The analysis of instrumental reason describes an atomism of abstract individuals striving to maintain their mere existence. The result is an increasingly incoherent, crisis-ridden process of social reproduction. As the whole grows more irrational, rationality is flung to the outside and to the outsiders who refuse to submit. But if the totality is truly total, these outsiders are insiders, needed to keep the system functioning through what Paul Piccone calls a "dialectics of negativity."[18] Either the instrumental reification is total, in which case critique is at best immanent and ultimately affirmative; or the critique is external to the totality it criticizes, in which case there is no guarantee that the results of the critique will be received by the intended addressees. In the one case, the possibility of critical theory excludes its intended political results; in the other, the intended political results cannot be grounded theoretically.

The source of the dilemma is the overly narrow conception of civil society which Critical Theory inherited from Marx. Hegel knew that the structures of modern civil society *pose a problem* which has to be resolved at the level of the political state. Marx took this problem to be *a solution*. By equating modern civil society with capitalist society, Marx developed a theory of political economy which showed why capitalist society creates the subjective and objective conditions of the possibility of its own overcoming. Marx did not, however, demonstrate the necessity that this possibility be realized. The theoretical consequence is drawn in the first sentence of Adorno's *Negative Dialectics*: "Philosophy, which once seemed obsolete, lives on because the moment to realize it was missed."[19] The political consequence need not be the pessimism of Horkheimer and Adorno's *Dialectic of Enlightenment*.

A conception of modern civil society which does not equate it with the capitalist economy permits the reintroduction of the standpoint of totality. Horkheimer and Adorno treat the Enlightenment from the point of view of a philosophy of the subject. Conceptualization of the Enlightenment as political was suggested already by Kant, for whom the creation of a lawful civil society was the problem of modernity.[20] Kant's solution turned around what historians, conscious of the paradox, call "Enlightened Despotism." The circle is familiar, but it is not hermeneutic; it is political. The equation of modern societies with capitalist (or socialist) *economic* formations is erroneous. The classical question of the Good Life in the City has not disappeared. On the contrary, modernity has made it more acute by robbing society of its traditional political institutions. The turn to economics, to subjective reason or to objective instrumental reason, obscures this fundamental fact.

Hermeneutics and Critical Theory as Methodology

The necessity of both a subjective and an objective foundation for a modern philosophy results in a paradoxical "dialectic" in which either one or the other, but not both, demands can be met. Without a demonstration of the conditions of the possibility of philosophy, the adventure loses its rational seal. Modernity introduces self-doubt into philosophy, thrusting it toward the subjective pole. When the doubt becomes anxiety, philosophy seeks an objective anchor in the positive world. With this, it sacrifices it's self in order to maintain itself. The other option is the ontological "identity philosophy" which subsumes the particularity of the world under the lawfulness of philosophical reason. The resulting monism veers toward solipsism when it avoids schizophrenia. This paradoxical structure is the result of a philosophy of subjectivity which cannot ground itself without losing the world, or ground the world without losing itself.

If modern society is conceived as political, the dispute between Bernstein's critical theory and Gadamer's hermeneutic can be resolved by showing each to be correct — but for the wrong reasons. The immanence of the political *as a question* to modern society means that Gadamer's insistence on the possibility of political judgment and practical *phronesis* is justified. The difficulty, however, is to show *when* and *how* this *phronesis* functions. That demands a theory of those *particulars* which make necessary political reflection; and it demands a theory of judgment which avoids the subsumption by which "identity philosophy" reduces otherness to mere appearance. This is where Critical Theory enters, following the model suggested by the relation between Adorno's *Negative Dialectics* and his aesthetic theory. The "existential judgment," "mimesis," and "phantasy" are grounded in the immanence of the political question within the modern. This is only the first step. The goals Bernstein and Horkheimer postulate as *telos*, or totality, guiding the critical theory could not be grounded because of the Marxian tendency to equate civil society with the capitalist economic form, neglecting the political question of the theoretical and institutional foundation of the being-together of society. This question emerges when particular events or institutions release practical energies whose repression constitutes social injustice. The result is that possibility is completed by necessity, and particularity is completed by totality, without their conflation or their irreparable separation.

Hermeneutics explains the conditions of receptivity that ground the necessity of the particular assertions whose possibility is designated by Critical Theory. Critical Theory stands as the political pole whose task is the articulation of particularity; hermeneutics provides the philosophical complement whose universality assures that this politics is grounded. Their relation is thus one of inclusion; excluded is only the economistic Marxism – accepted by the first generation of Critical Theory – which denies the immanence of the political question to civil society. Inclusion is not identity. Each approach has its legitimte place and domain. This limitation transforms the nature of both hermeneutics and Critical Theory. Neither can make the totalizing claims which their philosophical formulation suggests. Each, rather, becomes a methodological moment within a theory of modernity that transforms both. In this context Bernstein's political critique of Gadamer is perfectly correct. Gadamer is a political *naïf*, . . . but there is no need to treat him as a political philosopher. The political philosophy of a non-economistic Critical Theory shows hermeneutics its proper limits and place, just as hermeneutics shows Critical Theory its own. Whether this reconstruction of a contemporary Critical Theory is compatible with the variant proposed by the second generation's *summum*, Habermas's *Theorie des kommunikativen Handelns*, is a topic which will no doubt return in ongoing discussions.[21]

Notes

1. Hans-Georg Gadamer to Richard Bernstein, 1 July 1982, trans. James Bohman, Appendix to *Beyond Objectivism and Relativism: Science, Hermeneutics and Praxis*, by Richard Bernstein (Philadelphia: University of Pennsylvania Press, 1983), p. 262.

2. Ibid., p. 264.

3. Bernstein, *Beyond Objectivism and Relativism*, p. 231.

4. Hans-Georg Gadamer, *Wahrheit und Methode*, Vierte Auflage (Tübingen: J. C. B. Mohr, Paul Siebeck, 1975), pp. 258, 259.
Gadamer criticizes Horkheimer and Adorno's extension of the notion of enlightenment to the *Odyssey*, implicitly rejecting the notion of "instrumental reason" to which we will return below.

5. Ibid., p. 283.

6. The modern hermeneutics that sets itself off from the "philosophy of consciousness" typical of historicism, Dilthyian *Einfühlungsphilosophie*, or methodological *Verstehen*, makes a virtue of necessity – it literally ontologizes its own embarrassment. It explains that we cannot pose the question of foun-

dations because these foundations found our very being-as-questioning. We cannot pose the question of beginning because we have always already begun. Whether the hermeneutic circle is conceived ontologically, as with Gadamer, or linguistically, as with Apel, the dilemma remains. Philosophy cannot rule out the question of foundations without risking the accusation of irrationalism. But a modern philosophy cannot invoke foundations whose normative character it cannot justify immanently.

7. Hegel argues, for example, that "Peoples without a state may have passed a long life before arriving at this their destination. And during these periods, they may have attained considerable development in some dimensions." He continues more explicitly, "It is the state which first presents subject matter that is not only adapted to the prose of history, but involves the production of such history in its very being. Instead of government issuing merely subjective mandates sufficing for the needs of the moment, a community that is acquiring a stable existence as a state requires formal commands and laws, comprehensive and universally binding prescriptions. It thus produces a record as well as an interest in understandable, definite transactions and occurrences which have results that are lasting . . . ." G. W. F. Hegel, *Werke*, vol. 12: *Vorlesungen über die Philosophie der Geschichte*, ed. Eva Moldenhauer und Karl Markus Michel (Frankfurt am Main: Suhrkamp Verlag, 1970), p. 83.

8. This is argued explicitly by Hegel in the resigned tones of his Preface to the *Philosophy of Right*, trans. T. M. Knox Oxford: Oxford University Press, 1967), for which philosophy can only "paint its grey on grey" after the fact, when "the owl of Minerva" has taken flight. For a theoretical argument making this point from the perspective of Critical Theory, see Jürgen Habermas, "Hegel's Critique of the French Revolution," in *Theory and Practice*, trans. John Viertel (Boston: Beacon Press, 1973), pp. 121–42.

9. Max Horkheimer, *Sozialphilosophische Studien*, ed. W. von Brede (Frankfurt am Main: Fischer, 1972), pp. 33–46.

The research proposed for the Institute asks why the working class has not fulfilled its designated function. The changed economic, psychological, cultural, legal and religious conditions of modern capitalism are to be examined empirically and integrated theoretically by the renewal of that "social philosophy" whose inadequate foundation in German Idealism will be completed by the equivalent of a modern Marxism. Nowhere does the lecture put into question the adequacy of the Marxist manner of posing the questions. It questions only the 19th century solutions offered by orthdox Marxism.

10. Max Horkheimer, "Traditionelle und Kritische Theorie," *Zeitschrift für Sozialforschung* 6 (1937): 245–92; Max Horkheimer and Herbert Marcuse, "Philosophie und Kritische Theorie," *Zeitschrift für Sozialforschung* 6 (1937): 624–31 (Horkheimer), 631–47 (Marcuse). Marcuse's contribution to the essay is translated as "Philosophy and Critical Theory," in *Negations*, trans. Jeremy J. Shapiro (Boston: Beacon Press, 1968), pp. 135ff.

11. Horkheimer, "Traditionelle und kritische Theorie," p. 630.

12. Marcuse's interpretation of Descartes, like Marx's presentation of Epicurus in his *Dissertation*, sees a different implication in this subjectivism. Horkheimer's argument is concerned with the methodology of the social sciences whereas Marcuse's concern is to ground a Critical Theory which can no longer appeal to the proletariat. See Marcuse, "The Concept of Essence," in *Negations*, p. 50.

13. Marcuse, "Philosophy and Critical Theory," pp. 135–6. (I have changed Shapiro's translation of the penultimate sentence to stress that both *must* [*soll*] be brought together, i.e., that this imperative is an active task.)

14. Cf. the brilliant argument of George Schrader, "The Status of Teleological Judgment in the Critical Philosophy," *Kantstudien* 45 (1953–1954): 204–35. I have developed this argument in a broader context in my *From Marx to Kant* (Albany: SUNY Press, 1985) whose entire fifth chapter is devoted to "The Logic of Receptivity."

15. Jean-Paul Sartre, *Critique de la raison dialectique* (Paris: Gallimard, 1960), passim.

16. Jürgen Habermas has pointed to the major problems of this proposal. See the concluding chapter to his *The Theory of Communicative Action*, vol. 1: *Reason and the Rationalization of Society*, trans. Thomas McCarthy (Boston: Beacon Press, 1984), pp. 339–403. To summarize Habermas's point, it is not possible to reduce a social totality to one form of reason. Communicative (and emancipatory) reason must always function alongside instrumental reason if the society is not to be pulled apart by the centrifugal weight of the individual atoms seeking self-preservation at the cost of destroying the mechanisms of social reproduction.

17. Herbert Marcuse, *One Dimensional Man* (Boston: Beacon Press, 1964).

18. Paul Piccone has argued this position in numerous essays in the journal *Telos* of which he is the editor. Its political consequences can be quite problematic, as for example in the assertion that the feminist movement is simply necessary for the expanded reproduction of a blocked capitalist society.

Two other positions are possible within the framework of the political goals of Critical Theory. Along the lines of Walter Benjamin or Theodor Adorno, one could attempt to recover an intimation of the suppressed totality through the lightening of a mimetically based critique founded either in art or in the structures of the everyday. Or, along the lines of Ernst Bloch, one could propose a kind of "anticipatory hermeneutics" which develops the immanent futurity that traditional hermeneutics covers over through its classical orientation. On the former see Habermas, *The Theory of Communicative Action* 1:339–403; on the latter, see Burghardt Schmidt, *Ernst Bloch* (Stuttgart: G. B. Metzler Verlag, 1985).

19. Theodor W. Adorno, *Negative Dialectics,* trans. E. B. Ashton (New York: The Seabury Press, 1973), p. 3.

Habermas's reconstruction of Marx's philosophical debt to German idealism expresses this difficulty by speaking of the need for a "Fichtean moment": since ego is itself only in the act of relating to the world, there must be a moment of intersubjectivity which transcends the subject philosophy of the Kantian "I think" and unifies and makes my representations mine. This Fichtean moment is translated as the phenomenon of class consciousness in Marx's reconstruction of the capitalist civil society.

20. This is most explicitly stated in Kant's theses on "The Idea of History from a Cosmopolitan Point of View." For an interpretation of Kant from the perspective to which I can only allude here, see my essay "Kant's System and (Its) Politics," *Man and World* 18 (1985): 79–98, and my *From Marx to Kant.*

21. See the Afterword to the second edition of *The Marxian Legacy* (Minneapolis: University of Minnesota Press, 1987) for a detailed discussion of this problem.

Part III.
Phenomenology
and Dialectics

5. Phenomenology and the Problem of Action

Jacques Taminiaux

The topic of this short paper is to a large extent the result of a meditation on the works of Hannah Arendt. It has also much to do with the issue of the overcoming of Metaphysics, an issue which is more than familiar in the debates of our society. To put it bluntly, the question I wish to raise can be phrased this way: Might it be that phenomenology, though it leads in many regards to a post-metaphysical way of thinking, has often maintained and favored a very traditional approach to the problem of action? Let me try to articulate the question in the light of Arendt's teaching.

I. At the very foundation of the tradition of Metaphysics, i.e., in Plato, we find not only a distinction between two ways of life, action and contemplation, but also the assumption that action is of a lower order than contemplation: *the relation between action and contemplation is of a means to an end.*

Accordingly, the founders of Metaphysics approached the distinctive forms of active life in terms of the help they provided towards the ends of contemplation: labor produces the consuming goods necessary to keep the human body alive, the activity of work ($\pi o i \eta \sigma \iota s$) creates a habitation to shelter the human body, the activity of $\pi \rho \tilde{\alpha} \xi \iota s$, which means action in the public realm, organizes living together in order to assure the atmosphere of civil peace which is a precondition for the tranquility of theoretical life. As Arendt insisted time and again, this very description of active life by philosophy, because it is done from the viewpoint of contemplation, tends to minimize and obliterate the phenomenal articulations of active life. This is particularly clear in Plato who, much more than Aristotle, is inclined to obliterate the distinction between ποίησις and πρᾶξις and to understand political activity in the light of the activity of the craftsman, the τεχνίτης, who works according to a preconceived model and tries to realize it with adequate means. By the same token, Plato subordinates πρᾶξις to ποίησις. This subordination is itself ruled by the privilege of contemplation to the extent that the craftsman is like a contemplator: he beholds a model, an Idea, before and during the process of shaping the piece of equipment he wants to produce.

Consequently, in order to disclose and describe the phenomenal articulations of active life, Arendt had to go deeper than the patterns set by Metaphysics and had to break them in many regards. To accomplish this phenomenological task, she found significant, but not exclusive support in the Presocratic texts which testify to the way the Greeks evaluated active life prior to the foundation of Metaphysics. Let me recall briefly the phenomenological result of her investigation.

1. First of all a distinction has to be made – and it is supported in every European language by etymological evidence – between labor and work. Linguistically labor (πονεῖν, *laborare*, *travailler*, *arbeiten*) has a connotation of painful bodily experience. The word obviously signifies an activity linked with the biological process of the body. As Aristotle said, the laborers "administer with their bodies to the needs of life." Labor is an activity submitted to the necessity of biological survival. Its products are essentially perishable: they are to be consumed by the body. Because the biological process is an endless circle, implying the eternal recurrence of needs and satisfactions, exhaustion and regeneration, labor is an endless repetition, which does not leave behind any durable product. It corresponds to the *natural* condition of *life*, with its succession of troubles and rewards, and can be accompanied by a very deep form of happiness, stemming from confidence in the fertility of nature.

2. Unlike labor, work (ἐργάζεσθαι, *ouvrer*, *werken*) produces beyond the cycle of natural life a stable region of lasting things. Its products are not consumer-goods but use-objects which do not disappear by being used. Whereas labor is attached to nature, work interrupts or violates the natural processes. By transforming natural matter into a material for shaping non-natural things, it establishes an artificial environment which protects men from nature, houses them from birth to death, stabilizes their life, and assures them a continuity and identity related to the durability of the artifacts. In other words, *work* institutes a *world* which is irreducible to the natural environment

of biological life. Distinct from labor in its product, work is also distinct from labor in its very process. Indeed, the process of fabricating has a definite beginning and a definite and predictable end. Its beginning is the planning of the artifact by the maker; its end occurs when the artifact is finished. The process itself is distinct from the product; it is a means to an end. In the laboring process the body is both the means and the end: it produces what it consumes, it eats in order to labor, it labors in order to eat, endlessly. While the activity of labor is a cycle which dominates the laborer, the activity of making is a linear sequence, in which the *maker* is like a *master*.

However, though it constitutes a world as a stable realm beyond the devouring cycle of nature, the activity of working is not able to take in view the world itself. It is indeed thoroughly determined by instrumentality. In it the end justifies the means, selects them, and rules the work process itself. But as soon as the end is reached, i.e., the finished product which is a use-object, it takes its place in a new means-end sequence, and becomes a means for further ends. The stability established by work is again and again threatened by the utilitarian mentality of the working man, the *homo faber*. The worldly consistance and objectivity of the work product is constantly threatened by the loss of its intrinsic worth: as soon as it is generalized, instrumentality destroys any permanent meaning. There seems to be an easy solution to this contradiction: Man is the only end, an end in itself, never a means. But the trouble with this formula, though it prevents utilitarianism, as it does in Kant who invented it, from ruling human interactions, is that it is exclusively anthropocentric and not at all cosmocentric; it refuses worldly things and the world itself any intrinsic worth, hence increasing the threat of a falling back of activity into the eternal recurrence which characterizes labor.

3. Work is the *necessary condition* of a world, i.e., of a stable home outlasting the life-span of mortal beings, but it is not yet a *sufficient condition* for the durability of a world. For this, another activity is required. There is a world, in Arendt's notion of the word, "only inasmuch as it transcends both the sheer functionalism of consumer goods and the sheer utility of use-objects." The main features of the world in her sense are *appearances* and *common-ness*. The world is real inasmuch as it appears. And its appearance is publicly open – it is perceived, it can be seen and heard by all, it is communicable by all. Hence, as far as the world is concerned, the metaphysical distinction between *appearance* and *reality* is not valid, nor the metaphysical distinction between the *one* and the *many*, *identity* and *difference*. The world's identity is linked to a plurality of perspectives upon it. Its

oneness as a common space disappears as soon as it is seen in a single perspective. But it also transcends the sum total of the perspectives which are open on it at a given time, for it does not only relate together those who live now, it also relates them to those who were and to those who shall be born in it. The world in this sense is strictly correlated to the human conditions of *plurality* and *natality*. Plurality is not equal to multiplicity. Every living species is multiplied in a manifold of individual organisms, but human beings have the capacity of taking upon themselves the naked fact of their otherness and the distinguishing features which individualize them. In other words, not only are they distinct, but they can distinguish themselves. Their birth introduces a distinctive impulse to express who they are, in front of others who are their equals in this regard.

The only activity which corresponds to this condition of plurality and natality and, therefore, to the preservation of an appearing and common world is *action*. The unique individuality of the agent, who is similar to but distinct from all others, is disclosed by action. Action is not what relates an individual to life, like labor, nor is it what relates him to things like work. Action is what discloses the life of an individual in relation to other individuals. And action discloses this by being intimately linked with speech. Through action − and this implies an open series of initiatives − everyone actualizes the fact that by birth he is a new beginning. Through speech he declares who he is; he actualizes his belonging to plurality. Since it comes from the living *"who"* of an individual who cannot be defined except in general terms, action in this sense is never without ambiguity. Since, as speech and interaction, it inserts itself, by virtue of plurality, in a pre-existing network of human relations, it is always unpredictable, and the agent is a patient as well as a doer. Moveover, by virtue of an ever-renewed natality, its impact is almost endless. All these features − ambiguity, unpredictability, endlessness − denote a sharp distinction between acting and making. They show the essential fragility of human affairs. The pre-metaphysical remedy to this fragility was the invention of the Greek πόλις, conceived as a stable public space for the *sharing* of deeds and words, and as an institution enabling them to be remembered. In other words, political life, especially in its democratic form, was instituted for the sake of an appearing and common horizon for a *meaningful* sharing of renewed actions and words. The remedy did not intend to suppress the fragility of human affairs but to cope with it. But the same fragility is precisely what Metaphysics, at its beginning, was inclined to get rid of. Recognizing the lack of clarity of human affairs, Plato argues that the mortals are like puppets manipulated by a hidden God who is the author or the maker of the play.[1] This amounts implicitly to abolishing the distinction between action (πρᾶξις) and fabrication or work (ποίησις). Furthermore, it is well known that he conceived of the solution of the political problem in terms of a fabrication of the city-state, in which everything and everybody are means to a predefined end, as everything and everybody must be in a workshop.

II. In the light of this short and much too schematic recall of Arendt's analysis of the *vita activa*, let us consider the approach to the theory of action within phenomenology.

About Husserl, I will be very short. First of all, it is obvious that, in contradistinction to both Plato in the old world and Descartes in the modern world, Husserl made a tremendous contribution to the rehabilitation of perception. By showing that the density (the *Leibhaftigkeit*) of the perceived world is the strict correlate not only of the unification of my sensible experiences but also of the intersubjective communication of experiences by a plurality of perceiving beings, and by insisting, moreover, upon the contribution of a legacy of *artifacts* to the constitution of a common *Lebenswelt*, he seems to recognize what Arendt calls the "common world" which is a basic condition of action in the strict sense of the word. In Husserl's description of the perceived world, the one and the many are not opposed as they were since the beginning of Metaphysics. As he says: "Wir sehen, wir hören nicht bloss nebeneinander, sondern miteinander."[2] However this recognition of plurality on the level of perception does not lead him to the recognition of an essential link between plurality and action. Indeed, there is no doubt that the revival of the old predominance of the *vita contemplativa* upon *vita activa* was part and parcel of Husserl's phenomenology. The highest activity for him was the activity of the philosopher devoted to the problems of transcendental constitution which have their center in the Ego. It is not surprising, therefore, that when he deals with topics like social interaction or history, Husserl tends to obliterate their link to plurality and revives in his treatment of these topics the Platonist confusion between πρᾶξις and ποίησις. Indeed, when he deals with human interaction, Husserl insists that in order to constitute a community this interaction not only must be based upon a set of common cultural acquisitions, but also must be supported by a collective will and unified by a center, which is the collective equivalent of an Ego. In such an analysis, the correlate of a common world (*gemeinschaftliche Welt*) is not a plurality but a "collective subject," in which, as Husserl says, "the communicating multiplicity operates like a unique subject."[3] In agreement with this tendency to condense plurality in a unique center, which, of course, amounts to abolishing it, Husserl finds the best example of a community in the modern concept of the centralized state, unified by a constitution, a government and an administration. The nation-state, he says, is a "unique will" which is "centered in the way of an Ego in analogy with the individual Ego." In this view the focus is not upon the pluralist debate and interaction between equal citizens but upon the execution of a centralized will, which means that the civil servants, the "functionaires," are the true members of the body politic, and that the interlocutory interaction is less important than a unified management. In other words, Husserl's concept of "community" is "poietical" more than practical. If you claim that *Gemeinschaft* reaches its accomplishment when the persons composing it act as though they were one person, then the organization of work in a workshop is certainly an ideal of community. But the predominance of ποίησις over πρᾶξις is also obvious in Husserl's approach to history. Let me quote a very significant excerpt of a manuscript which deals with what Husserl calls the degrees (*Stufen*) of historicity on the individual level:

> A vagabond who lets himself go adrift without goal has his experiences, his deeds and misdeeds. But he has no history, he is not a possible subject-matter for a biography, if biography must be a mode of history. There can be a genuine historicity only for a man who has beforehand designed the unified sense of his life, like the one who freely decided to devote his life to a vocation and thereby has prescribed to all his future willing and doing a rule, a norm; by maintaining it in spite of all changes, by being faithful to himself, he lives in the history of his vocation a unified life full of meaning.[4]

The word I translate by vocation is *Beruf,* which also means profession. If I translate it by vocation, it is because I suppose that what Husserl had in mind was his own activity as a philosopher. Now, if his transcendental vocation was what he really had in mind, we may immediately object that the "history of his vocation" can be, of course, a subject-matter for the historian of his philosophy but not at all a subject-matter for a biography. When a philosopher is fully dedicated to the activity of thought, he withdraws himself, most of the time, from his fellowmen; he no longer inserts himself in the pluralistic interaction which characterizes the third degree of active life, and this is why his biography, being void of events, can be easily summarized in the way Heidegger once presented the biography of Aristotle: He was born, he worked, he died. Now supposing that by *Beruf,* Husserl meant "profession," then again we might object – and the more so, if the ideal profession is civil service – that professional activity, as such, is rarely a fascinating topic for a biography. But my point is not irony, rather that the very concept of history as a process which is ruled by a prior design is not based upon the phenomenal experience of action as interlocutory interaction. In this realm, prior designs or intentions, if there are any, are not maintained in spite of changes; they are always open to changes. Husserl's concept is based upon the phenomenal experience of work. In the activity of production there must be a prior design. But a prior design in the field of action is always a threat to the essential plurality and unpredictability of human affairs. In this regard Husserl's denial of any historicity to the vagabond is significant. It could indeed be objected that if plurality and unpredictable innovation are essential to human relations, there must be an essential element of "vagrancy" or at least of adventure in history.

Let me look at Heidegger. I will restrict my remarks to the "phenomenological" period of his thought, the period of fundamental ontology. As is well known, the description of everyday $\pi\varrho\hat{\alpha}\xi\iota\varsigma$ plays an important role in the existential analytic of Heidegger. If we admit that the aim of fundamental ontology was to achieve Metaphysics as the science of the sense of Being, may we suspect that the metaphysical bias about the $\beta\iota\varsigma\ \pi\varrho\alpha\varkappa\tau\iota\varkappa\acute{o}\varsigma$ guides Heidegger's approach to action? Let me put the issue with some precaution: Do we find in fundamental ontology traces of the Platonist understanding of active life in terms of a priority of work or $\pi o\acute{\iota}\eta\sigma\iota\varsigma$? And if this is the case, is this priority ruled by some form of Plato's rejection of the doxa pervading human affairs to the benefit of $\dot{\epsilon}\pi\iota\sigma\tau\acute{\eta}\mu\eta$ or $\theta\epsilon\omega\varrho\acute{\iota}\alpha$? To this first question, I am afraid that the answer has to be positive. Heidegger describes the activities of Dasein in everydayness as belonging to a comportment called preoccupation (Besorgen). Such a preoccupation is almost entirely interested in goals which are to be accomplished in the environment (Umwelt) and in the adequate means to reach them. Readiness-at-hand (Zuhandenheit) is what characterizes the mode of Being of the beings with which such daily comportment is concerned. This comportment is enlightened by what Heidegger calls a practical circumspection (praktische Umsicht). A close scrutiny of the texts devoted to everydayness during the Marburg period would show that he himself conceived of his analysis as a retrieval of the description of human affairs or of active life by the founders of Greek ontology and especially by Plato. To be sure, such a retrieval is not a sheer repetition. Heidegger's thesis is that Greek ontology was right in starting from an analysis of active life in order to discover the basic ontological categories. By so doing, Greek ontology discovered correctly that ontological categories were related to Dasein's comportment. However, the mistake of Greek ontology, in Heidegger's view, was to pay such exclusive attention to the practical comportent of Dasein, that it was unable to recognize underneath the practical circumspection of preoccupation its a priori, i.e., Concern or Care (*Sorge*) as the fundamental structure of our mode of Being. Consequently, the privilege they gave to everydayness led them to understand the sense of Being only in terms of what Heidegger calls *Vorhandenheit*, presence before the hands. *Vorhandenheit* as an ontological category is indeed intimately related to the horizon of understanding of the practical comportment we assume most of the time in everydayness. More precisely, it is linked to productive comportment: ". . . to *pro*-duce, to place-*here*, *Her*-stellen, means at the same time to bring into the narrower or wider circuit of the accessible, here, to this place, to the *Da*, so that the produced being *stands for itself on its own account and remains able to be found there and to lie before there* (vorliegen) as *something established stably for itself*."[15] Heidegger's thesis during the period of fundamental ontology was that all the ontological categories of Greek philosophy (ὁμσία, μοϱφή, εἶδος, ἐνέϱγεια, ὁϱισμός, and so on) had their basis in productive comportment. Fascinated, as it were, by daily productive comportment, the Greeks were then unable to realize that only a being whose mode of being is *Existence* and neither *Zuhandenheit* nor *Vorhandenheit*, can be related to things ready-at-hand and present-before-the-hands.

What is puzzling in this retrieval is that Heidegger never seems to be suspicious about the phenomenological adequacy of the Greek philosophical approach to active life. He does not seem to ever suspect that this approach to active life in terms of an overwhelming predominance of ποίησις is less the result of a patient examination of active life than of a rejection of active life. He does not seem to suspect that the pre-philosophical records of Greek political life testify to a sharp differentiation between the activity of the worker and the activity of the citizen. In other words, he takes for granted Plato's confusion of πϱᾶξις with ποίησις. Moreover, his own description of everydayness is done in the light of ποίησις, as though no phenomenological distinction were to be made between work and action. This explains in *Being and Time* the emphasis put on utensils, the workshop, the means-ends relation, the *Bewandtnisganzheit*, and so on. Moreover, when the analysis, replying to the question, "Who is the Dasein?", introduces, as essential determinations of the Dasein, the notions of *Miteinandersein*

[Being-with-others], *Mitsein* [Being-with], *Mitwelt* [the with-world], *Mitdasein* [Dasein-with], we face undoubtedly a tremendous endeavor to overcome the traditional metaphysical approach of the problem of the other in terms of a pure theoretical distinction between a Self given to itself and others confronted by the Self. Such an overcoming of the prejudice of a pure contemplation of entities supposedly determined by their being-before-the-hands, their *Vorhandenheit*, reveals that Dasein is essentially characterized by an *active* relation to the others as well as to the world. However, the analysis of this active relation to others is mostly done in the light of the activity of ποίησις. The analysis insists that, primarily and most of the time, the *Mitsein* is encountered in many ways in the context of the innerworldly utensil, and that we discover the others "at work."[6] To be sure, the active relation to others is misunderstood when the other is treated like a utensil: the relation to the other is not preoccupation but *caring-for.* Now caring-for, as described by Heidegger, seems to oscillate between two extreme possibilities: either to take upon oneself the other's preoccupation, or help him to take upon himself what in him is deeper than this preoccupation and essential to his existence, i.e. his *Concern* (*Sorge*). In the first case we are either on the level which characterizes labor − life as a cycle including pains and pleasures − or on the level of work, but we are not on the specific level of πρᾶξις. Is the second case on the level of πρᾶξις? I do not think so, and here is why. Heidegger insists that the first form of assistance is inauthentic, whereas the second one is authentic. So we must raise the question: Does authenticity, as described by Heidegger, account for the possibility of what, with Hannah Arendt, we called action in the strict sense of the word? We have seen that action, essentially linked with plurality and natality, implies a common world for the sharing of deeds and words. There is no avail to look for some sort of equivalent of these notions in Heidegger's analysis of authenticity. If, as he says about anxiety, unhomeliness has to be understood on the existential and ontological level as the most originary phenomenon, then authenticity implies the denial of a common world, i.e., of the public home which is necessary for enabling men to act.[7] If the existential and ontological meaning of the world is revealed through anxiety in the experience of Nothingness, then the authentic world is not only without things but also beyond the plural interrelations of men. If the Dasein is authentic when facing its ultimate possibility, or what it essentially is as a thrown-project, in the full awareness of its own mortality, then, again, authenticity is beyond the daily realm of human affairs, beyond any sharing of deeds and words. This is not at all to say that Heidegger's description of the public world in terms of inauthenticity should be discarded. On the contrary such a description is full of insights as far as society is concerned. But, precisely, society should not be confused with the public realm of action. Indeed, what Heidegger describes as the public *Mitwelt* of the They, corresponds in many regards to the market place in the modern sense of the word, i.e., to a public realm where indeed everybody is nobody, because what counts in it is either consuming or producing. In other words the public *Mitwelt* of the They corresponds to a mixture of labor and work. It does not correspond to action, i.e., to a form of activity which in the pre-philosophical, but political experience of the Greeks had to prevent both labor and work from invading the public realm. And the reason for this is precisely that they believed that in both labor and work everybody is nobody, and that the "who" of the agent could not appear in those activities. All this amounts to suggesting that Heidegger's distinction between inauthenticity as the basic feature of the public realm as a whole, and authenticity as a way of being which, as it were, is determined by what he himself calls somewhere "existential solipsism," reproduces the metaphysical disdain for human affairs.[8].

Here I reach the second question I was raising. Are we allowed to say that such a disdain is ruled by some form of the metaphysical distinction between δόξα and ἐπιστήμη? Ἐπιστήμη in Heidegger's sense – at the time of *Being and Time* – is the science of the meanings of Being. Now, this science finds its field and basis in the phenomenology of the being that we ourselves are. It claims to limit itself to a conceptual thematization of an understanding each of us already has or already is. Or to put it in other words, the vision (θεωρία) of the theorist of this science conceptually duplicates a vision which already pervades the existence of Dasein. About Dasein's vision, Heidegger insists that a distinction must be made between the practical round-view (*praktische Umsicht*) Dasein has in everydayness of its environment (*Umwelt*), as a correlate of its preoccupation, and the essential view it may have of its existential situation in the state of resoluteness. Resoluteness, as a state in which we take upon ourselves and see the radical finiteness of our existential time, is animated by a specific vision (the vision of the *Augen-blick* in a specific sense). According to several textual indications, Heidegger conceives of the everyday vision which animates both preoccupation and caring-for as a form of δόξα. Only the vision animating resoluteness thoroughly escapes δόξα. However, Heidegger himself once suggested that his notion of resoluteness was the result of an existential retrieval of Aristotle's concept of φρόνησις. This suggestion is a sort of condensation of the whole point I treat here. There is no doubt, indeed, that Aristotle's concept of φρόνησις in *The Nicomachean Ethics* takes place in a meditation upon the public realm which, in contradistinction to Plato, not only tries to maintain a distinction between πρᾶξις and ποίησις, but also to avoid any form of radical disdain for the sphere of human affairs. Accordingly, when he treats of φρόνησις, Aristotle acknowledges not only the necessity but also the dignity of δόξα in the realm of human affairs. This political background is what disappears altogether in Heidegger's retrieval of φρόνησις, which in this regard is more Platonist than Aristotelian.

I do not have enough time to carry on this brief investigation with an examination of French phenomenology. Just a few words about Sartre. To be sure, Sartre, like Merleau-Ponty for that matter, never paid much attention to the Greek world. Therefore we do not have to expect from them any explicit retrieval of the Greek philosophical approach to active life. But philosophers cannot escape the spell of the past by ignoring it.

Let me introduce what I have in mind by a short quotation. "La vérité est une, l'erreur est multiple. Ce n'est pas un hasard si la droite professe le pluralisme."[9] Truth is one, error is manifold. If the right teaches pluralism, this is no accident. This was not written by Sartre, but by his best pupil, Simone de Beauvoir, certainly in agreement with him on this point. Apart from the historical context in France at that time, the sentence means that the political realm must be approached in terms of a sharp distinction between truth and error, the One and the Many. This is exactly the type of approach claimed by Plato. It amounts to denying that plurality is essential to human affairs and that their light results from the expression of plurality. It amounts in contradistinction to δοξα to endowing those who are dedicated to truth, i.e., to the theorists, with the right to solve human affairs.

To be sure, in Sartre's theory of action the place of the theorist is no longer the heaven of Ideas; it is existence itself, the existence of each individual in its original movement. In *Being and Nothingness*, this movement is described as a conscious project whose internal unity, fluidity and transparency are threatened by others. In the *Critique of Dialectical Reason*, which is an existentialist retrieval of Marx, the subject-matter of the investigation is no longer the movement of consciousness but the relation between individual *praxes*. The individual *praxis*, though dedicated to the transformation of Nature with the help of tools, retains the basic features of consciousness: unifying project, transparency, apprehension of the situation and the goal. However, the conflict among individuals seems to be no longer essential; it depends on a contingent fact, the scarcity of economic resources, which generate and perpetuate in human conditions. A fully human relation between individuals would presuppose the overcoming of scarcity, the achievement of plenty. It would consist in a reciprocity between praxes, i.e., a recognition by each praxis of the praxis of the other.

In light of the phenomenological distinction I recalled at the beginning, the metaphysical bias of this analysis is almost obvious. To be sure, what is thoroughly un-Greek – in either the pre-philosophical or the philosophical sense – and typically modern in this analysis is the idea that an unbridled expansion of the labor sphere (achievement of abundance of consumer goods) would favor a truly human interaction. Nevertheless, what Sartre calls "individual praxis" is analysed in terms of the specific features of what the Greek called ποίησις: we are the makers of our life; we are the makers of history just as the craftsman is the lucid maker of a work. Moreover, his very definition of "recognition" shows the same metaphysical bias. "La *praxis* de l'un, dans sa structure pratique et pour l'accomplissement de son projet, *reconnait* la *praxis* de l'autre, c'est-à-dire au fond qu'elle juge la dualité des activités comme un caractère inessentiel et l'unité des praxis en tant que telles comme un caractère essentiel".[10] This is an explicit denial of plurality. It amounts to saying that history would be fully dialectical if it were not the adventure of men but the working process of one man.

Notes

1. Plato *The Laws*.

2. Edmund Husserl, manuscript K III, 3, pp. 19–20. "We see and we hear, not merely next to one another, but with one another." (Manuscripts are housed in the Husserl Archives in Louvain.)

3. Edmund Husserl, manuscript GC II, pp. 12–13.

4. Edmund Husserl, manuscript K III, 3.

5. Martin Heidegger, *The Basic Problems of Phenomenology*, trans. A. Hofstradter (Bloomington: Indiana University Press, 1982), p. 108.

6. Martin Heidegger, *Being and Time*, trans. J. Macquarrie and E. Robinson (New York: Harper and Row, 1962), pp. 153–63.

7. Ibid., pp. 228–35.

8. Ibid., p. 233.

9. Simone de Beauvoir, "La Pensée de Droite, aujourd'hui," *Les Temps Modernes*, no. 111 (April 1955), p. 1539.

10. Jean-Paul Sartre, *Critique de la raison dialectique* (Paris: Gallimard, 1960), p. 207. *Critique of Dialectical Reason*, trans. A. Sheridan-Smith, ed. J. Rée (London: NLB, 1976), p. 131: ". . . each individual's *praxis*, in its practical structure and for the sake of the completion of its project, *recognizes* the *praxis* of the other, which means, basically, that it sees the duality of activities as inessential and the unity of *praxes* as such as essential to them."

6. Hegel and Husserl: Transcendental Phenomenology and the Revolution Yet Awaited

Merold Westphal

It turns out that 1984 is not only the year for reflection on contemporary nightmares about Big Brother but also the year for recollecting the somewhat older dreams of these two giants on whose shoulders we seek to stand — dreams of rigorous science and of rational human life. It was in 1964 that George Schrader gave us an illuminating comparison of Hegel and Husserl.[1] Then in 1974 Quentin Lauer did the same,[2] suggesting to us that at least once a decade we need to reconsider what can be learned by generating a dialogue between these two thinkers, of whom it is not easy to tell whether it is the similarities or differences that run deeper. Now in 1984 we turn once again to that task.

The temptation is all but irresistible to focus on the *Phenomenology of Spirit* for Hegel's part of the conversation. Without even trying to resist, I do suggest that a comparison based on the theme of logic might also be very fruitful. But I shall stick to phenomenology rather than logic as the point of contact, and since I take Hegel's *Phenomenology* to belong to the tradition of transcendental philosophy (however un-Cartesian and un-Kantian it may be), the Husserl I shall seek to engage is the overtly transcendental phenomenologist we meet from 1907 on.[3]

To begin, let us note four major points of agreement between Hegel and Husserl. They are not, to be sure, total agreements in every detail. In fact, there are substantive disagreements related to each of these points. But the agreements are not for that reason merely verbal or superficial. On the contrary, they are deep and basic.

Philosophy as Rigorous Science

Two of these agreements are indicated by this familiar passage from Hegel's famous Preface:

> to help bring philosophy closer to the form of Science, to the goal where it can lay aside the title *"love* of knowing" and be *actual* knowing – that is what I have set myself to do. The inner necessity that knowing should be Science lies in its nature. . . . To show that now is the time for philosophy to be raised to the status of a Science would therefore be the only true justification of any effort that has this aim, for to do so would demonstrate the necessity of the aim, would indeed at the same time be the accomplishing of it.[4]

In the first place, then, Hegel agrees with Husserl that philosophy must be a rigorous science. It goes without saying that by this they do not mean that it should somehow try to imitate the procedures of the experimental sciences or that it should seek to ground itself on the results of the *Natur-* or *Geisteswissenschaften.* Both take the sciences in the most familiar sense of the term to be unfulfilled promises, themselves in need of clarification and grounding in spite of their dramatic successes.

Hegel's most general account of what would make philosophy a rigorous science has two key elements, each of which has strikingly Husserlian overtones. On the one hand, philosophy can be scientific only if it is without presuppositions. Hegel develops this point in detail in the Introduction to the *Phenomenology,* an utterly crucial text for understanding his relation to Husserl.[5] But this freeing of thought from prejudice, this negative preparation has a positive goal. And so, on the other hand, philosophy can be scientific only if it gets beyond the superficiality of first-order conceptualizations of experience and descends into the conceptual depths to encounter *die Sache selbst.* "Culture and its laborious emergence from the immediacy of substantial life must always begin by getting acquainted with *general* principles and points of view, so as at first to work up to conceptual thought of the subject matter [*der Sache überhaupt*] . . . " Even when this includes the ability to develop precise classifications and to give reasons for and against various claims, it is not enough. "From this beginning culture must leave room for the seriousness of life in its concrete fullness, which leads to the experience of the heart of the matter [*die Erfahrung der Sache selbst*]." But even this is not enough, for Hegel is no romantic. Just as the immediacy of substantial life requires conceptualization, so this deeper level of experience which gets beyond what Hegel views as mere Understanding must be brought to conceptual form. This final stage of *Bildung* occurs "when the heart of the matter has been penetrated to its depths by serious speculative effort [*der Ernst des Begriffs*]."[6]

This experiential and conceptual turn from superficial reasoning (*Verstand* in Hegel's sense) *zu den Sachen selbst* is not an automatic feature of everything that calls itself philosophy. It occurs only when philosophy gets beyond being "no more than a device for evading the heart of the matter [*die Sache selbst*]." Hegel's account of this latter kind of philosophy gives the negative image of a truly scientific philosophy. "For instead of getting involved in the real issue [*der Sache*], this kind of activity is always away beyond it; instead of tarrying with it, and losing itself in it, this kind of knowing is forever grasping at something new; it remains essentially preoccupied with itself instead of being preoccupied with the real issue [*der Sache*] and surrendering to it."[7] It is for the sake of this tarrying and this surrendering that philosophy seeks to free itself from presuppositions.[8]

Philosophy and Cultural Crisis

A second major agreement between Hegel and Husserl comes to light when Hegel says that "now is the time" for philosophy to become truly scientific. This seemingly incidental reference to Hegel's historical present is in fact anything but innocent. For he takes his time to be the *kairos* (in Tillich's sense) for scientific philosophy. On the one hand, it is a time of desperate need. If we consider "the stage which self-conscious Spirit has presently reached," we will see

that Spirit has now got beyond the substantial life it formerly led in the element of thought, that it is beyond the immediacy of faith, beyond the satisfaction and security of the certainty that consciousness then had, of its reconciliation with the essential being, and of that being's universal presence both within and without . . . Spirit has not only lost its essential life; it is also conscious of this loss, and of the finitude that is its own content. Turning away from the empty husks, and confessing that it lies in wickedness, it reviles itself for so doing, and now demands from philosophy, not so much *knowledge* of what *is*, as the recovery through its agency of that lost sense of solid and substantial being.[9]

Only the imagery of the prodigal son is adequate to convey the current cultural crisis.

On the other hand, however, Hegel sees the hopeful beginning of new things. For him

> it is not difficult to see that ours is a birth-time and a period of transition to a new era. Spirit has broken with the world it has hitherto inhabited and imagined, and is of a mind to submerge it in the past . . . But just as the first breath drawn by a child after its long, quiet nourishment breaks the gradualness of merely quantitative growth — there is a qualitative leap, and the child is born — so likewise the Spirit in its formation matures slowly and quietly . . . The frivolity and boredom which unsettle the established order, the vague foreboding of something unknown, these are the heralds of approaching change. The gradual crumbling that left unaltered the face of the whole is cut short by a sunburst which, in one flash, illuminates the features of the new world.[10]

We could summarize this second agreement between Hegel and Husserl by saying that both place the demand for a truly scientific philosophy in the context of an historico-cultural crisis whose resolution they hope it will be.

There are two fairly obvious objections to this way of putting their second point of agreement. From Hegel's side it has been said, "The very idea of a true crisis of man, with the fate of the human spirit undecided and hanging in the balance, is unthinkable in the context of the Hegelian 'theodicy.'"[11] Put this way the statement is unobjectionable, for Hegel surely has a deep, theologically rooted confidence about history which is lacking to Husserl. But the dictionary uses the term "crisis" to speak of the turning point or climax of a process and of an unstable situation which requires transformation or resolution; and I think it is clear that in these senses Hegel might well have entitled his book "The Crisis of European Culture and the Phenomenology of Spirit." The genuine difference must not be allowed to obscure the equally genuine similarity.

The other objection comes from the Husserlian side and goes like this. While the crisis motif is obviously central to Husserl's last great introduction to transcendental phenomenology, it is missing from *Ideas I* and from *Cartesian Meditations*. It does not belong to his idea of transcendental phenomenology as such. But this would be to overlook the way in which "Philosophy as Rigorous Science" serves as a kind of introduction to all the introductions. For the crisis motif is conspicuously present there. The task of a scientific philosophy concerns not only the demands of theory but also the requirement "from an ethico-religious point of view [of] a life regulated by pure rational norms." Yet not only has there never been a rigorously scientific philosophy, but also in the modern world the separation of science from wisdom and its ability to "unravel for us the riddles of the world and of life" has become so total that "the spiritual need of our time has, in fact, become unbearable. Would that it were only theoretical lack of clarity regarding the sense of the 'reality' investigated in the natural and humanistic sciences that disturbed our peace . . . Far more than this, it is the most radical vital need that afflicts us, a need that leaves no point of our lives untouched."[12] This is the passion which drives the sometimes tortured, hypertheoretical analyses of *Ideas I* and *Cartesian Meditations*.

Philosophy and Natural Consciousness

The third and fourth fundamental agreements between Hegel and Husserl concern, not the historical setting in which the need for scientific philosophy is keenly felt, but the further specification of its nature. They identify a twofold turning which philosophy must undertake, the turn against natural consciousness and the transcendental turn, the turn from the primacy of the world and the turn toward the primacy of the subject. If in Husserl the epoche and the phenomenological reduction are to be distinguished rather than identified, it is because the former prepares for the latter, clearing the way for the turn to transcendental subjectivity by suspending or putting out of play all beliefs in the world's existence and explanatory value, the whole of the natural attitude, which pervades both everyday common sense and the sciences.[13]

Husserl puts it dramatically by saying that from the perspective of the self-evidence which philosophy must achieve, "every ordinary appeal to self-evidence, insofar as it was supposed to cut off further regressive inquiry, [is] theoretically no better than an appeal to an oracle through which a god reveals himself. All natural self-evidences, those of all objective sciences (not excluding those of formal logic and mathematics), belong to the realm of what is 'obvious,' what in truth has a background of incomprehensibility. Every [kind of] self-evidence is the title of a problem, with the sole exception of phenomenolgical self-evidence, after it has reflectively clarified itself and shown itself to be ultimate self-evidence."[14]

Hegel speaks of natural consciousness rather than the natural attitude or standpoint, but he means the same thing. It includes common sense, the sciences, even philosophy insofar as it is not yet truly scientific. Already in his Jena essay on scepticism he had praised the scepticism of antiquity for being directed, not against philosophy but against the "dogmatism of common sense."[15] Now in the central third of the Introduction to the *Phenomenology* he presents his phenomenological journey as a radical scepticism directed against all forms of natural consciousness, from which philosophical science can liberate itself "only by turning against it."[16] In describing the systematic dispossession of natural consciousness, his imagery is more violent than Husserl's. True philosophy seems to natural consciousness like the attempt to walk on one's head and is experienced as a kind of death and despair.[17] It would not be surprising to find an implacable hostility in natural consciousness toward philosophical science.[18]

But while different metaphors bespeak a different rhetorical tendency, the issue is the same for Hegel as for Husserl.[19] Philosophy must free itself from natural consciousness because the latter is prejudiced; it proceeds on unexamined presuppositions. It appeals to principles whose truth has not been established and to concepts whose meaning has not been clarified.[20] This is why Hegel finds it necessary to say that "the familiar, just because it is familiar, is not really understood."[21] The willingness to let go of the familiar and undertake a self-transformation that at first looks like death, but is really the path to life, is the courage without which philosophy is impossible.[22]

Philosophy as Transcendental Reflection

The journey from the familiar into new and unknown territory leads into the domain of the cogito, discovered but unexplored by Descartes. The fourth and, for the present, final agreement between Hegel and Husserl is that we enter the path toward scientific philosophy by taking the transcendental turn.[23] Hegel's Preface indicates this in the most general way by saying that "the goal is Spirit's insight into what knowing is."[24] By itself, of course, this is not the phenomenological reduction, for there is no guarantee that the subjectivity which comes to view will not be naturalized, leaving us in the snares of psychologism.[25] This, on Husserl's view, is exactly what happened to the founders of the transcendental tradition he seeks to perfect, Descartes, Locke and Kant. But we cannot overlook the fact that they, along with Fichte, are the founding fathers of that tradition precisely by virtue of this first step of redirecting attention from the object known to the subject knowing. Reflection as such may not be the sufficient, but it is the necessary condition of transcendental philosophy.

In the Introduction Hegel becomes a bit more specific about the meaning of the reflective move. The task at hand is "an exposition of how knowledge makes its appearance [*Darstellung des erscheinenden Wissens*]."[26] This involves distinguishing the observed from the observing consciousness, what appears to the former and what appears, namely the former's activity, *für uns*. We, that is the phenomenological we, which is so crucial to Hegel's methodology, do not participate in the acts of the consciousness we observe. We are rather the *reine Zuseher* of reflection. "All that is left for us to do is simply to look on." For this reason phenomenology can be called the "Science of the experience of consciousness."[27]

It is only, however, in the chapters on Consciousness that the intentional nature of consciousness and its constitutive role come to full light.[28] These chapters are the phenomenological retelling of the Aesthetic and Analytic of Kant's first *Critique*. The analysis of the Here, the Now, and the I in the chapter on Sense Certainty is Hegel's deduction of space, time, and the transcendental unity of apperception as conditions of possible experience; and the chapters on Perception and Understanding develop the a priori nature of the concept of nature, substances (things with properties) in the totality of causal reciprocity. Moreover, it is in the analysis of Sense Certainty that we first encounter a phenomenological refutation of the view that sense experience is something that the object does to us. "The truth of Sense Certainty is in the object as *my* [*meinem*] object, or in *my intending* it [im *Meinen*]; it is, because *I* know it."[29] This expelling of Sense Certainty from the object is not the final truth of Sense Certainty, for merely as just stated it is capable of misinterpretation. Like Husserl, Hegel insists that the constituting I is not the momentary immediacy of the Cartesian "each time I think." It is a moment in the total life and thus is always the mediated part of a whole. But this discovery of its essential activity in knowledge is never abandoned.

On the contrary, it is reinforced in the transition from Sense Certainty to Perception, made with the help of a pretty bad pun. Hegel tells us that "experience teaches me what the truth of Sense Certainty in fact is: I point it out as a Here, which is one Here among other

Heres, or as in itself a simple togetherness of many Heres; i.e., it is a universal. I take it up then as it is in truth, and instead of knowing something immediate, I take it truly or perceive it [*ich nehme so es auf wie es in Wahrheit ist, und statt ein Unmittelbares zu wissen, nehme ich wahr*]."[30]

Hegel is here summarizing his phenomenological demythologizing of the myth of the given. He is translating the logical notion that every determination is a negation into the phenomenological insight that every perception (or any other knowing, for that matter) is the taking of something as something. I can perceive my copy of Kant's first *Critique* only by taking it to be there and not elsewhere, now and not then, book and not typewriter, red and not blue, hardbound and not paperback, etc. Without this taking, nothing is given. In Husserlian language intentionality constitutes its object in the act of meaning bestowal.

It is important to notice that while Hegel here focuses on the referential features of the object, the Here and the Now, this analysis looks ahead to the descriptive features as well, its properties, as the example of the book illustrates. And, in terms of properties, this same analysis applies just as fully to the material, empirical properties as to the formal, categorial properties. So I cannot but repeat my claim that "in this respect the theory of transcendental subjectivity which emerges from the discussion of the Now and the Here is, in spite of its obvious Kantian overtones, closer to the Husserlian principle of strict correlation between intentional act and intentional object, noesis and noema."[31] It would seem that Hegel and Husserl agree with Merleau-Ponty that philosophy is "the vigilance which does not let us forget the source of all knowledge."[32]

Turning now to the differences between Hegel and Husserl, I want to mention three. They are so closely interrelated that it is not easy to find the ideal order for presentation. I shall proceed from the theme of freedom to that of method and thence to that of transcendental subjectivity, the theme of the most basic disagreement.

Two Views of Freedom

My sketch of the different concepts of freedom in Hegel and Husserl will be sketchy indeed, leaving the fuller development of what I take to be a very important issue for another occasion. Borrowing a clue from Ricoeur, we might say that Husserl has a Cartesian concept of freedom while Hegel has a Spinozist concept.[33] According to the former, freedom is a permanent possession which can be exercised, so to speak "at will," at any time and in any circumstances. According to the latter, freedom is not a permanent possession to be exercised "at will" but a characteristic of my doings only under special circumstances, which we might call liberation. On both views it is possible to say that it belongs to our essence as human to be free, but in the one case it means we are always free while in the other it means we are not fully free until we achieve liberation.

In the case of Hegel and Husserl this difference is closely related to another. For Husserl the primary meaning of freedom seems to be that freedom from prejudice and sedimented tradition which makes it possible for me to be fully self-responsible (primarily for my cognitive acts). Performing the epoche and the phenomenological reduction are the primary acts of freedom. For Hegel, the primary meaning of freedom, in the *Phenomenology* at least, is reciprocal recognition (a primarily non-theoretical relationship). I do not become free by becoming a phenomenologist. In the one case freedom is independence, in the other interdependence.

I mention this difference between freedom as autonomy and freedom as community, if ever so incompletely, to alert us all to the political ramifictaions of the issues before us. It may well be true that Husserl has no politics, but his image of the self and its freedom is that of classical liberalism. The free self is the thin self, unemcumbered by any worldly identity, and therefore fully free, no matter what its choices, so long as it makes those choices in sovereign independence. The theory of right and of freedom is independent of all theories of the good. By contrast, Hegel's image of the self and its freedom belongs to the critique of classical liberalism.[34] Because the self which requires freedom is the concrete self, a thick self with worldly identity, freedom cannot be defined independently of its proper goals, nor can it be realized in circumstances where those goals are unrealized. In so far as the classically liberal concept of freedom prevails in our society, we can say that Husserl's phenomenology performs an ideological function, Hegel's a utopian function.[35]

Two Views of Method

I want to approach the second disagreement a bit obliquely. There is a conspicuous tendency in Husserl to identify certainty and truth. His passion not merely for apodicticity but for absolute apodicticity, even when he does not identify apodictic evidence with adequate evidence, is the permanent core of his project.[36] By contrast Hegel regularly distinguishes certainty from truth. It could be said, of course, that (as previously noted) neither takes the certanties of natural consciousness for truth and both see it to be the task of philosophy to find a knowing where truth and certainty coalesce.[37] But Husserl's path to this goal has a noticeably different direction from Hegel's, a difference we might indicate by calling Husserl's the path of piecemeal certainty.

Hegel places enormous emphasis on the requirement that philosophy be systematic, while this seems of little consequence to Husserl. I think it can be said that Husserl's recurring sketches of a comprehensive classification of regional ontologies is about as close as his phenomenology comes to being a philosophic system. Hegel's concept of system, inextricably tied up with such substantive theses as a) Substance is Subject, b) the Absolute is Spirit, and c) the True is the Whole, is dramatically more demanding.[38]

Quentin Lauer sees a link between these two differences. "Unlike Husserl, however, [Hegel] refuses to believe that the apodictic certainty of its knowledge will guarantee its rational adequacy. It is not the certainty of knowledge which constitutes its rationality; rather it is the grasp of reality in its total interrelatedness. Husserl can institute a phenomenology which piles up – and even relates – bits of certain knowledge . . . In this view phenomenology is phenomenology antecedent to any concrete investigation it undertakes; it is a sort of blueprint for future investigations. For Hegel phenomenology . . . is not complete as phenomenology until it somehow embraces the totality of consciousness. . . ."[39]

If, indeed, these two differences are linked, it may be that they will show themselves to be expressions of a deeper and more basic disagreement. And so they do. Far from being random or accidental, the differences on the issues of certainty and system show themselves to be corollaries of antithetical models of what genuine knowledge must be. Husserl is a foundationalist, Hegel a holist. Even if there were no other interesting point of contact between them, the crucial contemporary debate over foundationalism and the meaning of holistic alternatives to this long reigning epistemic paradigm in the larger philosophical community would make our *Auseinandersetzung* of Hegel and Husserl all but unavoidable.

The heart of classical foundationalism, whose paradigm of normal philosophy Husserl seeks to reformulate and perfect, is not simply the distinction between basic and derived or inferred beliefs by itself, but this distinction combined with a certain kind of restriction on what kinds of beliefs can be properly basic.[40] The three traditional criteria, self-evidence, evidence to the senses, and incorrigibility are clearly expressions of the same passionate quest for certainty which we find at work in Husserl's intuitionist theory of evidence. He moves immediately from the distinction between immediate and mediate or grounded judgments to the theory of evidence in terms of the fulfillment of intention. Fulfillment occurs when what is merely supposed or meant "from afar" or "at a distance" is fully present itself, a presence expressed in terms of viewing or mental seeing, on the one hand, in terms of having or possession, on the other.[41]

The mixture of metaphors is essential to Husserl's intuitionism. Not just any seeing will do, for, as just mentioned, to see "from afar" or "at a distance" is to see through a glass darkly, and this seeing cannot lay the sure foundation which the edifice of knowledge requires. Only the seeing which derives from the presence of possession will do. Husserl also expresses this in terms of the crucial concept of immediacy. So he can write, "*Immediate 'seeing,'* not merely sensuous, experiential seeing, but *seeing in the universal sense as an originally presentive consciousness of any kind whatever*, is the ultimate legitimizing source of all rational assertions."[42]

By making clear that the appeal to intuition is an appeal to immediacy, Husserl indicates the radicality of his foundationalist requirements. For on this theory of evidence, to be properly basic a belief must not only be *uninferred* from other beliefs, but also *free of all interpretation*. We are talking not only about *underived* propositions, but especially about *theory-free data*.[43]

It is perhaps in terms of immediacy that Hegel's holism is best distinguished from Husserl's foundationalism. For Hegel sets his phenomenological procedure against any appeal to immediacy, not just against the immediacies of everyday obviousness. For him science is mediated knowing, and the central text of Hegel's holism, the claim that "the True is the whole," is the introduction to an exposition of the essentially mediated character of true knowing. There can be no results unmediated by the process of their development, no part unmediated by the whole to which it belongs, and vice versa.[44] Hegel seeks to provide phenomenological grounding for this claim not only in his critique of any use of the mathematical model to support a rationalistic kind of intuitionism,[45] but above all in his critique of Sense Certainty, which functions in the *Phenomenology* as a critique not only of empiricist foundationalism but by extrapolation of all appeals to immediacy. It seeks to show that the object of knowledge is always doubly mediated, on the one hand by the context (world, horizon) in which it appears, and on the other hand by the subject to and for whom it appears, a subject which turns out itself to be mediated by its own temporality.[46] It is not language which introduces mediation into experience. Rather, language refutes every appeal to immediacy just because the experience it seeks to express is already filled with mediation.[47]

This difference over immediacy has two important ramifications. First, it brings the difference over system into clearer focus. For Hegel it follows directly from the mediated character of knowing that true knowledge must have the form of system.[48] For if no bit, piece, part, or building block of knowledge is intelligible or justified by itself but only in relation to something else, each relational constellation short of the whole will itself be a bit, piece, part, or building block. Only in the totality of relatedness or mediation can meaning or truth be adequately established. Short of that totality knowing cannot rest.[49]

Hegel's philosophy has to be a system, because it is a dialectical holism.[50] It is dialectical because everything immediate or finite shows itself to be relationally dependent rather than self-sufficient, and it is holistic because given the absence of anything immediate upon which to build, everything remains in flux until totality is reached. Perhaps the metaphor of the arch is helpful here, in which none of the stones will stay put until all of them are in place.

By contrast, Husserl's phenomenology cannot be a system, for there are only three methods for building a philosophic system, and he is cut off from all three. In addition to the dialectical system there are the constructive and deductive systems. Constructionist philosophical systems are not easy to characterize. What is clearest about the way Leibniz or Whitehead, for example, proceed, is that it is neither deductive nor dialectical. Beyond that I am tempted to characterize this strategy as non-dialectical holism, but that is more a promissory note than adequate exposition.[51] We need not be too concerned with this alternative, however it is to be defined and whoever its best examplars are, for it is not at issue between Hegel and Husserl. Each repudiates it as failing to live up to his own standards of genuine science.

If both dialectical and non-dialectical holism are unavailable to Husserl because of his intuitionism, there remains the deductive route, which Descartes, at least, found compatible with his own intuitionist foundationalism. But on Husserl's view, this was one of Descartes's most serious errors. For, to give but one reason, this involves presupposing the validity of logic, which rather requires its own grounding, one which obviously cannot be deductive.[52] This leaves Husserl with a foundationalism like that of the empiricists, which I earlier called "the path of piecemeal certainty," and which Quentin Lauer, more vividly, called "a phenomenology which piles up – and even relates – bits of certain knowledge." Given their shared repudiation of deductive and constructionist approaches, Hegel and Husserl find the question of immediacy deciding the question of system. Hegel denies immediacy and finds himself a dialectical holist. Husserl seeks to retain immediacy and finds the way to system blocked.

There is a second significant ramification of the disagreement over immediacy. The foundationalist model obviously lends itself to thinking of knowledge as built from the ground (a loaded word for both Hegel and Husserl) up. It is not difficult to find Husserl tying this imagery of *"Philosophie von unten"* as tightly as possible to the concept of scientific rigor.[53] But there are times when this spatial metaphor turns into or is joined by a temporal metaphor, as when Husserl writes that there

> emerges, as the *question of the beginning*, the inquiry for those cognitions that are *first in themselves* and can support the whole storied edifice of universal knowledge. Consequently . . . we meditators . . . must have access to evidences that already bear the stamp of fitness for such a function, in that they are recognizable as *preceding* all other imaginable evidences.[54]

Sometimes that which is "first in itself" is "prior" in a literal temporal sense. But usually, as the interchangeability with the spatial metaphor would indicate, the point is epistemic independence. The foundation can be what it is without the superstructure, and that which comes first can be what it is apart from what comes later. The primary priority is the "logical" priority of conceptual autonomy. In either case, the movement of thought is from what is subsequent to what is antecedent or primordial.

Hegel's thought moves in just the opposite direction. For him, as Ricoeur put it,

> consciousness is a movement which continually annihilates its starting point and can guarantee itself only at the end. In other words, it is something that has meaning only in later figures, since the meaning of a given figure is deferred until the appearance of a new figure. Thus the fundamental meaning of the moment of consciousness called Stoicism in the *Phenomenology of Spirit* is not revealed until the arrival of skepticism, since it itself reveals the absolute unimportance of the relative

positions held by Master and Slave before the abstract thought of
freedom. The same is true for all the spiritual figures . . . We can say,
therefore, in very general terms that consciousness is the order of the
terminal, the unconscious that of the primordial.[55]

Ricoeur is obviously developing his contrast between Hegel and
Freud, but on this point, ironically, Husserl's philosophy of consciousness plays the same role as Freud's theory of the unconscious.
Like Freud, in spite of obvious differences, Husserl plays archeologist
of the spirit to Hegel's teleologist of the spirit. When this difference is
applied to the philosophy of history we get the difference between
mythological and eschatological thought. On the one hand, the
historical process has its meaning only in relation to what happened
in illo tempore. On the other hand, historical events have a meaning
which is only fully available in the culmination of the historical
process.

But even when historical temporality is not an issue, there is all
the difference in the world between seeking to explain a phenomenon
(or justify it, or interpret it, or whatever) by reference to what is prior
to it in the sense of being fully independent of it and seeking to explain
(or whatever) the same phenomenon with reference to what presupposes, includes, and fulfills it. Husserl's foundationalism involves the
one habit of thought, Hegel's holism the other. Perhaps both are
necessary, and the real challenge is to find a way of uniting them.
Perhaps we must choose between them. Perhaps we'll find that one is
appropriate for some tasks, the other for other tasks. (Which for scientific philosophy?) In any case we need to see how sharply different
they are from each other and how the debate between "causal" and
"teleological" thinking in the philosophy of science is but one expression of a larger issue that cannot be left to the philosophers of science,
though we might learn a good deal from their debates.

Two Views of Transcendental Subjectivity

The third disagreement between Hegel and Husserl that I want to
discuss concerns the nature of transcendental subjectivity. Our point
of departure can be Husserl's lament: "Philosophy as science, as
serious, rigorous, indeed apodictically rigorous, science — *the dream
is over."*[56] There is general agreement that neither this lament nor
Husserl's later work in its totality is, in David Carr's words, a "death-
bed renunciation" of the dream on the part of Husserl himself.[57] There

is a second agreement, less general, but more interesting, that Husserl's lament is the verdict which *he* did his best to ward off, but which *we* are compelled to draw, not because of Dilthey or Heidegger, but on the basis of insights growing out of Husserl's own tenacious radicality.[58]

Thus, for example, Landgrebe speaks of Husserl's "reluctant" departure from Cartesianism. At issue, clearly, is not just the adequacy of the "Cartesian way" to the Cartesian goal, but the viability of the very goal itself. Husserl's breaking up of the traditions he sought to fulfill begins as early as 1923–1924 in *Erste Philosophie*, II, where, *"before the eyes of the reader,* occurs the shipwreck of transcendental subjectivism, as both a non-historial a-priorism and as the consummation of modern rationalism [read: foundationalism]. Today, primarily as a result of Heidegger's work, the 'end of metaphysics' is spoken of as though it were quite obvious. We shall first properly understand the sense of such language if we follow closely how, in this work, metaphysics takes its departure *behind Husserl's back* . . . . To be sure, neither Husserl nor those who were his students at that time were explicitly aware of this." For this reason the full impact of his later work in the *Crisis* is "partially obscured by the self-interpretation he gave it."[59]

No doubt the most familiar formulation of this thesis is Merleau-Ponty's:

> The most important lesson which the reduction teaches us is the impossibility of a complete reduction . . . . If we were absolute mind, the reduction would present no problem. But since, on the contrary, we *are in the world*, since indeed our reflections are carried out in the temporal flux on to which we are trying to seize . . . there is no thought which embraces all our thought. The philosopher . . . is a perpetual beginner, which means . . . that *radical reflection amounts to a consciousness of its own dependence on an unreflective life which is its initial situation,* unchanging, given once and for all. Far from being, as has been thought, a procedure of idealistic philosophy, phenomenological reduction belongs to existential philosophy: Heidegger's *"being-in-the-world"* appears only against the background of the phenomenological reduction.[60]

Whether one is sympathetic to this movement of phenomenology toward existentialism and hermeneutics, or, like Husserl himself, would prefer to resist it, Merleau-Ponty's formulation has the advantage of defining the issue with real precision. By juxtaposing two ways of putting the issue he helps us to see their equivalence. On the one hand, there is the question whether reflection can ever become total by freeing itself from its origins in life. Can I ever "grasp myself in pure reflexion," or is it rather the case that "human consciousness never possesses itself in complete detachment"?[61] In the *Ideas I* Husserl presents the phenomenological reduction as precisely the sought-after triumph of reflection over life without which rigorous science would not be possible. In response to the question whether we can really do this, he replies that it is not all that hard. Just as the geometer does it when doing geometry, so the philosopher does it when doing phenomenology.[62] In the *Crisis* the reduction is still understood in the same way.[63] But the discovery in the meantime that geometry itself has origins and that it was already tradition and not rigorous science for Galileo makes it clear that the quick assurance of 1913 will need to be more carefully supported.[64]

The other way of putting the question asks whether we who philosophize are inextricably in the world. For reflection to win full independence of its "initial situation" in "unreflective life" is for the transcendental ego to be established as "outside" the world in a sense Husserl seeks to make precise.[65] There are two ways of being in the world, the Cartesian and the Heideggerian. Husserl seeks to overcome them both.

Husserl complains regularly and bitterly that Descartes is a kind of Moses who leads us to the promised land but fails to enter in himself. A central reason why his discovery of transcendental subjectivity falls short of fruition is that he identifies the ego with the soul, which remains substantially and causally part of the world as nature. Descartes is a dualist, of course, and not a materialist, but his psychophysical dualism leaves us with a psychic world which, "because of the way in which it is related to nature, does not achieve the status of an independent world."[66] Husserl names the resultant point of view transcendental realism or transcendental psychologism, and regularly blesses it with the epithet Absurd.[67] This absurdity can also be expressed as what Husserl calls "the paradox of human subjectivity: being a subject for the world and at the same time being an object in the world."[68] The problem is obvious. A subjectivity which is part of the world cannot be the ground of the world. The acts of an ego conditioned by the world to which it belongs cannot be the unconditioned acts which have the foundational status required for rigorous science.

But on Husserl's view the paradox is only apparent. It disappears the moment we distinguish the empirical ego, which is clearly in the world as, for example, situated in the lived body, from the transcendental ego, for whom the world as a whole is transcendent.[69] In short, it is the work of the phenomenological reduction to dissolve the paradox. As Ricoeur puts it, "The subject which [in the natural attitude] is hidden from itself as part of the world discovers itself [in the reduction] as the foundation of the world."[70]

But there is another way of being in the world. If we call it the Heideggerian way, this is not meant to imply that Husserl's attention is drawn to it only through his reading of *Being and Time*. David Carr has shown us convincingly that there are powerful internal motives which lead Husserl to reconsider the adequacy of the reduction as first formulated for its liberting task.[71] To be in the world in the Heideggerian sense is to be given over to and thus conditioned by a universal network, not of causal interactions but of meaning constellations.[72] This world of meanings, which Husserl calls the life-world, is "the always already pregiven world."[73] Like the world of nature this is an actual world which "always precedes cognitive activity as its universal ground," and for this reason "we will not so easily find [in it] that ultimately original self-evidence of experience which we seek."[74]

But unlike the world of nature, this world stands as a challenge to the reduction and the goal of rigorous science as an explicitly historical world. For this world is "always a world in which cognition in the most diverse ways has already done its work." It is "always already pregiven to us as impregnated by the precipitate of logical operations. The world is never given to us as other than the world in which we or others, whose store of experience we take over by communication, eduction, and tradition, have already been logically active, in judgment and cognition." Thus "the world of our experience is from the beginning interpreted . . . "[75] In short, to be in the world in this Heideggerian sense is to be caught up in the hermeneutical circle.

In the *Ideas* and the *Cartesian Meditations* Husserl had already recognized that the world in which we always already find ourselves is a world of both nature and culture,[76] that this "already" represents a bondage or restriction from which we must be freed,[77] that it is the task of the phenomenological reduction to reflect us out of the world, both as nature and as culture,[78] and that phenomenology must flesh itself out as a theory of the constitution of both nature and culture.[79] But he came to think that in those works he had only developed the first step of the epoché.[80] The bracketing of nature and culture as defined by the sciences had left untouched the pre-theoretical life-world within which and on the basis of which the sciences arise, and this world, whose opacity must be transformed into transparency, is itself largely the product of cultural history. It is a world of linguistically mediated tradition.

In this context the reduction is redefined in order to be completed. One must still speak of the movement from *doxa* to *episteme*. But whereas *doxa* originally had the sense of belief as that which lacks the apodictic certainty of knowledge, it now comes to have the more determinate sense of tradition as that which lacks the self-grounding character of knowledge. In the Vienna Lecture, the Greek ideal of theory, of truth-in-itself as knowledge without presuppositions, is interpreted as freedom from every form of bondage to tradition.[81] Hence the identification of tradition with prejudice.[82] The reduction, which can now be called the historical reduction, becomes the "discovery-overthrow" of historical prejudices, the "dismantling" of sedimented tradition.[83]

This task amounts to moving the life-world from the subject side of the equation to the object side. When Husserl speaks of the life-world, with all its sedimentations of historical tradition, as the ground of all our cognitive activity, he gives it a constitutive role in everyday experience, in scientific research, and even in philosopical reflection.[84] As such he identifies it with the subject of knowing and speaks of "mankind as the subjectivity which, in community, intentionally brings about the accomplishment of world validity."[85] It is, to be sure, an "anonymous" subjectivity, marred by the opacity of unconscious mediation.[86] It is an intersubjectivity whose We is much closer to Heidegger's They (*das Man*) than to any I myself. But it nevertheless participates in subjectivity.

But the subjectivity which is enveloped in this anonymous subjectivity is not capable of *episteme*, for it is swimming in the *doxa* of traditional prejudice. Just as in the first instance rigorous science was to be possible only for a knower which had reflected itself out of the world of theoretical objectivity, so now it will be possible only by the switching off of one's interested involvement in the world of pre-theoretical subjectivity. This involves doing what has never been done before, making the life-world itself into a theme of scientific (phenomenological) investigation. The historical reduction and the science of the life-world are the same thing. In both cases the life-world itself becomes phenomenon, constituted not constituting, object not subject.[87]

Like the original version of the reduction, this one involves the eidetic reduction. The life-world has an essence, general structures which are not themselves historically relative, and these can be

brought to intuitive clarity.[88] But the eidetic reduction is never sufficient. Here as in the *Ideas* it must be completed by a reduction which
arises out of the epoche by which I disengage myself from interested
involvement *within* the world in question so as to rise *above* it. It is this
rising above which constitutes the phenomenological, and now, its
completion, the historical reduction.[89]

As the Sartrean self seeks to neutralize the threatening look of the
other by returning the gaze so as to objectify the other, I now seek,
as Husserlian philosopher, to neutralize the anonymous subjectivity
of the life-world, looking not at but through me, by making it the
object of my own philosopical gaze. At this point

> the gaze of the philosopher in truth first becomes fully free: above all,
> free of the strongest and most universal, and at the same time most hid-
> den, internal bond, namely, of the pregiveness of the world. Given in
> and through this liberation is the discovery of the universal, absolutely
> self-enclosed and absolutely self-sufficient correlation between the
> world itself and world-consciousness. By the latter is meant the con-
> scious life of the subjectivity which effects the validity of the world . . . .[90]

But this subjectivity is no longer the anonymous subjectivity of the
life-world. The self has raised itself above that in the very act of
"the reduction of mankind to the phenomenon 'mankind,' [which]
makes it possible to recognize mankind as a self-objectification of
transcendental subjectivity which is always functioning ultimately
and is this 'absolute.'"[91]

True philosophy for Husserl, like true religion for St. James, is to
"keep oneself untarnished by the world."[92] It now looks as if this task
is a good deal harder than it had looked earlier. The simple reflection
of the "Cartesian way" will have to be supplemented by an historical
reflection which is much more complicated.[93] But the passages cited
in the previous paragraph suggest that Husserl has little doubt that the
freedom and purity he sought could indeed be found. This impression
is confirmed in *Experience and Judgment*. Once the need is seen to
distinguish between the pregiven world, the life-world as spoken of up
to now, and the *original* life world, Husserl is confident that the regres-
sion from the former to the latter can be accomplished. In doing so
we move from a realm of experience which is already the result of
interpretation to "experience in its immediacy," to "pure experience," to
"immediate intuition," and to "original experience," which is "experience
in the ultimately original sense . . . an experience still unacquainted
with [unaffected by] any of these idealizations [historical traditions]

but whose necessary foundation it is."[94] This is the realm of pure experience which has been Husserl's goal since 1907. It is the home of that utterly antimundane subjectivity which Husserl calls transcendental.

It can easily be argued against this background that Heidegger, for example, is not a transcendental philosopher. Far from seeking a subjectivity "untarnished by the world," he emphasizes the inescapably worldly character of *Dasein*, not in the Cartesian sense of worldly but in the, well, Heideggerian sense. And he draws the obvious consequences about the hermeneutical circle and the possibility of philosophy as rigorous science. If Husserl is taken to be the paradigm of transcendental philosophy, we simply have to acknowledge that Heidegger stands outside its pale. In doing so we gain an important insight, but also close ourselves off from other insights. For in important senses Heidegger is a transcendental philosopher. *Dasein* is the totality of the conditions of possible experience, a "subjectivity" which gives meaning to the nature and culture in which it lives. It does so, of course, not absolutely, but as a mediated and conditioned source of meaning. Instead of simply denying that Heidegger is a transcendental philosopher, it might be more accurate to speak of his first taking the transcendental turn and then a post-transcendental turn, in which the worldly and relative nature of transcendental subjectivity is acknowledged without denying the import of the second Copernican Revolution.

I make this point in order to suggest the same for Hegel. Like Husserl, as I have already argued, he takes the transcendental turn.[95] But like Heidegger, he also takes the post-transcendental turn, and he does so by asking essentially the same question posed by the existential analytic of *Dasein*: Who is the transcendental subject? This Who? implies a thick self with a worldly identity which guarantees the historical relativity of all its acts. And yet Hegel is not, as Heidegger is, among those for whom the dream of rigorous science is over.[96] Precisely this is the genius of the *Phenomenology of Spirit*, that (to speak anachronistically) with Heidegger it takes the post-transcendental turn but with Husserl retains the dream of rigorous science. How does Hegel think it possible to do this?

The transcendental turn is essentially completed as the transition from Consciousness to Self-Consciousness takes place with "the necessary advance from the previous shapes of consciousness for which their truth was a Thing, an 'other' than themselves," to the discovery "that not only is consciousness of a thing possible only for a self-consciousness, but that self-consciousness alone is the truth of those shapes."[97] The post-transcendental turn begins immediately with the introduction of desire. As animal desire, self-consciousness is embodied, and thus embedded in nature. As human desire for recognition, self-consciousness is embedded in spirit, the I that is We and the We that is I. And this We to which I belong is not the We of Husserl's Fifth Meditation, but the historically concrete We whose struggles for reciprocal recognition include the brutalities of alienated labor. Who is the transcendental subject? The transcendental subject is Spirit embodied, working, dominating, fighting, and dying.[98] The subject which gives meaning to my life is the partially individuated self I am, immersed in a life-world, a *Sittlichkeit* which is as much a part of my identity as I myself am. And just as my practical freedom does not consist in the autonomy of dominating the other self, so my theoretical freedom does not consist in the autonomy of freeing myself from immersion in the world. In Hegel's eyes Husserl has been seduced by the most tragic of modernity's heresies, the equation of freedom with independence. He does not recognize that, beyond the inherent impossibility of ever becoming truly independent, to the degree that I do become independent, I become, not more free, but more abstract, less real.[99]

Philosophical thought is not immune to this worldliness. Already in his Jena essay on *Naturrecht* Hegel had spoken of "the historical aspect of Science," and invited us to see "the empirical condition of the world reflected in the conceptual [*ideellen*] mirror of Science." Philosophy pays its dues to necessity not by disdaining particularity as something merely positive and contingent, tempting it to flee the world. It rather rescues [*entreisst*] the ethical life of its people from contingency when "it permeates and animates it [*sie durchdringt, und belebt*]."[100] Here Hegel anticipates the famous formula from the Preface to the *Philosophy of Right*, "Whatever happens, every individual is a child of his time: so philosophy too is its own time apprehended in thoughts."[101]

In the *Phenomenology* Hegel expresses this theme not only by presenting philosophy as essentialy mediated by its own history,[102] but also as the fulfillment and expression of its own spiritual world. Thus, Science is the "crown of a world of spirit, the product of a widespread unheaval in various forms of culture, the prize at the end of a complicated, tortuous path of historical development."[103] One can feel Husserl's shudder when he hears Hegel saying, "That the True is actual only as system, or that Substance is essentially Subject, is expressed in the representation of the Absolute as Spirit — the most sublime concept and *the one which belongs to the modern age and its religion.*"[104] Prior to Marx we have here the makings of a theory of ideology, of philosophical thought as essentially conditioned by its world. But Hegel is not traumtized, for he sees no conflict between this relativity and the absoluteness philosophy requires to be scientific. Again we are forced to ask, How can this be?

It turns out that when Hegel says that "now is the time for philosophy to be raised to the status of a Science," he implies a double disagreement with Husserl as well as the double agreement pointed out at the beginning of this essay. On the one hand is the acceptance of science as having historical-cultural conditions, as being possible only in a life-world of a particular kind. On the other hand is the claim that these conditions are, at least in principle, currently actualized. When Hegel finds it not difficult "to see that ours is a birth-time and a period of transition to a new era," he is not speaking of just any historical transition but of the decisive one which finally makes philosophy possible as science. We are face to face with Hegel's so-called end of history thesis.[105]

It is easy to make either absolute or relative nonsense of Hegel's claim that his philosophy somehow brings the historical process to its conclusion, or, as he puts it at the end of the *Phenomenology,* that the triumph of the concept which he presents "annuls time" (*die Zeit tilgt*) or "sets aside its time-form" (*hebt er seine Zeitform auf*).[106] We get absolute nonsense if we make Hegel into a kind of evolutionary McTaggert, for whom at a particular time events cease occuring. We get relative nonsense if we hear Hegel saying, as I fear we must, that the historical world of his own time is the fulfillment of human history. But I want to try to see if we can find some sense rather than nonsense here.

We can begin to do so, I believe, by answering the question we have twice left hanging: How does Hegel harmonize the relativity of philosophical thought, on which he insists in terms of the thick, historical identity of the transcendental subject, with the absoluteness of philosophical thought, on which he insists with equal vigor, in terms of its scientific, systematic rigor? Hegel's "solution" is as simple as it is bold. Relativity is not bad in itself. Relatedness belongs to the very nature of the real (this being the ontological foundation of the holistic methodology). Thought is finite in a sense to be surpassed, not simply by virtue of its ties to its world, but by virtue of the finitude of that world. But what if the world had overcome its finitude by fulfilling the inner telos of human history? The thought which was the crown of that world would be the ideology of freedom actualized.

It would be relative and absolute at the same time, relative to its world instead of being self-grounding, but absolute because that world would be unsurpassable. Knowledge would no longer need to go beyond itself because its world would no longer need to be transcended.

If we inquire how Hegel describes such a world, which others have called the Messianic age, the Kingdom of God, the classless society, and so forth, we find that in the *Phenomenology* Hegel defines the fulfillment of history in terms of reciprocal recognition. On the analysis he develops there reciprocal recognition must be both uncoerced and universal to be completely realized. Since mental manipulation is as much a violation of freedom as physical force, this means that the world whose ideology would be science would have to be a global community free from both war and propaganda.[107]

Hegel's time may well have been a birth time of revolutionary change, but neither his time nor ours has been the advent of a global community free of war or propaganda. That fact counts against the element of realized eschatology in Hegel's thought but not in the least against his concepts of transcendental subjectivity, science, and freedom. Because of his deep affinities with Husserl he would find it important to be as clear as possible about the differences between them, and he might well summarize them this way, with apologies to Marx: the phenomenologists have only sought to perfect the reduction, the task is to hold forth a vision that will help to change the world. The task of philosophy as such is not directly to change the world. But precisely because its own fulfillment as science depends upon the world's fulfillment as the global reign of peace, justice, and love, its task is to be a partner in the revolution still awaited. This revolution will not be the triumph of either capitalism or communism in anything like the forms in which we know them. For while both aspire to be the global community, both have sold their souls to war and propaganda as the means to universality. The philosophy which wishes to be scientific in the spirit of Hegel's *Phenomenology* will be a subversive agent in relation to both contemporary theory and praxis — for its own sake and for the sake of the world from which it seeks no divorce.

Notes

1. George Schrader, "Hegel's Contribution to Phenomenology," *The Monist* 48 (1964): 18–33.

2. Quentin Lauer, "Phenomenology: Hegel and Husserl," in *Beyond Epistemology: New Studies in the Philosophy of Hegel*, ed. Frederick G. Weiss (The Hague: Martinus Nijhoff, 1974), pp. 174–96.

3. Naturally the central focus will be on *Ideas I, Cartesian Meditations*, and the *Crisis*, Husserl's three major introductions to transcendental phenomenology.

4. G. W. F. Hegel, *Phenomenology of Spirit*, trans. A. V. Miller (Oxford: Clarendon Press, 1977), pp. 3–4.

5. For my more detailed interpretation of this passage see *History and Truth in Hegel's Phenomenology* (Atlantic Highlands: Humanities Press, 1979), Section 1C, "Phenomenology as Criticism without Presuppositions." Since this occurs in the context of Hegel's attempt to distinguish his phenomenological critique of reason from that of Kant and the British empiricists, it is surprising that Husserl complains that "his system lacks a critique of reason, which is the foremost prerequisite for being scientific in philosophy." "Philosophy as Rigorous Science," in *Phenomenology and the Crisis of Philosophy*, trans. and ed. Quentin Lauer (New York: Harper and Row, 1965), p. 77. A detailed dialogue between Husserl and just this Introduction would be one very good way of thinking through the relation between the two thinkers.

6. Hegel, *Phenomenology*, p. 3. I have somewhat modified Miller's translation here and occasionally elsewhere.

7. ibid., pp. 2–3. On the cognitive significance of tarrying or lingering (*verweilen*), see ibid., pp. 16–17.

8. In view of the religious overtones of this language, drawn from the contemplative life, the metaphor of epistemological asceticism may be appropriate for the discipline of "world-denial" involved in Husserl's phenomenological reduction and its disengagement not just of belief in the world but also of all worldly interests. He himself compares the epoche to "a religious conversion." *The Crisis of European Sciences and Phenomenological Philosophy*, trans. David Carr (Evanston: Northwestern University Press, 1970), p. 137.

9. Hegel, *Phenomenology*, p. 4. Cf. Westphal, *History and Truth*, pp. 26–28.

10. Hegel, *Phenomenology*, pp. 6–7. This is a recurring theme in Hegel's thought. See my *History and Truth*, p. 54, n 46. Both Kant's Copernican revolution and the French Revolution are important themes behind this one.

11. David Carr, in his Translator's Introduction to *Crisis* p. xxxv.

12. *Phenomenology and Crisis*, pp. 71–73, 135–42. It is worth noting that in this text from 1911 Husserl has an almost Hegelian confidence missing from the *Crisis*: "There is, perhaps, in all modern life no more powerfully, more irresistably progressing idea than that of science. Nothing will hinder its

victorious advance" (p. 82). Cf. the concluding paragraph of Hegel's inaugural address at Heidelberg, *Hegel's Lectures on the History of Philosophy*, trans. E. S. Haldane (1892), Reprint ed. (New York: Humanities Press, 1963), p. xiii. It is also worth noting that Husserl begins the *Cartesian Meditations* with at least a hint of the crisis motif. *Cartesian Mediations*, trans. Dorion Cairns (The Hague: Martinus Nijhoff, 1973), pp. 4–5.

13. For helpful commentary on Husserl's "switching off" metaphor and the explanatory role of the world in the natural attitude, see Erazim Kohak, *Idea and Experience: Edmund Husserl's Project of Phenomenology in Ideas, I* (Chicago: University of Chicago Press, 1978), pp. 35–40. On the difference between the epoche and the reduction, see *Crisis*, p. 151.

14. Husserl, *Crisis*, pp. 188–9.

15. "Verhältniss des Skepticismus zur Philosophie," in *Jenaer Kritische Schriften, Gesammelte Werke*, ed. Buchner and Poggeler (Hamburg: Felix Meiner Verlag, 1968), 4:215.

16. Hegel, *Phenomenology*, p. 48. On the threeford radicality of Hegel's phenomenological scepticism in relation to natural consciousness, see my *History and Truth*, section 1b, "Phenomenology As the Way of Doubt and Despair."

17. Hegel, *Phenomenology*, pp. 15, 49–51.

18. See Hegel's *Differenzschrift*, in *Gesammelte Werke*, 4:21.

19. Gadamer suggests that the twentieth century critique of consciousness is more radical than Hegel's critique of subjective spirit because of the rise of a hermeneutics of suspicion in Marx, Nietzsche, and Freud. Since Husserl is essentially untouched by these analyses of personal and social self-deception, it could be said that his critique of everyday experience is, like Hegel's, a nineteenth century critique. See "The Philosophical Foundations of the Twentieth Century" in *Philosophical Hermeneutics*, trans. and ed. David E. Linge (Berkeley: University of California Press, 1976).

20. Westphal, *History and Truth*, pp. 5–6.

21. Hegel, *Phenomenology*, p. 18. It is for just this reason that Kohak regularly stresses the non-identity of the obvious and the evident for Husserl. See *Idea and Experience*. In the *Crisis* Husserl sounds as if he has Hegel in mind when he writes, "But the great problem is precisely to understand what is here so 'obvious'" (p. 187).

22. Hegel, *Phenomenology*, pp. 19, 51–52. Cf. the last paragraph of Hegel's *Antrittsrede* at Berlin. *Werke*, ed. Moldenhauer and Michel (Frankfurt: Suhrkamp, 1970), 10:417.

23. Were I to take time and space for a further agreement it would con-

cern Hegel's affinity in the *Phenomenology* for Husserl's eidetic reduction. Not only does the entire text have "patterns of consciousness" *[Gestalten des Bewusstseins]* for its theme; the discussion of Sense Certainty shows how the most immediate levels of sense experienced are saturated with universality. We express our sense experience in a language of universals because we have already perceived the world that way. Essences are pre-predicative. See my *History and Truth*, section 3c.

24. Hegel, *Phenomenology*, p. 17.

25. Husserl, *Meditations*, pp. 32–37. Transcendental psychologism can also be viewed as transcendental realism. See p. 24.

26. Hegel, *Phenomenology*, p. 49. The ambiguity in the adjective is probably intentional, indicating both that knowledge appears, becomes a theme for reflective thought, and that the knowledge which does thereby come under scrutiny is merely phenomenal knowledge, in a quasi-Kantian sense. It is not the genuine knowledge which reflective philosophy aspires to be.

27. Ibid., pp. 54–56. Cf. Ricoeur's formulation: "an 'uninterested' impartial spectator wrenches itself away from 'interest of life.' At this point the triumph of phenomenological 'seeing' over vital and everyday 'doing' is complete." With reference to both the epistemological asceticism mentioned above (note 8) and this splitting of the ego into observer and observed, Ricoeur is reminded of "the Platonic conversion by which the psyche, 'captivated' by reality, draws closer to the νοῦς from which it came." But he is nervous, not entirely sure whether he is dealing with spiritual heroism or, perhaps, neurosis. And so he asks "what motivates such a rupture?" *Husserl: An Analysis of His Phenomenology*, trans. Ballard and Embree (Evanston: Northwestern University Press, 1967), p. 94. Ricoeur is discussing *Meditations*, p. 35. Though Hegel himself is committed to a form of philosophical world-denial and to a reflective turn in which "we" distinguish ourselves from the forms of consciousness we observe, he raises the same question. With special reference to the way his transcendental forefathers made the second of these moves, he wonders outloud whether the fear of error which leads to reflection might itself be the error to avoid. He suspects that at least sometimes "what calls itself fear of error reveals itself rather as fear of truth" (*Phenomenology*, p. 47). The boundary line between sainthood and schizophrenia is not always well marked, and phenomenology's radicality seems to place it on that boundary. For an account of the "unmotivated" character of phenomenological reflection more sympathetic to Husserl, see Eugen Fink, "The Phenomenological Philosophy of Edmund Husserl and Contemporary Criticism," in *The Phenomenology of Husserl: Selected Critical Readings*, ed. and trans. R. O. Elveton (Chicago: Quadrangle Books, 1970), pp. 101–102. Yet Fink's own linkage of phenomenology with the traditional question of the origin of the world and with the aspiration to be an "absolute knowledge" of the world's "ultimate ground," "the world-transcendent knowledge of the absolute 'ground,'" suggests motivation; and he uses the term *hubris* himself (pp. 97–98, 103).

28. For Husserl there is a tight link between the idea of constitution and transcendentalism. See, for example, *Ideas Pertaining to a Pure Phenomenological Philosophy: First Book*, trans. F. Kerstein (The Hague: Martinus Nijhoff, 1983), pp. 209 and 239.

29. Hegel, *Phenomenology*, p. 61.

30. Ibid., p. 66.

31. Westphal, *History and Truth*, p. 89, n. 18.

32. *Signs*, trans. Richard C. McCleary (Evanston: Northwestern University Press, 1964), p. 110.

33. *The Conflict of Interpretations*, ed. Don Ihde (Evanston: Northwestern University Press, 1974), p. 191. Ricoeur frequently draws this distinction, but not, as far as I am aware, with reference to Hegel.

34. On Hegel as a critic of classical liberalism see my essay, "Hegel, Human Rights, and the Hungry," forthcoming from Humanities Press in *Hegel on Economics and Freedom*, ed. William Maker.

35. I'm using these terms as Karl Mannheim uses them in *Ideology and Utopia*, trans. L. Wirth (San Diego: Harcourt, Brace, Jovanovich, 1985).

36. Ludwig Landgrebe points out that Husserl identifies them in *Erste Philosophie*, II, but distinguishes them in *Cartesian Meditations*. "Husserl's Departure from Cartesianism," in Landgrebe, *The Phenomenology of Edmund Husserl: Six Essays*, ed. Donn Welton (Ithica: Cornell University Press, 1981), p. 76.

37. Thus both would agree with Ricoeur's notion of a "crisis in the notion of consciousness." See n. 33 above, *Conflict of Interpretations*, p. 101.

38. Hegel, *Phenomenology*, pp. 9–14.

39. See Lauer, "Phenomonology: Hegel and Husserl," p. 187. Cf. p. 189: "Because Husserl is more concerned with the apodictic certitude of the knowledge he can obtain than he is with the extent of that knowledge, his aim is to find in self-consciousness the guarantee of any knowledge, however trivial it may be. Since Hegel's aim is the attainment of knowledge which is truly knowledge only if it is total, he cannot be satisfied with anything less than . . . a knowledge which cannot stop short of the interrelatedness of all knowing and of all that is known." Since this could only be "absolute Spirit's absolute knowledge of itself," we can see why the substantive theses of the previous paragraph are embedded in Hegel's concept of system and why, as George Schrader puts it, it is "because Hegel's phenomenology is *ontological* that is must be *dialectical*." The converse is just as true. See his "Hegel's Contribution," p. 25.

40. My account of classical foundationalism is indebted to *Faith and Rationality: Reason and Belief in God*, ed. Plantinga and Wolterstorff (Notre Dame: University of Notre Dame Press, 1983), especially the essays by the editors. For a different kind of critique see Richard Rorty, *Consequences of Pragmatism* (Minneapolis: University of Minnesota Press, 1982).

41. Husserl, *Meditations*, pp. 10–13; cf. p. 57, where evidence means "the *self-appearance*, the *self-exhibiting*, the *self-giving*" of the intended so that the following becomes synonymous: "itself there," "immediately intuited," and "given originality." Ricoeur's summary: "Evidence . . . is the presence of the thing itself in the original . . . one would be tempted to say presence in flesh and blood, this is the self-givenness (*Selbstgegebenheit*) which Husserl calls 'originary.'" (*Husserl*, p. 101). Husserl speaks of the "*absolute nearness*" which is "*pure* givenness." (*Ideas*, p. 153).

42. Husserl, *Ideas*, p. 36. In *Erste Philosophie*, II, *Husserliana*, vol. 8, ed. R. Boehm (The Hague: Martinus Nijhoff, 1959), Husserl reinforces the equivalence of apodicticity and immediacy. "At the very start . . . there must be an immediate knowledge, possibly a field, coindicated by immediate knowledge, of entirely accessible and therefore itself immediate knowledge, and these immediacies must be certain in an immediate fashion" (p. 40). This is the meaning of the claim that "absolute justification thus presupposes absolute intuition" (p. 367). Quoted in Landgrebe, *Six Essays*, pp. 77–78.

43. Husserl, *Ideas*, p. 33, 38, 42. "The issue between Husserl and Hegel turns on whether description can be isolated from interpretation . . ." George Schrader, "Hegel's Contribution," pp. 23–24. This issue lies at the heart of the *Crisis* and motivates Husserl's attempt at an historical reduction based on the recognition that tradition is theory and that it affects not only thought but also perception. Perhaps the clearest statement of the problem is in Husserl's *Experience and Judgment: Investigations in a Genealogy of Logic*, trans. Churchill and Ameriks (Evanston: Northwestern University Press, 1973), pars. 6–11 and in David Carr's helpful commentary, *Phenomenology and the Problem of History* (Evanston: Northwestern University Press, 1974), ch. 9, esp. pp. 213–19.

44. Hegel, *Phenomenology*, pp. 11–13.

45. Ibid., pp. 24–28.

46. There is a kind of holism at work in Husserl's reflection on the concepts of horizon, world, and eventually life-world. Because he begins with a *phenomenology* of perception he avoids the atomism of Hume, and because he begins with a phenomenology of *perception* he avoids the atomism of the early Wittgenstein. But his holism always remains subordinated to his intuitionist evidentialism, however tense the relation between them becomes.

47. This sketchy summary of Hegel's critique of Sense Certainty is developed in detail in *History and Truth*, ch. 3. Hegel had already developed a critique of immediacy in the section on Jacobi in *Glauben und Wissen*, 1802

(*Gesammelte Werke*, 4:346–86). He repeats this informal treatment of the matter in paragraphs 61–78 of the *Encyclopedia*, with reference to Jacobi and Descartes, and in lectures 3–5 of his *Lectures on the Proofs of the Existence of God* in vol. 3 of *Hegel's Lectures on the Philosophy of Religion*, trans. Spiers and Sanderson (New York: Humanities Press, 1962) and in vol. 17 of the *Werke* (Frankfurt: Suhrkamp, 1969). In both versions of the Logic the opening triad, Being-Nothing-Becoming, plays the same role vis-á-vis all appeals to immediacy that the analysis of Sense Certainty does in the *Phenomenology*. See Hans-Georg Gadamer, "The Idea of Hegel's Logic," in *Hegel's Dialectic: Five Hermeneutical Studies*, trans. P. Christopher Smith (New Haven: Yale University Press, 1976), and Dieter Henrich, "Anfang und Methode der Logik," in *Hegel im Kontext* (Frankfurt: Suhrkamp, 1971). One cannot overemphasize the centrality to all of Hegelian thought of the critique of immediacy in any form.

48. Hegel, *Phenomenology*, pp. 13–14.

49. Ibid., pp. 50–51.

50. For a fuller sketch of Hegel's dialectical holism and its relation to contemporary holisms, see my essay, "Dialectic and Intersubjectivity," forthcoming in *The Owl of Minerva*.

51. Though Leibniz is not free of foundationalist rhetoric, I think the ultimate logic of his metaphysics is holistic. The same can be said for Spinoza, with perhaps even more right, in spite of what he says about proceeding *more geometrico*. In any case the Spinoza Germany came to love during the *Goethezeit*, mediated by Herder's *Gott*, was a holistic and not a geometrizing Spinoza.

52. Husserl, *Meditations*, pp. 7, 24.

53. See, for example, *Phenomenology and Crisis*, pp. 76, 122, 142; and Husserl, *Crisis*, p. 75.

54. Husserl, *Meditations*, p. 14. I have added italics to Husserl's. For this temporal imagery of what is first or prior, also see pp. 16, 18, 21–22, and 27, and *Ideas*, pp. 33, 38, and 42.

55. Ricoeur, *Conflict of Interpretations*, p. 113.

56. Husserl, *Crisis*, p. 389.

57. Carr, *Phenomenology and the Problem of History*, p. xxiii.

58. Those of a different disposition than Husserl may experience this compulsion as liberation. For an extreme example, see Rorty, *Consequences of Pragmatism*. Husserl's own efforts to avoid this verdict are the theme of Gadamer's discussion of the *Crisis*. So carefully does Husserl seek to preserve and perfect the transcendental reduction by keeping both the life-world and intersubjectivity relative to the constitutive activity of the transcendental ego, whose place is thus *not* taken by the life-world, that Gadamer writes, "The

Crisis attempts to give an implicit answer to *Being and Time.*" See "The Phenomenological Movement" and "The Science of the Life-World" in *Philosophical Hermeneutics*. Obviously Gadamer does not find Husserl's case convincing, but his account reinforces Landgrebe's suggestion that what occurs "before the eyes of the reader" takes place "behind Husserl's back." Carr agrees that if Husserl did in fact plant the seeds of the destruction of transcendental philosophy in the *Crisis*, he himself surely did not think so. Beyond that he argues, tentatively but hopefully, that Husserl's encounter with history and the life-world does not require that verdict. See Carr, *Phenomenology and the Problem of History*, p. xxv and chaps. 9–10.

59. Landgrebe, *Six Essays*, pp. 68–69. (My italics.) On the "Cartesian Way" into phenomenology, see p. 83 and 90 and *Crisis*, pp. 144–54.

60. M. Merleau-Ponty, *Phenomenology of Perception*, trans. Colin Smith (New York: Humanities Press, 1962), p. xiv. (My italics.) Still another, quite similar formulation comes from Ricoeur. In the *Crisis* and in *Experience and Judgment* "the decisive fact is the progressive abandonment, upon contact with new analyses [e.g., of the life-world as pre-given], of the idealism of the *Cartesian Meditations*. The reduction less and less signifies a 'return to the ego' and more and more a 'return from logic to the antepredicative', to the primordial evidence of the world. The accent is placed no longer on the monadic ego; instead the accent is placed on the totality formed by the ego and the surrounding world in which it is vitally engaged. Thus, phenomenology tends toward the recognition of what is prior to all reduction and what cannot be reduced. The irreducibility of the life-world signifies that the Platonic-mathematical conversion cannot be carried out all the way." *Husserl*, p. 12.

61. These formulations are from Merleau-Ponty, *The Primacy of Perception and Other Essays on Phenomenological Psychology, the Philosophy of Art, History and Politics*, ed. James M. Edie (Evanston: Northwestern University Press, 1964), pp. 21 and 40.

62. Husserl, *Ideas*, pp. 114 and 149. The differences between geometry and philosophy, pp. 161ff., are not relevant to this point.

63. Husserl, *Crisis*, p. 59.

64. Ibid., pp. 49ff, and appendix 6, "The Origin of Geometry," pp. 353–78.

65. It can be said that there are three selves in Husserl, the empirical ego, the transendental ego which comes to light as the subjective or noetic correlate of the world as phenomenon in the phenomenological reduction, and the philosophizing ego which carries out the epoché and the reduction. While Husserl is clear that rigorous science depends on a thoroughly non-worldly subjectivity, there is some ambiguity as to whether this is to be the second or third self or both. In the *Ideas*, for example, the correlation between *transcendental* ego and *transcendent* world (pp. 171 and 239) points to the second self, while the assurance that reflection can outflank life with

reference to geometry (n. 54 above) points to the third. See Eugen Fink, "Husserl and Contemporary Criticism," pp. 115ff.

66. Husserl, *Crisis*, p. 60.

67. Husserl, *Meditations*, pp. 24, 32; *Phenomenology and Crisis*, pp. 78–80; Husserl, *Crisis*, pp. 69, 79–88, 212, 215, 298.

68. Husserl, *Crisis*, pp. 178–80. Cf. p. 133, and, for Kant's entanglement in the same problem, pp. 115–18.

69. See n. 57 above. Cf. Gadamer, *Philosophical Hermeneutics*, pp. 160, 191–92.

70. Ricoeur, *Husserl*, p. 26.

71. In *Phenomenology and the Problem of History*.

72. Heidegger's *Verweisungsganzheit*, "referential totality," in *Being and Time*, pp. 99 and 91–148.

73. Husserl, *Experience and Judgment*, p. 41. On the "already," that is, the a priori role of the life-world, see pp. 37, 43, 47, and *Crisis*, pp. 110, 142.

74. Husserl, *Experience and Judgment*, pp. 30, 41.

75. Ibid., pp. 31, 42, 43.

76. Ibid.; *Meditations*, p. 25.

77. Ibid., pp. 76–77.

78. Husserl, *Ideas*, p. 131.

79. Husserl, *Meditations*, pp. 55, 63.

80. Husserl, *Crisis*, pp. 135 and 147. Cf. p. 155 on the limitations of the "Cartesian Way."

81. Ibid., p. 286.

82. Ibid., pp. 8 and 72.

83. See Carr, *Phenomenology and the Problem of History*, p. 117, and *Experience and Judgment*, pp. 47–48.

84. On the life-world as ground, see *Experience and Judgment*, p. 30, and *Crisis*, pp. 130–131, 155.

85. Husserl, *Crisis*, pp. 295–96 (The Vienna Lecture) and 175.

86. Ibid., pp. 111–13.

87. Ibid., pp. 112–13, 122–25, 137–48.

88. Ibid., pp. 123, 139–42, and 173–74.

89. Ibid., pp. 122 and 148–52.

90. Ibid., p. 151.

91. Ibid., p. 153. Cf. p. 113 where the life-world is presented first as constituting subjectivity and then as a constituted meaning construct, "the construct of a universal, ultimately functioning [*letztfungierende*] subjectivity."

92. James 1:27 (NEB).

93. See Carr's account of Husserl's use of *Besinnung* to express this difference. *Phenomenology and the Problem of History*, pp. 59–62.

94. *Experience and Judgment*, pp. 50, 43–45. I have omitted Husserl's italics.

95. In giving his imprimatur to Eugen Fink's famous defense of phenomenology from neo-Kantian criticism, Husserl claims that his own mode of doing transcendental philosophy is unique while acknowledging that other philosophical projects can rightly call themselves transcendental. ("Husserl and Contemporary Criticism," pp. 75 and 88–103.) The distinguishing feature of Husserl's version is the anteworldly character of the transcendental ego. (See pp. 95–99).

96. Quentin Lauer sees Hegel as a transcendental philosopher but with a difference, as "the exercise of the epoché and the reductions has permitted Husserl to elimiate whatever is idiosyncratic to individual subjectivity and has provided him with a sort of subjectivity as such." Though Hegel is in the transcendental tradition that seeks "a subject which will find in the consciousness of itself the consciousness of all reality, [he] does not come up with *such* a 'transcendental subjectivity,'" that is, a thin, pure, worldless kind. ("Phenomenology: Hegel and Husserl," p. 188, my italics.) When Lauer correctly adds that "Hegel . . . is not bothered by contingency," this does not mean he does not see and address the problems it raises for a philosophy that would be scientific (p. 196).

97. Hegel, *Phenomenology*, p. 102. See my *History and Truth*, chaps. 2–4.

98. See my *History and Truth*, chap. 5 and pp. 64–65. The difference, then, is not so much that Hegel moves more quickly and easily from I to We than Husserl does, but that for Hegel both I and We are naturally and culturally in the world. As Maurice Natanson puts it, "The Cartesian 'I' is the subject of the statement, 'I think.' It is an 'I' without depth . . . One slips into the 'I' as one tries on a shoe. There is no indication the 'I' can be ravaged, that the course of experience may be dark, that mood and desire are central to the ego. The 'I' . . . is apparently sexless – an epistemic neuter." *Edmund Husserl: Philosopher of Infinite Tasks* (Evanston: Northwestern University Press, 1973), p. 148. Hegel's departure from this Cartesianism is deliberate and conscious, Husserl's reluctant and unwitting.

99. I have developed this more fully in "Hegel's Theory of the Concept," *Art and Logic in Hegel's Philosophy*, ed. Steinkraus and Schmitz (New Jersey: Humanities Press, 1980).

100. Hegel, *Gesammelte Werke*, 4:419, 479.

101. It is just this idea which appalls Husserl in his discussion of *Weltanschauung* philosophy *Phenomenology and Crisis*, pp. 129ff.

102. Hegel, *Phenomenology*, pp. 1-2.

103. Ibid., p. 7. To emphasize the *essential* nature of the mediation involved, Hegel uses organic metaphors in this and the preceding passage: first bud, blossom, and fruit; then, acorn and oak. Science is the crown of a spiritual world as the top of a tree.

104. Ibid., p. 14. My italics.

105. See Reinhart Klemens Mauser, *Hegel und das Ende der Geschichte*: *Interpretation zur Phänomenologie des Geistes* (Stuttgart: Kohlhammer Verlag, 1965).

106. Hegel, *Phenomenology*, p. 487.

107. See my *History and Truth*, secs. 2b-2d, 6c-8b, and "Dialectic and Intersubjectivity" for a fuller account.

7. From Immediacy to Mediation: The Emergence of Dialectical Phenomenology

James L. Marsh

The purpose of this paper is to lay out what might be described as a movement from suspension to suspicion in the history of phenomenology as it extends from Husserl to Ricoeur. Suspension, present in Husserl's bracketing of scientific and common sense claims, leads into a moment of interpretation present in appropriations of tradition such as those of Husserl, Gadamer, and Ricoeur. Recovery of tradition, however, leads into a suspicion and critique of tradition. This is exemplified in the three masters of suspicion, Nietzsche, Marx, and Freud, and is incorporated by Ricoeur into the phenomenological project.[1]

The relevance of such a paper to a discussion of Hegel and Husserl is that this movement from within the phenomenological tradition, having its origin and inspiration in Husserl, approximates in several significant respects claims about method and content present in the Hegelian-Marxist tradition. There is a movement from immediacy to mediation, description to dialectic, immediate evocation of the given to interpretation of the given, receptive openness of experience to critique of experience. Much as Hegel advises in the *Phenomenology*, we watch the phenomenological tradition's various attempts at a one-sided immediacy self-destruct from within and give way to mediation. In spite of its own best stated intentions, phenomenology as it develops becomes less Husserlian and more Hegelian.[2]

Because I see this history in its unfolding as having three moments, a descriptive, a hermeneutical, and a critical moment, I

appropriately divide the paper into three parts. These parts correspond to what we might call three reductions: the phenomenological,
the hermeneutical, and the critical.

The Phenomenological Reduction

As Husserl executes his famous reduction in *The Cartesian Meditations*, we are invited to put out of play all prior common sense and
scientific truth claims about the world and to search for a starting
point which is solid and cogent. As Husserl develops his argument
meditating on the idea of science, the criterion that emerges for the
legitimacy of this starting point is that of apodicticity. If we begin our
reflection on the starting point with the ideal of science, then that
turns out to have two possible variants, adequacy and apodicticity. Of
these two, apodicticity is preferable because it gives us stronger certainty and can be present even when adequacy is lacking.[3]

The search for a starting point, then, turns into a search for an
apodictic starting point. As Husserl argues the point, neither cultural
institutions, nor the physical world, nor my own psychological and
physical constitution will do, because these are dubitable. The only
domain that measures up to the criterion of apodicticity is that of consciousness itself. Because I cannot even doubt without presupposing
the reality of the ego that doubts, the ego itself is present to me in an
indubitable way. Even if the world were but a coherent dream,
nonetheless the *ego cogito* remains real, because it is essential for the
occurrence of the dreaming itself. What emerges as a method is a
strictly descriptive stance in which the ego's awareness of itself is
unfolded in a presuppositionless manner.[4]

Almost as soon as this very rigorous Husserlian formulation
appears on the scene, however, it begins to dissolve in the so-called
existential phenomenological responses of Heidegger, Merleau-Ponty,
Sartre, and early Ricoeur. First, there is the problem of embodiment.
If the ego in its higher activities of logical, scientific, and philosophical
reflection is founded on perception, as even Husserl admits,[5] and
perception is essentially embodied, then the ego is essentially embodied and the distinction between transcendental and empirical ego
breaks down. Secondly, there is the issue of intersubjectivity. If others
are given to me only through their bodies, then it is difficult to see
how I can reach the real ego of the other. There is a contradiction
between Husserl's claim that we know others and the distinction
between transcendental and embodied ego.[6]

Thirdly, there is the problem of language. What begins to emerge in the existential phenomenology is the awareness that language and thought do not remain external to one another, but rather inter-penetrate. Language is not external clothing on thought otherwise complete in itself, but is essential for thought to become definite and complete. An artist painting a picture, a poet creating a new poem, and a philosopher writing a philosophical treatise do not know what they wish to say until they have said it. The full reality, therefore, is hyphenated ("thought-expression") and indicates two aspects related internally but not reducible to one another. Expression completes thought, and thought forms language in the search for the correct expression.[7]

Fourthly, there is the problem of the so-called presuppositionless character of Husserl's starting point. If reflection is dependent on embodiment, language, and history, then such reflection would seem to be operating on the basis of presuppositions for which it itself has not accounted. What the reduction seems to show is, in Merleau-Ponty's words, "the impossibility of a complete reduction."[8] Fifthly, there is the problem of apodicticity. If there are regions implicit in my experiences that can never be fully thematized, and if experience itself is essentially expressive, embodied, and historical, then how can I be totally certain that I have considered all relevant examples or counter-examples in imaginative variation upon a putative eidetic essence?

Sixthly, if thought is necessarily expressive and linguistic, then language is necessarily part of a tradition. I think within a tradition, even when I try to escape that tradition. As Gadamer puts it, Husserl's attempt to think without prejudice or presupposition is itself a prej-udice deriving from the tradition of modern philosophy.[9]

To summarize this section of the paper, I wish to argue that the descriptive phase of phenomenology has two stages, a transcendental and an existential phenomenological. As the existential phenom-enological phase comes into its own, the pure ego of Husserl gives way to various kinds of exteriority such as the body, the human other, language, and tradition. An immediate Husserlian immanence self-destructs from within; immediacy gives way to mediation.

The Hermeneutical Turn

Within the phenomenological tradition, there are many who executive the hermeneutical turn: Heidegger, Ricoeur, Gadamer, and, to some extent, Husserl in the *Crisis*. By a hermeneutical turn, I mean a shift from description to interpretation as a way of gaining access to meaning. Although description is not rejected totally, there is at least the sense that it has to be complemented by an interpretation of tradition that moves beyond immediate articulation of conscious experience.[10]

There are at least three reasons for making such a turn. The first is the conviction that there are phenomena of various kinds, personal, social, or religious, which we cannot adequately understand from a purely descriptive standpoint and which therefore must be interpreted. Symbols such as the omnipotent father arising from the unconscious, social symbols such as the fetishized commodity, and religious symbols such as the Cross, require an approach that reveals what is hidden, not immediately present or describable. Certain experiences that we can describe, such as neurotic behavior, evil, or openness to the transcendent, require an interpretation that carries us beyond description.[11]

Secondly, in a way that is related to the first, there is a necessary moment of explanation within interpretation. Otherwise we would not understand certain structures of languages and institutions that influence our experience. For example, the formal structure of the Oedipus Myth described by Levi-Strauss is necessary for the full illumination of our experience of family and society. As Ricoeur argues the point, there is the movement from an initial interpretation involving guess and hypothesis to a structural explanation back to a fuller interpretation including such explanation as a moment of itself. Structural analysis of myth is a necessary explanatory moment, but requires grounding in the life-world if such an analysis is to make sense. Hidden structures of language and intuitions must, therefore, be related to our experience of the life-world in a way that contributes to our understanding of that world. In such a move, however, an explanatory moment is united with interpretative and descriptive moments. Once again we relate immediacy to mediation.[12]

Thirdly, it becomes apparent that history and tradition ingress into the act of philosophizing itself. Heidegger, Gadamer, and Ricoeur all make this point;[13] here I will dwell upon Husserl's argument in the *Crisis*. Such a recognition is significant, I think, because Husserl makes the point in order to continue his own transcendental project, but the move undermines his project. Almost in spite of himself, Husserl is forced to recognize the historical, mediated character of his own philosophical project.

As Carr argues the point in his excellent book on Husserl, Husserl's very desire to uncover all presuppositions leads him to historical reflection, historical reduction, in order to complete the project.[14] The ideal of a presuppositionless starting point, the notion of apodicticity, and the project of a transcendental turn into the subject, all emerge from history. Historical figures such as Descartes or Kant are no longer mere instances of a truth or an untruth known in a pure, transcendental, phenomenological realm, but are essential for the emergence of phenomenology itself. Let Husserl speak for himself on this point:

> What is clearly necessary (what else could be of help here?) is that we reflect back, in a thorough historical and critical fashion, in order to provide before all decisions for a radical self-understanding; we must inquire back into what was originally and always sought in philosophy, what was continually sought by all the philosophers and philosophies that have communicated with one another historically; but this must include a *critical* consideration of what, in respect to the goals and methods (of philosophy) is ultimate, original and genuine and, which, once seen, apodictically conquers the will.[15]

History, then, is essential for phenomenology itself; phenomology is a product of the historical development of modern philosophy. Husserl begins such a task by reflecting on Galileo, who conceived the idea of a universal, systematic, physical science. In so doing, however, Galileo and his successors are guilty of forgetting the origins of science in the pre-scientific life world of perception. Because there is such forgetfulness, we mistake scientific abstractions for reality and occlude the many pre-scientific, qualitative dimensions of the life world. The origins of scientism and positivism lie in such occlusion.[16]

Descartes takes over Galileo's project and conclusions with the resulting problems of mind-body dualism, the subjectivism of secondary qualities, and cognitive inaccessibility of the external world. He gives rise to a double tradition in modern philosophy dialectically at odds with itself, physicalistic objectivism, enamored with the model of physical science, and transcendental subjectivism. Phenomenology is the historical product of this dialectic between physicalistic objectivism culminating in Spinoza and Leibnitz and transcendental subjectivsm culminating in Hume and Kant.[17]

The encounter with Kant is the last step in Husserl's analysis. With Kant, a new kind of transcendenal subjectivism emerges, one that has learned from Hume but more properly is the successor to the rationalist tradition as has developed through Christian Wolff. Kant's is the first fully worked out transcendental philosophy attempting to exhibit the a priori structure of human knowing, moral activity, and aesthetic perception. To that extent, he takes a step forward. He does, however, accept the world as described by science and does not inquire into the life-world as the ground of science. The lack of an intuitive exhibiting method in Kant's approach leads him to attempt to deduce concepts a priori rather than to reflectively disclose them through eidetic description. Because he is too much influenced by the naturalism and objectivism of modern philosophy, his concept of experience is too narrow, confined to either external or internal sensations. For these reasons he falls into paradoxes and contradictions, such as claiming that things-in-themselves exist but claiming at the same time that we cannot know them; or using categories such as cause, substance, and existence, initially restricted to phenomena, to talk about things-in-themselves.

The history of modern philosophy as it culminates in Kant, therefore, is a dialectic between transcendentalism and objectivism. Transcendental phenomenology emerges as the truth of such a dialectic. In contrast to Descartes, Husserl's ego is intentionally present to the world. In contrast to Kant again, and many others as well, the life-world comes into explicit thematic focus as the ground of science. In contrast to Kant and the empiricists, human experience is not simply experience of sensuous objects, but is experience of myself as a conscious self who perceives, imagines, remembers, understands, judges, and chooses. As Husserl says in the *Ideas*, "If by 'positivism' we are to mean the absolute unbiased grounding of all science on what is 'positive', i.e., on what can be primordially apprehended, then it is we [phenomenologists] who are the true positivists."[18]

When we phenomenologically theorize, the life-world initially appears as the subjective-relative in contrast to the objective revealed by science. The life-world appears simply as a partial problem appended to thinking the objectivity of the sciences. However, as we reflect, this contrast between subjective and objective begins to turn on its head. For we first discover that perceptions in the life-world, which are in their own way objective, are necessary to ground science. The falling bodies which I think are initially perceived by me, and experiments verifying the law of falling bodies, terminate in life-world perceptions. If these are merely subjective and not objective, then the hypotheses of science would be merely subjective. Moreover, certain presuppositions, such as the intersubjective nature of truth, are themselves derived from the life-world. Einstein uses the Michelson experiments and researchers's corroboration of them.

But Einstein could make no use whatever of a theoretical psychological construction of the objective being of Mr. Michelson; rather he made use of the human being who was accessible to him, as to everyone else in the prescientific world, as an object of straightforward experience, the human being whose existence, with this vitality, in these activities and creations within the common life-world, is always the presupposition for all of Einstein's objective-scientific lines of inquiry, projects, and accomplishments pertaining to Michelson's experiments.[19]

Not only does the life-world ground science, but the life-world in another sense includes science. When we see that science is just one project among many that human beings undertake in the life-world, and that the results of science are themselves products of an activity that is chosen and operates according to certain criteria and values, then we see scientific theorizing as part of the life-world conceived as the totality of projects.

Therefore, Husserl relativizes science's claim to be absolutely the only form of knowing in two senses: Science is founded on life-world perception and science is part of the life-world. Still a third overcoming of scientism and positivism occurs when we reflect on phenomenological theorizing itself. For what we have been doing is reflectively trying to ground science in the life-world. An ungrounded science, one that leaves its presuppositions unexamined, is not fully scientific. The only way, however, to fully ground science is to transcend science as positive science and recover it phenomenologically as grounded in the life-world. Not only does phenomenology emerge as a crucial counter instance to scientism, but the life-world, rather than being a part, a mere subjective appendage to the objective sciences, has become the whole. Science has been seen to be not only objective but subjective, not whole but part. The life-world has been seen to be not only subjective but objective, not part but whole.[20]

In the *Crisis*, Husserl makes a breakthrough to history and life-world. On the other hand, these very breakthroughs tend to explode even more the Cartesian immanence with which he began in *Cartesian Meditations*. If history is essential for philosophical self-understanding, and historical judgments about history and history of philosophy are contingent and not apodictic, how can apodicticity be possible in phenomenology? Moreover, if the very turn to history uncovers some presuppositions, does not this same turn make it seem unlikely that a total account of all presuppositions is possible? Recovery of the life-world as the ground of all thought gives us another inexhaustible fount that can never be thematized.

Finally, if perception founds all thought and is essentially embodied, can the distinction between transcendental and embodied ego, established in *Cartesian Meditations* and reiterated in the *Crisis*,[21] be maintained? Is not such a distinction in Husserl a Cartesian remnant that his discovery of the life-world should force him to expunge? Husserl's very attempt to expand his project of presuppositionless phenomenology leads him to discoveries that undermine that project.

The Critical Turn

If the hermeneutical turn is necessary, then so also is the critical turn. I will reflect on the formal necessity of such a turn in discussing the Habermas-Gadamer debate. Then I will reflect on the content involved in such a turn, the psychological content that emerges from Ricouer's encounter with Freud and the social content that emerges from critical theoretical reflection on scientism.

The necessity of a critical turn emerges in the Habermas-Gadamer debate. Habermas argues that if one admits that interpretation of tradition is necessary, then we also have to concede the possibility of its being flawed or distorted by various kinds of class bias and class domination. Is not Gadamer's approach to the text excessively passive? Is not the model of dialogue inappropriate when the tradition is implicitly ideological and, therefore, violates the conditions for fruitful dialogue? What is necessary, Habermas argues, is an ideology critique in which the repression hidden in various forms of historical communication is articulated and revealed.[22]

As the debate between them develops, and others such as Ricoeur enter it, what emerges is a notion of hermeneutics in which both respectful openness to tradition and critique of tradition are essential. Moreover, such a suspicion is a necessary complement to eidetic descriptive phenomenology itself. If hermeneutical, interpretative encounter with history is necessary for eidetic, descriptive phenomenology, as even Husserl saw in the *Crisis*, and if suspicion leading to and culminating in ideology critique is a necessary component of hermeneutics, as both Gadamer and Ricoeur have admitted, then ideology critique is essential for eidetic phenomenology. Hermeneutics is the essential middle term between eidetic, descriptive phenomenology and ideology critique.[23]

Suspicion or critique, therefore, becomes necessary on both a psychological and social level. There is a psychological and social unconscious that forces us to move beyond both a strictly descriptive and a strictly receptive hermeneutical approach. As Ricoeur argues in his book on Freud, there are certain phenomena such as parapraxes, dreams, and neurosis that cannot be accounted for in a strictly descriptive approach. When I as chairman of the board, declare at the beginning of the meeting that it is closed, or when I lose a gift from my wife and recover it after getting over a secret anger toward her, a conflict manifests itself between a conscious intention and subconscious wish.[24]

Secondly, a phenomenological account of conscious experience in various forms of implicitness or partial givenness approximates, but does not equal, the unconscious. The hidden side of the thing, the hidden dimensions of another person, the implicit presence of my body, and the background out of which a perceived thing emerges, though implicit, are still conscious and, therefore, can be articulated through a reflective description. Such a description, however, cannot adequately explain the parapraxes mentioned above, which have causes that are not conscious in any sense.[25]

Thirdly, such phenomena as the above find their adequate explanation in an account of the unconscious as both force and meaning, dynamism and intelligibility. The force is present in such phenomena as compulsive guilt, a repressive super-ego, and a dynamic id. The meaning is present when, for instance, dreams signify something. My feelings or hostility towards a female figure in my dream can be seen to originate in a repressed hostility towards my mother; my delight in insulting a male figure in my dream who resembles my father can reveal a deep-seated desire to assert myself against my father.[26]

Fourthly, the move to a personal unconscious demands a shift from a Husserlian to a Hegelian model of phenomenology. The shift that emerges is a unity of conscious and unconscious, immediacy and mediation, archeology and teleology. In such a shift, Freud is both retained and overcome. He is retained insofar as he has made valid discoveries concerning psychoanalytic method, sexuality, and the unconscious. He is overcome insofar as he misinterprets his method, sinks into a realism of the unconscious, posits a total determinism of the unconscious, and denies any teleology. In such a dialectical, Hegelian version of phenomenology we do not give up either description or interpretation, but complement and qualify them with suspicion and critique.[27]

If Ricoeur's appropriation of Freud is a compelling argument for a psychological unconscious, similarly a phenomenological appropriation of Marx and critical theory is a cogent argument for a social unconscious. I propose to exemplify such an approach here by engaging in a further reflection on scientism. Because of limitations of space, I here assume the superiority of a Marxian, critical theoretical form over other possible modes, such as the Weberian, Shutzian, Heideggerian, or Derridean. Such a superiority I have argued for elsewhere.[28]

In criticizing scientism theoretically, Husserl makes an important first move, but scientism nonetheless hangs on. In spite of many twentieth century attempts to refute them theoretically, scientism and positivism are still with us. Why has one-dimensional thought survived long after it has been refuted?[29]

The answer has to be that theoretical one-dimensionality survives because it is rooted in practical one-dimensionality. Theoretical positivism is rooted in capitalism as one form of lived positivism. Because of this fact, any merely theoretical overcoming is incomplete, because it leaves practical, lived positivism and objectivism untouched and uncriticized. What becomes necessary for a fully complete phenomenology, therefore, is a description, explanation, and critique of practical lived objectivism, rooted in capitalism as a form of life.

For the sake of its own radical self-responsibility and orientation towards lucid self-possession, phenomenology must inquire into the relation of scientism to capitalism as a social form of life. To do less is to fail to ask all the relevant questions and to remain unclear about the relation of the part, scientism, to the whole, capitalism, as a social form of life. Yet Husserl's project is one of grounding parts in wholes and becoming clear about their relationship.[30] A phenomenology that remains content to examine scientism in a one-sided theoretical fashion, leaving its relationship to capitalism unclear, is incomplete even as phenomenology, because it leaves one crucial part-whole relationship unexamined and unclarified.

I propose to outline such a sketch here in four steps. First is the domination of exchange-value over use-value. What becomes important in capitalism is profit as determined by abstract labor time, which is quantitatively determined homogeneous labor with qualitative differences ignored or minimized. Because commodities can only be exchanged on the basis of something quantitative, only abstract labor time, abstract because it is the average socially necessary amount of labor time required to produce a given commodity, can be that common element. The homogeneous, abstract, anonymous society, criticized by both Kierkegaard and Heidegger, has its roots in this domination of exchange-value over use-value.[31]

A second major step in the development of scientism is the emergence of money as the god of commodities. Because exchange-value must be measured in money, money becomes privileged among commodites. As capitalism develops, three functions of money emerge: money as measure of the value in commodities, money as medium of exchange, and money as a representative of wealth. If making money in the form of profit is good, then making more money is better, and making the most money is best. Built-in medieval moral and religious limits to making money break down, and an infinite striving emerges in capitalism to break down limits to production, consumption, and exploitation of nature. With money coming into its own as an end in itself, the origins of exchange value in labor time are forgotten and a commodity fetishism develops in which relations between human beings appear as relationships between things. The reification, self-forgetfulness, and loss of self so criticized by phenomenologists and existentialists have one of their most powerful roots in such fetishism.[32]

Thirdly, the development of science and technology is crucial to capitalism when relative surplus-value, labor-time acquired by shortening the working day, begins to acquire an ascendancy over absolute surplus-value, acquired by lengthening the working day. By surplus-value, I mean the amount of labor-time that goes to the capitalist over and above necessary labor-time, the amount of time the laborer must work to reproduce his own labor-power. Because the value of necessary labor-time can be decreased by a higher productivity rooted in technology and machinery, thus cheapening the commodities necessary to keep a worker alive, relative surplus-value can increase as more and more is invested in technology and machinery compared to labor. Because science is necessary for the development of such technology and machinery, science at this point becomes a productive force essential for capitalism.[33] Division of labor occurs in which the worker is progressively deskilled and the mental control of the work passes to the capitalist manager and machine. Division between mind and body appears in both labor and capital.

Fourthly, with the development of the modern corporation and modern state, technical, scientific reason extends from the economic into the social and political spheres. Late capitalist societies develop a problem of finding enough people to consume the goods produced, a problem solved by socially controlled, technically manipulated, and scientifically researched advertising.[34] Also, as the capitalist state moves from a laissez-faire state to a welfare state, a tension develops between its two goals: serving capitalist accumulation through devices such as defense spending, and public education support, which derive legitimation from arguments that appeal to the general interest.

Because there is general public perception that the economy is being manipulated and controlled by corporations and labor unions working with the state, economic evils can no longer be passed off as the working of an invisible hand that we cannot control.

The state, therefore, has difficulty legitimating decisions that serve particular capitalist interests before and above all other interests. It solves this legitimation problem by turning practical problems into technical problems, moral problems into administrative problems. An ideology of scientific expertise emerges in which popular political participation, which Habermas calls symbolic interaction, is discouraged as anachronistic and obsolete. Techniques proper to the economic sphere, such as advertising, encroach more and more on the political sphere through short political advertisements and television debates that avoid discussion of serious public issues. Technical manipulation is substituted for dialogue, the rule of the best and the brightest is substituted for popular political participation, formal bureaucracy is substituted for substantive democracy. In late capitalism, science and technology become both productive force and ideology, legitimizing the reign of one-dimensional capitalism.[35]

Conclusion

What emerges, first, is the sense of phenomenology as a unity of description and interpretation, receptive openness to tradition and critique of tradition, immediacy and mediation, description and explanation. Phenomenological method comprises, then, three reductions: the hermeneutical, rooted primarily in the past modality of time-consciousness, the descriptive, rooted primarily in the present, and the critical, rooted in and primarily oriented to the future.

Secondly, the necessity of interpretation and critique must force us to modify our previous enthusiasm for description. If all descriptive attempts are essentially influenced by tradition and history, then to a certain extent all description is an "interpreting as." If the precept of Wittgenstein, "don't think, look," and that of Husserl, "return to the things themselves" in a descriptive way, were clarion calls that pushed philosophy forward fifty or sixty years ago, now, if taken as exhaustively defining philosophical inquiry, they act as straitjackets on such inquiry. Now the appropriate motto is "don't look merely, but interpret and criticize." There is more in heaven and earth than one can dream of in a strictly descriptive approach.

Thirdly, the "merely" in the above motto is important because it retains a limited place for description. Description is necessary in order for us to be clear in a way that is not presuppositionless about what we experience, to ground basic fundamental concepts used in interpretation and critique, and to develop criteria for interpretation and critique. For example, I cannot criticize false consciousness adequately unless I know what consciousness is, I cannot criticize the loss of freedom in late capitalist or state socialist societies unless I know what freedom is descriptively and eidetically, and I cannot criticize contemporary loss of community unless I know what intersubjectivity is. Eidetic, descriptive phenomenology then, and I have argued this point more fully elsewhere,[36] can function as an element in and foundation for ideology critique.

Fourthly, what emerges as a result of the historical dialectic within phenomenology is a qualified, chastened version of the concrete universal, the unity of universal and particular.[37] To the extent that phenomenology is descriptive and eidetic, it attains to universal claims that have at least a putative historical and cultural invariance. To the extent that phenomenology is interpretative and critical, it reflects on particular individual and social histories. Universal and particular do not just lie together like two estranged lovers, but interpenetrate and interact. Eidetic description functions as a foundation for, and element in, interpretation and critique; these, on the other hand, make fully concrete and realize eidetic description.

Notes

1. The term "suspension" refers to the *epoche* as it occurs in Edmund Husserl's philosophy. For a representative sample, consider his *Cartesian Meditations*, trans. Dorion Cairns (The Hague: Martinus Nijhoff, 1977), pp. 7–26. The term "suspicion" refers to Paul Ricoeur's definition as it occurs in his *Freud and Philosophy*, trans. Denis Savage (New Haven: Yale University Press, 1980), pp. 32–36.

2. G. W. F. Hegel, *Phenomenology of the Spirit*, trans. A. V. Miller (Oxford: Clarendon Press, 1977), pp. 53–57.

3. Husserl, *Cartesian Meditations*, pp. 10–16.

4. Ibid., pp. 17–20.

5. Edmund Husserl, *Formal and Transcendental Logic*, trans. Dorion Cairns (The Hague: Martinus Nijhoff, 1969), pp. 208–9.

6. Husserl, *Cartesian Meditations*, pp. 89–157; James L. Marsh, "An Inconsistency in Husserl's *Cartesian Meditations*," *The New Scholasticism* 53 (Fall 1979): 460–74.

7. Maurice Merleau-Ponty, *The Phenomenology of Perception*, trans. Colin Smith (Atlantic Highlands, NJ: Humanities Press, 1962), pp. 174–99; James L. Marsh, "Consciousness and Expression," *Southwestern Journal of Philosophy* 9 (Spring 1978): 105–9.

8. Merleau-Ponty, *Phenomenology of Perception*, p. xiv.

9. Hans-Georg Gadamer, *Truth and Method*, trans. ed. Garrett Barden and John Cumming (New York: Continuum, The Seabury Press, 1975), pp. 240–45.

10. See Martin Heidegger, *Being and Time*, trans. John Macquarrie and Edward Robinson (New York: Harper & Row, 1967), pp. 424–55; Paul Ricoeur, *The Symbolism of Evil*, trans. Emerson Buchanan (New York: Harper & Row, 1967); Gadamer, *Truth and Method*.

11. Paul Ricoeur, *The Philosophy of Paul Ricoeur*, ed. Charles Regan and David Stewart (Boston: Beacon Press, 1978), pp. 86–108.

12. Paul Ricoeur, *Interpretation Theory: Discourse and the Surplus of Meaning* (Forth Worth: Texas Christian University Press, 1976), pp. 80–87.

13. Gadamer, *Truth and Method*, pp. 153–311; Heidegger, *Being and Time*, pp. 424–55; Paul Ricoeur, *Hermeneutics and the Human Sciences*, ed. John Thompson (Cambridge: Cambridge University Press, 1981), pp. 101–28.

14. David Carr, *Phenomenology and the Problem of History* (Evanston, Illinois: Northwestern University Press, 1974), pp. 110–33.

15. Edmund Husserl, *The Crisis of European Sciences and Transcendental Phenomenology*, trans. David Carr (Evanston, Illinois: Northwestern University Press, 1970), pp. 17–18.

16. Ibid., pp. 23–82.

17. Ibid., pp. 73–90.

18. Edmund Husserl, *Ideas*, trans. Boyce Gibson (New York: Collier Books, 1931), p. 78. Cf. *Crisis*, pp. 70, 91–93.

19. Ibid., pp. 125–29.

20. Ibid., pp. 129–35.

21. Ibid., pp. 182–83.

22. Jürgen Habermas, "A Review of Gadamer's *Truth and Method*," in *Understanding and Social Inquiry*, ed. Fred R. Dallmayr and Thomas A. McCarthy (Notre Dame: University of Notre Dame Press, 1977), pp. 335–63; Hans-Georg Gadamer, *Philosophical Hermeneutics*, trans. and ed. David E. Linge (Berkeley: University of California Press, 1976), pp. 26–42.

23. Gadamer, *Philosophical Hermeneutics*, pp. 26–42; Ricoeur, *Hermeneutics and the Social Sciences*, pp. 63–100.

24. Ricoeur, *Freud and Philosophy*, pp. 390–418; Sigmund Freud, *Introduction to Psychoanalysis*, trans. Joan Riviere (New York: Pocket Books, 1953), pp. 19–83.

25. Ricoeur, *Freud and Philosophy*, pp. 375–90.

26. Ibid., pp. 419–58.

27. Ibid., pp. 459–93.

28. See my "Heidegger's Overcoming of Metaphysics: A Critique," *Journal for the British Society of Phenomenology* 16 (January 1985): 55–69; "Dialectical Phenomenology: From Suspension to Suspicion," *Man and World* 17 (Fall 1984): 121–43.

29. See Herbert Marcuse, *One-Dimensional Man* (Boston: Beacon Press, 1964), p. 12, for a definition of one-dimensionality: "Thus emerges a pattern of one-dimensional thought and behavior in which ideas, aspirations, and objectives that, by their content, transcend the established universe of discourse and actions are either repelled or reduced to terms of this universe. They are redefined by the rationality of the given system and of its quantitative extension."

30. Robert Sokolowski, *Husserlian Meditations* (Evanston, Illinois: Northwestern University Press, 1974), pp. 8–17.

31. Soren Kierkegaard, *The Two Ages*, trans. and ed. Howard V. Hong and Edna H. Hong (Princeton, NJ: Princeton University Press, 1978), pp. 68–112; Heidegger, *Being and Time*, pp. 210–24; Karl Marx, *Capital*, vol. 1: *A Critique of Political Economy*, with an Introduction by Ernest Mandel, trans. Ben Fowkes (New York: Random House, Vintage Books, 1976), pp. 125–77.

32. Karl Marx, *Grundrisse*, trans. Martin Nicolaus (New York: Vintage Press, 1973), pp. 140–240.

33. Marx, *Capital*, 1:283–306, 320–39, 492–639.

34. John Kenneth Galbraith, *The Affluent Society* (Boston: Mentor Books, 1958), pp. 114–30; Stuart Ewen, *Captains of Consciousness* (New York: McGraw-Hill, 1976).

35. Marcuse, *One-Dimensional Man*, pp. 101–20; Jürgen Habermas, *Towards a Rational Society*, trans. Jeremy Shapiro (Boston: Beacon Press, 1970), pp. 81–122; Jürgen Habermas, *Legitimation Crisis*, trans. Thomas McCarthy (Boston: Beacon Press, 1975), pp. 68–75.

36. See my "Phenemonology as Ideology Critique," *Philosophy Today* 24 (Fall 1980): 272–84.

37. G. W. F. Hegel, *The Logic of Hegel*, trans. William Wallace, 2nd ed. (London: Oxford University Press, 1965), pp. 287–97.

Part IV.
Knowledge and Critique

8. Heidegger and Peirce: Toward New Epistemic Foundations

Patrick L. Bourgeois
Sandra B. Rosenthal

Heidegger's initial efforts in fundamental ontology can be clearly shown to have overcome the false dichotomy between idealism and realism found in modern philosophy. Not so evident is the manner in which his fundamental ontology can be brought to bear, by means of extrapolation, on the equally false dichotomy in epistemology between empiricism and rationalism. Indeed, an attempt to overcome that dichotomy requires deepening his notion of epistemology,[1] and, at the same time, an integration of this expanded notion with his fundamental ontology. This effort, however, is fruitful, not only because it expounds his philosophy's relevance to contemporary issues of perennial philosophical interest, but also because it reveals affinities between his philosophy and that of another leading twentieth century philosopher, C. S. Peirce. This paper, consequently, will hopefully show that both Heidegger and Peirce overcome once and for all the modern split between empiricism and rationalism.

The central role of the Kantian scheme can be seen to be a key factor for both Heidegger and Peirce in their respective returns to lived experience. Further, it will be seen that, for both Heidegger and Peirce, undercutting the rationalist-empiricist distinction leads to an uncovering of meaning in being-in-the-world in which the Kantian schema has an essentially central role. For Heidegger and Peirce alike, the schema has a central role in the fundamental level of unity or of meaning in man's basic rapport with the given: a level of meaning and a field below the distinctions between subject and object; between external matter or body and internal consciousness or spirit; and finally, between acts of imagination and understanding.[2] Thus their common Kantian heritage, when explicated, will be seen to reveal a basic rapport between their respective philosophies which has been for too long hidden from view.

For Heidegger, a world projected from the fore-understanding is the general context for the encounter with any particular unity, requiring a certain anticipatory structure on the part of man's mode of being.[3] This anticipatory structure is an orientation to receive, allowing for the senseful encounter with any entity given to man. The full dimension of Heidegger's context of meaningful encounter in being-in-the-world will be left behind in turning to an expansion of one limited aspect of it.[4] It is to this expansion of Heidegger's fundamental ontology, adjusted to account for epistemic foundations, that the present discussion will now turn.

Although Heidegger's fundamental ontology has successfully overcome the epistemological dichotomy between the subject and the object, and, at the same time, has undercut nineteenth century epistemological controversies concerning methods in the natural sciences and the human sciences, his philosophy has failed to investigate the full depths and originary dimensions of being-in-the-world from the epistemic point of view. For Heidegger, traditional epistemology itself has failed to get below the derived mode of Being of the present-at-hand to the foundational level of existence. However, some contemporary epistemologies, not so limited and restricted, seek the origins of the epistemic aspect of existence in order to reach the fullness and richness of meaning at the ground level of lived experience as existence.

On the fundamental level of the being of the knower the meaning structure of Dasein is explicated in fundamental ontology. As such, it grounds epistemology, derived from comprehension as constitutive of Dasein's Being structure; but, at once, it *is* epistemology in the sense that fundamental ontology, as involving primordial knowledge, uncovers the fundamental epistemic strata of Dasein, looked at from the point of view of epistemology, i.e., the description of the whole gamut of epistemic levels, including that of origins. And, indeed, it is from this epistemological point of view that Heidegger's fundamental ontology can be seen to overcome the falsely exclusive alternatives of rationalism and empiricism, with the schema, rooted in the structure of being-in-the-world, having a central epistemic role.

For Heidegger, the function of schemata, to the extent that he refers to it at all in the context of strict fundamental ontology, has an essentially ontological role. Schema, just as the understanding, sensibility, and all the celebrated Kantian themes, is considered within the uniqueness of Dasein's existence and the ontological priority of Dasein as ontological. In this context, the mediation between the understanding's projecting of a world and the fulfillment of meaning in sense is an existential of Dasein.

Although Being-in-the-world in *Being and Time* is the presupposed background of *Kant and the Problem of Metaphysics*, and although the orientation and problematics of the latter work are different from that of *Being and Time*, *Kant and the Problem of Metaphysics* contains certain epistemic dimensions making it relevant to the present study. This epistemic dimension is manifested in the Kantian context in which the schemata are dealt with, even though "repeated"[5] in the context of fundamental ontology. In this book, Heidegger expresses the view that ontological, primordial Knowledge is "made up of transcendental determinations of time because transcendence is temporalized in primordial time."[6] Primordial, originary time is the basis and origin of all else in human finite knowledge and existence. As such, it is a source of the categories, of the conditions of objectivity and of subjectivity, in their primordial unity. Primordial time gives rise to transcendence by forming the horizon of transcendence in the schemata, thus exfoliating the conditions of possibility of the objectivity of the object. The practical reason, together with the schemata, is grounded in the Kantian transcendental imagination, which is rooted in primordial and originary time. And the horizon of transcendence, as the schemata, is the derived time-formation which Kant focuses on explicitly but fails to carry further to its source in primordial originary time. Heidegger says explicitly that "the pure schemata as transcendental determinations of time form the horizon of transcendence."[7] The schemata of the transcendental imagination, as forming the horizon of transcendence, are produced by the transcendental imagination, constitute the temporalization of primordial time itself.[8] And it is primordial time which allows the pure formation of transcendence to take place. Thus, primordial time makes possible transcendental imagination, as essentially spontaneous receptivity and receptive spontaneity. "Only in this unity can pure sensibility as spontaneous receptivity and pure apperception as receptive spontaneity belong together and form the essential unity of pure sensible reason."[9] This interpretation, chiefly in the context of Kant's language and problematics, indicates how Heidegger pulls Kant in the direction of the presupposed ontology from which he is operating, and in terms of which he has extended the transcendental imagination as Care in *Being and Time*.[10]

According to Heidegger's interpretive appropriation of Kant, the schema, formed as a mode of sensibilization, is bipolar. For, although it must be distinguished from the image, it necessarily possesses the "character of an image," which character has its own nature.[11] This image character of the schema Heidegger calls the schema-image; yet the schema is the representation of the rule, which necessarily remains relative to a possible schema-image to which no particular thing can claim to be the only possible example. "The concept 'dog' signifies a rule according to which my imagination can delineate the figure of a four-footed animal in a general manner, without limitation to any determinate figure such as experience, or any possible image that I can represent in concreto actually present."[12]

Heidegger indicates that for Kant, the aspect of an entity immediately represented does not attain that which is represented of it in the concept; or the aspect of the thing immediately present does not "attain" the empirical concept of the thing. And he interprets Kant further: not attaining the concept means not presenting it 'adequately', thus the necessity for the schema-image, which is the image of the concept.[13] The empirical aspect, or the object immediately on hand, contains everything in the concept, if not more. But the aspect does not contain its object in the manner in which the concept represents it, i.e., as the one which applies to many.[14] Further, the inadequacy between the empirical aspect and the empirical concept requires the mediating function of the structural relation of the schema-image to the schema. This mediating function expresses the regulative function of the concept in providing a possibility of an image or of an empirical aspect, revealing the centrality of schema and schematism.[15]

> This relation [between schema-image and schema] makes the schema-image a possible representation of the rule of presentation represented in the schema. This means, at the same time, that beyond the representation of this regulative unity the concept is nothing. What in logic is termed a concept is based upon the schema. The concept "always refers directly to the schema."[16]

The importance of this is that the image derives its intuitive character from the "fact that the schema-image comes into being and from the way in which it comes into being from a possible representation which is represented in its regulative function, thus bringing the rule within the sphere of a possible intuition."[17] This means that the image derives its intuitive character from above – not from the content of sense. The rule is brought to bear on the possible intuition. Thus, one must clearly distinguish between image and the image character of the schema as the schema-image. Expressing the relation between the concept and the schema, Heidegger, using Kant's example of the five points, explains that the image has its possibility already formed in the representing of the rule of presentation. The true aspect in the schema as the schema-image is the possibility. The possibility of the image is already formed in the act of representing the rule of presentation.[18]

Thus, for Heidegger, the schema-image cannot be separated from the concept, but rather it is generated by, and gains its character from, the regulative function of the rule which generates it. Nor can the specific sensory content experienced be separated from the schema-image, for only within the possibilities presented by the schema-image can sensory content come to awareness.

Heidegger's ontological context for considerations of this originary level does not totally and exhaustively account for it. Before the "change-over" and narrowing to the present-at-hand, there are epistemic dimensions of schematization which underlie the subject-object split and the derived modes spoken of by Heidegger in *Being and Time*. If understanding (as a mode of Being) and schemata, extended to the ontological level of intentionality, demand fundamental ontological unveiling, they also require an investigation into their epistemic ramifications. And this epistemological consideration obtains the originary level just as does any fundamental ontology. This originary level, epistemic precisely as grounding all cognitive levels, must be unveiled and investigated from that epistemic point of view. And, indeed, it is precisely this originary epistemic level which overcomes the traditional distinction between rationalism and empiricism by revealing the fundamental meaning-structure at the level of lived experience or of being-in-the-world.

Heidegger's epistemic dimensions latent in efforts toward a fundamental ontology and in his interpretation of Kant's *Critique of Pure Reason* in the context of fundamental ontology emerge in the realization that to investigate the pre-reflective or originary level grounding any knowledge is already to investigate in some way the epistemic substrate for knowledge, as it involves the explication of the structures and process of the being of the knower. In this shift of focus from the strictly ontological to the epistemological considerations, the perspective upon the schemata is no longer limited to the context of the Being of entities encountered in Being-in-the-world. Rather, the fore-understanding grasps the schemata from the point of view of any possible cognitive access to these same entities, coming to grips, from the cognitive point of view, with how they are meaningfully grasped. The epistemic focus changes the attitude toward the schemata, but retains the legacy of existential phenomenology as the deepening of intentionality, in one way or another, below that of acts of awareness to the underlying structure, which includes schemata and schematization.

It has been seen that a latent epistemic dimension of Kantian schemata can be explicated from Heidegger's fundamental ontology, and that his "repetition"[19] of the Kantian problematic is a laying of the foundation of metaphysics. This latent element, once manifest, is a bridge to the philosophy of Peirce, which develops the Kantian schema at this primordial level of vital intentionality. Thus, it is to Peirce's explicitly epistemic development of Kantian schema at this primordial level that the ensuing discussion will now turn.

Peirce, in appropriating Kantian schemata, takes from Kant the fundamental insight that concepts are empirically meaningful only if they contain possibilities for their application to sensible experience. Further, the imagery which makes possible the application of a concept cannot be abstracted out from sense experience but rather must be provided before meaningful perceptual content can emerge within experience. However, Peirce's pragmatic appropriation of these insights radically alters Kant's understanding of the schema. Such a schema is no longer a product of productive imagination as distinct from the understanding as the faculty of judgment. Rather, both understanding and imagination are unified and transformed into the creative functioning of habit which provides a lived or vital intentionality between knower and known. Indeed, such an interactional unity of knower and known, rooted in man's mode of existing in the world in terms of purposive activity, is incorporated within the internal structure of meaning through the functioning of the little-mentioned Kantian schemata.[20]

For Peirce, meanings are to be understood as logical structures,[21] not as psychological or biological facts.[22] Meanings are to be understood as relational structures emerging from behavioral patterns, from the lived-through response of the human organism to that universe with which it is in interaction. Or, in other terms, human behavior is meaningful behavior, and it is in behavior that meaning is rooted. Only within the context of principles embodied in purposive behavior does the sensory come to awareness. And such interpretive relationships are embodied in the internal structure of the meanings through which man interacts with his world, for meanings are reducible neither to pure principles or patterns of response apart from the character of the sensory, nor to the sensory as existing apart from the pattern of response. For Peirce, sensuous recognition and conceptual interpretation represent two ends of a continuum rather than an absolute difference in kind. His view that sensuous recognition involves interpretive aspects, in some yet to be determined sense, is fairly clear-cut and can be found in his view that there are no first impressions of sense.[23] However, Peirce's view that conceptualization requires imagery is open to some confusion. He states that "I will go so far as to say that we have no images even in actual perception." Yet, he objects to Kant, not because Kant requires a schema for the application of a concept to experience, but because he separates the schema from the concept, failing to recognize that a schema for the application of a concept to the data of experience is as general as the concept.[24] And if the schema is to allow for the application of a concept to sense experience, then imagery, in some sense at least, would seem to be required.

The resolution of this difficulty lies in the definition of image which Peirce so emphatically rejects in the former statement, that is, the definition of image as an absolutely singular representation, a representation absolutely determinate in all respects.[25] Thus, Peirce accepts imagery as part of conceptual meaning, but refuses to equate such imagery with determinate, singular, representation. In the schematic aspects of conceptual meaning, then, there would seem to be an inseparable mingling of the sensuous and the relational as the vehicle by which we think about and recognize objects in the world. It is to the relation between habit and schematic structure that the ensuing discussion will turn.

Peirce holds that conceptual meaning must include within itself the emotional, energetic and logical interpretants.[26] Or, in other terms, it must include the elements of Firstness, Secondness, and Thirdness, found, in some form, in all analyses in this case. Firstness is the feeling core or sensuous content, Secondness response or set of acts, and Thirdness structure or resultant image.[27] Imagery, then, as part of the internal structure of meaning, is inseparably connected with sense content as Firstness and pattern of reaction as Secondness. As Peirce observes, "To predicate a concept of a real or imaginary object is equivalent to declaring that a certain operation, corresponding to the concept, if performed upon that object would . . . be followed by a result of a definite general description."[28] Or, in other terms, "How otherwise can a habit be described than by a description of the kind of action to which it gives rise, with the specification of the conditions and the motive?"[29]

Here it should be noted that habit gives rise to certain kinds of action in the presence of certain kinds of conditions to yield certain kinds of results. And if the act is dependent upon the condition or sensory content, then different sensory cues will give rise to different acts. Thus, there is not one act but an indefinite number of acts corresponding to an indefinite number of possibile sensory conditions. For example, varying perspectives yield varying appearances and hence varying resulting acts. Habit does more than unify three pre-existent elements – sensory condition, act, and result. Only as habit performs its function of unifying possible sensory conditions and possible reactions does an intended objective structure emerge at all. As Peirce notes, "the general idea is the *mark* of the habit."[30] And, perhaps even more significant, it is habit which determines reaction, and it is reaction which partially determines the nature of the sensory condition. Thus, it is habit, ultimately, which partially determines the nature of the sensory cue. As Peirce stresses, "Feeling which has not yet emerged into immediate consciousness is already affectible and already affected. In fact, this is habit . . . ."[31] Or, in other terms, "Thus, the sensation, so far as it represents something, is determined, according to logical law, by previous cognitions; that is to say, these cognitions determine that there shall be a sensation."[32]

Peirce's position can perhaps be clarified by taking the term "image" as "aspect". For example, one may quite correctly say that an ocean presents a turbulent image or aspect. And, while the specific empirical content of experience is best understood as one particular among many, the image of the schema for the application of a living habit to experience is best understood as the one which determines the many. Indeed, the importance of the content of the image of the schema lies in the way in which it comes into being. Such an image represents an aspect of the dispositional structural order by which it is regulated, whether the resultant image is taken at the level of appearance or of objectivity. Such an image as representing an aspect of an ordering cannot be reduced to the content of any experience, whether imagined or actual. Rather, it represents principles or possibilities in terms of which sensory content can emerge within experience.

An examination of the internal dynamics of the meanings by which objects come to conscious awareness indicates that habits are partially constitutive of immediate perceptual experience. Pure "feeling core" or pure Firstness or pure "sense content" is "there" in experience as the logically or epistemically final basis and ultimate referent for all cognitive activity. In this sense it is epistemically primitive. Further, such a "feeling core" held apart from particular experiences must be "there" as part of the image if concepts are to be applicable to experience. But such a core is precisely the senuous core of the schematic image, and as such partakes of the generality of the image. Neither the image nor its sensuous core can be apprehended independently of the structural orderings of habit, for their character is partially determined by the generative functioning of habit. Habit is thus the living meaning which generates acts of response in relation to criteria for grasping the situations in terms of which such activity is appropriate. In brief, all perceptual experience is shot through with the relationship between human action and apprehended content, for such felt dispositions and tendencies to act enter into the very tone and structure of any experienced content. Thus, meanings emerge from organism-environment interaction as precise relational structures unified by habit as a rule of generation and organization, and they contain activity and temporal reference in the very heart of their logical structure.

It is meaning in terms of habit which provides, further, the source of a sense of the concrete unity of objectivity as more than a collection of appearances. Just as a continuum may generate an unlimited number of cuts within itself, so a disposition as a rule of organization and generation contains within itself an unlimited number of possibilities of specific acts to be generated. As Peirce states, "a true continuum is something whose possibilities of determination no multitude of individuals can exhaust," while a habit or general idea is a living feeling, infinitesimal in duration and immediately present, but still embracing innumerable parts.[33] That such an objective concreteness which transcends any indefinite number of appearances is built into our very sense of objectivity is evinced in Peirce's description of habit as the "living continuum" indicated above. In such an "absense of boundedness a vague possibility of more than is present is directly felt."[34] Or, as he emphasizes, a pragmatist must subscribe to the doctrine of real possibility because nothing other than this can be so much as meant by saying that an object possesses a character.[35] Habit, then, is the source of our sense of a reality of physical objectivities whose possibilities of being experienced transcend, in their very nature, the experiences in which they appear.

Thus, the conceiving mind cannot, by the very nature of meaning, be tied down to a consciousness which apprehends actualities only, for the implicit content of our concepts includes meaningful assertions about potentialities which reach out beyond that which will ever be actualized. Embodied in the actuality of our conceptual structures as dispositional, then, is a sense of a reality which transcends actual occasions of experience. That readiness to respond to more than can ever be made explicit, which is "there" in the functioning of habit, is immediately experienced in the passing present and gives experiential content to the "more than" of objectivities which can never be exhaustively experienced, to the "feel" of unactualized possibilities of being experienced which pervade every grasp of the world around us and which belie the conclusions of reductionistic empiricism. And schemata, as embodying the principles of organization by which man experiences his world, present the possibilities in terms of which the sensory can emerge within experience. The sensory emerges in experience within the structure of the possibilities of appearing contained in the images of the schemata, images which are generated by, and in turn reflect the structure of, the dispositional modes of response in terms of which we experience a world of objectivities. Possibilities of experience cannot be separated from the structure of the image of the schema, nor can any specific empirical content, as it emerges within experience, be separated from the structure of the image. There is thus incorporated within the structure of behavior a fundamental intentional or interactional unity of knowner and known which traditional rationalism and traditional empiricism have each tried, unsuccessfully, to break apart. And, for both Heidegger and Peirce, such a unity of man and world – at once ontological and epistemic – is provided by the seldom mentioned but pervasive role of Kantian schemata.

Notes

1. For a further elaboration and clarification of this expansion and deepening of Heidegger's notion of epistemology, see Patrick Lyall Bourgeois, "Fundamental Ontology and Epistemic Foundations," *New Scholasticism* 60 (Summer 1981): 373–80.

2. Merleau-Ponty, in a different context, well depicts this deepening expansion of understanding and other Kantian themes: "Finally, after sense experience, understanding also needs to be redefined since the general connective function ultimately attributed to it by Kantianism is now spread over the whole intentional life and no longer suffices to distinguish it." Maurice Merleau-Ponty, *The Structure of Behavior*, trans. Alden Fisher (Boston: Beacon Press, 1961), p. 176. When phenomenology deepens and broadens the notion of intentionality, it requires this redefinition of understanding, so that it now can encompass the whole intention of unique and concrete human existence.

3. If a being is to be given to a man, a finite being, man must be receptive or orientated to receive it beforehand. The horizon within which something is encountered must be "an anticipating proposition of something which has the nature of an offer," (Martin Heidegger, *Kant and the Problem of Metaphysics*, trans. James S. Churchill [Bloomington: Indiana University Press, 1962], pp. 94–95.) and one which is "perceptive as a pure aspect the formation of which is brought about by the pure imagination." Heidegger distinguishes two roles of the pure imagination in the formation of this aspect. "Not only does the pure imagination 'form' the intuitive perceptivity of the horizon, in that it 'creates' *this horizon* by the free turning-toward, but also in this act it is 'formative' [*bildend*] in yet a second sense, namely, in that it provides for the possibility of an 'image' [*Bild*] in general." Martin Heidegger, *Kant and the Problem of Metaphysics*, p. 95.

4. Certain affinities with Peirce which will be revealed here raise the suspicion that there are more far-reaching affinities as well.

5. Martin Heidegger, *Being and Time*, trans. John Macquarrie and Edward Robinson (New York: Harper and Row, 1962), p. 437. The role of "repetition" in Heidegger's philosophy is an essential aspect of his entire project, for it is central to the hermeneutical approach to the history of ontology and must be aligned with his attempt to destroy that history. This notion of repetition must not be trivialized by considering it simply as representing the past, or taking it up again. Rather, it requires coming to grips with those possibilities of existence which have come down to us. Since the cornerstone of the temporal exstases is the future, and since he is dealing with possibilities, repetition of possibilities is in terms of the future, so that his research into the history of ontology is in terms of possibilities.

We must keep in mind that the working out of historicality is simply a more concrete working out of temporality, and is interrelated with the resoluteness of Dasein. "The resoluteness which comes back to itself and hands itself down, then, becomes the repetition of a possibility of existence that has come to us. Repeating is handing down explicitly – that is to say, going back into the possibilities of the Dasein that has-been-there" (*Being and Time*, p. 437). This repetition, strictly in terms of possibilities, does not attempt to make past actualities recur. And anticipatory resoluteness is the existential ground for the authentic repetition of a possibility of existence that has-been-there, thus allowing, as Heidegger says, "the possibility that Dasein may choose its hero" (*Being and Time*, p. 437). In the choice of Kant, we have an instance of such a repetition. Kant's role in the history of ontology is decisive for that history, and merits repeating as delving into the latent possibility to be handed down from the future. Since "the laying of the foundation (or metaphysics) is based on time" and since "the first and only person who has gone any stretch of the way towards investigation of the dimension of Temporality or has even let himself be drawn hither by the coercion of the phenomena themselves is Kant," Heidegger approaches Kant as playing a decisive role in the tradition of ontology.

Thus, in making the task of *Kant and the Problem of Metaphysics* to explicate the *Critique of Pure Reason* as a laying of the foundation of metaphysics,
Heidegger reaches for the revelation of the internal possibility of ontology.
Heidegger proceeds to give an ontological interpretation, based on Kantian
texts, especially from the edition of 1781, to the Copernican revolution, showing that Kant does not wish to establish that all knowledge is ontic, nor does
he want to exclude what that presupposes – ontological knowledge. For "ontic
knowledge can be adequate to the essent only if the essent is already manifest
beforehand as essent, that is, if the constitution of its Being is known . . . . The
manifestation of the essent (ontic truth) depends upon the revelation of the
constitution of the Being of the essent (ontological truth)." *Kant and the Problem
of Metaphysics*, pp. 17–18.

6. Martin Heidegger, *Kant and the Problem of Metaphysics*, p. 203.

7. Ibid., p. 204.

8. Ibid., pp. 201, 202.

9. Ibid., p. 202.

10. Thus, it must be kept in mind that Heidegger's account of the Kantian
pure a priori schematization of the concept for an image is really an attempt
to show how Kant almost speaks of the fundamental originary level of
schematizing and reception of an entity and the structure of Dasein in terms
of its comprehension of Being. He is less interested in the a priori and pure
dimensions of Kant's account than he is in interpreting the cognitive synthesis
as an ontological synthesis presupposing the synthesizing of temporalizing
primordial time, which produces the horizon in the schemata: "The pure
schemata as transcendental determinations of time form the horizon of
transcendence" (*Kant and the Problem of Metaphysics*, p. 204). Likewise, this
level of primordial knowledge is his concern in turning to discuss the empirical dimension of schema, image, and concept. For Heidegger, the experience
of an entity demands that the experiencing entity must have this anticipatory
structure as its mode of being, must "bring a schema of all possible being." In
turning to the empirical dimension of Kant's analysis, we are closer to the context from which we can ask Heidegger questions more crucial and critical
than the almost myriad questions posed in the last few pages of *Kant and the
Problem of Metaphysics*.

11. Ibid., p. 102.

12. Immanuel Kant, *Critique of Pure Reason*, trans. Norman Kemp Smith
(New York: St. Martin's, 1965), pp. 182f. (180/B, 141/A) [English translation
modified], as quoted by Heidegger, *Kant and the Problem of Metaphysics*, p. 103.

13. Ibid., p. 102.

14. Ibid., pp. 102–3.

15. Although Heidegger's interpretation of Kant's *Critique of Pure Reason* gives the central place to the interpretation of schematism, it is beyond the scope of this paper to investigate its role. In a summary fashion, suffice it to say that the Kantian "Deduction" justifies the categories in the sense of what must be for knowledge, whereas the schematism, in the section of the *Critique* on the principles, deals with the application of the categories for knowledge – with the "how" of the rules for the application of the categories. Further, if we develop this distinction between schematized categories and schematism far enough, we can find certain Husserlian elements. For the schemata, as time determinations, or as constituted time, can lead to their root in originiary or primordial time, giving rise to the synthesis involved in the time determinations.

16. Martin Heidegger, *Kant and the Problem of Metaphysics*, p. 102; phrase quoted from Kant, *Critique of Pure Reason*, p. 182.

17. Ibid., p. 101.

18. The role of the concept is such that the concept, as a represented universal, cannot be represented by a singular representation or intuition, because of the distance between the concept and the sense presentation. Thus a mediation is required. This leads Heidegger to the "how" of the concept – to its regulative function in providing a possibility for an image: to "that which regulates and predetermines how, in general, something must appear in order to be able, as a house, to present an aspect correspsonding to its nature. The predetermination of the rule ... is a 'distinguishing characteristic' (*Auszeichnen*) of the whole of that which is intended by 'house'" (*Kant and the Problem of Metaphysics*, p. 100). This 'intended' must be represented as regulating the possibile inserting of the complex "house" into an empirical aspect. This means that it is represented as unifying and regulating the possibility of the concept into a possible aspect. "If, in general, a concept is that which serves as a rule, then the conceptual representation is the supplying, in advance, of the rule insofar as it provides an aspect corresponding to the specific way in which it regulates" (*Kant and the Problem of Metaphysics*, p. 100). Since this representation of the rule as a regulative action of structural necessity refers to a possible aspect, as a mode of sensibilization, it does not give an immediate, intuitive aspect of a concept. Thus, Heidegger concludes that "the rule is represented in the *how* of its regulation, that is, according to the manner in which, in regulating the presentation, it inserts itself in, and imposes itself on, the aspect which presents the presentation. The act of representation of the *how* of the regulation is the free (i.e., not bound to a representation) "construction" (*Bilden*) of a sensibilization. The latter, in the sense just described, is the *source* of the image." *Kant and the Problem of Metaphysics*, p. 101.

19. See note 5 above for a clarification of "repetition" in Heidegger's philosophy.

20. Peirce does not accept Kant's absolute system of categories with their transcendental schemata, for experience is not limited by modes of intuition and fixed forms of thought. Rather, all schemata are schemata of empirical concepts. For Peirce, the essential criteria for the application of any empirical concept to experience are given in the schema for the production of an image.

21. Charles Sanders Peirce, *Collected Papers*, vols. 1-6, ed. Hartshorne and Weiss (Cambridge, Massachusetts: The Belknap Press of Harvard University, 1931-1935); vols. 7-8, ed. Burks (Cambridge, Massachusetts: Harvard University Press, 1958); 4:9. (Hereafter cited using only conventional two-part number signifying volume and page number.)

22. 8:326; 8:332. It must be emphasized that purposive biological activity, as the foundation of meaning, cannot be understood in terms of scientific contents. Rather, it is the "lived through" biological activity of the human organism and, as such, is capable of phenomenological description.

23. 5:416; 5:213; 7:465.

24. 5:531. (See also 7:407 for a discussion of Kant's schema in relation to Peirce's position.)

25. 5:298-99.

26. For Peirce, an interpretant is that response in an interpreter which relates a sign to its object.

27. Peirce refers to such an analysis both as logical and as "phaneroscopic" or phenomenological.

28. 6:132.

29. 5:491. The use of "motive" here seems analogous to "anticipated result."

30. 7:498. By "general idea" here Peirce means, of course, not the generality of a Lockean type of abstract idea but the generality of a schematic image.

31. 6:141.

32. 5:291.

33. 6:170, 6:138.

34. 6:138.

35. 5:457.

9. Shifting Paradigms: Sartre on Critique, Language and the Role of the Intellectual

Thomas Busch

In two interviews he gave shortly before he died, Sartre made some remarkable statements.[1] He explicitly rejected the ontology of *Being and Nothingness*[2] calling it "false and incomplete."[3] Deploring his previous ontology for stressing "ruptures" between consciousnesses, he now claims that there are levels where consciousnesses enter into one another ("il y a des plans où elles entrent les unes dans les autres: il y a des plans communs à deux").[4] In the same spirit he rejects Marx's theory of superstructures for basing human relationships upon work and production and not recognizing the more primal bond of fraternity. He gropes for a language in which to express himself, at one time using the term *bifide*, or double-edged reality, to depict the unity of relationships, at another time approvingly referring to totemism and myth as a more adequate discourse than what is available today.

I take these remarks seriously and instead of attributing them to senility or to an abrupt turnabout in his thought, I see Sartre as giving full conscious expression to a development in his thought that had been percolating and steadily growing in influence for some time. Specifically, I will try to show that these remarks are intelligible in terms of a paradigm shift in his thought of which Sartre only gradually became aware.

Sartre's thought took shape under two major influences, the Cartesian/Husserlian and the Heideggerian.[5] In his attempt to creatively synthesize these influences in *Being and Nothingness*, the Cartesian/Husserlian influence dominated, for it was the basis for the ontology of freedom. Freedom is first located in the power of consciousness to hold objects at a distance, to change attitudes toward objects, and to escape entrapment by any objective situation. This power of consciousness is itself grounded in the "presence to self" which conditions every contact of consciousness with otherness, throwing consciousness back upon itself, creating a subjectivity which recognizes itself as being beyond the determination of objects. The ontological distinctions of *Being and Nothingness* – being-for-itself, being-in-itself, being-for-others – express the *differences* which constitute self, world and other selves.

If the Cartesian/Husserlian paradigm was taken up by Sartre to defend the autonomy of consciousness, he took up Heidegger to defend the implantation of consciousness in the world and to avoid idealism. Sympathy toward Heidegger's being-in-the-world runs throughout *Being and Nothingness*; "The concrete is man within the world in that specific union of man and world which Heidegger calls . . . 'being-in-the-world.'"[6] Texts bearing the stamp of Heideggerian immersion in the world and, as well, of Cartesian/Husserlian distance from the world, run parallel throughout *Being and Nothingness* without integration.

> . . . In what we shall call the world of the immediate, which delivers itself to our unreflective consciousness, we do not first appear to ourselves, to be thrown subsequently into enterprises. Our being is immediately "in situation"; that is, it arises in enterprises and knows itself first in so far as it is reflected in these enterprises . . . . But as soon as the enterprise is held at a distance from me, as soon as I am referred to myself. . . . I emerge alone and in anguish confronting the unique and original project which constitutes my being. . . . Anguish . . . appears at the moment that I disengage myself from the world . . . . In anguish I apprehend myself at once as totally free and as not being able to derive the meaning of the world except as coming from myself.[7]

There can be no doubt, however, that the Cartesian/Husserlian influence was primary. Consciousness, even on the immediate level of being-in-the-world, is structured as present-to-itself-as-it-is-present-to-objects, with the implication, Sartre claims, that "*presence to* always involves duality; . . . Presence incloses a radical negation as presence to that which one is not. What is present to me is not me."[8] This "presence to self" on the level of being in the world reveals itself in a lucid pre-reflective cogito, entailing "an awareness of being aware," in which subjectivity unavoidably grasps itself as outside of determination by the world. Heidegger is explicitly criticized because "he begins the existentialist analytic without going through the *cogito*."[9] Situatedness, in *Being and Nothingness*, is relegated to the status of a background or occasion for the flexing of the power of consciousness over it.

The beginning of the end of the dominance of the Cartesian/Husserlian paradigm was Sartre's study of Genet. This work evidences a "turn" in Sartre's thought reflecting his growing awareness of "the force of things" and, in particular, of the problem of the conditioned consciousness. The lesson Sartre claimed to learn from World War II was that consciousness could be hoodwinked, deluded, unaware of factors influencing it "behind its back." A close reading of the Genet book makes it apparent that, while Sartre attempts to handle Genet within the categories of *Being and Nothingness*, these categories begin to strain, smoke, and come apart in the effort. Young Genet did not know that he was free and thus did not fit into either of the alternatives offered by *Being and Nothingness*, bad faith (self-deceptive flight from freedom) and authenticity (acceptance of radical freedom and responsibility). Genet had to discover that he was free and only then could Sartre accuse him of bad faith. A new type of alienation has appeared. Sartre describes its victims:

> . . . They internalize the objective and external judgments which the collectivity passes on them, and *they view themselves in their subjective individuality* on the basis of their "ethnic character," a "nature," an "*essence*," which merely express the contempt in which others hold them.[10]

The presumption of this phenomenon of the conditioned consciousness is that the previously claimed clarity and lucidity of consciousness to itself be dimmed to admit an obscurity and ambiguity of self-knowledge. Furthermore, the relation of a person to his or her situation cannot be simply compressed into that of a subject that has objects confronting it. Somehow the situation must deeply influence the subject, into even its most intimate thoughts. The phenomenological tools he had appropriated from Husserl were unequal to the task of handling this new type of alienation and so, after the Genet book, Sartre was pressed to search for a more adequate method.

Sartre found his new method in the dialectic: "We cannot conceive of this conditioning in any form except that of a dialectical movement

... ."[11] In the *Critique of Dialectical Reason* Sartre situated consciousness within praxis and praxis in a dialectical relationship with the practico-inert.[12] The result of this move (the full implication of which he was unaware) is to radically decenter consciousness, to challenge its dominance over meaning and structure, and generally to subvert subject/object discourse. Remnants of the Cartesian/Husserlian vocabulary remain, but it is clear that Sartre is trying to twist them into a new context. Praxis, he tells us, is "the moving unity of subjectivity and objectivity."[13] In the same vein he claims that "the subjective contains within itself the objective, which it denies and which it surpasses toward a new objectivity, and the objectivity by virtue of *objectification* externalizes the internality of the project as an objectified subjectivity."[14] This tortured language is aimed at overcoming the distantiations inherent in the Cartesian/Husserlian paradigm. Actually, Sartre was already moving toward not so much a revised method as toward recognition of the failure of an old paradigm and the need for a new one. I will examine certain key and interrelated issues in order to explore how Sartre came to change his mind about them and how this change of mind may indicate the direction of his thought as he shifted from the Cartesian/Husserlian paradigm. The issues are *critique* (the power of consciousness), *language* (meaning and structure), and *the role of the intellectual* (political action).

Critique

Sartre's initial project of founding an ethics and politics was formed around the possibility of a radical critique deriving from Descartes's doubt, but more especially from Husserl's epoché and reduction. Sartre's appropriation of the latter consisted in what he called "pure" or "purifying reflection." Purifying reflection allows one to grasp the constitution of the ego as a transcendent object and, indeed, the constitution of all meaning and value by consciousness' original project. Anguish is the experience of the functioning of this critical reflection. Anguish, Sartre writes,

> ... appears at the moment that I disengage myself from the world where I had been engaged — in order to apprehend myself as a consciousness which possesses a preontological comprehension of its

essence and a "prejudicative" sense of its possibilities. Anguish is opposed to the mind of the serious man who apprehends values in terms of the world and who resides in the reassuring, materialistic substantiation of values . . . . The meaning which my freedom has given to the world, I apprehend as coming from the world and constituting my objections. In anguish I apprehend myself at once as totally free and as not being able to derive the meaning of the world except as coming from myself.[15]

Purifying reflection, made possible by the "presence to self" constitutive of consciousness on the pre-reflective level, played a crucial role in Sartre's early philosophy, for it was both an instrument of critique and the path to an authentic life.

In his later philosophy the insertion of consciousness within praxis, as a "moment" of praxis, radically situates consciousness. Praxis itself is in dialectical relation with the practico-inert and with other praxes. Sartre drops his earlier Cartesian notion of the pre-reflective cogito, in which the self grasped itself as outside of objects. In its stead, he employs the notions of le vécu (lived experience) and comprehension, more holistic forms of experience, which admit of an obscurity on the part of consciousness.

Today, the notion of "lived experience" represents an effort to preserve that presence to self which seems to me indispensable for the existence of any psychic fact while at the same time this presence is so opaque and blind before itself that it is also an absence from itself.[16] Reflection is not denied but situated "as a moment of the action itself – the action, in the course of its accomplishment, provides its own clarification."[17] Sartre explicitly drops his previously held distinction between pure and impure reflection:

. . . Later I discovered that nonaccessory [pure] reflection was not different from the accessory [impure] and immediate way of looking at things but was the critical work one can do on oneself during one's entire life, through praxis.[18]

Critique can arise only from within a situation, when the situation becomes "unlivable" or "intolerable," that is, from contradictions within the situation. Sartre came to refer to his earlier notion of freedom as abstract. The new "concrete" freedom he comes to embrace is not the projection of possibilities upon a situation, but the recognition of certain structured, objective possibilities of the situation itself, among which is the possibility of altering the situation in some new direction.

Language

In *Being and Nothingness* language is relegated to a brief discussion tucked away in the chapter on the body. Here, language is presented as a tool, transparent in its usage, which is lived by a controlling consciousness. In some of his essays in *Situations*, where Sartre becomes more explicit about language, it is clear that he locates language within the Cartesian/Husserlian paradigm. Subjectivity is in full control of language.

> . . . when I am conscious of understanding a word, no word is interpolated between me and myself. The word, the single word in question, is there *before* me, as *that which is understood* . . . . Otherwise it is merely an idle sound . . . . The effectiveness of the cogito — its eternity — lies in the fact that it reveals a type of existence defined as the state of being present to oneself without intermediary. The word is interpolated between my love and myself, between my coverage or cowardice and myself, not between my understanding and my consciousness of understanding. For the consciousness of understanding is the law of being of understanding. I shall call this the silence of consciousness . . . . I know what it is that I want to express because I am it without intermediary. Language may resist and mislead me, but I shall never be taken in by it unless I want to, for I can always come back to what I am, to the emptiness and silence that I am, through which, nevertheless, there is a language and there is a world.[19]

It is clear that this view of the relationship between consciousness and language is dependent upon Sartre's understanding of the translucency of the pre-reflective cogito. Note particularly his claims that the cogito reveals one's existence as "being present to oneself without intermediary" and "I know what it is that I want to express because I am it without intermediary." Here Sartre can be seen to conflate the notions of presence to self and knowledge of self. However, as consciousness becomes decentered, self-knowledge mediated by one's involvement in the world, and an obscurity and mystification allowed to befall consciousness (for these are the necessary ingredients in making intelligible the conditioned consciousness) Sartre's view of language correspondingly changes.

In *Critique of Dialectical Reason* language takes its place among the phenomena which comprise the practico-inert, which is the sedimented basis for all thought and action. Culture, tradition, institutions of any sort, make up the practico-inert. In *Critique of Dialectical Reason* language becomes thick with its own being, which is that of a self-referential totality.

> . . . the totality of language as a set of *internal* relations between objec-
> tive senses is given, for and to everyone; words are simply specifications
> expressed against the background of language; the sentence is an actual
> totalisation where every word defines itself in relation to the others, to
> the context and to the entire language, as a integral part of a whole. To
> speak is to modify each vocable by all the others . . .; language contains
> every word and every word is to be understood in terms of language as
> a whole.[20]

For the later Sartre there can be no thought without language. There
may be, he says, "something to say," but this "something is nothing
sayable, nothing conceptual or conceptualizable, nothing that
signifies."[21] In this view there is no translucent cogito behind language
directing it by its knowledge. Recall that Sartre exchanged his earlier
notion of the pre-reflective cogito for the notions of *le vécu* and *comprehension*. He refers to *le vécu* as "the ensemble of the dialectical process of psychic life, insofar as this process is obscure to itself because
it is a constant totalization, thus necessarily a totalization which cannot be conscious of what it is."[22] The speaker or signifier is not in
possession of meaning prior to its expression, and there is now
recognition that nothing can be signified, not even the speaker to him
or herself, except through the medium of a linguistic field of possibilities with all the limitations involved.

The Role of the Intellectual

Paralleling his early position on critique, when Sartre first turned
his attention toward politics and social change, he envisaged a prominent role for the intellectual. In *What Is Literature?* he looked to the
writer to be the yeast of liberating social change. Literature itself
became the model of authentic relations, since it was reciprocal, based
upon acknowledgement and respect of freedoms for one another. The
writer would provoke, lead, teach, transform the reading audience to
work for the establishment of "the city of ends," the classless society.

> We must *historicize* the reader's good will, that is, by the formal agency
> of our work, we must, if possible provoke his attention of treating men,
> in every case, as an absolute end, and, by the *subject* of our writing,
> direct his intention upon his neighbors, that is, upon the oppressed of
> the world. But we shall have accomplished nothing if, in addition, we
> do not show him — and in the very warp and weft of the work — that
> it is quite impossible to treat concrete men as ends in contemporary

society. Thus he will be led by the hand until he is made to see that, in effect, what he wants is to eliminate the exploitation of man by man. . . . [23]

Literature, then, is to function as a sort of purifying reflection for the purifying action of changing an alienated society: "The collectivity passes to reflection and mediation by means of literature."[24]

Later, Sartre's critique of "critique," leading to the decentering of consciousness, brought him to a revised conception of the role of the intellectual in effecting political change: "this historical agent is entirely conditioned by his circumstances and his consciousness is precisely the opposite of an overview."[25] His revised theory of critique as arising from contradictions within the situation leads him to a complex analysis of the intellectual's situation in society. The intellectual is a privileged member of society, racked by the contradiction of commitment to universal knowledge, on the one hand, and the particularity of his or her social position, on the other. Because of the later Sartre's preoccupation with the conditioned consciousness, he views the particularity of the intellectual's social position in terms of bias and suspicion. Thus, Sartre holds that if the intellectual "wishes to understand the society in which he lives, he has only one course open to him and that is to adopt the point of view of its most underprivileged members."[26] On the other hand, the intellectual's situatedness does not allow the intellectual to become one of the masses or its organization except in his or her own unique way: "he can never renounce his critical faculties." There is no formula, the intellectual must constantly live in "tension."

Conclusion

I believe that this analysis sheds light upon those remarkable statements Sartre made shortly before his death.

The ontology of *Being and Nothingness* presented "absolutely separated regions of being."[27] This ontology was meant to support the radical differentiation between subject and object. The conditioned consciousness, however, could not be understood in those terms and so Sartre turned toward dialectic. At first he used the dialectic as a device to try to piece together subject and object. Gradually dialectical relatedness became dominant and he found the old language of subject and object no longer relevant.

In each of the areas just examined – critique, language, the role of the intellectual – there is apparent a move away from the terms of a relationship (consciousness/situation, consciousness/language, agent of change/social situation) and toward the reality of relationship. The terms of a relationship are abstract. Concrete reality is the relationship itself. Sartre expressed this in one of the interviews in question when he told his interviewer that "what is real is . . . the relationship of you to me and of me to you."[28] What Sartre's concrete philosophy became sensitive to was mediation, overlapping, intertwining – what Merleau-Ponty had referred to as the "interworld."

No one can say where Sartre's thought would have pushed on from these interviews, but it is safe to say that when he reached out for the word *"bifide"*, he had finally worked his way out of the Cartesian/Husserlian paradigm into a new one.

Notes

1. "Jean-Paul Sartre et M. Sicard: Entretien," *Obliques*, nos. 18–19 (1979); "The Last Words of Jean-Paul Sartre," *Dissent* (Fall 1980), pp. 397–492.

2. Jean-Paul Sartre, *Being and Nothingness*, trans. Hazel Barnes (New York: Philosophical Library, 1956).

3. "Sartre: Entretien," *Obliques*, p. 15.

4. Ibid.

5. In an interview he gave in 1975, Sartre was asked: " . . . how have you 'programmed' yourself in relation to the philosophical thought of the time?" He responded: "That is a difficult question. *L'Etre et le Néant* was the phenomenology and existentialism . . . (existentialism is the wrong word) . . . let us say the philosophy of Heidegger and Husserl. I took from them what appeared to me to be true and I tried to develop my own ideas from there." "An Interview with Jean-Paul Sartre," *The Philosophy of Jean-Paul Sartre*, ed. Paul Arthur Schilpp (La Salle, Illinois: Open Court, 1980), p. 25.

6. Sartre, *Being and Nothingness*, p. 5.

7. Ibid., pp. 39–40.

8. Ibid., p. 173.

9. Ibid., p. 73.

10. Jean-Paul Sartre, *Saint Genet: Actor and Martyr*, trans. B. Frechtman (New York: Mentor, 1963), p. 44.

11. Jean-Paul Sartre, *Search for a Method*, trans. Hazel Barnes (New York: Random House, 1968), p. 34.

12. Jean-Paul Sartre, *Critique of Dialectical Reason*, trans. Alan Sheridan-Smith (London: NLB, 1976).

13. *Search for a Method*, p. 97.

14. Ibid., p. 98.

15. Sartre, *Being and Nothingness*, pp. 39–40.

16. "The Itinerary of a Thought," in *Jean-Paul Sartre: Between Existentialism and Marxism*, trans. John Mathews (New York: William Morrow, 1974), p. 41.

17. Sartre, *Search for a Method*, p. 32.

18. Jean-Paul Sartre, "On the Family Idiot," in *Jean-Paul Sartre: Life Situations*, trans. Paul Auster and Lydia Davis (New York: Pantheon Books, 1977), pp. 121, 122.

19. Sartre, *Critique*, p. 99.

20. Jean-Paul Sartre, "Departure and Return," in *Literary and Philosophical Essays*, trans. Annette Michelson (New York: Collier, 1962), pp. 171–72. A very fine analysis of this essay can be found in Joseph Fell, *Heidegger and Sartre* (Ithaca: Cornell University Press, 1979), pp. 280–88.

21. Jean-Paul Sarte, "A Plea for Intellectuals," p. 272.

22. Sartre, "The Itinerary of a Thought," p. 41.

23. Jean-Paul Sartre, *What is Literature?*, trans. B. Frechtman (New York: Harper, 1965), pp. 269–70.

24. Ibid., p. 291.

25. "A Plea for Intellectuals," p. 255.

26. Sartre, *Being and Nothingness*, lxiii.

27. Ibid.

28. "The Last Words of Jean-Paul Sartre," p. 413.

10. Merleau-Ponty and the Problem of Knowledge

Henry Pietersma

That Merleau-Ponty recognizes a problem of knowledge is clear, although it is, of course, true that his philosophy as a whole offers much more than a theory of knowledge. Already in the introductory chapters of his *Phenomenology of Perception*, particularly chapter three, Descartes's evil genius is mentioned, and his general stance with respect to the Cartesian tradition briefly but clearly indicated. The first chapter of part one opens with the question as to the epistemic role of our ineluctably perspectival perceptions. Later chapters offer at various points lengthy discussions of the distinctions between appearance and reality, certainty and doubt, error and truth. And in the chapter entitled "The Cogito," he tackles the central issues of the problem of knowledge, in particular the relation between the evident and the true, and offers what may be taken to be the core of his theory of knowledge. In *The Visible and the Invisible* the concern with knowledge is even clearer. The opening pages of chapter one, entitled "Perceptual Faith and its Obscurity," are almost entirely devoted to epistemic questions. The lengthy discussion of Sartre in chapter two shows that one of the main objections he has to *Being and Nothingness* is its failure to recognize a problem of knowledge. I will try to show that the introduction of the concept of flesh in the fourth chapter is an attempt to secure our perceptual knowledge of the world.

In this paper I will concentrate on *The Visible and the Invisible*, making only occasional references to his earlier work. I want to begin by calling attention to a point about which the author makes only a few remarks but which is crucial in my discussion, because it sets out the limits within which the main discussion of the work is kept. Having just noted that my certainty of seeing my table gets contested as soon as I become aware of the fact that this is *my* perception,[1] he proceeds to say that one should not primarily think in this connection of the common argument from dreams, madness, or illusions, suggesting to us that we should examine whether or not what we see may be false.

> For to do so the argument makes use of that faith in the world it seems to be shaking: we would not know even what is false, if there were not times when we had distinguished it from what is true. The argument therefore postulates the world in general, the true in itself; this is secretly invoked in order to disqualify our perceptions and cast them pell-mell back into our "inner life" along with our dreams, in spite of all observable differences, for the sole reason that our dreams were, at the time, as convincing as they are — forgetting that the "falsity" of dreams cannot be extended to perceptions since that falsity shows up only in relation to perceptions, and that if we are to be able to speak of falsity, we do have to have experience of truth.[2]

The point is a familiar one to philosophers who have concerned themselves with skepticism. To declare that something is a dream is to discredit it as knowledge of an objective reality. But on any occasion when we do this, we presuppose that we know what is true, partly at least on the basis of perception. Hence, we cannot declare all beliefs or claims to be dreams, because that would nullify even the knowledge presupposed in making that very declaration. It would destroy the contrast between perceptions and dreams, or more precisely, as the author himself puts it, the ontological worth or value of that contrast.

It is clear that the skeptic of the philosophical kind will not be impressed by this, since he denies, precisely, not that we make such a distinction, but that in the last analysis it can be justified. At the end of his First Meditation Descartes has already acknowledged that we do ordinarily make this distinction with confidence, but his meditation leads him to a further point, namely, that there is a possibility that he may be dreaming while he sits in his room by the fire and takes himself to be awake, even if he himself cannot tell whether that possibility is realized. Merleau-Ponty seems to be not entirely unaware of this, because he hints that the skeptical argument has validity, if we assume what he himself immediately brushes aside as a naiveté. It is the idea that our perceptions constitute knowledge if and only if they apprehend an objective reality *beyond all experience*. Pyrrhonist arguments reflect the illusions of the naive person, he says; they vaguely allude to the idea of a being completely in itself and set over against that, as states of consciousness, all our perceptions and imaginations.[3] I think he is certainly right about the connection of philosophical skepticism and this notion of objectivity. It is the notion of being, which does not include any reference to cognitive capacities. Being does not imply either that it is possible or that it is impossible to know it or to make rational assertions about it. Yet our beliefs are true only by virtue of what exists in this sense. And if they are not true, they cannot amount to knowledge. No matter what has gone into the formation of a belief, no matter what natural or historical events may have shaped a state of mind, the truth of the belief depends on nothing else. According to this view no analysis of a belief as such can show that it is true. In slightly different terms, the relation between the knower and what he knows is an external, not an internal, relation. So what Merleau-Ponty stresses, namely, that perceptions are in our awareness different from dreams, does not prove that they amount to knowledge of the objective, real world.

At the very beginning of his book, then, the author wants to make sure that we realize that he is not going to deal with this form of skepticism and that he in fact rejects the conception of being associated with it. I have elaborated the point he makes somewhat, because I think it is very important to appreciate the full import of this rejection. As I said a while ago, this rejection defines the limit within which the discussions engaged in by the author of *The Visible and the Invisible* are conducted. His reasons for rejecting being-in-itself are not stated here. He merely calls it naive and urges that we re-examine the concept of being. As we will see, what emerges from his own deliberations is a concept of being which relates it essentially to our experience of being. Entities have being only within our experience.

What this means is, of course, not at all clear. In fact, we might read the remainder of the book as an attempt to define at least two different ways in which that statement might be taken. As the author puts it, it is a critical examination of philosophies of reflection. He wants to set forth his own view and distinguish it from those philosophies. But as he clearly indicates, it is a dispute within a community of thought. Both he and his opponents agree in rejecting the notion of being-in-itself.[4] Both parties contextualize entities, i.e., consider them as entities existing only within contexts of belief. With regard to philosophical skepticism this means that both parties think of themselves as having overcome it: yes, we do have knowledge of the world. The price paid for this victory, of course, is clear. They pay for it, as I just put it, by contextualizing being, by rejecting the age-old conception of entities that exist whether or not they are known by anyone. If in Kant's philosophy we disregard the doctrine about the thing-in-itself, we could say in Kantian language that what is empirically known as real is nonetheless, transcendentally speaking, ideal.

Given this concept of being it follows, of course, that entities can be known, that they fall within the scope of our cognitive power. Any *general* doubt of the kind expressed by Descartes at the end of his First Meditation is not just mistaken. It is meaningless, since if flies in the face of what is now to be meant by the term "being." There is no problem of knowledge, if by that we mean an attempt to answer that doubt on its own terms. There cannot be such a general doubt, because the concept of contextualized objects entails that entities and a certain cognitive power – whether perception or intellect – form a unitary matrix or framework, which specifies both what kinds or categories of objects exist and the general way in which we can establish whether a particular entity of a certain kind exists or what properties it has. This much, I think, can be said about the ideas held by both Merleau-Ponty and those he refers to as philosophers of reflection. To go much further would run the risk of distorting one or the other of the parties to the dispute.

What, then, is the problem of knowledge which Merleau-Ponty does recognize as a problem to be addressed? It is the problem as it arises in our everyday and scientific experience of the world. It is simply the problem we may be said to have whenever certain cognitive claims are contested and we set out to evaluate them. That there is a sense, as I just indicated, in which objects exist within our experiences of them does not mean that a given perceptual act and its objects are one and the same thing. Merleau-Ponty argues against a Bergsonian view which stresses coincidence of subject and object.[5] As we know, that was not Kant's view either, in spite of his thesis about objects being transcendentally ideal. And we face a problem of knowledge in a genuine sense as soon as a percipient becomes aware of another person looking at the same thing. As he quite perceptively notes, there emerges then a distinction between two objects:

> The thing perceived by the other is doubled: there is the one he perceives, God knows where, and there is the one I see, outside of his body, and which I call the real thing – as he calls real the table he sees and consigns to the category of appearances the one I see.[6]

He does not mean to say that each percipient takes himself to be confronted in a literal sense by two objects. He speaks of a doubling of objects, because this is a situation of epistemic appraisal. And such an appraisal begins by distinguishing, on the one hand, the real or true object which the appraiser takes himself to see out there in front of him and a certain distance from the body of the other percipient, and, on the other hand, the object as the other percipient claims to see it. The question to be decided is whether these two objects are actually one and the same object existing out there in the actual world. But until that has been decided, there are indeed two objects. And the one is necessarily taken to be real, because otherwise the appraisal could not be what it is: the asking of a question, whether or not expressed in words, as to whether what the other claims he sees is real, whether his claim is knowledge. The other object is contextual, a mere appearance or, in orthodox phenomenological language, an intentional object or noema. If I find that the other's claim is correct, I identify the two objects as the same, not just qualitatively similar but numerically identical.

The experience of having my perceptions appraised by another person, according to the author, opens my eyes for the fact of the relativity of my perceptions.[7] In his discussion of Sartre he states that when alone the experience of seeing suggests a kind of sovereign ownership of the world before me with nothing separating me from what I see.[8] But the other person is precisely the radical calling into question of this impression; my sense of seeing everything there is to see is repudiated.[9] My competence to say what the world is like and in so doing speak for all is contested.[10] The others's hesitation and appraisal of my perceptual claims, however brief and unexpressed, give me the awareness that there is a problem of knowledge, that from my beliefs about something it is not immediately and in all cases apparent that they are correct.

Although the example discussed a moment ago is very simple, it illustrates the kind of problem the author recognizes, that of the subjectivity and relativity of all our cognitive claims, in particular our sensuous perception of the external world. While a perception is a claim to apprehend the object *itself* (it is not screened from us in any way or separated from us by spatial or temporal distance), the fact is that a perception is an act of an embodied subject activating psychological and physiological powers, acquired dispositions, and confronting an object in terms of a perspective or situation which is not only spatio-temporal but also cultural and historical. We are not simply a Sartrean *néant*, but an embodied percipient whose shadow falls on what we take to be there, as the author documents with an overwhelming array of examples in his *Phenomenology of Perception*. What is important for my discussion is the fact that Merleau-Ponty emphatically situates the problem of knowledge in a setting in which it can be overcome. In the discussion of the above example I deliberately emphasized the fact that one of the percipients may have doubts about the other's perception but he has none about his own. He assumes that he can evalute that perception by using his own eyes to see what is really there in the world. Clearly, if he had doubts about his own perceptions, he would not be able to tell whether the other really perceived what was there in the world. If later he should come to have doubts about his own earlier perception, it would again be on the strength of what he then took himself to be perceiving unproblematically. In other words, the problem of knowledge our author recognizes is one that cannot be generalized so as to make the entire world problematical. The doubts I have in everyday life and in science are everyday doubts and scientific doubts, not the kind of doubt the philosophical skeptics have about *all* of our perceptions. Merleau-Ponty makes this point by introducing the Husserlian concept of horizon. Every particular perception has its horizons. That is to say, it implicitly indicates both earlier perceptions and those later perceptions that may either confirm or refute it. These pertain either to the same object, which we then say we see from different sides, or to objects in its vicinity. Each perception is thus directed upon an object or a group of objects but also, though not explicitly, upon its wider context. If the object of a given perception turns out not to be there or to be different from what it was taken to be, this eventuality requires occupation of a standpoint within this horizon. And what is seen from that standpoint, it is presupposed, is there and is thus and so without the percipient having any doubt about it.[11] While a perception is pervaded by a sense of its fallibility, of its possibly being doubted or rejected, that very sense, in the author's view, requires a certainty that there is something out there, that there is a world. The skeptics on whom Merleau-Ponty turned his back right at the beginning of this work are lacking, as he says, appreciation for this peculiar presence of the world as horizon.[12] From his own perspective this criticism does indeed seem to be so. To suppose that we might not know anything at all of the world is to take the expression "world" as a totality or set of objects but to fail to see that in consigning this totality to non-existence or unknowability we must perceive something truly, i.e., have truth. This is, of course, making the point already formulated earlier: not all of our perceptions can at one and the same time be taken as mere states of mind failing to reveal the world.[13]

What about the so-called philosophers of reflection? As I pointed out, they share with Merleau-Ponty a rejection of that conception of being which functions importantly in the position of philosophical skepticism. Positively stated, all that which exists falls within our cognitive power. We have just seen that Merleau-Ponty worked this out in terms of the cognitive power of perception. This power is such that it will always transcend doubt; more precisely, there is doubt only when it has already been transcended. Since there is no being in itself, no evil genius needs to be feared. He would not be able to fool us, if being itself is contextual. Now, the philosophers of reflection, as the author makes clear, also think that the evil genius can be overcome and they too reject being in itself. The difference is that they contextualize being with respect to the power of *thought* in sharp distinction from sense perception. Their reason is that they construe the problem of our perceptual knowledge to be a problem that cannot be solved by perception. What is called for, obviously, is epistemic appraisal, but this cannot, they hold, be carried out by what is in turn a perception, since that would involve the same problem of knowledge. We should, therefore, change our attitude and adopt one that does not involve perception. Whatever term is used (reflection, reason, intellect, thought, or whatever), it is important that this new standpoint does not commit us to anything in perception.

Who were these philosophers? The author does not give a list but the figures most frequently mentioned are Descartes, Spinoza, Kant, and Husserl. If Descartes is to be included here we have to think of him as one who in the last four meditations answered the skepticism set forth in the first. Spinoza is mentioned or alluded to many times in both the *Phenomenology* and the present work, remarkably enough many times with approval. As to Husserl, the author's attitude to this philosopher is ambivalent. As a Cartesian and a rationalist who held that a philosopher cannot with full rational justification assert the existence of the spatio-temporal world, Husserl clearly falls under the criticism directed at philosophies of reflection. After all, who urged more strongly than he that the philosophical attitude is one of detachment from the natural attitude of perception and science? Yet there is also a phenomenological strand in Husserl's philosophy, to which Merleau-Ponty clearly felt very sympathetic. In my remarks I will not discuss the historical accuracy of the author's views of these men.

When I cease to make use of any of my senses and adopt an attitude of reflection toward my everyday perceptions of the world, everything is different. Merleau-Ponty puts a great deal of emphasis on this difference. The ordinary objects of perception are replaced by different objects, called cogitata, ideata, or noemata (by Descartes, Spinoza, and Husserl, respectively). The act of perceiving as I perform it in everyday life, with its phenomenological sense of having attained knowledge of the world around me, is now, as Merleau-Ponty often repeats after Descartes, simply called a form of thought: I think I perceive.[14] It seems but a pale shadow of its former self, the sense I had when I actually perceived something under optimal conditions. Our natal bond with the world is loosened, he says. The noemata, unlike the corresponding objects of first-order perceptions, are defined by their certainty, their resistance to doubt, even to the mere suggestion that they might not exist.[15] They exist, it is said, even if the corresponding objects of ordinary sense perception do not.

He emphasizes the differences, because he thinks they might be overlooked. It might be thought that the philosophical reconstruction of the world, the world we actually do know, is really the same world we encounter in perception, the only difference being that we now see without being confused by sense or distracted by our embodied state. Reflection, we might thus say, is nothing but perception returning to itself.[16] We now "see" things better, closer-up, so to speak. Now in our everyday exploration of the world we do indeed assume that walking up to a tree for a closer look, the tree we see close-up is the same as the one we saw from a distance, the only difference being that we are now in an epistemically more favourable position to know that tree.[17] But such an objective identity is defined by the context of embodied exploration of the external world. We cannot simply transport it to the inner realm, as we would be doing if we straightforwardly identified the noema with the sensible object of the same name. Reflection introduces a different object, and it is itself also in its very nature a modification of an antecedent perception.[18] One must not overlook the fact that first "there was a thing perceived and an openness toward this thing, which reflection neutralized or transformed into perception-reflected-on and thing-perceived-in-a-perception-reflected-on."[19]

This emphasis on the differences between reflection and perception calls attention to several points that are certainly valid. A noema or intentional object is no doubt different from the tree in the garden that corresponds to it: the noema is the tree indexed with reference to a perceptual form of consciousness, the tree-as-perceived. The tree itself, on the contrary, is an object which the percipient takes himself to know as a real existent and which he therefore does not feel he needs to index. As Husserl said, the tree is a physical object out there in the garden which can burn up, but the tree-as-perceived cannot

undergo such a transformation. This noema is internal to the perceiving in the sense that it "exists" even if the perceptual belief is false. As
Merleau-Ponty says, in being resistent to doubt it amounts to a negation of negation,[20] thus giving us a certainty which is quite different
from the certainty we have that there is a world.[21] Yet as we noticed
earlier, the peculiar logic of epistemic appraisal, at least the kind prac-
ticed in everyday circumstances, is such that, if a certain belief is
found to be correct, its noema is identified with a really existent
object. Or in the terms I have been using on occasion in this paper,
the external object is nothing other than the indexed object. Discourse
of noemata, then, is discourse about a possibly real object. (The adjec-
tival qualification "possibly real," it should be observed, reflects the
standpoint of the appraiser, not that of the percipient who takes
himself to know that it is real.)

It seems to me that in his discussion of philosophies of reflection
Merleau-Ponty ignores this second aspect of the logic of appraisal. He
stresses merely the difference between noema and perceptual object,
and, correlatively, that between thinking and perceiving. Consequently, philosophical discourse, in which noemata rather than ordinary objects of perception are referred to, is made to look like nothing
more than a *different* kind of concern about *different* objects. What we
lose is the appreciation of the fact that philosophical reflection was
meant to have cognitive import for the cognitive status of perception.
In fact, ordinary perception was thought to have been shown not to
deserve fully the title of knowledge of the real world. The real world
was thought to be better known by science and better still by
philosophy. Nevertheless, whatever the outcome of the philosophical
reflection on perception, it was assumed to be relevant for perception
as a web of claims to knowledge.

One might counter this criticism by pointing out that Merleau-
Ponty sees in reflective philosophy a wholesale condemnation of
perception and an attempt to replace its image of the world by that of
a world constructed by thought. In other words, what he objects to is
the rationalism and the idealism associated with it. I think this is true.
The following quotation shows this quite well:

> It is therefore essential to the philosophy of reflection that it bring us
> back, this side of our *de facto* situation, to a center of things from which
> we proceeded, but from which we were decentered, that it retravel this
> time starting from us a route already traced out from that center to us.
> The very effort toward internal adequation, the enterprise to reconquer
> explicitly all that we are and do implicitly, signifies . . . that the world

is our birthplace only because first we as minds are the cradle of the world.[22]

In this kind of statement he clearly attributes to men like Descartes, Spinoza, and Husserl the desire to re-establish, from the viewpoint of a thinking distinct from perception, the totality of our human experience, including perception. As noted earlier, it is indeed a form of idealism inasmuch as being is essentially correlated with the cognitive subject; the skepticism associated with the conception of a being independent of the subject is no longer a threat to this idealism. The only kind of skepticism to be taken seriously is that skepticism which accepts our capacity for knowing the truth and which in its name calls into question whatever cognitive results do not yet fully satisfy the intellect. Hence the concern on the part of these philosophers to ward off doubt, to make sure that none of their steps are open to doubt, a posture which is really just the reverse side of their attempt to satisfy the demands of thought or reason, to attain what in the quotation he calls internal adequation and what in another passage he fittingly calls "le consentement de la pensée à la pensée."[23] (It should be noted that here skepticism plays a role analogous to that which Merleau-Ponty assigns to it in the realm of perception.)

The author's objection to this tradition of philosophy is that reflection is an attitude which presupposes a first-order perceptual attitude to the world. We already noted his emphasis on this point, namely that it is a modification and in fact a neutralization of perception. Since the construction of the world from the point of view of reflection necessarily fails to include this transformation from which that point of view originates, the philosophy cannot pretend to re-constitute the *totality* of experience.[24] In a similar vein, but now with special reference to Kant, we are told that in the latter's attempt to isolate the necessary conditions for the possibility of an experience of a world "rests upon the fact that I can see the world," that "his guideline is furnished him by the unreflected image of the world" and that its resultant principles or categories are not "so much the foundation as the second-order expression of the fact that for me there has been an experience of a world".[25] He also complains that this type of philosophy fails to understand the actual world, does not clarify it, and transforms it into a noema.[26]

Such criticisms show, it is to be observed, that the author's attention is shifting away from the problem of knowledge. For *if* the philosophers in question are taken to be giving an epistemic evaluation of the experience of our everyday world, what Merleau-Ponty says is beside the point. Such an evaluation of course presupposes that certain claims to knowledge have been made, in this case the claims inherent in our perceptual experience. And it also goes without saying that the approach taken in such an appraisal is *different* from the approach taken in the claims to be appraised. And it is in some perfectly straightforward sense *guided* by those everyday claims about the world. Without understanding what is being claimed and the circumstances in which it is claimed, the evaluation would not be relevant, would in fact be impossible. But epistemic appraisal of experience *strictly speaking* does not set itself the task of clarifying and in some sense re-establishing the *totality* of our experience by way of an exhaustive phenomenological description. Its focus is on what is believed and on the grounds that are offered, or could be offered, for that belief. The crucial presuppositions made in such a philosophical evaluation of experience is that in our perceptual experiences we claim to know something about the world. That the reflective point of view involved a transformation and in a certain readily intelligible sense a neutralization of that pre-reflective attitude is true, but it is accounted for by the distinction that is made between object and noema. That the reflective appraisal does not address critical questions to itself is likewise true, but this is part of the very logic of appraisal as set forth earlier in this paper. The appraiser can only proceed to evaluate other claims by taking himself to know something, in the light of which knowledge other claims can then be assessed. To put it in terms of the Spinozistic phrase so frequently quoted by Merleau-Ponty himself, the philosopher assumes that we have a true idea (*habemus ideam veram*).[27]

In the criticism I urged above I stated that it appeared from the manner in which the author presents the position of the so-called philosophies of reflection that their arguments could not have any cognitive import for the perceptual experience, that their noema-talk is to be taken as simply about altogether different objects; that it accordingly shows nothing about the cognitive status of perceptual objects; that it could not possibly either endorse or confute their cognitive status. Having taken a closer look at his criticism of those philosophies, I think that my criticism still stands. In fact, the nature of his criticism confirms it. What becomes quite clear from his remarks is the fact that he is in the last analysis saying that the philosophical attitude, in his own language the attitude of reflection, cannot be taken as a clearer version of the attitude of everyday perception, as being nothing more and nothing less than perception freed from its confusion and its liability to error; the objects, so to speak, generated by this attitude could not possibly be in some sense identified with the objects of ordinary perception. In other words, he rejects reflective philosophy, because he attributes to it the pretension that its construction could be looked upon as a substitute for perception as it exists pre-reflectively. That this construction might have to be taken as an epistemological evaluation of perception does not figure in his rejection. I have tentatively put forward the idea that it might have to be taken that way and that, if taken that way, Merleau-Ponty's critical remarks can be set aside as irrelevant. An evaluation of the cognitive status of claims does not have to reproduce, let alone re-enact, the attitude that lies at the basis of those claims. In fact, inasmuch as the purpose of the evaluation is to assess only their truth, the attitude is strictly irrelevant. The one who conducts the evaluation *shows* this in fact by adopting a different attitude, hoping that by using this different approach the truth of those claims can be established. To conclude, the emphasis our author places on attitudes seems to me to show that the problem of knowledge plays no role in his discussion of the philosophers of reflection, although the reader is at first led to believe that they will be shown to have made mistakes in their evaluation of perception.

As stated earlier, Merleau-Ponty's disagreement with the philosophers of the tradition of rationalism and idealism has to do with the *nature* of the cognitive power in correlation with which entities are to be considered – alternatively, with respect to which they are contextualized. For those philosophers, as he interprets them, this power is that of reason, intellect, or thought. He does not disagree with their concern to ward off the threat of the evil genius and their rejection of the concept of being which that philosophical skepticism brought into play. He too rejects the time-honoured idea of being, of entities that are what they are whether or not anybody knows them or can ever know them. Like them he recognizes only contextual objects, which as such fall within the scope of some cognitive power or other. But in his view it is the power of pre-reflective, ordinary perception. Now if an object is considered strictly contextually, it is defined by whatever specific context is indicated in the initial introduction of it. And it logically follows that it cannot be identified with any object outside that context; it can at most be said to be exactly similar to such an object. Although he himself does not argue at such a high level of abstraction, it does seem to me that one would not do a serious injustice to him if one said that by virtue of the logic of contextualization the issue was decided the moment he insisted that objects like noemata, cogitata, or ideata are different from perceptual objects and defined by the reflective attitude which introduces them.[28] For it follows from that point that a discourse which makes no direct reference to any objects other than noemata can at best only sketch a belief-context which has a certain degree of resemblance to the belief-context defined as perception, a resemblance which our author does not think exists.

Merleau-Ponty, then, rejects rationalistic idealism. As he already remarked near the beginning of his *Phenomenology*,[29] to ward off the evil genius and to ensure that we have a true idea, as he puts it with a clear allusion to Spinoza, we do not have to follow reflective analysis and postulate a well-nigh divine subject having within its cognitive scope a system of absolutely true thoughts capable of coordinating all phenomena. We do not need to follow this route, because there is one human act which at one stroke cuts through all possible doubts, namely, the act of perception. How this can be so was explained earlier. The only doubt possible with regard to a perception or a group of perceptions is one which presupposes the truth of those perceptions which make up the standpoint of the doubter. Merleau-Ponty therefore rejects an essential point of philosophical skepticism, namely that there might be grounds to doubt all perceptions at once, that there exist in fact grounds to think that none of them is true. The philosophers of reflection, on the other hand, did not reject that point and accordingly undertook to show without making use of perceptual data that we nonetheless have knowledge of what may be called an external world, albeit a world not accessible to sense perception. Since Merleau-Ponty, however, rejects that point, one could say that he did not think there was a need for a detailed examination of those philosophers's attempts to refute the skeptic, confining himself, accordingly, to the observation that the picture of the world that emerges from them clearly does not resemble the world of sense perception.

Merleau-Ponty's own account of perception is profoundly phenomenological, an attempt to let perception, as it were, speak for itself. Throughout he turns back theories or interpretations on the grounds that they fly in the face of phenomenological data. Perceptual faith as it actually functions, the percipient's body as it is alive in his perceiving of the world, have in a certain sense already solved the problem of knowledge as it pertains to perception. It is the task of philosophy to understand this and to express it in suitable words. No doubts occur here which would call into question perception as such; on the contrary, each falsity can be found out only by virtue of a move that leaves intact the cognitive power of perception as such. Yet I do think that the author recognizes a problem regarding perception which must be dealt with by philosophy. To that end, as I see it, he introduces at the end of *The Visible and the Invisible* the concept of flesh. What is that problem?

II

As I pointed out in the first part of this paper, Merleau-Ponty shares with his rationalist-idealist opponents a contextual view of being. Like them he rejects the realist view according to which being is independent of the knower. While for the realist an entity is at best contingently related to a knower, on the contextual view entities cannot exist in themselves and cannot possibly be unknowable. In terms that have gained currency in the history of modern philosophy, entities are internal to experience.[30] There is, accordingly, no problem of knowledge in the usual traditional sense and no occasion for the radical kind of skepticism voiced by Descartes in his First Meditation. It is strictly inconceivable that we might not possess truth about the world.

On the contrary, it is rather the possibility of error that has at times seemed endangered. For how can a cognitive act fail to correspond, or to be in accord, with its object, if that act defines its own object, if the latter is what it is for that act? We might, therefore, say that on this contextual view of being the possibility of error is more of a problem than the possibility of truth. I think that the history of post-Kantian idealism shows this and Josiah Royce, in fact, formulated it in this way.[31] For the idealist, in order to salvage the possibility of error, it became necessary to elaborate the distinction between a finite and an absolute mind in such a way that it could become intelligible how the object of consciousness might yet escape and leave the finite mind in error. What this distinction amounts to, at least when regarded with this problem in mind, is the admission that the finite mind is after all confronted with an external reality to which it must correspond if its thoughts are to be true, namely the reality of absolute mind. It is here, of course, essential *not* to let this externality be interpreted in the spirit of realism. The reality with which the finite mind can fail to be in accord is not in its essence so far removed from that mind as to be completely foreign to it. It, too, is mind, or consciousness, or spirit. In other words, to salvage the possibility of error we should not endanger the possibility of truth. It is, therefore, to be insisted that this is an externality within a unity. If my thoughts, or the thoughts of a community of individual minds, are to be repudiated as erroneous, it is not being in itself which repudiates them but a higher mind, to whose thoughts entities are internal and with whose thoughts mine do not cohere. From the standpoint of this higher mind the well-known definition of truth as coherence comes into play, because the idea of correspondence was felt to leave the door open for a kind of ultimate skepticism.

Now Merleau-Ponty is not an idealist in the tradition of Hegel, Bradley, Bosanquet, and Royce. But as I stressed from the beginning of this study, his view of being is contextual. And if there is this much community of thought between them and himself, should we be surprised to find analogies between his problems and their's as well as analogies between his way of dealing with them and the way they dealt with them?[32] What separates him from the traditional idealists I have thus far formulated in the thesis that the cognitive power with respect to which he contextualizes is perception, not reason or intellect defined in sharp contrast to perception. And perception is emphatically said to be a power that can never become clear about itself, that is not self-transparent. Its cognitive claims remain beset by the problems arising from their relativity and subjectivity. In the sense that a perception is always vulnerable to conflicting cognitive claims, its object always remains external to it.[33] To be sure, the problem of knowledge thus arising is one that is dealt with within the domain of perception itself, but the object remains external in the sense just indicated. Merleau-Ponty is, in the final analysis, confronted with the question whether the object might not be foreign to our perceptual knowledge claims in the sense in which realists hold that it is, a sense which skeptics fastened upon to present their case. We might put it this way. I stated at the beginning that Merleau-Ponty rejects that kind of skepticism as meaningful because of its assumption of the validity of the concept of being in itself. He now has to assure his readers in an explicit way that the externality which he too attributes to the object of perception is not going to threaten the prospect of arriving at truth about it. In short, he owes his readers a doctrine of being.

Now, to repeat, he is not a contextualist in the same sense as the idealist philosophers mentioned above. Yet he too will have to present a doctrine of being such that it becomes clear that the externality of the world in relation to the finite percipient is not ultimate, that there is also a sense in which there is unity. For only then can it appear plausible to hold that the percipient's inescapable subjectivity does not stand in the way of knowledge, that the percipient has a true idea, as we heard him say it again and again by means of Spinoza's phrase. The metaphysics set forth by Merleau-Ponty is accordingly monistic.

The unity of subject and object envisaged by him is expressed by the term "flesh." But he emphatically states, in terms which again recall Spinoza, that the underlying concept is neutral with respect to the natures of either subject or object. The term "flesh" is, therefore, used here in a very unusual way. It was chosen because the idea behind it is really an extrapolation from what the author thinks is a remarkable situation. It is the situation in which we use our hands. One and the same hand can function as a cognitive organ of touch but also as an object touched by the other hand. The metaphysical position elaborated shows a striking resemblance to Spinoza but even more so to the neutral monism William James set forth in his *Essays in Radical Empiricism* by means of the term "pure experience."[34]

Let us now try to become clear about the precise manner in which this metaphysical doctrine contributes to the author's view of perceptual knowledge. I begin with a quotation that may help us on our way. He states:

> Between the exploration and what it will teach me, between my movements and what I touch, there must exist some relational principle, some kinship, according to which they are not merely, like the pseudopodia of the amoeba, indefinite and ephemeral deformations of corporeal space, but initiation to and openness toward a tactile world.[35]

It would seem that the author's point has to do with the conditions that have to obtain if movements I perform for the purpose of exploring, for example, the tactile qualities of an external object may be taken to have the cognitive value which I in fact ascribe to them, and to be for that reason different from the movements of the amoeba's pseudopodia. The movement of my hand, as we read in the *Phenomenology*, "traverses space like a rocket to reveal the external object in the place it occupies," but the same hand when touched by another hand is nothing more than "a system of bones, muscles and flesh compressed in a place within space."[36] The first distinction involved here is, of course, that between movement as an intentional action and movement of an object from one place to another in space. But the author's real concern is with a question which presupposes this distinction. How can an intentional action have the peculiarly *cognitive* role which it has for the one who performs it? For it to have that role, he goes on to say in the text of *The Visible and the Invisible* immediately following the above quotation, it should take place in the same universe or matrix as the objects it explores. The movements of objects and the places they occupy, as he puts it, should be recorded on the same map as the intentional movements of the percipient's exploring hand and whatever other sorts of movements are involved in our sensuous exploration of the world around us. More precisely, the movements I make, which in some respect are just episodes in my personal life, are also movements on the way to the place where the object is. My sense of where I am now, where I just came from, and where I am going, my sense of where to look for the object I am interested in, are bearings taken within the same universe in which objects exist. But this should not be understood as an attempt to reduce the inner sense of what we are doing and where we are going to the external world of observable space. Inner space and outer space are not to be contrasted as subjective and objective space, so that something taking place within inner space, the space of motor-intentionality, would automatically be suspect as a movement revealing to us something about the external world. We are rather to take them, so it seems, as two distinct but equally legitimate "readings" of the same reality. Neither can claim to represent the nature of reality, to which the other must be shown to be reducible if it is not to be declared illusory.

As stated before, what he is after is a metaphysics such that the ineluctable subjectivity and relativity of the percipient need not be counted against the cognitive status of perceptual knowledge claims. The philosophers of reflection held that the subject with reference to which entities are contextualized is potentially a self-transparent subject, whose powers of thought can be exercized according to broadly logical rules. But the subject which our author brings into play is not at all like that. Its powers are those of the body and are obscure. However, if these powers are somehow of the same "nature" as the objects which by their means we apprehend, their exercise in a perceptual act, so the author seems to think, cannot be cited as a reason for thinking that our perceptual access to the world might be discordant with the reality of that world. To be sure, the knower does not stand outside that which he knows, as the philosophical realist would have it. But if he bears sufficient resemblance to it, he may rely upon his own being to give him knowledge of realities other than himself. In the terms of the situation envisaged in the above quotation, the movements as I sense them from within may be relied upon by me to lead me to a position in which I can be sure that I know what are the object's tactile qualities. The sameness of spatial matrix, it is now suggested, should be taken as representative of the metaphysical state of affairs. *Prima facie* the author's position seems to be a throw-back to the very ancient view that like knows like.[37] But it is clear that the idea of resemblance should not be taken in the sense in which a picture-theory of knowledge would take it or in that broad sense in which all representationalist theories worked with that idea. For Merleau-Ponty has no use for sensations, images, and other mental items that function representationally in perception. His own view of perception is phenomenological and Husserlian: in perception the object itself is taken to be present. There are actually several ideas, beside that of resemblance, which in the text before us compete for our attention. We read, for example, that the access to things through our body is communication, inasmuch as the approach through "the thickness of the body"[38] is constitutive of that thing's visibility. And a few pages further we are told that, since things are not only in front of us but also within us, the embodied percipient employs his own being to participate in the being of things.[39] Without dwelling on the precise meaning of these various assertions it is safe to conclude that Merleau-Ponty interprets the relation between perceptions as a subjective act and the objects upon which it is directed as some kind of part-whole relation. The unitary matrix underlying perception and accounting for its *cognitive* status is, as he says, "a relation of the visible with itself that traverses me and constitutes me as a percipient."[40]

There can be no doubt that this last statement quoted is not to be understood as asserting a causal determinism. Flesh is not to be understood in a physical or physiological sense; it is neutral with respect to the physical as well as the mental. But, to recall my earlier discussion, we do have here an attempt to articulate the unity in spite of externality between subject and object. And if that is so, the contextualism which Merleau-Ponty shares with idealism in the traditional sense suggests that it might be illuminating to inquire about the possibility of error. As I stated earlier, the idealist version of contextualism had the problem of showing the possibility of error, granted its view of the unity in difference that underlies finite consciousness. The realist framework had no problem with respect to error. The non-existence of an object is quite conceivable in spite of a belief in its existence. And on this realist view there may be error, *although* it is never discovered to be error, a point which no contextualist, idealist or otherwise, can possibly admit. The question we want to address to Merleau-Ponty is this: Is the unity he postulates with his concept of flesh such that it has room for the possibility of error?

Before tackling this issue I want to consider a statement which does not yet contain the idea of flesh but does have a direct bearing on the author's doctrine of being.

As for being, I can no longer define it as a hard core of positivity beneath the negative properties that would accrue to it from my vision . . . . The negations, the perspectival deformations, the possibilities which I have learned to consider as extrinsic denominations, I must now reintegrate into being . . . .[41]

What he sets himself off from is clearly the realist view of being in itself, the being of entities indifferent to the subjectivity of our cognitive approach to them with its mistaken and distorted vision, in short its relativity. As the contextualist has it, such modes of appearing belong to being itself, inasmuch as there is a unity of subject and object. Merleau-Ponty shares this view with his idealist opponents. These modes of appearing cannot be said to exist only within a knower who stands outside of the world, as being that part of him which he makes use of in trying to acquire knowledge of the external world. As we already noticed in connection with the statement quoted earlier, the cognitive moves made by a percipient are to be recorded on the same map as the movements of the object explored. And as he says elsewhere,[42] if each perception is embedded in a horizon of possible perceptions, the world itself is horizonal.

Turning now to the question about error, the unity or intimate correlation just noted applies to perceptions quite apart from their being considered as true or false. For all equally exemplify subjectivity and relativity; all are activities of an embodied percipient. And if we regard the unity introduced as the concept of flesh as designed to safeguard the attainment of truth from the threat of ultimate skepticism, then one is not surprised to read that perceptions are all "true".[43] For all of them are occurrences within the same unity of being. We cannot distinguish between them on the basis of the fact that some have objects corresponding to them and others do not, whether or not beings merely human can actually discern that distinction. Even the suggestion of the possibility of an error not recognized as such makes no sense from the anti-realist, contextual point of view held by Merleau-Ponty. To him this would look like a gaping hole in a cohesion which, as he says, does not like a vacuum.[44] Why does it not like a vacuum? Because the purpose a philosopher has in introducing this kind of concept is precisely to capture the unity of all things, in particular, of course, the unity of subject and object. From Merleau-Ponty's point of view, an error conceived as simply a failure to perceive correctly, which would be an error whether or not it was recognized as such, presupposes the idea of being in itself, external to the knower in a sense which his concept of unity was designed precisely to contain. As he sees it, I fall into error only when at the same time the possibility of correction is given.[45]

In what sense then does perception deal satisfactorily with the problem of knowledge, which the author does recognize as a genuine problem? As we showed earlier in this study, perception itself has doubts about some of its own performances and distinguishes between the true and the false. But we have now come upon the concept of a unity according to which all perceptions are true. As I have tried to show, this concept of unity was introduced to secure the possibility of truth, i.e., knowledge. But what if in effect it wipes out the difference between true and false, knowledge and error? To be sure, to the extent that Merleau-Ponty recognizes a problem of knowledge at the level of perception he is committed to a view in which such distinctions play a role. And his epistemological discussions use much of the language of traditional theories of knowledge. Yet the discussion of this paper has led us to a point where we should press the question: Precisely in what sense are perceptions cognitive? Perceptual claims get challenged, we noted, but what is the nature of that challenge? I think we can find an answer to these questions by turning to the discussion in the *Phenomenology* where he deals with the relation between the evident and the true, a topic that is epistemologically crucial in several ways.

What I just called the evident Merleau-Ponty refers to by using the French noun *évidence*. It designates an epistemic experience or situation in which, as we would say in contemporary English, some proposition is so related to a person's mind that it is evident to that person that the proposition is true. Since the English word "evidence" nowadays suggests accredited facts which have a bearing on the epistemic worth of a certain claim or hypothesis, it cannot be used to translate the author's term. What is at issue here is what one might call the epistemic, as opposed to the ontic, aspect of truth: truth as it enters into that relation which we call apprehension by a cognitive being. And in this connection in the phenomenological tradition since Brentano something is spoken of as *evident*, a term which serves to indicate the degree of justification that a cognitive being has for affirming a proposition as true. I called a discussion of the relation between the evident and the true epistemologically crucial for the following reason. When we distinguish between the evident and true, as we must if we are to speak of their relation, we are distinguishing what in an actual, lived epistemic situation is *not* distinguished. What is taken to be evident is believed or affirmed to be true. In making the distinction we have distanced ourselves from that situation and in proposing to talk about the relation we seem to suggest that the degree of justification a particular individual has for making his affirmation of truth might not be sufficient. Such a skeptical conclusion might not actually be reached, but the possibility is suggested by such a stance of detachment. Now if we assume for a moment that the degree of justification someone has for a claim is the highest *anybody* can possibly have for a given kind of proposition, the threat of a skeptical conclusion about the relation between the evident and true becomes very serious for the prospects of attaining truth. If in relation to a large and important domain of propositions such a conclusion were actually drawn, and if the conclusion could not be refuted, it would amount to an acknowledgement that that entire domain is external to the knower in the sense that he could not know anything about it. As I suggested above, it was for this reason that Merleau-Ponty, like his idealist opponents, introduced a concept of unity to keep the true within the bounds of the evident. And we are now concerned to measure, so to speak, the consequences of this move. For that reason I preface my discussion of his text with these remarks that delineate the issues involved, if not stated, therein.[46]

Right at the beginning of his discussion of the evident a reader who is familiar with traditional epistemology will be struck by the fact that the author does not introduce the idea of justification but the ideas of time and motivation. A state of mind in which something is experienced as evident is said to involve experiences not made explicit, and a sedimented history, as he puts it with a Husserlian expression. Something evidently appears to a person to be thus and so, we are told, *only because* of the historical background of the belief in question as well as the framework of ideas in which he operates. If this background and this framework were not left implicit but were made explicit, certitude would vanish and be replaced by doubt.

> Every appearance of a "something" or of an idea presupposes a subject who has suspended self-questioning at least in that particular respect. Which is why, as Descartes maintained, it is true both that certain ideas are presented to me as in fact evident and compelling, and that this fact is never valid *de jure*, and that it never does away with the possibility of doubt arising as soon as we are no longer in the presence of the idea. It is not perchance that what is evident can itself be called into question, because *certainty is doubt*, inasmuch as it carries forward a tradition of thought which can only be condensed into an evident "truth" on condition that I give up all attempts to make it explicit.[47]

In this passage the italicised claim that certainty is doubt is at first puzzling in the extreme. How can certainty *be* doubt. Surely, as G. E.

Moore once pointed out, you cannot evince certainty by saying that it is raining and at the same time say that you doubt that it is raining. Our author, however, is not concerned to sanction this immediate kind of conjunction of the attitudes of certainty and doubt. What he means is, for example, that *within* a tradition or framework of thought something may be evident and certain, while it is doubtful to a person *outside* that context, even to the very same person at a later time when he is "no longer in the presence of the idea."

I think that all of this is in a certain way very plausible. We can all think of examples where it is not merely plausible but obviously true. If we regard belief as a doxastic attitude adopted by a person, it appears to be an act performed and in this perspective it will connect up with a past history of experiences which may be seen as having motivated the formation of that belief, the adoption of that attitude. And becoming explicitly aware of this background of our present beliefs may affect those beliefs so that we distance ourselves from them. But this way of regarding beliefs is not the only way in which we regard them. No matter how closely related they may be to earlier experiences and beliefs, we also regard them as in need of justification, as claims to be defended against challenges. And from this perspective we hold that our beliefs are at least in part due to the objects of those beliefs. In this spirit we say that we believe what we do believe because we see that things are that way. And if pressed further we might say that we see things that way because they *are* that way. The phenomenological credentials of this second view of beliefs are as good as those of the first.

Why does Merleau-Ponty not mention it? Does he hold that perceptual claims are to be considered *merely as attitudes* which might emerge from a historical background of motivations and can only remain what they are as long as that background does not become foreground? Let us look at the kind of challenges he envisages. As noted on more than one occasion, the author emphasizes the general idea that perceptual claims always remain vulnerable to challenge. In fact, I used a situation in which one percipient challenges another as an illustration of that problem of knowledge which he recognizes as genuine. But there are all sorts of challenges issued by one person to another or by one community of culture to another. And not all of them are usually considered as damaging the validity of a belief or claim. When I encounter a tradition of thought foreign to me what is believed may seem to me novel, surprising, strange, bizarre, and even suspect. And those within that tradition will adopt a similar attitude to the things I consider evident and true. By the exchange of various epithets ("strange," "uncouth," etc.), challenges are issued, let us assume, by them to me to change my ways of thinking. Whether I do or not, we would agree that no epistemic question has been decided. I may experience upon first encounter an incipient doubtfulness about the truth of those "strange" beliefs, but one would hardly call that a case of entertaining serious doubts for which I have grounds. Similarly the mere passage of time would hardly as such be considered good enough as a ground for doubt, although Merleau-Ponty seems to attribute this view to Descartes in the text quoted above. We thus rule out certain challenges as irrelevant to the epistemic worth of one's claims. Why does the author not distinguish the peculiarly cognitive challenges in a discussion ostensibly dealing with the question of knowledge?

Does the fact that he does not apparently recognize a distinctively cognitive challenge show that, contrary to what we have maintained throughout this paper, he does not recognize a distinctive problem of knowledge in perception at all? Is his clearly epistemological language in the last analysis misleading? We have noticed that a challenge to a claim to certainty can come from almost anywhere, from any person or consciousness who does not share the background which motivated the making of the claim. Hence, the affirmation that certainty is doubt. Earlier we were led to the conclusion that all perceptions are true, a conclusion that wipes out the distinction between truth and falsity, which one would have thought to be a distinction made as a result of epistemic challenges. It seems to me that both ideas stem from the same source, which is the author's metaphysics. The author's epistemological language is misleading in the sense that his doctrine is better expressed in thoroughly metaphysical terms.

At the beginning of the second part of this study I singled out the problem about the possibility of error, mainly drawing on traditional idealism. I suggested that similar issues might come up in Merleau-Ponty's thought, because of the fact that he too has a contextual view of being. Josiah Royce could present an argument to the effect that, since error is manifestly possible, there must exist an infinite mind or thought. This type of argument is not available to Merleau-Ponty, because he rejects that version of contextualism. Rejecting its critique of the cognitive worth of perception, he contextualizes being with respect to this perceptual power emphatically affirmed as finite. Hence being is itself finite. That means that it is on the scene everywhere, in a perception said to be erroneous as well as in the other perception which confutes it, in the claim of certainty as well as in the one who challenges it for whatever reason. That is ultimately why the evident is the same as the true, the true the same as the false, certainty the same as doubt.

Notes

1. Maurice Merleau-Ponty, *Le Visible et l'invisible* (Paris: Galimard, 1964), p. 19 [5]. Here and in the following notes the first page reference is to the French edition, the next, in square brackets, is to the English translation: *The Visible and the Invisible*, trans. A. Lingis (Evanston: Northwestern University Press, 1968). Quotes follow the original translation fairly closely. Departures from it are not specially noted.

2. Ibid., p. 19 [5].

3. Ibid., p. 21 [6].

4. Ibid., p. 53 [32].

5. Ibid., p. 163 [122].

6. Ibid., p. 25 [9–10]. Italics omitted. While it is not always clear whether a text expresses the author's point of view, here we need not have any doubt, as can be seen from the fact that the same terminology is used in connection with his later development of the concept of flesh. Cf. Ibid., near bottom of page 177 [134]. Students of Merleau-Ponty may think that my talk of epistemic appraisal is inappropriate in view of the author's remarks on the anonymity of perception and his general tendency to view perception as a non-self-consciously enacted performance. But it seems to me that epistemic appraisal is not necessarily a highly self-conciously and deliberately enacted procedure and that speaking of appraisal at the level of perception is unavoidable in a philosophical discussion that wants to give an account of the cognitive aspects of perception. It is for similar reasons that the author himself often speaks of the body as engaged in problem-solving, as being invited or being questioned, when he obviously does not want these terms to be understood in the sense they have at a more sophisticated level of consciousness.

7. Ibid., p. 189 [143].

8. Ibid., pp. 105–6 [75].

9. Ibid., p. 109 [78].

10. Ibid., p. 111 [79].

11. Ibid., p. 63 [40].

12. Ibid., p. 21 [6].

13. Cf. M. Merleau-Ponty, *Phenoménologie de la perception* (Paris: Gallimard, 1945), pp. 458, 466; *Phenomenology of Perception*, trans. C. Smith (London: Routledge and Kegan Paul, 1962), p. 400, 407. (Page references to this work will follow the practice stated in note 1 above.)

14. *The Visible and the Invisible*, pp. 49–50 [29].

15. Ibid., pp. 75, 62 [50, 39].

16. Ibid., p. 59 [37].

17. Ibid., p. 60 [37–38].

18. Ibid., pp. 60–61, 104 [38, 73].

19. Ibid., p. 60 [38].

20. Ibid., p. 62 [39].

21. Ibid., p. 59 [36].

22. Ibid., p. 54 [33].

23. Ibid., p. 51 [30].

24. Ibid., p. 55 [33–34].

25. Ibid., p. 56 [34].

26. Ibid., p. 59 [36], p. 62 [39], p. 67 [43].

27. The phrase is alluded to three times in the text at the moment under discussion (51, 56, 69 [30, 34, 44]). It occurs in Spinoza's *Tractatus de intellectus emandatione* (*Opera* [ed. Gebhardt] II, p. 14). In Spinoza's text the phrase occurs within parentheses, reminding the reader very briefly of a point elaborated elsewhere. That point is Spinoza's central contention that "a true idea must necessarily first of all exist within us as an innate instrument" (ibid., p. 14). It is aimed to avoid the infinite regress which is generated by Descartes's view that the discovery of truth requires an antecedently devised method. The devising of such a method would presuppose the possession of a cognitive power. We should, therefore, begin by actually accepting the fact that some of our thoughts are true and then proceed by using the power envinced in such thoughts to extend our knowledge of truth by devising ever better instruments of inquiry. It is no use to want to refute skepticism and to exorcise the evil genius by a method which ostensibly bestows upon a given recognition of truth a worth over and above its own intrinsic worth. In short, this is what he says by means of his well-known aphorisms, "truth needs no sign" (ibid., p. 15) and "truth is both its own norm and that of falsity" (*Ethics* II, Prop. 43). Although the *nature* of the cognitive power is a point of disagreement between Spinoza and Merleau-Ponty, the general logic of their positions is the same.

28. Husserl was, I think, more subtle in this matter. The central importance of the phenomenological reduction in his thinking led him, of course, to emphasize the difference between the natural and the transcendental-phenomenological attitudes and their correlative objects, but in the fourth part of the *Ideas* he argued that within the object of the phenomenological attitude we have to distinguish a kind of central point which is not essentially defined by any one set of predicates ascribed to it in a given belief-context. In consequence, an object contextualized as object of such and such beliefs

could be identified meaningfully and truly as the same object which also exists in reality. See my elaboration of this issue in "Husserl's Concept of Existence," forthcoming in *Synthèse*.

29. *Phenomenology*, p. 50 [40].

30. *The Visible and the Invisible*, p. 53 [32].

31. Josiah Royce, *The Religious Aspect of Philosophy*, (New York: Harper, 1958), chap. 11.

32. A reader of S.B. Mallin's monumental study, *Merleau-Ponty's Philosophy* (New Haven: Yale University Press, 1979), cannot fail to be struck by the frequent mention of Hegel (e.g., pp. 98–99, 106, 208, 241, 266).

33. See Professor Mallin's remarks about the social dimension of being in the final chapter of his book.

34. It seems, therefore, that he is mistaken when he remarks that what he calls flesh "has no name in any philosophy" (p. 193 [147]).

35. *The Visible and the Invisible*, p. 176 [133].

36. *Phenomenology*, p. 108 [92].

37. *The Visible and the Invisible*, p. 179 [135].

38. Ibid., p. 178 [135].

39. Ibid., p. 181 [137].

40. Ibid., p. 185 [140].

41. Ibid., pp.107–8 [76–77].

42. Cf. ibid., pp. 116, 136 [84, 100].

43. Ibid., p. 65 [41].

44. Ibid., p. 184 [140].

45. Cf. *Phenomenology*, p. 344 [297].

46. Ibid., pp. 452–56 [395–408].

47. Ibid., p. 454 [396].

Part V.
Hermeneutics of Persons
and Places

11. Place: A Certain Absence[1]

Joseph C. Flay

Hegel presented, in his system of philosophy, a complete meta-physics. It was a metaphysics of presence in the traditional sense that all that which is stands as a whole and has meaning as a whole, and is to be encompassed in one, complete account of what it means to be, i.e., of what it means to be present. For such a metaphysics, everything which exists is understood to exist in terms of a place which I shall call "objective place," a place which is structured by various sorts of categorial systems and which, ideally, could be comprehensively comprehended in terms of an ultimate categorial system. If one is confronted with an immanentist metaphysics such as Hegel's, the ultimate ground of what-is is taken to be what-is itself, structured in terms of the categorial system. If one is presented with a pre-Kantian, transcendent metaphysics, then the ultimate ground of what-is is taken to be God or Nature or some other kind of being which exists, ultimately in mystery, outside of or in some way transcendent to objective place. But in all such systems, immanentist or transcendent, there is a metaphysics of presence in the sense that the task is to make intelligible what is present in being, i.e., to articulate and explain the Being of beings. Everything, in the end, is reduced to the ground of presence.

At the same time, all such traditional accounts of the Being of beings evidenced a certain absence which could not be reduced to absence as simple non-presence, which could not be understood simply as the presence of non-presence, a dialectical difference which left absence still a matter of presence. The ground of presence, be it God, Nature, or the concrete Absolute Idea, referred us to an absence which could not be spoken of as interchangeable in objective place with other beings; for God, Nature and the Absolute Idea were not the sort of thing that could appear and disappear, be present or absent, in the way in which all else that exists could be either present or absent. Therein lay the great difference between necessary being and contingent being: the ground was claimed to have necessary being, what was grounded and was present or absent in objective place had only contingent being.

Thus, God, Nature, and the concrete Absolute Idea could not appear in the place of a particular person, a chair, or a government, as could you or I or physical objects or institutional objects. Rather, in the case of the ground there was a radical absence from that domain of being which it grounded, an absence which was radical not only in the sense that it was not simply non-presence at this or that time in this or that space − not simply non-presence in place − but, to the contrary, an absence which was radical precisely in the sense that it was radically present, everywhere and at all times, such that it could not be relatively absent. The omnipresence and eternality of the ultimate ground was just what made it possible for it to be only relatively absent or relatively present. It was present without limitation; but because it was present in this way, it was also absolutely absent. The only way it could be made present, for example, for a Spinoza or a Hegel, was for us to reach a special level of insight or knowing. The great quest for certainty in the tradition was the quest for this ultimate domain.

In an interesting way, then, just that which was to be understood as absent through not being only relatively present in objective place, was made present as absolutely present. Mystery indicated its radical absence, necessary being indicated its radical presence. Although, by resort to analogy or dialectics, there was a tendency to try to make this radical absence and presence present in a place "like" objective place, there was equally a tendency to assign it to a special place, a primordial place, a place whose characteristics violated the space-time properties of objective place.

It was this inescapable *difference* between primordial and secondary or objective place which always threatened to emerge as a dangerous fissure in metaphysics. Metaphysics was fragile precisely because the radical difference could not be totally ignored, and yet could not be embraced in the comprehensive speech. Neither mystery nor recognition of an ontological difference, neither analogy nor dialectic, prevented the fissure from finally cracking open in the widespread rejection of the traditional metaphysics. Many of the attacks on Hegel and the tradition, emerging after Hegel's "completion" of metaphysics, focused on precisely this weakness, this hiatus, this difference which could not really be articulated and made intelligible, not even by the great Hegel. Hegel's failure dialectically led to Nietzsche, Kierkegaard, Russell, and the main traditions of the subsequent history of western philosophy through both Heidegger and the later Wittgenstein.

But this liberation from the hegemony of metaphysics in turn threatens now to become a new tyranny which aims to place paradox, unintelligibility, mysticism, and perhaps even nihilism in the place of the great metaphysical systems. This seems to be a case — to employ a different metaphor — of throwing out the baby with the bath water. In this paper I want to suggest, in the context I have laid down, that the split created by the pressure of that radical *difference* should not lead to a catastrophic destruction of intelligibility and belief in systematic categorial analysis, but, rather, that it should allow us to glimpse a light not seen before, a light which illuminates the true significance of that sense of place which involved radical presence and radical absence.

I want to take seriously the notion of two senses of presence and two senses of absence, and of two senses of place. First I will examine the traditional sense of place, objective place, the place of ordinary presence, and argue that it cannot be ignored in any adequate description or analysis of experience and reality. Then I shall show that, although there is a radical *difference* involved, primordial place is necessary for the other sense of place, albeit not as the locus of God, Nature or the Absolute Idea, but as a constituent of experience, coexistent with objective place. The two senses of place, while radically different, are at the same time connected. It is radical *difference* which makes experience possible, and which preserves the categorial nature of objective place in relation to the non-categorial nature of primordial place.[2]

Objective Place

The traditional sense of place is that which gives us the usual kind of referent, e.g. place which is geographical, social, practical, physical. These kinds of places are places to which we refer as the *place in which* we are or the *place in which* things, other person, events, etc., are to be found. As such, place denotes certain sets of space/time coordinates understood in terms appropriate respectively to geographical or social or practical or physical place, and I call it "objective" place. Objective place is the place thematized by and depended upon by the natural attitude. It is the sort of place dominated by presence, the presence of beings, and is the place within which things, persons, and events are present.

Objective place gives us a matrix of relative places, i.e., places which are locatable relative to each other, within a more or less clearly designated set of time/space coordinates. Thus, to use an example of geographical place, the place which is Chicago in October, 1985 is a place within another place designated as Illinois in October, 1985; furthermore, within that place designated as Chicago in October, 1985 are many pacticular places, among them the places in which are located this section of Chicago, this campus, this room, this lecturn, those chairs, all of them as they are in October, 1985. The same is true of the temporal dimensions of place. October, 1985 is within the general year 1985 which, in turn is within the 20th century; and within October, 1985 itself are the weeks, days, hours, etc. which count October 1985 as a matrix.

So, Chicago-in-October-1985 is a place within Illinois-in-the-20th century, etc. No particular place within any given place and framework is absolute; rather, all are temporally as well as spatially present or absent relative to all the other particular places which can be fixed as present or absent within the framework. There is no privilege to one place or another within objective place and thus no privilege to any object or event present in such places. Whether something can be designated as present or absent depends primarily on which general framework (e.g. the geographical) and which space/time coordinates encompass the various places. You and I and this room are to be found here and now if the framework is geographical and the coordinates involve Chicago, Illinois, on October 17, 1985; but neither you nor I nor this room are to be found here and now if the coordinates involve New York, New York, on October 17, 1985, or if they involve Chicago, Illinois, on October 1, 1878. The same relativity would be found if we used other spatio-temporal indexicals such as here and then, there and then, there and now. For example, I am absent there and now if reference is being made to State College, Pennsylvania on October 17, 1985, while my wife (one hopes) *is* there now.[3] Such places (and, *mutatis mutandis*, historical, geological, physical, etc., places) are easy to understand and they are the sorts of place to which we ordinarily refer and which have as one of their major characteristics presence and absence in the latter's ordinary relative senses.

As the particular places are relative to each other, so the determination of presence and absence is relative. My presence here before you is relative to your presence before me, within the walls, etc. The presence of that wall (as opposed to any other wall) is relative to the presence of you and I and the specific furniture in this room. Absence is thus rightly determined as the non-presence of something relative to what is present, and consequently absence *can* be defined in terms of presence. This is the heart of the traditional analyses of relations which dominated the traditional metaphysics of presence.

I find nothing wrong with this and, in fact, find it quite correct. Contrary to what some might hold, it is not the supremacy of presence in the domain of metaphysics (and by derivation in other philosophical domains) which signifies an error in the tradition. I see no other way of dealing with the dialectics of objective place and of the identity and difference to be found there. The error has been, rather, in making that metaphysics a metaphysics without limit, a metaphysics of presence which encompasses all modes of being.[4] Attempts to dismiss such a metaphysics *as a whole* seem to me, as I said in my prefatory remarks, to be acts of the proverbial baby-thrown-out-with-the-bath-water variety. If we are truly to understand what has grown out of the critique of Hegel and the "end of metaphysics," best shown perhaps in Heidegger's attempts to discuss *Dasein* and the ontological difference for itself as radically different from what is dealt with by the traditional metaphysics, we must preserve the metaphysics of presence; for it belongs, authentically, to objective place, and objective place belongs authentically to reality and to our experience.

Primordial Place

Tradition, it can be said, gave primordial place to God or Nature or the Absolute Idea by default. In one of several ways it was established that there had to be necessary being such that it transcended in some sense contingent being. Primordial place arises as a kind of place because it functions as a necessary condition for the possibility of what exists in objective place. But I should like to show that the omnipresence and eternality which was attributed to primordial place through the place of God, Nature or the Absolute Idea, in fact is a constituent of experience itself, and not merely by default.

I find myself *in* this room with you, and thus can "place" myself in objective place. I am, in terms of the classical analysis, here-now.

This morning in Chicago (again a secondary place which is one of the possible contextual places for this room) I was in a restaurant eating breakfast. If I stick to my objective mode of discussing place, I can say that I was there-then, i.e., in the restaurant at 7:30 a.m., etc. In keeping with the relativistic nature of place, in so far as I was there-then, I was not here-then. My absence here-then (i.e., in this room at 7:30 a.m.) is fully determinable by my presence there-then and *vice-versa*. Likewise, my presence here-now (in this room at 1:15 p.m.) determines my absence there-now. There is also the relativity of my being here-now (at the present moment in this room) and my being there-then. The *place in which* I can be located as a content can be determined by the dialectic of those indexicals, given an overall geographical framework within which to work.

But in this discussion of objective place something constantly occurred which indicates another sort of place, a place which is in no way a place within the objective matrix. One of the facts about such spatio-temporal matrix is that, given the whole of the place as a matrix, all places are equally present; and within that matrix, there is relative presence and absence, each being only the negation of the other. Thus there is no way in which to give a privilege to one of the places over all the others such that the one place can uniquely and alone identify the other places. And yet, in talking quite naturally about the fact of my being here in this room now excluding my being in that restaurant now, I did distinguish some sort of privileged place. In order to use the indexicals properly, I designated here and now as in this room at 1:15 p.m. ("here" as in this room and "now" as 1:15 p.m.), and being in the restaurant this morning as there and then, i.e., "there" as being in the restaurant and "then" as 7:30 a.m. If I had extended my examples, all other times would have been designated by "then" and all other places by "there." This means that privilege is to be given to this room as the only "here" in the present discourse and 1:15 p.m. as the only "now" in the present universe of discourse. How does this come about?

When I ask this rhetorical question, I sense that most of you probably see a simple answer, which either I am going to give − in which case this will be a simple-minded paper − or I am going to miss and put in its place a needlessly complicated answer to a simple question − in which case this will be an even more simple-minded paper since I did not even see the simple-minded answer. I think there is a third alternative, so please give me a few more minutes before the jury discusses the case.

The simple answer is, of course, that the privilege is due to the designator, in this case myself. There is here only an apparent violation of the "neutrality" of objective place, a violation due to arbitrary or purposive designation on the part of some designator. Objectively, each place is simply what it is relative to other places, and is always that. This room and my presence in it at 1:15 p.m. today, put in objective geographical terms, was exactly this room with my presence in it at 1:15 p.m. today even 50 or 100 or 1,000 years ago, and will be in the future. Nothing changes objectively; and as due to the designator, in this case me, no real violence is in fact done to objective place; for my ability to change designations relies precisely upon the "calm" presence of objective, geographical place. I range over the map, designating and redesignating; or I speak from different places which are relative to each other. This seems to introduce an ambiguity of place, as ambiguity due to the relativity of perspective of the designator who, himself, changes in terms of objective, geographical place. However, the ambiguity seems easily resolved, for as long as one keeps straight just where I am and of what I am speaking, one has no trouble understanding me.

But if we now examine this claim of privilege, a complication arises. Let us imagine that I am in that restaurant this morning at 7:30, talking to someone about this session we are in right now. What would be happening in this case is that this morning at 7:30 in the restaurant would be designated as here and now and this session we are presently in would be designated as there and then. So what is at one moment here and now (while I am reading this paper, this room at this time is here and now) was there and then (as I talked this morning at breakfast about this room at this time) and what is at one moment there and then (while I am reading this paper, the restaurant at 7:30 a.m. is there and then) was earlier in time and in the space of the restaurant designated as here and now (while I was eating breakfast this morning at 7:30 a.m.). In terms of privilege appearing, it not only appears, but radically changes designations of each and every place in terms of the indexicals. What is at one place called here and now is at another place called there and then. There is no objective constancy; rather there is a loss of that stability present in pure, objective place with all positions fixed relatively to all other positions.

The easy answer is, therefore, disturbed by a simple fact: each occasion on which I designate a place, *regardless* of the *place in which* I find myself, I am myself always and everywhere here-now. I never am, as designator of secondary, objective place, any place but here-now. Primordially I am always here-now. This is not to say that I always *am in* the same place; it is to say that I always *am* the same place. What is the referent of place which I am now calling 'primordial,' the place which *I am?*

The referent, in extensional terms, is simply what has been traditionally referred to as the self or person as designator of the spatio-temporal indexicals (i.e., here-now, here-then, there-now, there-then). But it is not the self as a substance of one sort or another; it is, rather, the self as place. It is, to borrow Heidegger's old word, *Dasein,* the "there" or "*da*" of "being-there." It is, literally, the place or clearing in which what appears appears, in which what is present (or absent) is present or absent. But for just this reason – for just the reason that it is always and everywhere the place which and the place "from which" all that is present or absent is present or absent – it is a radically different kind of place. It is a place which is structured as radical absence and radical presence. It is radical presence, for in *whatever,* place I am located objectively – as an object – I exist there not only as indexed or indexible in various objective terms, but as always and everywhere here-now.

There are two possible objections which might arise to this designation of the primordial here-now as an eternal and omnipresent presence. The first is that when I refer to myself as having been in the restaurant this morning I refer to myself as being there and then. Thus, I am as relative as this room at this time or the restaurant this morning. But this is not an objection, for when I refer *to* myself *I* am referring, i.e., it is in terms of and from the primordial place of here-now that I refer to myself *as an object in objective place* there and then. Secondly, the difference between the primordial and the objective is not contradicted by the fact that all objects in objective place preserve identity relative to other objects over changes in place. If it were simply a matter of general preservation of identity through change, there would be no uniqueness of reference.

Presence as primordial place, then, is not relative to an absence; for the place *which I am* is never absent, even when I refer to myself in the past or the future. But, on the other hand, that radical, enduring, all-pervasive presence is also a radical absence; for as place of designating, as clearing, it is not and can never be made present. It is a certain absence which is different from relative absence. As primordial place it is precisely an absence from the presence-absence of secondary, objective place which makes the relativity of presence-absence possible. That it is a *radical* absence is evidenced by the fact, already alluded to, that it is a constant presence, a presence which is never effaced, never metamorphized or relativized into absence. The primordial here-now is always and everywhere here-now, regardless of what occurs in the relativized place of secondary frameworks.

For example, here-now is presently designated by me as this room at a certain time on October 17, 1985. Yesterday, here-now was designated by me as somewhere else at some other time, and if I were now back at Penn State, here-now would be designated by me as somewhere else at this very time. But this "violation" of objective places has no effect on what is present or absent in those places (save the presence or absence of myself as one of the objects located in that objective place, and the fact that it can be designated by me as here-now). My presence *qua* primordial place is, to be sure, linked to my presence *in* secondary place; but *qua* primordial place I make no difference. It is as though my "presence" as this eternal, omnipresent place were invisible or did not exist; and yet my presence as such is the only locus of the power to be the origin of indexical designation for secondary place.

The radical presence is, therefore, a constant which gives privilege to place. All secondary places are simply relative and thus no indigenous privilege belongs to them. They are present *or* absent, depending on the context. But as primordial place I am never absent in that sense in which something can be *either* present *or* absent. This constancy gives the stability which allows for designation.

The radical presence is self-referential as well as being other-referential. As indicator, as indexer, I refer to various objective places. But in each such reference, the constancy of primordial here-now is also necessarily referred to; for it is that constancy which anchors the reference made in the objective indexing. Here-now is always and everywhere the place *in which I am*, and it is so *derivatively from the pure here-now which I am*. This does not mean that there is an identity between the place *which* I am and the place *in which* I am; for the place *in which* I am retains all of the characteristics of relative, objective place and the sort of presence/absence which constitutes it as such a place. It means, rather, that they "co-exist;" and they-co-exist in such a way that there is an asymmetry in their relation as places. The sort of presence belonging to the place which I am is completely absent from the place in which I am; but the presence/absence of the place in which I am is a presence/absence not only relative to other objects in that place and places related to it, but also relative to primordial presence.

This latter characteristic is an important one; for the asymmetry is what gives birth to the tension and ambiguity which structures any complete analysis of "self" and experience. There is a kind of eternity and omnipresence to the self as place. It is an eternity and omnipresence because it itself does not change: here-now is always and everywhere here-now, and the experiencing self *qua* experiencing self is *never* there-then. It is an eternal present, if you wish, a present in both the spatial and the temporal senses of that term. But it is an odd sort of eternity and omnipresence if we take for a paradigm the traditional sense of being an infinite instant with no change; for while the here-now is always here-now, it is *also* true that the content changes in the sense of constantly involving new secondary places which have not yet occurred before and in that particular space. The "change of place" involved objectively is also involved in this eternity. But that does not alter the fact that the place which the experiencing self *is* does not change. This ancient puzzle – that the self is permanent in the sense of preserving identity over time and space *and* that the self is ephemeral in the sense of changing identity over time and space – is rooted in this double sense of place structured in an asymmetrical way. The primordial here-now *is* eternal and omnipresent only in contrast with and in coexistence with the changing of places and thus the changing of experiences. What is indexed by any person *qua* primordial here-now is constantly of a differing character and is in constantly changing objective places. The primordial here-now exists only in tension with the secondary and designated here's, there's, now's, and then's which are "indexed" from a point of reference which is nothing other than the primordial here-now.

Conclusion

The conclusion I wish to draw from this at the present time, and the notion on the basis of which I want to think it through further, is that the metaphysics of presence, with its traditional categorial schemes, must be an integral part of any adequate analysis of what it means to be as one who experiences the world. As an integral part, it is not something that can be left aside in order to talk either of that which cannot be reduced to presence in the conventional sense, or in order to talk about the radical *difference* which holds between objective and primordial place. Without the kind of eternality and omnipresence which belongs to primordial place as "I," presence does indeed become an all-devouring monster which destroys the essence of being human, which effaces what is means to "be there." However, without the dialectics of presence and absence or non-presence captured only by the recognition of *relative* difference, the *radical dif-*

ference between relative presence-absence on the one hand, and radical presence and radical absence on the other hand, must be lost. Thus, in that radical difference between the two modes of presence-absence, there is contained as well relation, not as a difference held within an identity, but as a difference which needs both the radicalness of presence and absence *and* the relativity of presence and absence in order to be radical difference. It is a difference held within two differences.

The fissure which destroyed the traditional metaphysics does not appear here; for there is no primordial place postulated as a necessary being on the grounds of necessity for the possibility of reality. The difference of which I speak, rather, evidences itself in a phenomenological unity, with no question of necessity and contingency, of actuality and possibility entering into the matter. But as a phenomenological unity it does not remain purely descriptive; there is a great explanatory power there also, for example with respect to the structure of referring and thus of intentionality. Presence is not to be effaced, but to be refined.

Notes

1. In the whole of my discussion it is to be understood that place involves necessarily space/time, and is not to be taken as synonomous with space. Both space and time are by themselves abstract; for every lived space is space at some time and every lived time in some space. Contemporary discussions which focus on temporality alone as central – misled, I think, by Kant – are in the end abstract and have themselves been misleading and even self-defeating. Thus, the terms 'present' and 'presence' will refer to space/time, and not to time alone or space alone.

2. In what follows, I want only to concentrate on one aspect of this difference, that of the spatio-temporal difference or the difference of place in this sense only. I do not want to claim that this is the only nor that this is necessarily the most important aspect of the difference in the senses of place. I find it important to insert this proviso here – a limitation not explicitly made in the original presentation at SPEP in Chicago, but certainly intended as a limitation to be understood – because of the excellent and constructive commentary offered by James Risser and by many in the audience. In general, this essay is among the first attempts to flesh out what I have suggested in my earlier essay, "Categories of Comportment," in *Categories: A Colloquium*, ed. Henry W. Johnstone, Jr. (University Park: The Department of Philosophy, The Pennsylvania State University, 1978), pp 121–41, and in the final chapter of my *Hegel's Quest for Certainty* (Albany: State University of New York Press, 1984).

3. I shall now make use of the spatial indexicals "here" and "there," and the temporal indexicals "now" and "then." There are four possible indexical combinations: here-now, there-now, here-then, and there-then. The indexical combinations involving "then" indicate both past and future. To these, of course, can be added the pronominal indexicals (I, you (singular), she, etc.), yielding a much more complex set of combinations. But there is no time to consider these in the present paper.

4. That they did not do this is one of the virtues of the thought of both Jaspers and Levinas.

12. I and Mine

Bernard P. Dauenhauer

For centuries, one of the staples of Western thought has been a rather specific conception of what a human person is. On this conception, the person is understood, as Clifford Geertz has put it, as "a bounded, unique, more or less integrated motivational and cogitive universe, a dynamic center of awareness, emotion, judgment and action organized into a distinctive whole and set contrastively both against other such wholes and against a social and natural background."[1] Though Descartes was by no means the father of this conception of the human person, the self, the Cartesian *cogito* provided it with a powerful and influential articulation. In the wake of Descartes, Enlightenment thought in its various dresses has often exalted the self to quasi-divine status, or at least ascribed to it an angelic independence from the physical and cultural context in which it acts.

Recent years, however, have witnessed a considerable reassessment of what is to be claimed for and about selves. A number of influential arguments have been advanced which deny that the individual human person is the source of any significant originality. Rather, according to these analyses, the human person, the self, is fundamentally a product or a result of some other set of forces or factors. The self is, to use Cartesian terminology, nothing more than a particular intersection of basically extensional properties.

Thus, one finds today analyses of man in terms of his genetic make-up, or in terms of his social functions or roles, or in terms of power relations of some sort. For sociobiologists, all of a person's performances are ultimately explicable in terms of survival of gene pools. The individual person is nothing but the bearer of a particular configuration of genes. For Levi-Strauss, the self is not an historically

216

located actor, but rather is simply a set of structural transformations.[2] For Althusser, human actors do no more than occupy positions within effectively self-contained structures.[3] For Benveniste, at least on one reading, the I is not the author but is the effect of the act of speaking.[4] Or, turning to the Anglo-American philosophical scene, for Anthony Kenny, the pronoun "I" does not refer. Citing Wittgenstein, Kenny argues that mind is simply a second order ability which consists totally in the ability to acquire first order abilities.[5]

The ultimate sense of any analysis of these sorts is that, in principle, either alone or with other analyses also dealing exclusively with extensional properties, it can deal exhaustively and comprehensively with its subject matter, namely human beings and their performances. On all such analyses, what Geertz calls the Western conception of the person, the self, appears nowhere. The self, if it is mentioned at all, explains nothing. Rather, it is itself simply an *explanandum*, something to be explained by factors other than itself.

In this paper, I have no intention of trying to reinstate some Cartesianesque Western conception of the self. But the recent reaction against that conception appears excessive. Some version of the traditional Western conception of the person, the self, seems to me to be indispensable for a thorough account of human phenomena.

Following clues to be found in Heidegger, Ricoeur,and others, I want to argue that though structures and causal sequences of various sorts are admittedly necessary conditions for the occurrance of any human phenomenon, they are not sufficient conditions for all human performances. They are not sufficient conditions for the occurrence of qualitively new human phenomena. Even if all human performances, once they have occurred, are fully analyzable in extensional terms, there is genuine novelty in human matters and this novelty is not fully explicable without resort to something like the Western conception of the self. After having defended this thesis, I will briefly suggest a way of characterizing this self.

The sort of self for which I intend to argue is in all respects historical. History is not without structures. But these structures do not constitute a closed field, a field which precludes genuine initiative. As Anthony Giddens has said,

> every process of action is a production of something new, a fresh act; but at the same time all action exists in continuity with the past, which supplies the means of its initiation. Structure thus is not to be conceptualized as a barrier to action, but as essentially involved in its production.[6]

The possibility of novelty does not require a self which stands outside of history and episodically intrudes itself into the historical field. It does not require a Cartesian subject. It does, however, require an agent who can constitute events by causally intervening in the ongoing processes which make up the world. Intervention of this sort entails that the agent could have acted otherwise.[7]

Before proceeding to present evidence in support of my thesis, let me say something about the logic of my argument. First, I do not claim that I can definitively prove that selves exist as sources of novelty. So strong a claim risks falling into the fallacy of ignorance. I must admit that even if presently proposed sets of necessary conditions for the occurrence of all human phenomena do not amount to sufficient conditions, it is not logically impossible that some as yet unformulated proposals might articulate both necessary and sufficient conditions for all human phenomena.

Rather, my argument claims that, given the set of phenomena that I will point out, it makes sense to acknowledge the existence of selves to account for them. My argument, therefore, deals with "contingent necessities." It has both factual and conceptual elements. None of the phenomena to which I will point out necessarily exists or occurs. But if they do occur, then there is good reason to acknowledge the existence of selves.

Second, the evidence supporting my thesis, because it is drawn from relatively independent lines of inquiry, can be said to be "robust." In scientific investigations, a result is called robust to the extent that it is invariant under a multiplicity of at least partially independent processes across which invariance is shown.[8] There is more reason to have confidence in robust results than in those issuing from just one line of investigation. Considerations of robustness are applicable to the determination of both entities and properties.[9] I take it that they are applicable to the question of the existence and character of things like traditionally conceived selves.

One last caution. My claim that we should admit the existence of something like a self does not entail either that every member of the biological species *homo sapiens sapiens* is a self nor that a self is of intrinsic moral or a aesthetic value. Though I happen to believe both of these things, they are fundamentally unrelated to the argument that I wish to make here.

Let me begin my case by turning to *Being and Time*. Heidegger provides there the ontological characterization of the sort of self for which I wish to argue. Consider first his discussion of mineness. Mineness, along with existence, is a distinguishing characteristic of

Dasein's way of being. Dasein is always mine to be in one way or another. It is always a decided upon way of comporting itself toward its ownmost unique possibility. That Dasein can be either authentic or inauthentic is rooted in its essential mineness.[10] Because of its essential mineness and existence, Dasein cannot be treated as merely a special case of entities in the world. "Because Dasein has *in each case mineness*," Heidegger says, "one must always use a *personal* pronoun when one addresses it: 'I am', 'you are'. "[11] On this basis Heidegger can go on to discuss Dasein's way of Being-in-the-world in such a way that though it is never worldless, neither is Dasein just another constituent item in the world. In the final analysis, if the things of the world are to make sense, they can do so only by reason of Dasein's distinctive way of being, by reason therefore of its mineness.

The mineness characteristic of Dasein is made fully explicit when it is considered in terms of death. "Death, as the end of Dasein, is Dasein's ownmost possibilty – non-relational, certain and as such indefinite, not to be outstripped. Death is, as *Dasein's* end, in the Being of this entity *towards* its end."[12]

And Heidegger continues:

> Death does not just "belong" to one's own *Dasein* in an undifferentiated way; death *lays claim* to it as an *individual Dasein*. The non-relational character of death [as opposed, to the context of relations making up significance or meaning], as understood in anticipation, individualizes Dasein down to itself. This individualizing . . . makes manifest that all Being-alongside the things with which we concern ourselves, and all Being-with Others, will fail us when our ownmost potentiality-for-Being is the issue.[13]

Later, in "*Was Heisst Denken?*" Heidegger gives further specificity to man's distinctive way of being when he distinguishes between capability and possibility. Only men are capable. To be capable of something means: to allow something to be close to us in accordance with its own being and constantly to look after what has been allowed close. That of which we are capable (*vermögen*) is always what we desire (*mögen*), that to which we are devoted in that we let it come.[14] Man's way of being, then, is not merely to be the outcome of any set of antecedent conditions upon which he depends.

These ontological considerations of Heidegger's, inimical though they clearly are to any doctrine positing Cartesian subjects, by no means require that the Western conception of the person be completely jettisoned. Rather, they point to a distinctive entity, a self, which can act into the world and take responsibility for what it does. Further, these same considerations can be filled out and made robust by paying attention to a cluster of phenomena all having to do somehow with language and its deployment. Let me concentrate here on four of these sorts of phenomena.

Consider, first, Alasdair MacIntyre's arguments, in *After Virtue*, for the systematic unpredictability of human affairs. These arguments, as he points out, do not preclude the logical possibility of the universal predictability of human affairs. But no available *material* evidence butresses this mere logical possibility. Indeed, just what could count as material evidence for universal predictability is conceptually opaque.[15]

Of the four arguments which MacIntyre marshals to defend this thesis, let me focus on the one he presents against the possibility of predicting specific conceptual innovations. He asks us to imagine a discussion in the Old Stone Age concerning the possibility of predicting the invention of the wheel. Someone asks: "Wheel? What's that?" The forecaster then describes the wheel. His interlocutor can then reply: "No one is going to invent the wheel. You have just done it." As MacIntyre explains:

> In other words, the invention of the wheel cannot be predicted. For a necessary part of predicting an invention is to say what a wheel is; and to say what a wheel just *is* is to invent it . . . . Thus the notion of the prediction of radical conceptual innovation is itself conceptually incoherent.[16]

The point I wish to stress for purposes of the present argument is that since there have in fact been conceptual innovations, there have been unpredictable events in human history. But if analyses of human activity in terms of antecedent structures or causal sequences could be exhaustive, then one would expect at least the prospect of total predictability. In the absence of such a prospect, however, there is no basis for insisting that all human phenomena can be accounted for without admitting human initiative. There is, then, room for an efficacious self.

MacIntyre goes on, however, to set forth a refinement of considerable importance. Unpredictability, he notes, does not, by itself, entail inexplicability. Unpredictability, he says, is logically compatible with a strong version of determinism. Nonetheless, it is logically impossible that anyone be able to predict his own decisions, innovations, etc. Therefore MacIntyre concludes:

Insofar as the observer cannot predict the impact of his future actions on my future decision-making, he cannot predict my future actions any more than he can his own; and this clearly holds for all agents and all observers.[17]

Determinism, then, is not logically refuted by the unpredictability of innovations. Yet one could give a coherent deterministic account of his own innovations or decisions, and its impact on others, only if he abandoned first-person descriptions of what he had done in favor of third-person accounts. But this shift itself begs for explanation. To give a complete, comprehensive deterministic account of his total conduct, one would have to explain his shifting from one sort of description to the other sort in a third, "neutral" language. There is, however, no material evidence to support the claim that such a neutral language could be discovered.

MacIntyre's reflections on conceptual innovations, and the evidence they provide for an initiating self, bear striking similarities to central features of Paul Ricoeur's theory of metaphor. And Ricoeur's metaphor theory also points to a self capable of efficacious agency.

In *The Rule of Metaphor*, Ricoeur shows that genuine, fresh metaphors are not merely decorative or ornamental. They are cognitively significant. They both introduce new meaning and necessarily claim to articulate something true.[18] Such metaphors, according to Ricoeur, hold in abeyance direct or ordinary linguistic reference. They promote, and are themselves part of, a redescription of reality, a redescription which alters the way in which men inhabit the world. The truth articulated in fresh metaphor is not that of straightforward correspondence with an already established, routinized concept of reality. Rather, the truth of metaphor is that *aletheia*, that unconcealing of the previously hidden, of which Heidegger speaks. In Ricoeur's terms, the truth of metaphor is a tensive truth, a truth that says of p both that it is and that it is not q. The tensive truth of metaphor does not pretend to simply mirror the world. Rather, it effects a fresh relation between man and world.

These metaphors involve a semantic impertinence. They thus overstep the bounds of established linguistic usage. Once fresh metaphors have been produced, they may, Ricoeur acknowledges, be analyzed in terms of antecedent structures or causes. But these analyses cannot account for the *event* of the actual production of new meaning. And, I would add, the fresh metaphors, rather than being simply the consequences of antecedent patterns and structures, themselves modify the antecedent conditions whence they spring. Unless one reifies these conditions, there is no reason to think that the fresh metaphor for which they supply necessary conditions will not, when actualized, affect their own efficacy. To the contrary, such a modification is precisely what one would expect.[19]

The existence of fresh metaphors points to the existence of an author. This author is not, of course, Descartes's imperial ego. Nor is he the romanticist's genius. He always inhabits a language and a social matrix containing numerous elements whose functions are predictable. But this author is not merely an intra-systematic functionary. While living within the system, he both keeps the system from total closure and modifies the system by bringing something distinctive, namely his semantic initiative, to the structural resources of the system.

Once the author has effected an innovation, that innovation can be studied and analyzed without reference to him. But without his initiative there would be nothing new to be analyzed. All of this is simply another way of saying that a) if language can be said to have a history, and b) if history is something other than mere process, if history involves novelty as well as routine,[20] and c) if history is intelligible *qua* history, then authorial initiative must be acknowledged.[21] But to acknowledge authorial initiative is in fact to acknowledge the existence of selves.

Let me shift now from discussions of initiatives and novelties within language to a consideration of certain features of language and discourse themselves, which also point to the existence of a self as a sort of entity fundamentally distinct from other kinds of things. Attention to these features is particularly appropriate inasmuch as arguments relying on certain results of linguistic investigations have furnished a large part of the impetus for the movement to dismantle the traditional Western conception of the self.

For some years now, analyses of language employing the techniques of modal logic have concluded that the first person singular pronoun enjoys a special status among linguistic elements. Hector-Neri Castanada's conclusion is representative of the results of these studies. He says:

> The first-person pronoun has . . . an ontological priority over all names, contingent descriptions of objects, and all other indicators: a correct use of "I" cannot fail to refer to the entity to which it purports to refer; moreover a correct use of "I" cannot fail to pick up the category of the entity to which it refers. The first-person pronoun, without predicating selfhood, purports to pick out a self *qua* self, and when it is correctly tendered, it invariably succeeds.[22]

What can and cannot be said consistently about the I to which the first person pronoun refers shows that the I never has properties, e.g., weight, in just the same way that other entities have them. And so, Castanada concludes: "The I is not an entity that either exists contingently or necessarily. It is not, in that sense, an entity in the world but an entity outside the world that must be identified in terms of entities in the world."[23]

One need not subscribe to Castanada's talk of the I as an entity "outside the world" to find evidence in his analysis for the existence of selves. But it is useful for present purposes to notice his conclusion that the I must be identifiable in terms of entities in the world.

Further, to find evidence for the existence of selves, one need not claim, as Castanada does, that the first person pronoun has an ontological priority over all other indicators. It is sufficient to notice the linguistic irreducibility of what Colin McGinn calls "the subjective view." McGinn argues that the indexicals "now" and "here" are just as secure against reference failure as is the I.[24]

One of McGinn's central theses is that perceptual experience and direct cognitive awareness cannot be articulated in a language devoid of indexical concepts and concepts of secondary qualities. He argues that we must distinguish between two sorts of thought. Non-indexical thought is the sort of thought employed in mathematics and the sciences. In such thought, "the world is conceptualized without selecting any particular point of view as privileged."[25] Indexical thought is the sort of thought connected with engagement in practical affairs in the world. In McGinn's words: "What phenomenologists would call 'being-in-the-world' presupposes indexical thought."[26] And he adds: "Similarly, to have perceptual experience of an object the object must be perceived to have qualities whose instantiation conditions make essential reference to properties of the perceiver, i.e., to the kinds of experience he enjoys."[27] Thus if secondary qualities are to be ascribed in any way to the world, then this ascription must proceed through reference to a subject of awareness from which they spring.[28] And this reference to a subject cannot fail.

In McGinn's general argument there is a somewhat latent dimension which is particularly pertinent to the case I am presenting here.[29] If indeed there are these two distinct sorts of thought with their respective appropriate vocabularies and grammars, and if one and the same entity deploys each of them in turn, then there is reason to claim that this entity, if it can switch from the one to the other, must be relatively independent of each of them, must, in effect, be a self.

One might of course say that because an entity is independent of each sort of thought does not entail that it is independent of their conjunction. True enough from the purely logical standpoint. But just what the conjunction of these two distinct sorts of thought would amount to is fundamentally opaque. Until this opacity is removed, there is no reason to discredit this sort of evidence for the existence of selves.[30]

One finds the kind of switching indicative of selves in other guises. Consider the following feature of discursive practice. All discourse has the following form: A says p about x to B.[31] In any deployment of discourse, the emphasis can be placed primarily either on saying what is most appropriate about the topic x or what is most accessible to the audience B. So far as I can tell, no actual instance of discourse avoids emphasizing one rather than the other, though neither emphasis necessarily obliterates concern for the unstressed constituent. The apparent necessity for selecting one emphasis rather than the other constitutes one of the principal problems for all pedagogy. When and how are these emphases to be distributed?[32]

The relevant point here is that discursive practice shows the possibility of selecting and shifting emphases. Though there are customary guides to appropriate selections and shifts, these guides are both questionable and regularly questioned. Specific selections and shifts are made possible by but are not fully determined by either discourse, the topic, or the audience. In their concrete specificity they point to an agent, a self exercising initiative, a self who is responsible for the shifts and selections actually made.[33]

This consideration provides a basis for challenging Kenny's claim that a pronoun "I" does not refer to anything. Kenny would analyze the human being into a set of first-order abilities and their exercise, together with a second-order ability to acquire first-order abilities. The exercise of every first-order ability involves some bodily vehicle, e.g., eyes for seeing. His analysis, however, does not account for the person's ability to switch from exercising one ability, of either order, to exercising another ability. This ability to switch is not of the same sort as either the first-order or the second-order abilities recognized by Kenny. The ability to switch from one sort of ability to another, an ability which is applicable to all of the abilities Kenny acknowledges, points to a responsible agent, a self who deploys its several specific abilities on its own initiative.

This ability to switch among abilities, each of which has a determinate field of exercise, is closely connected with the ability to perform silence. Silence is a complex, positive phenomenon.[34] It does not, however, have a well defined object belonging to a determinate field of activity. As such, performances of silence show their performers possess a relative independence from each determinate field of human endeavor. They show their performers to be selves.[35]

This congeries of evidence, drawn from several relatively independent lines of investigation, yields the robust result that there are indeed selves. The powers of these selves resemble in important respects those connected with what Geertz has called the "Western conception of the person."

None of the evidence I have adduced, however, implies that the self can be the topic of direct inspection or study. On the contrary, the thinkers upon whose results I have drawn hold, either explicitly or implicitly, that however this self is to be described, its description is achieved indirectly, by examining the contexts into which it is born, in which it lives, and from which it expires. Many of the contexts are "extensional" contexts. All of these results are consistent with Heidegger's description of how a self comes to grasp itself. He says:

> Because as existents we already understand world beforehand, we are able to understand and encounter ourselves constantly in a specific way by way of the beings which we encounter as intraworldly. . . . In understanding itself by way of things, the Dasein understands itself as being-in-the-world by way of its world.[36]

Unlike Cartesianesque selves, then, the historical self can be understood only in the worldly inscriptions of its doings and sufferings. The evidence I have assembled here by no means warrants any claim that the positive essence of the self has been disclosed. Nonetheless, it does furnish non-trivial grounds for proposing something like the following sketch of the self.

The self appears in its linguistic, fabricational, and actional performances. None of these performances is uniquely privileged or radically decontextualized. There is, therefore, no "key" to the self. Nonetheless, the self is experienced and encountered in and through its multiple performances as an abiding complex agent. The self is a sort of story. It has a theme, but the theme is, as long as it lives, never irrevocably settled.

This self neither shows nor knows itself as a whole. But neither is it a mere product of a fabrication or the outcome of a process to which it contributes nothing. What has it, it also has. It cannot be without being had by antecedent contexts. But it, in turn, stamps these contexts as at least partially its own.[37] The self somehow both works on its context, which presents itself as either problematic or maleable, and authenticates the results of its work. The self, in Giddens's terms, reflexively monitors both its own performances, the performances of other actors, and the setting of their interaction.[38] To quote Giddens:

> The communication of meaning in the processes of interaction does not just "occur" over time. Actors sustain the meaning of what they say and do through routinely incorporating "what went before" and anticipations of "what will come next" into the present encounter.[39]

The self's power to monitor both its own performances and its setting makes it possible for the self to seek absent or new meanings. It can move beyond the traditional certainties and confident beliefs into which it was born. In living out its own undoing of its established sense of itself, the self discovers that its unity is, in Edward Ballard's terms, a dramatic unity.[40] Its unity is one of "non-identity."

Such a self, of course, has no private knowledge. What it knows of itself is, in principle, knowable for others. But it always knows itself as something other than an empty frame upon which the structural and causal contexts it inhabits can inscribe just whatever they will. This self can both address and be the addressee of spatio-temporally specific moral, political, religious, and artistic claims. For example: "Will you help me now?" It is capable of both freedom and responsibility. And of alienation. It is autarchic, but never angelic.

In sum, then, the evidence I have adduced gives robust support for the conclusion that selves, in the traditional Western sense, exist. These selves and their doings cannot be exhastively analyzed in purely extensional terms. This same evidence provides no succor to those who would defend a Cartesianesque, substantial self. The self described in this evidence is a curious tale, a tale which tells itself. It finds itself already begun and, though it senses its ending, it must leave the sense of its ending as well of as its beginning to its equally curious fellow tales.[41]

Notes

1. Clifford Geertz, "From the Native's Point of View," in *Interpretive Social Science*, ed. Paul Rabinow and William M. Sullivan (Berkeley: University of California Press, 1979), p. 229.

2. See Anthony Giddens, *Central Problems in Social Theory* (Berkeley: University of California Press, 1979), p. 29.

3. See Louis Althusser and Etienne Balibar, *Reading Capital* (London: New Left Books, 1970), pp. 180–89. "The structure is immanent in its effects in the Spinozist sense of the term, . . . *the whole existence of the structure consists of its effects* . . . . (The structure) is merely a specific combination of its particular elements, is nothing outside its effects" (pp. 188–89). For a good overview of this and other continental analyses which claim to undercut the distinctiveness of the self, see Giddens, *Social Theory*, pp. 9–48.

4. See Samuel Ijsseling, "Hermeneutics and Textuality," *Research in Phenomenology* 9 (1979): 10.

5. Anthony Kenny defended this position in the untitled paper he read at the "Continental and Anglo-American Philosophy: A New Relationship?" conference at the University of Chicago, May 11–13, 1984. See also G.E. M. Anscombe, "The First Person," in *Mind and Language* ed. S. Guttenplan (Oxford: Clarendon Press, 1975), p. 59.

6. Giddens, *Social Theory*, p. 70.

7. Ibid., pp. 55–56.

8. See William Wimsatt, "Robustness, Reliability, and Multiple Determination in Science," in *Scientific Inquiry and the Social Sciences*, ed. Marilyn M. Brewer and Barry E. Collins (San Francisco: Jossey-Bass, 1981), pp. 124–63, esp. pp. 126–28.

9. Ibid., pp. 144–47.

10. See Martin Heidegger, *Being and Time*, tr. John Maquarrie and Edward Robinson (New York: Harper and Row, 1962), pp. 67–69.

11. Ibid., p. 68. See also Heidegger, *The Metaphysical Foundation of Logic*, tr. Michael Hein (Bloomington: Indiana University Press, 1984), pp. 188–89.

12. Heidegger, *Being and Time*, p. 303.

13. Ibid., p. 308.

14. Heidegger, "Was Heisst Denken?" in *Vorträge und Aufsätze* (Pfullingen: Neske, 1967), Vol. 2, p. 3; *Basic Writings*, ed. David Krell (New York: Harper and Row, 1977), p. 345.

15. See Alasdair MacIntyre, *After Virtue* (Notre Dame: Notre Dame University Press, 1981), pp. 96–97.

16. Ibid., p. 89.

17. Ibid., p. 91. My emphasis.

18. See Paul Ricoeur, *The Rule of Metaphor*, tr. Robert Czerny with Kathleen McLaughlin and John Costello (Toronto: University of Toronto Press, 1977), p. 7.

19. Ricoeur himself suggests something of this "rebound" effect. See his *Rule of Metaphor*, pp. 87–89.

20. See in this connection Hannah Arendt, "The Concept of History: Ancient and Modern," in her *Between Past and Future* (New York: Viking Press, 1965).

21. For a discussion of this issue from another angle, see my "Authors, Audiences, and Texts," *Human Studies* (1982): 137–46.

22. H.-N. Castanada, "On the Phenomeno-Logic of the I," *Akten des XIV Internationalen Kongresses für Philosophie*, Wien, 1968, p. 261. Husserl, it should be recalled here, speaks of the "primal 'I' . . . which can never lose its uniqueness and indeclinability." See his *The Crisis of European Sciences and Transcendental Phenomenology*, tr. David Carr (Evanston: Northwestern University Press, 1970), p. 185.

23. Ibid., p. 266.

24. Colin McGinn, *The Subjective View* (Oxford: Clarendon Press, 1983), pp. 53–55. He explicitly criticizes here G.E.M. Ancombe's position referred to above, and thereby implicitly attacks the Kenny thesis I have mentioned.

25. Ibid., p. 91.

26. Ibid., p. 91.

27. Ibid., p. 91 fn. 32.

28. Ibid., p. 93.

29. McGinn does deal, under another heading, with the dimension with which I am concerned. He recognizes that his position poses problems for physicalist accounts of experience. He himself, though, does defend a specific version of physicalism. See the *Subjective View*, pp. 137–45.

30. This argument parallels MacIntyre's contention, discussed above, that a full account of determinism would have to be couched in a "neutral" language, but that no such neutral language is either available or in prospect.

31. See in this connection Richard Bauman, *Let Your Words Be Few* (Cambridge: Cambridge University Press, 1983), p. 14.

32. See in this connection, Paul Ricoeur, *Interpretation Theory* (Fort Worth: TCU Press, 1976), p. 22.

33. The possibility of shifting emphasis between the topic and the audience also makes possible the historical distinction between rhetoric and science. However much one might today want to attenuate this distinction, it is hard to claim that all discourse has the same manifest emphasis. Styles of discourse differ from one another and are deployed at the discretion of the speaker.

34. See Bauman, *Let Your Words Be Few*, pp. 10–11 and 30.

35. For more detailed argument, see my *Silence: The Phenomenon and Its Ontological Significance* (Bloomington: Indiana University Press, 1980), esp. pp. 54–82. Arendt makes a comparable point in terms of thinking and its independence from space-time. See her *Between Past and Future*, p. 13.

36. Heidegger, *The Basic Problems of Phenomenology*, tr. Albert Hofstradter (Bloomington: Indiana University Press, 1982), p. 171. See also H-G. Gadamer, *Philosophical Hermeneutics*, tr. David E. Linge (Berkeley: University of California Press, 1976). Gadamer says: "Self-understanding only realizes itself in the understanding of a subject-matter and does not have the character of a free self-realization" (p. 55).

37. Emmanuel Mounier makes something of this same point from another standpoint. See his *Personalism*, tr. Phillip Mairet (London: Routledge and Kegan Paul, 1952), pp. 39 and 59–64.

38. Giddens, *Social Theory*, pp. 56–57.

39. Ibid., p. 84.

40. For an interesting account of the self, see Edward Ballard's *Man and Technology: Toward the Measurement of Culture* (Pittsburg: Duquesne University Press, 1978), esp. pp. 124–29, and his *Principles of Interpretation* (Athens: Ohio University Press, 1983), esp. pp. 216–25. See also Heidegger, *Foundation of Logic*, p. 139.

41. I am grateful to James Bernauer for his stimulating, incisive comments on an earlier version of this paper.

13. Individuation, Mimetic Engulfment, and Self-Deception

Bruce Wilshire

I.

What is an individual self?

The response of the man in the street is perhaps to laugh a bit and to point at one. Why ask questions which have obvious answers? There's one — call it number one — and there's another — call it number two. Just as one number cannot be another number, so each self is itself and not another. Each self is right there in its own place — and two things cannot be in the same place at the same time. When a self moves, it carries its identity within the envelope of its skin, in the way that it carries its guts or its brain. With stunning clarity Bishop Butler said, "Each thing is itself and not another thing," and he spoke both for the common man and for many theorists.

The surest way to beg the question of the identity of a self is not to see that it is a serious question. But if we beg the question we ought to feel guilty, I think, because if people are just as separate as their bodies, then why is their behavior so lacking in individuality so often? Why is it that contagions of imitative or mimetic behavior have swept through human history so regularly? Why are the mass movements and mob movements such fundamental and pervasive phenomena — from the Saint Vitas dance of the Middle Ages, to Nazi masses saluting, to fads of consumption and display in our industrial societies, to single styles of thought and expression that clamp themselves on "individuals" paid and tenured to keep open minds and to think for themselves — college professors working in the mainstreams of their professional specialties? Something particularly opaque, pre-rational, and elusive must be going on between human beings imitating one another, something very difficult to see. It challenges the common assumption that beings we call "individuals" *are* individuals, that is, independent existences.

The locution "individual self" turns out to be seriously ambiguous. The first sense is dominant and is used by ordinary persons in the run-of-the-mill activities of life — pointing out different persons, keeping the children straight at home, issuing summonses to court, etc. Somewhat remarkably, it is also the sense dominant in most traditional philosophical and technical psychological systems: the third-person point of view of the detached observer and thinker summoning human "substances" or "subjects" (read: *objects*) one after another before his eyes, or before the "eye" of his mind. The conditions which individuate a body, and which are sufficient to pick it out from others, are assumed to be the same as those which individuate a self. One body equals one self: it is all or nothing; there is no room for degrees of individuation of self.

But there is another less obvious sense of "individual self" which crops up occasionally in ordinary life. It revolves around the first-person point of view — the complex experience of one's own identity. It shows up, for example, when we say of an adolescent, "He's having an identity crisis," or when he says "I am trying to find myself." Everyone knows how to pick out the adolescent's body from others's bodies, but the crisis of individuation of that *self* remains. This sense of "individual self" leaves room for degrees of individuation, and for notions such as compromised or imperfect individuation. Although experienced in what we call "the first person," this sense of individual identity is related in distinctive and subtle ways to the identity of the group.

It is this complex and subtle sense that I believe to be much more revealing of the reality of our lives, and I will dwell upon it. Before I do, however, I will review briefly the dominant tradition of the third-person point of view and its cruder sense. When the question of identity of an individual self is raised in this cruder sense only, the question which ought to be raised in the more complex sense is concealed — and begged.

Now it might be objected that my characterization of the third-person point of view as crude is itself far too crude, at least with respect to the work of philosophers. Has not Wittgenstein already

shown that while the man in the street may think that he is pointing
out independent existences, he can point out individual humans only
because he tacitly supposes a sense of what they have in common?
The ordinary man differentiates within a presupposed grouping
which he cannot articulate. Only this enables him to discriminate one
human from another. And thousands of years ago Aristotle maintained
that every *this* is a this some*what*. There is a common essence. Why
should not this explain the contagions of mimetic engulfment which
I claim to be misunderstood and neglected?

Without wishing to minimize the importance of Aristotle's point
– and its various embellishments in the history of philosophy – I con-
tend that its conception of the common, or universal, is inadequate to
explain mimetic engulfment. It is too schematic, taxonomical,
biological.[1] It does not grasp how *our experience* of others experiencing
our common human traits is constitutive of who we *are* as individuals.
A being might be picked out as an individual and not experience at all
the other who picks him out.

And why assume that this other who does the picking is a human
individual? Because somebody else picks *him* out? But why assume
that the one who picks out the one who picks out is an individual self?
We are involved in an infinite regress. Some conditions of experience
of self are being overlooked.

Aristotle said many profound things, e.g., that it is our nature to
gain a second nature, that we gain it through socialization, and this is
largely imitative. But his analysis of how we experience this being-
with-and-for-others – the psychological aspect – is incomplete. It is
only when we newly and radically understand the first-person point
of view – understand how I experience myself experienced by others
as human – that we can avoid assuming what ought to be proved: my
identity as an individual self.

There is a vivid example of the depth of the prejudice which I
have stigmatized as the crude third-person point of view. It occurs in
the *apparently* radical first-person viewpoint of Descartes in the seven-
teenth century. Given his conviction that only measurement secures
a reading of objective reality, the question "What is pointed out when
we point at a human being?" generated the answer, "Only movements
of an organism along various metrics." No mind, no awareness, can be
pointed out in *rerum natura*. Luckily, however, one mind, the observer's or the thinker's, points directly at itself. All perceiving is a
perceiving of itself as a perceiving – and of a perceiver – said
Descartes and John Locke. Mind is conceived to be a mental substance
that in pointing perpetually at itself constitutes itself within itself –

an immaculately conceived individuation and identity. The skeptical problem, arises, do other minds exist at all? Etc., etc. Mind points itself out and forgets the question of how it can do so.[2]

Hidden within the apparently radical first-person point of view of Descartes is the third-person point of view that simply assumes that separate substances exist and point out themselves and each other. The only difference is that mind has become such a substance, and the question of individualization of self is begged in a new way. (The individual self is supposed to be a composite of individual mental and physical substances.) There is a new conception of what is common to such mental substances, but the old prejudice lies under the surface, because it is assumed that the conception of what is common is adequate merely if it is adequate *for the purposes of pointing out.*

Let us try to do something very difficult: to free our minds of prejudice of reference and to describe phenomena or appearances just as they appear – in this case the phenomenon of perceiving. When we do we confront Descartes at the foundations, it seems clear that most perceiving is *not* perceptive of itself, and so *a fortiori* not perceptive of the perceiver; that perceiving is characteristically lost and absorbed in the thing perceived. And the key question of just how one unsticks oneself from the perceived and becomes conscious of one's individual perceiving and individual self is not asked by Descartes, and thus begged in the crudest way. Is it not quite apparent that all reflexiveness must arise from a pre-reflective and pre-rational absorption in the world, that the very models and paradigms of selves are those other bodily selves appearing right there in space – but they need not appear *as* other – and that we must raise and answer the question of how self-reflexiveness and self-identity can arise?

II.

Atomistic notions of individuation and reference prompt us to beg the question of individuation of self, i.e., the question of identity of individual self. This can be avoided only by taking a completely different approach to the question. We need a "field" approach. On this view individuals do not first exist and then get assembled into fields or communities. A field of reciprocating recognition individuates selves to certain degrees at particular points within the field. The whole is primordial, the individual derivative. At first glance this is Hegel's view, and certainly he provides many profound insights. The self arises only when it recognizes another self, recognizing it to be human. This is profound, yet Hegel leaves a crucial ambiguity. Need the other be recognized *as* other? If so this begs the question of individuation of self, for if the other is recognized *as* other, then I must be tacitly recognized as distinct from this other. My self must be regarded as already individuated, and the question of individuation of self is begged, not confronted. Differently put, Hegel seems to suppose that the "it" which recognizes another recognizing it to be human is already an individual consciousness. But this is already too much; it begs the question.

Hegel, "the German Aristotle," does in fact perpetuate in subtle ways Aristotle's tendency to overvalue traits which distinguish and individuate at the expense of traits which are shared.[3] There can be no doubt that there is *the* Absolute and *the* Concept and that it precisely alienates itself and distinguishes itself within itself. Hegel's remorseless attacks on his erstwhile mentor, Schelling, are well motivated. For he discerns that Schelling's notion of identity as the locus of differences is not sufficiently precise to ground a dialectical logic.

There is something right about Hegel's critique; he was right to feel threatened by Schelling. But Schelling's views have great compensations and values, particularly for an inquiry such as ours. Contrast presupposes kinship; and, ironically, the contrast tends to eclipse the kinship, the common ground, which makes the contrast possible. The deeply intuitionistic and artistic Schelling was ever aware of how opaque – and in a sense bottomless – this common ground is. Everything figural and individuated appears in this world only for moments, and appears only against a background that cannot ground itself. Schelling cannot find the logic of the Concept that will set the dialectical oppositions going, and thereby spin-out the content of the empirical world. Schelling can talk about individuals "as such" in their "whatness," but there is always left over an unclarified residuum which they share. This "ground," from which the rationalist would like to derive the world, turns out to be an abyss, an *Abgrund*. Ultimately we must find what is shared by identity and difference. This can only be the identity of non-difference, the "night in which all cows are black," as Hegel put it sarcastically. Hegel, the logician, could not imagine this to be the luminous darkness, the fertile darkness, of which the mystics speak.

Schelling could never completely give up his rationalistic ambitions, and his metaphysics is pushed forcibly and creatively into an impasse, as Heidegger says.[4] Here we can only touch in the most cursory way some implications of his thought for philosophical anthropology and self-deception. Schelling suggests that we need not beg the question of individuation of self. The look of the authoritative other falls into the *ground* and excites it.[5] The ground is not outside the self, but it is not within it either. The individual self with its powers of deliberate control has not yet crystallized. The look of the other excites a craving for unification within the ground. But this craving is blind; it cannot clearly distinguish the unity which is the group, the corporate individual, from the unity which is "the individual self" – the being we so easily call the individual and assume to be located in an individual organic body. That there are individual organic bodies is a fundamental fact; yet this guarantees no primordial "mineness" of self, individuality of self.

Schelling's artistic talents and sensibilities go hand in hand with a great phenomenological skill for capturing and describing the elusive phenomenon of constitution of self within community. He suggests new approaches to self as a complex field phenomenon, one in which individual bodies experience themselves through others, from "the first person." But they gain sharply demarcated self-referentiality and clearly marked individuation as selves only occasionally.

It is chastening to realize that Edmund Husserl himself – the founder of a phenomenological science of consciousness and appearance – seems to have given excessive emphasis to the cruder sense of "individual self" as something referred to, and to have begged the question of identity. Chastening because his whole intent was to record things just as they appeared, hot off the griddle of our contact with the world, unprejudiced by theoretical preconceptions about the role of "referents" – "objects" or "substances," mental or physical, causal or otherwise. The hope was that we can then go on to distinguish leading from misleading appearances.

Just how do selves appear, according to Husserl? His phenomenological method varied their appearances in his imagination until he reached the various limits of their appearance, and these limits marked the concept or essence – the suchness – of what they appear to be. At what points does what presented itself as a self cease to present itself as such? The limits of appearance determine the "shape" of the concept of the self as it appears.

But Husserl seems not to have examined just how he was raising the question of how selves appeared. He seems not to have examined the primal "how" of his own imagining. It was while sitting alone in his armchair reflecting. He just assumed that it was *a* consciousness, *his own* stream of consciousness. He just assumed his own individual identity. His act of critical reflecting was uncritical of itself and of its own assumptions and conditions, and he wound up in his *Cartesian Meditations* saddled with an elaborate and tortuous version of the Cartesian argument from analogy to try to explain how other minds and selves can be at all. He remains committed to a primordial mineness of individual self.[6]

Despite the advances of Husserl's phenomenology, he stays loyal to a tradition in which the world is polarized into individual subjects and the individual objects they point out. We must break through this question-begging individualism and ego-centrism and its corollary thesis of objects which are posited and scrutinized by this ego-soul. We must explode the presumption of an ego that turns its tunnel-vision hither, thither, and yonder, fixing, objectivizing, denuding, and casting into question everything it spies – everything, that is, except itself.

Well, what if basic ideas of self, soul, ego, person, individual are derived from *others*, and as they *relate* to others? What if every self must understand every self (including itself) in general terms applicable by any self to any self? Thinking this way, we will have completely reversed the problem of "other minds" inherited from the Cartesian tradition. The problem now becomes: How does one know one's own mind and one's own self? *Is* there an individual self? Might there be degrees of individuation at different times? Destructive enough? How can terms and traits applicable to anyone by anyone – hence general terms and traits – get applied to oneself so that one's particularity is not utterly drowned out, assuming it to exist at all? For we certainly cannot assume that one's particular self exists in splendid isolation from one's experiencing and understanding of that self. A self is supposed to *be* self-conscious – self-conscious in its being. We are dealing not merely with epistemology but with ontology. The question is thorny: since we must understand ourselves in terms applicable to anybody, to what extent are we *individual* selves at all?

III.

By *mimetic engulfment* I mean a situation in which two or more human bodies, ("selves" in the crude sense) are imitating each other undeliberately. It is reported that infants only two weeks old learn rapidly to imitate adults' facial expressions.[7] It is either highly doubtful or inconceivable that this could be done deliberately. But this mimetic engulfment is not limited to infant behavior. It has been noted by students of "kinesics" and "body language" that adults often imitate each other without being aware of it; hence, they must be doing it undeliberately. This is voluntary behavior in some broad and important sense, but it is typically not deliberate. It is not a chosen act preceded by deliberation.

Aristotle's concept of the voluntary is very broad and it will help us some. He defined it negatively as any action not done from compulsion or from ignorance.[8] By compulsion he meant some force external to ourselves which renders us helpless to defeat its effect upon us (like a hurricane moving our small ship), and by ignorance he meant ignorance of the situation in which we act which is nonculpable, that is, ignorance of things that destructively deflect our actions from their intended ends and of which it cannot reasonably be claimed that we ought to have apprised ourselves of their presence. Voluntary actions comprise an immense set, of which "chosen" acts – voluntary actions preceded by deliberation – are but a small sub-set. Voluntary actions are all actions which proceed from ourselves rather than from another person or agency, and which are not significantly mediated by factors in our situation of which we ought to have been aware.

This analysis is helpful, but it is not sufficiently fine-grained for our purposes. Aristotle's conception of what is internal to one as opposed to external, of self and other, of self and situation, is too rough for us. This renders his notion of non-culpable ignorance too rough. It does not fit some of the facts. An action can arise from oneself and be destructively deflected by *another* of one's intentions of which it *can* be reasonably said that one ought to have been aware of it. *I* want to regard this as a voluntary action. I think we must make room for such actions if we would explain self-*deception*. In a definite sense of the terms we voluntarily and intentionally keep ourselves from fully recognizing our own intentions, and we do this by voluntarily and intentionally keeping ourselves from fully recognizing how we become mimetically engulfed in others.

We can, in fact, be *somewhat* aware of intentions to conceal ourselves from ourselves, and *somewhat* aware of losing ourselves in mimetic engulfment with others in order to bring this about. We must very carefully describe phenomenologically these chiaroscuro modes of awareness. In some instances of self-deception it is just because we can verbally acknowledge that our intention with respect to the other is A, that we can prevent ourselves from acknowledging what we dimly recognize nonverbally: that our intention with respect to the other is non-A. In instances of self-deception which involve greater degrees of engulfment and of lack of awareness it may be difficult to tell how we voluntarily conceal ourselves from ourselves. There may be no capacity for even nonverbal acknowledgement to self of the intention to conceal one's intentions from oneself in one's mimetic situation with the other. Perhaps we must direct our attention a step backwards to that shadowy area of consciousness in which we voluntarily undermine our capacity for any awareness on any more voluntary and more focally conscious level. At the deepest level of engulfment the greatest philosophical perplexities arise. Here we suppose that there is no recognition of the other as the other, hence no recognition of one's individual self because no recognition of oneself as other from the other. But at a preceding moment there may have been enough awareness of self to voluntarily set in motion that mode of interaction which prevents even the capacity for self-awareness to be present in the next mode.

At this deepest level the most difficult questions arise, not only with regard to self-deception but also identity of self. *Is* there an individual self at those moments when there is no capacity for self-awareness? Is what we call identity of individual self really, at best, an occasional matter, and is the identity of the corporate individual, the culture, with all its mimetic patterns of engulfment and attunement – inherited or emergent – the more fundamental identity?

How is self-deception possible? How is it possible to *voluntarily* keep one's *own* conscious project, one's *own* intention in *some* sense, concealed in some degree from oneself? There must be an intention to conceal the intention and this meta-intention must be concealed. We must hide and hide the hiding; the very project of self-deception must itself be in self-deception, as Sartre has said. The logical mind may be inclined to dismiss this out of hand as impossible, inconceivable. But our visceral intuition is that something very like this happens frequently and often with momentous effect. If it is actual, it must be possible – now how? First, we appropriate a fundamental distinction of William James's phenomenology of consciousness in *The Principles of Psychology*, that between the focus and margin of consciousness.[9] We must finally get clear on the vague, James says. In the field of consciousness the focus is the tiny portion which we clearly perceive or apprehend. Thousands of elements and relations hover on the nebulous fringe; they may become focal the next instant, they may not. Here is a clue: out of the corner of the eye we can apprehend an intention in the margin as "not to be faced squarely." In our analysis as philosophers we are forced to use these words to describe what is being apprehended as having this character, but really it is being apprehended *nonverbally in the margin*. And the intention to *keep* the intention in the nonverbalized margin *is itself* marginal, nonverbalized, unfaced. We hide and hide the hiding.

In this type of self-deception I wish to discuss how a powerful added factor abets the self-deception of the project of self-deception. It insulates it from the focus, from that which is clearly perceivable and acknowledgeable to self, typically verbalizable to self, and perhaps even to others. It is the other person as apprendend by self – but not apprehended distinctly *as* other – and with whom the self stands in mimetic attunement or engulfment. This is my development of Schelling's notion of ground, the idea of a prereflective, pre-individual, anonymous mimetic field. It is plausible to suppose that some of the facial expressions imitated undeliberately by the infant have become permanent imitative tendencies, permanent susceptibilites in certain social situations. Engulfment is almost inevitably regressive and archaic.

But if the field is truly pre-individual and anonymous how can a condition for self-deception be met, that the intention to deceive oneself be one's *own*? As already suggested, in Schellingian fashion I affirm the temporality of existence and experience. For self-deception to *begin* there must be some sense of individual self, otherwise we get some sort of radical self-mistaking, a self-obliterating which is not a self-deceiving. But it is possible to assign some responsibility which was shirked at an *earlier* moment. We voluntarily set in motion behaviors which we sense will result in self-obliteration, or near self-obliteration, at a later moment. This sensing is not focal or thematic. Even if we maintain that the self is a body (though not one exhaustively analyzable physiologically), it is a body already formed mimetically through others, and which can so allow itself to slip under the influence of others that it can come to believe that it is only what it believes the other believes it to be. That is, the body as imperfectly individuated self becomes mimetically engulfed in the other's apparent belief about it; this is voluntary in the broad sense. And if the other's supposed belief is counter to what the body-self does not want to face and believe about himself, this reinforces his own denial. Indeed, if he can construe his mimetic partnership with the other as owing to motivations different from self-concealment – as he so easily can – then he can both hide the to-be-hidden and hide the hiding; the feat is accomplished. All that he can acknowledge is that feature of himself which is the object of the other's supposed construal; he cannot acknowledge his manipulation of self and other which has produced his construal of the other's construal.

IV.

It would be a mistake to suppose that Husserl has nothing to teach us about self-deception. His technique of free − or fictive − variations can help us show the nature of self-deception. The technique is not limited to formal subject matters such as mathematics and geometry but can illuminate the murkiest levels of experiential content. (Indeed, he himself suggested that the productions of artists can serve as free variations on experiential possibilities, but this suggestion has been almost completely ignored, and the development of Schelling's insights neglected in the bargain.[10]

I am supposing that mimetic engulfment is the key to a certain prevalent sort of self-deception. As engulfment increases, the clarity and degree of individuation of individual self decreases. Depth of self-deception should be directly proportional to this decreased individuation, and by depth I mean the degree of difficulty of breaking the spell of self-deception. So I propose that we freely vary examples of self-deception along with a continuum of increasing degrees of mimetic engulfment. Let us see if self-deception increases in depth as we do so.

We should also be able to discern those factors which remain present and invariable as we go through this continuum of variation from the least to the greatest degrees of engulfment. We will conclude that the invariable factors are essential to the phenomenon of self-deception we have chosen to study. Let me anticipate. *In all our examples of self-deception the same general pattern will be evident: a voluntary engulfment in the other that presents his view of one as being such that one's motivations in voluntarily engulfing oneself in him are concealed from oneself.*

The least degree of mimetic engulfment would seem to be cases which resemble games. We engage in them practically deliberately, and our awareness of our hiding and our hiding of our hiding is almost focal, and we prevent it becoming so just for the fun of it. Some flirtations are of this sort. Perhaps because we are aware that the other is playing the same game and we sense that no destructive consequences could issue from our sport. These cases barely count as self-deceptions and we break out of them at will. At the other end of the spectrum is profound, deeply archaic self-deception which is difficult or impossible to acknowledge even under the most favorable circumstances and with the best will. Let us delve in this direction along the continuum. We will be exhibiting increasing degrees of mimetic engulfment, further variations on how we voluntarily confuse and blur together our own desires and feelings and the other's desires and feelings. (It is a clarification, I believe, of what psychiatrists call "the defense mechanism of projection.") In each case we corrupt our ability to reflectively grasp ourselves by corrupting our ability to utilize what a truly candid and perceptive other might have told us about ourselves. From more or less innocent games we soon become involved in serious matters.

Take next what we like to call "frank" discussions. It is possible to accomplish the feat of apprehending one's projects non-thematically and vaguely as the to-be-hidden, and to hide from oneself the hiding of them, if one can allow oneself to so slip under the influence of the other (as one understands the other) that one can believe one is just what the other believes one to be, and the other believes one is not hiding anything. Both persons are being "frank" and "open," so how could one's motivation for undertaking the discussion *possibly* be to hide oneself from oneself and to hide the hiding? Thus the strange aura that hovers about many "frank" discussions, as if it were a cloud of vaporized acid secretly corroding everything. It smells almost sweet. We squirm and love every minute.

This case exhibits a greater degree of mimetic engulfment that did the first, and this is required if the appearance of frankness or seriousness is to be maintained. This appearance may or may not become so self-deceptive that one or more of the parties involved are "carried away" and come to take it seriously. If so, serious words become serious deeds. In the next case we increase the mimetic engulfment and the seriousness of the behavior. We see that it is now difficult or impossible to break the spell of the self-deception; the difficulty is directly proportional to the depth of self-deception, and both are proportional to the degree of seriousness. For the more serious the matter to be concealed from self by self, the deeper must be the self-deception.

Let us appropriate an example from Sartre and turn it to our own purposes.[11] A young woman is invited out by a man who, she knows, will try skillfully to seduce her. This troubles her. Nevertheless she accepts his invitation, for she finds him attractive, and, while engaged in an intellectual conversation, allows him to take her hand, a move which she knows − in a nonthematic and vague way − sets the seduction in motion. She falls into self-deception. But perhaps the woman is hypocritical, not self-deceived, it might be objected, for she can see that that hand opened to his is *hers* and that *she* has accepted his advances. No, not so; she can acknowledge it at the time, and later she may tell us sincerely, "It happened in a dream."

In order that the young woman's nonthematic sexual project and desires be non-thematizable by her, she allows herself to so slip under the influence of the other that she believes she is just what he believes her to be, and that he believes her to be incapable of sexual desires and projects. Let us say their conversation is about Platonic love. Since the explicit topic of the conversation is the reverse of what she means to accomplish in the project of her self-deception – the conversation is about the value of nonsexual relationships when what she means to accomplish through this is the hiding of sexual desires, the hiding of the hiding, and the accomplishment of a sexual relationship – then the assertion of the conversation as her goal will subvert her awareness of it as her means (to the opposite); indeed, she will acknowledge it as her goal precisely in order not to be able to acknowledge it as the means which it is. She is pathetically sincere.

The woman does what she deeply wants to do: she imitaties his belief about her – or rather what he appears to her to believe about her. And he appears to her to believe this because she tacitly wants him to appear this way. She wants him to appear in such a way that she is relieved of responsibility for herself; indeed, relieved from an awareness of this desire to be relieved. Self-deception is self-reflection that defeats self-reflection; it is Cartesian nightmare.

What we have said is correct, I believe, but it is overly simplified because overly intellectualized. It is not simply that the young woman is voluntarily engulfed in the seducer's apparant belief about her. She is mimetically engulfed in his body, as this appears to her. In all likelihood she is acting out archaic responses to those early authority figures who molded her mimetic life. She allows him to stand in for her, and for key figures in her life who stood in for her earlier, and who interpreted her to herself. Here is one of her archaic "roles" into which she can slip nonthematically: "nice little girl for the big, nice man." At this moment she is an individual self in only a compromised sense. The man is a skilled seducer because he understands that she is to become aware of her flesh, but only through the obscuring mediation of his flesh. She and the man conspire to make her aware of her flesh, but not *as* hers, and certainly not *as* her conspiring adult self. She colludes with him to relieve herself of responsibility, and she does this by becoming engulfed in his body.

In the next case we increase still further the degree of mimetic engulfment and find a correlative increase in self-deception. This must be the case because what must be concealed is "plainly" aggressive and destructive behavior. Here the voluntary engulfment is a discounting and discrediting of the other as witness rather than a flattering masquerading of him. (Of course, even in the preceding case the woman subtly discounts and degrades the man, in counterpoint to his obvious degrading of her, in the sense that she discounts whatever capacities he might have for engaging in a nonseductive relationship.) There is a way in which I condemn another for being picky and squeamish – imagine that we are at dinner together – that discounts him as a witness to my behavior – he is "simply disgusting," an "insensate lump." The more picky I find him, the more my pickiness concerning his pickiness is obscured. The to-be-hidden is my pickiness; the hiding is an absorbing engulfment in the other's pickiness, a repetition of archaic, communal, and habitual modes of rejection; the hiding is itself hidden because in seeing him to be a disgusting, insensate lump I cannot see him seeing me to be anything at all, therefore, cannot see that I see him this way in order not to see the pickiness in me. I am connivingly merged in the other's apparent blindness. My own pickiness and squeamishness dissolves, blurs, and undermines self-recognition; the world is reduced to a mass of slime. And so on, e.g., aggression against the other's aggressiveness undermines the capacity for reflective recognition of my aggressiveness.

Let us vary the example slightly. Again, I look down upon the other for what I condemn myself for, if I had not undermined my ability to accurately reflect – let us say this time the voraciousness and sloppiness of my own eating. Self-rejection slips into other-rejection – a magical but in its way very real consumption of the other. The bodies emerge experientially because they are colludingly isomorphic, as if two mirror images collapsed into each other. I condemn another with the very words which, if I could reflect, I would know apply to myself. Indeed, I already know, in the sense that an incompletely individualized self has a pre-reflective consciousness. The self which refuses to let itself be penetrated by its own knowledge of itself is the self willingly absorbed in a diffused, rejecting, mimetic community shared with the other.[12] My expressivity is knowable for my own reflection only because initially it is known pre-reflectively through the expressive and responsive bodies of others. Reflection can be undermined if – on the pre-reflective and sneakingly voluntary level – the other can be either flatteringly masqueraded or discredited as a witness of my bodily being. For since my sense of individual self involves being other than the other and yet also *for* the other, and since he is distorted or discounted as a witness of my behavior, I blur my sense of individual self. Self-rejection which has remained at the pre-reflective level is dissipated through the atmosphere of one's mood and attitude. One's world is guilty.[13]

It should not surprise us if this behavior is a remnant of cannibalistic impulses – a symbolic expression which, nevertheless, given the reality of the eating at the table and the blurring of selves, is quite close to factual reality. Often self-deception involves the emergence of tabooed behavior: cannibalism in this case, and incest in the case of the woman being seduced.

The last example I will give develops Freud's assertion that in the unconscious one's own death is inconceivable, and hence the belief that one does die must be self-deceiving. I think that this is the deepest level of self-deception we have discussed so far; it seems to be the deepest there is. The seriousness of what must be concealed from self achieves the status of terror, the terror of the uncanny, i.e., that a condition of all one's experience of the world, a condition of all meaningfulness as one immediately lives it, is somehow removed; one's life ends. If our projection of the essential features of self-deception in these free variations is correct, we should expect the mimetic engulfment to be greatest in this case. This we do find, I believe.

Let us say that one is providing for his family by planning for his funeral and that he envisions it. The image of himself laid out as a corpse presents itself to him. He must think of this sight as being experienceable if it is to make any sense to him, and he cannot neatly distinguish its being experienceable by him from its being experienceable by anyone. Thus he can pre-reflectively and self-deceivingly lose himself in that ongoing body of persons that he envisions looking on at his corpse. In this picturing of his funeral his eye looks on at his corpse, but it is an eye that is merged with other's eyes, and it is disowned by him. At an unthematized level of his experience, he thinks himself to be living on with the others; he thinks himself to be immortal; he flees from his death in self-deception. He cannot see that he is doing this just because in thematically seeing himself as dead he cannot see that he is seeing, thinking, or doing anything. In massive mimetic engulfment – in an indefinitely large group – he hides his belief in immortality and hides his hiding.[14]

This is extraordinarily deep self-deception. One reason is that it derives from basic, universal characteristics such as having a particular, mortal body and yet experiencing it unavoidably through the intersubjective structures of the ongoing community of persons as possible experiencers. A corollary of the difficulty is that since the self-deception is presumably universal, there may not be those others who do not "go along with one," and who could, if they existed, startle one into self-recognition. However, persons self-deceived about their own deaths may not be self-deceived about others's deaths, and may, therefore, startle them into self-recognition.

V.

This helps us to formulate the question: What is that criterion of identity which allows for what is evidently needed – degrees of individuation of self at different times? I do not pretend to have the whole answer, for I have not precisely coordinated the cruder and the more subtle senses of "individual self." But I do know that the question of the criterion of identity of the corporate body, the culture, must be considered. We achieve what we call identity as an individual self only because we incorporate dumbly, mimetically, and undeliberately others's attitudes and perceptions (including others's attitudes and perceptions of ourselves). Inevitably, then, "what I am" (or its nonverbal equivalent) must include "what we are" (or its nonverbal equivalent). At some moments what distinguishes a self from others is in relative ascendency, at other moments what is shared. When the latter occurs self-deception can be rampant. It is fostered when the identity of the corporate body involves mimetically induced social role playing which can be used to mask one's asocial or anti-social or super-social intentions from oneself – "frank discussions," "strictly intellectual conversations," "just dining together," "prudentially planning one's last rites," etc.

The identity of the particular mimetic community typically conspires to blur one's sense of individuality and to facilitate one's self-deception. Successful role playing is essential to the cohesion and survival of the group. Only the exceptional other who, for some reason, cares for one and is willing to risk ostracism or alienation, will dare to run counter to one's self-deceptive project (perhaps because he or she loves one). In these matters, compassion seems to be an essential ingredient in perceptual capacity.

The creature . . . never gains complete control over the ground. It shatters itself upon it and remains . . . burdened by its gravity. Thus, the veil of sadness which is spread over all nature, the deep, unappeasable melancholy of all life.[15]

Notes

1. One measure of the skeletal quality of Aristotle's conception of the universal is that he consistently overvalued what *distinguishes* humans as a species from other species, *and* what distinguishes particular humans from each other. Hence, while we are essentially animals, the emphasis falls on the differentia: *rational* animals (and rationality as related to divinity). Hence,

while each individual must exhibit a universal form, each is a point-outable one, a *this* somewhat. He tended simply to assume that having an individual body is sufficient for being an individual self. He inadequately grasped the blur of mimetic phenomena, the ancient message of Dionysus, the wierd whole of others, of nature, and of fertility in which we are caught up (although he is not oblivious to it — for just one example, he observes tellingly that for the young child all men are "father"). Thus, while he gives to imitation a central place in the formation of the self, he creates certain obstacles for the understanding of its range and depth.

2. Descartes thought that the soul is a non-extended and invisible substance separate from the body and brain. But it is likely that in addition to Descartes's views on reference his scientific theory of the causal role of brain in the production of mental events influenced furtively and uncritically his ideas of mind and soul. For, as the brain is just mine, hidden within my skull, so mind or soul is just mine, hidden from others, but directly and indubitably apparent to myself. How do I know any other selves exist at all? One branch of this tradition tends to argue from analogy that there are other selves: Since I know both my mind and my body, and since I know that distinctive bodily motions of mine appear and are correlated with distinctive mental states of mine — and since my body is similar to what appears to be other human bodies — therefore it is likely that there are other similar minds correlated with these other similar bodies, and that other selves exist.

3. See note 1.

4. Martin Heidegger, *Schelling's Treatise on the Essence of Human Freedom* (Athens, Ohio: Ohio University Press , 1985) p. 161.

5. Ibid, pp. 136–42.

6. Edmund Husserl, *Cartesian Meditations*, trans. D. Cairns (The Hague: Martinus Nijhoff, 1973), p. 100.

7. Meltzoff and M.K. Moore, "Imitation of Facial and Manual Gestures by Human Neonates," Science 198 (Oct. 1977).

8. *The Nichomachean Ethics*, Book III, chaps. 1 and 2.

9. *The Principles of Psychology* (New York: Henry Holt, 1890), chap. 9. See also my *William James and Phenomenology: A Study of 'The Principles of Psychology'* (Bloomington: Indiana University Press, 1968).

10. I use theatre as free variations on the nature of mimetic engulfment in my *Role Playing and Identity: The Limits of Theatre as Metaphor* (Bloomington: Indiana University Press, 1982). Most phenomenologists have found nothing to say about this salient feature of the book.

11. *Being and Nothingness*, trans. Hazel Barnes (New York: Philosophical Library, 1953), part 1, chap. 2.

12. The idea of the self which does not let itself be penetrated by its own knowledge of itself is Gabriel Marcel's. See his *The Mystery of Being*, trans. G.S. Fraser (Chicago: Gateway Books, 1960), vol. 1, pp. 79 and 119 ff.

13. Concerning the inability to clearly localize guilt, see Max Scheler, "On the Tragic," *Cross Currents* 4 (1954): 185–7. On the connection between self-deception and what İ call tragic choice, see my *Role Playing and Identity*, pp. 173–86 and 209–10.

14. With regard to the Vietnam War Helen Caldicott writes, "Nuclear war and weapons were forgotten, much to everyone's subconscious relief, for to contemplate nuclear war is to entertain the concept of the end of immortality, not just the idea of death". *Missile Envy* (New York: W. Morrow, 1984), p. 14. This is a shocking passage. Is it sufficiently shocking to knock one out of his self-deceptive projects with respect to death? Perhaps at some moments. But at other moments the thought of nuclear war is not in our minds, or not forcefully there. Perhaps we can say that the distinct possibility of nuclear war gives us the probably unprecedented opportunity to dislodge this deeply seated project of self-deception with respect to death. Whether we are responsible enough to take it, I do not know.

I should add a qualifier to my words, "In massive mimetic engulfment – in an indefinitely large group . . . ." If this group is all possible human experiencers, then this logically entails, of course, the human race. But psychologically it need not involve this. Psychologically we tend to equate humanity with our own nation or culture (see my *Role Playing and Identity*, p. 296).

15. Heidegger on Schelling (see note 4), p. 160.

Final note: This paper overlaps with, and develops, material previously published. See my "Self, Body, and Self-Deception," *Man and World* 5 (1972): no. 4; *Role Playing and Identity*, chap. 12; and "Mimetic Engulfment and Self-Deception," a contribution to a collection of articles on self-deception [ed. Amalie Rorty and Brian McLaughlin (University of California Press, forthcoming)].

Part VI.
Critique of
Cognitive Psychology

14. Information Processing and the Phenomenology of Thinking

Christopher M. Aanstoos

This paper will demonstrate a particular contribution of Merleau-Ponty's work in relation to contemporary cognitive psychology. Specifically, it will show how Merleau-Ponty's phenomenology of consciousness helps to overcome conceptual problems at the heart of the current cognitivist theory of thinking as information processing. Before developing that position, two preliminary points must be made. First, it should be noted that the cogito of philosophy is not synonymous with the cognition of psychology. That difference does not indicate a deficiency in either discipline. Rather, it is the entirely appropriate consequence of the fact that philosophy and psychology pursue different projects, even when both are phenomenologically based. The philosopher's cogito has an ontological status, whereas psychology, as an ontic science, uses cognition in that more restricted sense. This divergence does not mean that one is irrelevant to the other. It only means that care must be taken when insights are appropriated from one field to the other.

Merleau-Ponty's work provides an especially fecund source of insights for psychology. Indeed, especially through his major works, *The Structure of Behavior* and *Phenomenology of Perception*, Merleau-Ponty engaged in a detailed dialogue with the major psychological systems of his day: Gestalt psychology, psychoanalysis, and behaviorism. But this range of dialogal partners raises the second preliminary point. Since Merleau-Ponty's work antedates the coalescence of contemporary cognitive psychology, he did not have an opportunity to discuss their foundational commitments. Nevertheless, his work is especially valuable in resolving some highly problematic conceptual foundations which have become popular as a result of cognitivism's recent rise to paradigmatic prominence. This paper will thematize that relevance in the following way. First, the information processing approach will be briefly reviewed. Second, Merleau-Ponty's basic understanding will be summarized. Third, a dialogue between the two will be developed in order to clarify how Merleau-Ponty provides an alternative to the cognitivist theory of thought. Fourth, this critique will then be supported by phenomenologically based psychological research on thinking in order to bring the discussion to the concrete, empirical level.

The Cognitivist Theory of Thinking

The contemporary cognitive psychology of thinking, while not completely monolithic, is dominated by the information processing approach formulated by Newell and Simon. It is with their work that this dialogue will be developed. First, the selection of Newell and Simon needs to be briefly justified by reviewing their position in the field. Their pioneering efforts have deservedly earned them recognition as the founders of the information processing approach to psychology. Indeed, a recent history states that Newell and Simon's influence "on computing and cognitive psychology so pervades those fields that their discoveries and models are simply taken for granted"[1] Likewise, in his text on systems in psychology, Robinson even concludes that "'information processing' has become something of a synonym for cognitive psychology itself."[2]

Though some cognitive psychologists, most notably Neisser, dispute this information processing model in areas such as memory and perception, it has achieved pre-eminent status especially with regards to thinking. For example, the 1978 *Annual Review of Psychology* noted in its survey of the psychology of thinking that "the information processing language is almost universal".[3] Also, Mandler, a prominent historian of the psychology of thinking, has similarly described the information processing approach as being "synonymous" with the field as a whole.[4]

This new paradigm was initiated by Newell and Simon in the 1950's on the basis of the computer as an exemplar case of an information processing system. Thus, the fundamental justification for the information processing hypothesis has been the implementation of computer simulation models. While these models are now being applied to simulate a very diverse range of psychological phenomena, Newell and Simon's primary interest has always been the simulation of thinking, and they have devoted the major portion of their research efforts in this direction. Their information processing model presents thinking as the construction of a new representation through a series of elementary or primitive processes, combined serially according to explicit and predetermined rules, each process of which is a formally definite operation for the manipulation of information in the form of discrete and contextless bits.[5] Thus, thinking is seen as a processing that is avowedly mechanistic and elemanlistic. Both of these characteristics are readily affirmed by information processing theorists. Regarding the former, Newell and Simon have long agreed that "information processing theories of human thinking . . . provide explanations of behavior that are mechanistic."[6] Similarly, they have repeatedly asserted that thinking is composed of hypothetical "elementary information processes,"[7] and that any composite processes are actually "compounded from the more elementary ones in a few characteristic ways".[8]

A leading advocate of this approach has summarized its view of thinking more succinctly as follows: "Thought is the achievement of a new representation through the performance of mental operations."[9]

The consequences of accepting this representational conception of thinking becomes more explicit in this lengthier elaboration by another prominent supporter of the information processing model:

> The reality which we experience is quite artificial . . . for the world of which we are conscious is the product of a series of processes applied to sensory data. . . . Our "immediate" contact with the world is illusory . . . . Our experiences are representations based upon the processing of our private sensory experience.[10]

This emphasis on the representational character of the psychological was the information processing approach's reaction to the previously dominant insistence by behaviorism on its completely instrumental nature. Whereas behaviorism had argued that psychological life could be conceptualized without reference to cognition at all, the new cognitivist paradigm insists that "at heart every psychological phenomenon must be seen as a cognitive one".[11] Thus, where behaviorism had conceptualized psychological reality as blind associations of stimuli and responses, cognitivism has even reinterpreted phenomena such as conditioning[12] and partial reinforcement[13] as involving information processing. Maki and Levin claim to have demonstrated information processing in pigeons undergoing operant conditioning.[14] And Bever, Straub, Terrace and Townsend argue that information processing models rather than S-R links are necessary to explain serial behavior in humans and pigeons.[15]

Hence, this new cognitivism claims to have achieved a "paradigmatic revolution" in psychology.[16] In the above sense it certainly has. The information processing approach did so, however, while conserving an even more basic assumption of traditional psychology. Since its inception as an experimental science, psychology has borrowed more from natural science than its method. It has also uncritically assumed the conceptual foundation underlying that methodology, namely, objectivism – the thesis that psychology's subject matter must be treated as objects, in the sense of mechanisms for causal analysis. Contemporary cognitivism, as information processing, has been able to reintroduce "cognitive processes" into psychology by retaining the fundamental presupposition that these processes are mechanistic – as demonstrated by computer models. The question is whether this new paradigm is any more faithful to the essential nature of psychological life.

Merleau-Ponty's Approach to Thought

Through his thesis of the primacy of perception, Merleau-Ponty argued that the fundamental synthesis of perceiving subject and perceived world form a strictly wholistic system. He disputed the notion that this synthesis was constructed by a founding act of pure thought. While the refutation of that conception of thought was Merleau-Ponty's most direct concern, his thesis does more than that. It not only clears away a misunderstanding, it also suggests the basis for a more adequate understanding of thought. Merleau-Ponty's elaboration of consciousness in general as embodied in the world explicitly so describes thought as well. He noted "we are through and through compounded of relationships with the world".[17] What Merleau-Ponty asserts about thinking is that it is, like all consciousness, fundamentally contextual or worlded. To be worlded, for

Merleau-Ponty, is to be engaged, or involved, in situations, thereby grasping them from within this involvement with them. Such a grasp is hence necessarily perspectival, and such perspectivity necessarily implies horizons of indeterminacy. Thus thought, though an original mode of psychological life, must be considered to be just as intentive of horizonal indeterminacy as is perception, through its similar foundation in a world which it grasps only perspectivally. The fundamental thrust of this understanding of thought is to ground it, or found it, in such a way that rationality is recognized as rooted in human presence, rather than purely absolute and detached. In his own words, "the perceived world is always the presupposed foundation of all rationality".[18] This conclusion was not meant to deny rationality as such but only its disembodied caricature as pure calculation (such as forms the basis for information processing models). He reminded his audience that "this thesis does not destroy . . . rationality . . . it only tries to bring [it] down to earth".[19] Thinking is not reduced by the recognition of its inherence in the world. On the contrary, it is thereby welcomed home.

This primordial engagement means that thinking is always situated, and thus perspectival. Yet, as Merleau-Ponty so ably demonstrated with regard to perception, perspectivity must not be understood naturalistically. Rather, horizons and temporality are always included in perspectivity. In the case of thinking, Merleau-Ponty states "we must define thought in terms of that strange power it possesses of being ahead of itself, of launching itself and being at home everywhere".[20] In this sense, thinking launches itself beyond the sensible, toward latent possibility. Merleau-Ponty notes that "ordinary questions . . . are the lack and the provisional absence of a fact or of a positive statement, holes in a fabric of things."[21] These latencies, however, are not random, disconnected. Rather, like the unfinished part of a tapestry, they portend a connectedness and coherence. That is, any latency of thought refers to a larger whole, through its participation in it. As Merleau-Ponty points out, "every question, even that of simple cognition, is part of the central question that is ourselves, of that appeal for totality to which no objective being answers".[22] Crucial here is the point that this appeal to totality is one that exceeds objective answers. The positivity of the objective is insufficient to conclude thought, which dwells in the realm of possibility, negativity – in "holes in the fabric of being."

This larger panorama is the referential totality which thinking opens. Hence, the field of thought, far from being closed by predetermined boundaries, implicates an unending horizon. "Reason's labors presuppose such infinite conversations."[23] This is the sense in which thinking transcends the bounds not only of the sensible givens, but also of any pre-established thought. This continual overturning act of transcendence by thought means that rationality, as lived, should be understood in an expanded sense, in the sense that "the highest form of reason borders on unreason".[24] Through this movement of spontaneous thought beyond its own previous achievements "we are invited to discern beneath thinking which basks in its acquisitions, and offers merely a brief resting place in the mending process of expression, another thought which is struggling to establish itself".[25] Thinking thus contacts the abyss at the edge of the sensible. "But," as Merleau-Ponty recognizes, "an abyss is not nothing; it has its environs and edges. One always thinks of something, about, according to, in the light of something . . . . The opening is in principle immediately filled, as if lived only in a nascent state. If it holds out, it does so through and by means of the sliding movement which casts it into the latent".[26]

This process is through and through temporal. Thinking "follows in the wake of previous thoughts. . . . Time and thought are mutually entangled. In the dark night of thought dwells a glimmering of Being."[27]

To summarize, Merleau-Ponty characterizes thought as fundamentally contextualized in the same sense that all embodied consciousness is. As situated consciousness, what is particular to thought is its structure of perspectivity/transcendence. That is, thinking is perspectival, yet its very perspectivity provides thinking its launching, its movement beyond the givens to the latent horizons of possibility and, through them, to further possibles which they imply.

Merleau-Ponty and Cognitivism: A Critique

Cognitivism holds that all psychological phenomena are fundamentally cognitive. Merleau-Ponty, on the other hand, states that "the world is not what I think, but what I live."[28] This position is not a return to behaviorism. It does not deny a cognitive dimension, for one does also think about the world one is living. Rather, it grounds the cognitive by relating it to the precognitive. Cognition is founded on precognitive experience but emerges from it as a specialized and original form of presence. In other words, a conception of human presence as representational is not the only alternative to instrumentalistic conceptions. Merleau-Ponty cuts between cognitivism's representationalism and behaviorism's instrumentalism, and, instead, describes human involvement as primordially presentational. The difference between viewing psychological life as "presentational" versus viewing it as "representational" are crucial. The term presentational is meant to indicate the emergence of meaning within the involvement of person and world, or, in Merleau-Ponty's words, the emergence of rationality within being-in-the-world, at the very juncture with irrationality. Such a view differs from a representational model, in which rationality is a construction, indeed a reconstruction that is imposed by a detached and contextless Thought that is not primordially engaged *in* the world.

By failing to contact this basic engagement of person and world, information processing theory perpetuates a variation of the "retrospective fallacy" of putting the researcher's conception in place of the subject's own experience. Thus, cognitive psychology's latest paradigm commits the very psychologism, or "category error," that Merleau-Ponty so vigorously disputed, as indeed had Husserl and James before him. Specifically, cognitivism took the calculative representational concept of thinking derived from one category — the computer model — and posited it onto another category — that of the experiencing person. In doing so, assumptions were carried over uncritically from the former category to the latter. For example, Simon argues that information processing theory need not consider "whole man," but only "thinking man" — in other words, thought independent of existence.[29] He has also noted that, as represented for a computer, "all problems look alike" in the sense that "they all can be attacked with processes that are indifferent to real-world content" — in other words, thought independent of world.[30] These cognitivist premises differ fundamentally from Merleau-Ponty's work. An information processing system, operating as a series of elementary and predetermined processes independent of existence and the world essentially lacks situatedness, and so perspectivity — the very foundational characteristic of rationality upon which Merleau-Ponty most vigorously insisted. One could even say that the computer model's formal representational character cannot be disclosive of human thinking's situated character, but is only compensatory for the lack of a presentational mode of presence.

An Empirical Phenomenological Psychology of Thinking

Contemporary cognitivist theory is refuted not only by Merleau-Ponty's work, but by recent empirical phenomenological research on the psychology of thinking. An example is Cloonan's work, which demonstrated the importance of one's perspective for understanding.[31] Another example, more relevant to this dialogue, is this author's phenomenological study of thinking in chess.[32] It was undertaken specifically in order to compare results with those of information processing. Such an empirical comparison is urgently needed in this area. The question of the adequacy of the computer simulation model has been heatedly debated in philosophy for three decades. In fact, philosophers have long advanced both *a priori* arguments in favor of the computer model as well as *a priori* arguments against it.[33] Nevertheless, contrary evidence has not been forthcoming within empirical psychology, thereby permitting information processing advocates to defend their model by arguing that it is better than the lack that had existed prior to its emergence;[34] that there is no evidence contrary to their position;[35] or at least that there is no evidence to the contrary that can establish its sufficiency.[36]

Given this background, the aforementioned phenomenological research study was conducted in order to obtain the solid, descriptive findings needed to address this issue. First, thinking was circumscribed more specifically: it was studied in the context of chess playing. Chess playing was selected because it has long been identified by information processing researchers as their own "type case"[37] or "natural arena."[38] Indeed, chess playing became so important a task for computer simulation efforts that it has been referred to as the "fruit fly" of that field.[39].

The method for this study involved the use of descriptive data in the form of think aloud protocols, collected from five subjects, all of whom were U.S. Chess Federation tournament players (with ratings ranging from Master through Category III). Each subject thought aloud while playing an entire game of chess against an evenly matched opponent (who wore headphones so as not to be able to hear the subject). Their verbalizations were tape recorded and then transcribed. The theoretical justification for the use of the think aloud data has already been discussed elsewhere.[40].

Each of these protocols was then analyzed by means of the phenomenological method adapted to psychological research by Giorgi and Wertz.[41] This analysis remained faithful to the descriptive nature of the data, in order to disclose its essential meaning directly, rather than on the basis of an inferential framework. The aim was not to test hypotheses, but to discern the essential meanings of the subjects' experience.

The results of that analysis are structurally interrelated essential themes which disclose how thinking is manifested in chess playing. This general structure included a description of the noetic mode characteristic of thinking and the noematic objects of thought, as well as thinking's relation with other psychological processes involved in chess playing.[42] These findings also provide a concrete illustration of the essential aspects of Merleau-Ponty's description of thought, and it is that exemplification that will be discussed here.

One such example concerns the issue of the perspectivity of thought. The chess player always thinks about the game from a point of view. That is, not all possible combinations of future moves are thematized. It would be impossible to do so, as there are millions of alternative combinations available. Only a small number are thought about. Those that do occur to the thinker are those which appear relevant to his plans and the position of the pieces on the board. In other words, the selective thematization of possible moves to be considered is based upon the particular perspective that thinking brings to bear in the game. From this perspective, certain piece relations and moves are thematized and not others, and these implicate certain possible futures and not others.

Far from being a disadvantage, such perspectivity allows thinking to consider relevant combinations without wasting time on irrelevant ones. Furthermore, it is this very perspectivity that is lacking in computer simulation models. Computer chess programs must search and evaluate a much larger number of alternative combinations in order to select a move. Indeed, they typically must search hundreds of thousands or even millions of alternatives.[43] Information processing psychologists acknowledge that programs which search thousands of positions per move "are almost certainly proceeding differently than humans."[44] Even Berliner's effort to rectify this anomaly by designing a program that searches more selectively still reveals the essential problem, as it still must search five thousand possibilities – far more than any human player.[45] Thus, thinking's embeddedness in the situation allows it to thematize possibilities in a focussed way that is not simulated by computer models, which much rely on a more extensive, because more arbitrary, search process. This difference is inherent precisely because the computer is not situated, that is, because it is essentially "contextless" as Simon was earlier quoted as acknowledging.

The second major point also illustrates this difference between thinking's context-relatedness and the computer model's lack of it. This issue has to do with the way in which thinking concerns itself with maxims, or guidelines – general strategies learned from books, other players, or previous experience. The computer model relies on such predetermined rules to guide and limit its search and evaluation processes. The results of this study do show that general principles are involved in thinking in chess. However, rather than simply adhering to predetermined guidelines as sheer facticities, thinking took them up as guidelines, as objects of thought. As such, they were questioned, as possibilities. For example, one subject followed the principle of posting a knight on the sixth row when he had an opportunity to do so, as an explicit following of a maxim that it is advantageous to do so. But the maxim itself was thematized as a question, and following it meant extending that questioning to the position on the board. In other words, the maxim did not serve to limit thinking, but to evoke it. So, even when followed, maxims serve as signifiers rather than as rigid rules. Perhaps an even clearer example of this difference between thinking's flexibility and the model's rigidity occurred in those instances when thinking took up again as questionable the very possible moves it had already rejected on the basis of pre-established guidelines. For example, one subject repeatedly reconsidered playing "pawn takes pawn" after having decided against it "on general principles." Such data provides ample support for the distinction that thinking determines the applicability of guidelines within the context of the game or situation, in contrast to the predetermination that is made for the program's heuristics. Again, the essential difference here is between thinking as situated involvement, and the computer model as essentially uninvolved and contextless.

The third major exemplification of Merleau-Ponty's work to emerge from this research concerns the notion of "symbol." Merleau-Ponty emphasized that the object of thought is one that cannot be reduced to an objective answer. In this study, thinking was seen as taking up implicatory relations among the pieces on the board. Their character was implicatory specifically in the sense that it implied further, unthematized relations — ultimately a referential totality of relations among the pieces. This referential totality itself was never thematized as a whole; it was only implied, rather, through its partial manifestation in specific relational configurations. It was in this sense that thinking's objects are symbolic — they symbolize an implicit significance never captured in an objective manner. The computer model, however, uses the notion of symbol in a very different way. The information processing approach, viewing thinking as calculation, understands symbol manipulation in the same sense that computer processing is.[46] In other words, symbol manipulation as a definition of thinking means that thinking is essentially a series of primitive processes, combined serially according to explicit and predetermined rules, each process of which is a formally definite operation for the manipulation of information in the form of elemental and discrete bits. Newell repeats explicitly many of these points, for instance that symbols are "discrete" and that thinking is seen as the "processes that manipulate these symbols." He goes on to point out that "the central notion" to "the view that man is an information process . . . is that of the symbol, which is taken to mean essentially what it does in computer science."[47] And just what does the symbol mean in computer science? It is the binary digit (hence the neologism "bit" of information). Such digits, transmitted through on-off switches, represent information in the technical sene of a mathematical reduction of randomness by a series of binary choices between previously equally probable alternatives. While the engineers who first formulated this concept of information in the late 1940's pointed out that it was not concerned with meaning at all,[48] cognitive psychologists applied it so uncritically that they now assume that the term "information" is synonymous with "knowledge."[49] Such a presumption thereby assumes as true the computer model's preconception that thinking involves calculative choices between discrete and elemental alternatives. It assumes the very objectification of thought which Merleau-Ponty so vigorously disputed.

The descriptive results of this research showed that this objectification does not correspond to the phenomenon as lived. They showed that such a presumption is a distortion that rests upon a fundamental misuse of the term "symbol." The binary digits of computer science may be known as symbols in the technical jargon, but they are not symbolic in the full sense of that term. Symbols are a type of signification. Binary digits are also signifiers, but they are not the same type of signifiers as symbols are. Rather, they are the type known as signs. The difference is critical. A sign bears an essentially different relation with what it signifies than a symbol does. The former has an objective "one to one" relationship, whereas the latter has a "one to many" relationship, one that may involve an essential participation with that which it signifies.[50]

It is this characterization of symbol that was confirmed by the descriptive research. It showed thinking's symbolic objects as implicatory of a referential totality. Indeed, that is what thinking essentially is – the quest for and explicitation of understanding through the grasp of the implications of its symbolic objects. In that sense, thinking essentially cannot be simulated by processes for the manipulation of binary digits, for binary digits are not symbolic in that sense – they do not refer to a referential totality.

Conclusion

This paper has sought to demonstrate that Merleau-Ponty's work can provide important foundational clarifications for the contemporary psychology of thinking. Indeed, it provides a decisive alternative understanding of thought to that of the currently dominant information processing approach. This alternative is supported by empirical phenomenological research on thinking in the context of chess playing, the very context deemed most important to information processing models.

Notes

1. P. McCorduck, *Machines Who Think* (San Francisco: Freeman, 1976), p. viii.

2. D.N. Robinson, *Systems of Modern Psychology* (New York: Columbia University Press, 1979), p. 303.

3. J.R. Erickson and M. Jones, "Thinking," *Annual Review of Psychology* 29 (1978): 61.

4. G.A. Mandler, "What Is Cognitive Psychology? What Isn't?, paper presented at the meeting of the American Psychological Association, Los Angeles, 1981.

5. A. Newell and H. A. Simon, *Human Problem Solving* (Englewood Cliffs, N.J.: Prentice-Hall, 1972).

6. H.A. Simon and A. Newell, "Information Processing in Computers and Man," *American Scientist* 52 (1964): 283.

7. See A. Newell, J.C. Shaw, and H.A. Simon, "Elements of a Theory of Human Problem Solving," *Psychological Review* 65 (1958): 165-66; A. Newell and H.A. Simon, "Computer Simulation of Human Thinking," *Science* 134 (1961): 2013; H.A. Simon and A. Newell, "Information Processing in Computers and Man," *American Scientist* 52 (1964): 290-94; H.A. Simon and A. Newell, "Human Problem Solving: The State of the Theory in 1970," *American Psychologist* 26 (1971): 149.

8. H.A. Simon and A. Newell, "Information Processing in Computers and Man," p. 290.

9. M.I. Posner, *Cognition: An Introduction* (Glenview, Ill.: Scott, Forseman, 1973), p. 1947.

10. G. Underwood, ed., *Strategies of Information Processing* (New York: Academic Press, 1978), pp. 9-10.

11. A.G. Reynolds and P.W. Flagg, *Cognitive Psychology* (Cambridge: Winthrop, 1977), p. 13.

12. W. Brewer, "There is No Convincing Evidence for Operant or Classical Conditioning in Adult Humans," in Weimer and Palermo, eds., *Cognition and the Symbolic Process* (Hillsdale, N.J.: Erlbaum, 1974).

13. J. Feldman, "Simulation of Behavior in the Binary Choice Experiment," *Proceedings of the Western Joint Computer Conference* 19 (1961): 133–44.

14. W.S. Maki and T.C. Levin, "Information Processing by Pigeons," *Science* 176 (1972): 535–36.

15. T.G. Bever, R.O. Staub, H.S. Terrace, and D.J. Townsend, "The Comparative Study of Serially Integrated Behavior in Humans and Animals," in Jusczyk and Klein, eds., *The Nature of Thought* (Hillsdale, N.J.: Erlbaum, 1980).

16. H.A. Simon, "The Behavioral and Social Sciences," *Science* 209 (1980): 76.

17. M. Merleau-Ponty, *Phenomenology of Perception*, trans. C. Smith (New York: Humanities, 1962), p. xiii.

18. M. Merleau-Ponty, *The Primacy of Perception*, trans. J. Edie (Evanston: Northwestern University Press, 1964), p. 13.

19. Ibid., p. 13.

20. M. Merleau-Ponty, *Phenomenology of Perception*, p. 371.

21. M. Merleau-Ponty, *The Visible and the Invisible*, trans. A. Lingis (Evanston: Northwestern University Press, 1968), p. 105.

22. Ibid., p. 104.

23. M. Merleau-Ponty, *Signs*, trans. R.C. McCleary (Evanston: Northwestern University Press, 1964), p. 19.

24. M. Merleau-Ponty, *Sense and Non-Sense*, trans. H.L. Dreyfus and P.A. Dreyfus (Evanston: Northwestern University Press, 1964), p. 4.

25. M. Merleau-Ponty, *Phenomenology of Perception*, p. 389.

26. M. Merleau-Ponty, *Signs*, p. 14.

27. Ibid., pp. 14–15.

28. M. Merleau-Ponty, *Phenomenology of Perception*, pp. xvi–xvii.

29. H.A. Simon, *The Sciences of the Artificial* (Cambridge, Mass: M.I.T. Press, 1969), p. 25.

30. H.A. Simon, "Information Processing Explanation of Understanding," in *The Nature of Thought*, p. 43 (see n.15).

31. T.P. Cloonan, "Body Subject and Dialogue of Perspective in the Perception of Letters Traced on the Head," in Giorgi, Fischer, and Murray, eds., *Duquesne Studies in Phenomenological Psychology*, Vol. 2 (Pittsburgh: Duquesne University Press, 1975).

32. C.M. Aanstoos, *A Phenomenological Study of Thinking As It Is Exemplified During Chess Playing, Dissertation Abstracts International* 43 (1983): 26–27B (Doctoral Dissertation, Duquesne University, Pittsburgh, PA., 1982); "A Phenomenological Study of Thinking," in Giorgi, Barton, and Maes, eds., *Duquesne Studies in Phenomenological Psychology*, Vol. 4 (Pittsburgh: Duquesne University Press, 1983), pp. 244–56.

33. See D.M. Mackay, "From Mechanism to Mind," *Trans. Vict. Inst.* 85 (1953): 17–32; H.L. Dreyfus, *What Computers Can't Do*, rev. ed. (New York: Harper and Row, 1979).

34. L. Uhr, "Computer 'Simulations' of Thinking Are Just (Working, Complete, Big, Complex, Powerful, Messy) Theoretical Models," in Voss, ed., *Approaches to Thought* (Columbus: Merrill, 1969), p. 290.

35. H. Hunt and S. Poltrock, "The Mechanics of Thought," in Kantowitz, ed., *Human Information Processing* (Hillsdale, N.J.: Erlbaum, 1974), p. 344.

36. A. Newell, J.C. Shaw, and H.A. Simon, "Elements of a Theory of Human Problem Solving," p. 156.

37. A. Newell, "The Chess Machine," *Preceedings of the 1955 Western Joint Computer Conference*, pp. 101–8.

38. A. Newell, J.C. Shaw, and H.A. Simon, "Chess Playing and the Problem of Complexity," *IBM Journal of Research and Development* 2 (1958): 320–35.

39. E. Hearst, "Man and Machine: Chess Achievements and Chess Thinking," in Frey, ed., *Chess Skill in Man and Machine* (New York: Springer-Verlag, 1978), p. 197.

40. C.M. Aanstoos, "The Think Aloud Method in Descriptive Research," *Journal of Phenomenological Psychology* 14 (1983): 243–66; A. Giorgi, "Verbal Reports As Data: A Phenomenological Response to Nisbett and Wilson" (paper presented at the meeting of the Human Science Research Association, Carrollton, GA, 1984).

41. A. Giorgi, *Psychology As a Human Science* (New York: Harper & Row, 1970); "An Application of Phenomenological Method in Psychology," in Giorgi, Fischer, and Murray, eds., *Duquesne Studies in Phenomenological Psychology*, Vol. 2 (Pittsburgh: Duquesne University Press, 1975), pp. 82–103; Ibid., pp. 72–79; and F.J. Wertz, "Procedures in Phenomenological Research and the Question of Validity," *West Georgia College Studies in the Social Sciences* 23 (1984): 29–48; and also "From Everyday to Psychological Description: Analyzing the Moments of a Qualitative Data Analysis," *Journal of Phenomenological Psychology* 14 (1983): 197–241.

42. C.M. Aanstoos, "A Phenomenological Study of Thinking As It is Exemplified during Chess Playing."

43. P.N. Johnson-Laird and P.C. Wason, eds., *Thinking* (Cambridge: Cambridge University Press, 1977), p. 529; and J. Kaplan, "Not Bad — For a Machine," *Sports Illustrated*, September, 18, 1978, p. 74.

44. A. Newell and H.A. Simon, *Human Problem Solving*, p. 751.

45. H.J. Berliner, "Some Necessary Conditions for a Master Chess Program," in Johnson-Laird and Wason, eds., *Thinking* (New York: Cambridge University Press, 1977).

46. A. Newell and H.A. Simon, *Human Problem Solving*, p. 5.

47. A. Newell, "Artificial Intelligence and the Concept of Mind," in R. Schank and K. Colby, eds., *Computer Models of Thought and Language* (San Francisco: Freeman, 1973), p. 27.

48. E.g. R.W. Weaver, *Ideas Have Consequences* (Chicago: University of Chicago Press, 1948).

49. A.L. Glass, K.J. Holyoak, and J.L. Santa, *Cognition* (Reading, Mass.: Addison-Wesley, 1979), p. 2.

50. G.M. Kinget, *On Being Human: A Systematic View* (New York: Harcourt Brace, Jovanovich, 1975); also J.R. Royce, *The Encapsulated Man* (New York: Van Nostrand, 1964), pp. 133–34.

15. Merleau-Ponty and the Cognitive Psychology of Perception

Frederick J. Wertz

During Merleau-Ponty's career, he skillfully dialogued with virtually every significant school of psychological thought from both Europe and America. Only a few years before his death, a new movement in the United States was getting under way. That approach, cognitive psychology, has now emerged as the dominant force in the field. Its adherents view themselves as having achieved a status equal to psychoanalysis and behaviorism.[1]

One consequence of this trend is that perception, as an experiential process, has received revitalized attention in psychology. Of central concern to the early Structuralist Psychology of Wundt and Titchener as well as the Gestalt School in Germany, perception ceased to fascinate the Behaviorist dominated psychology from the 1920's into the 1950's as mental processes as such were considered to be beyond the limits of the "objective science of behavior." Piaget's anti-behaviorist developmental psychology and Chomsky's explicit critique of the behaviorist theory of language led the way in a renewed interest in cognitive functioning, exemplified by the Bruner, Goodnow, and Austin study of thinking.[2] Ultimately more consequential for American psychology was the 1958 paper by Newell, Shaw, and Simon which suggested the use of a computer model in the analysis of human phenomena. It was the fact that computers seemed to "do many things that humans did – learn to store, manipulate, and remember information as well as use language, solve problems, and reason"[3] that lent a new reality to these processes and provided terms for their exact specification, namely the language of computer programs. Indeed this new approach in psychology has defeated behaviorism; even elementary forms of behavior have been understood in terms of "plans" and "feedback loops."[4]

Now, after twenty years of proliferation, cognitive psychology in the broad sense, including such diverse theorists as Piaget, Chomsky, Bruner, Bandura, and Schacter, must be distinguished from the more narrowly homogeneous group of psychologists who utilize cybernetic, information processing models, represented for instance by Simon. While the latter has gained a tremendous following and power in American psychology, consistent with the unmitigated reverence for sophisticated technological advance, perceptual psychology has reemerged riddled with controversy. Most interesting in this light is the work of Ulrich Neisser, who wrote what is accepted as the first successful textbook in the field of cognitive psychology, called *Cognitive Psychology*,[5] which features the study of perception. Originally a sympathizer with information processing theory, Neisser has, largely through his interchange with the Gibsons, come to question the cybernetic approach, articulate an unresolved antinomy in the contemporary conceptualization of perception, and propose a new and integrative perceptual theory which places him within cognitive psychology in the broad sense but in opposition to cybernetic theorists. The question we will address is: Do these latest developments in perceptual psychology converge in any way with Merleau-Ponty's largely ignored phenomenology of perception, and to what extent does the latter offer a valuable contribution to the cognitive psychology of perception?

The Information Processing Theory of Perception

American perceptual psychology has characteristically viewed its subject matter from an empiricist standpoint. In laboratory experimentation, physical properties of stimuli have constituted the independent variables and perception has been viewed as stimulus-determined, the perceiver as a passive sufferer of the ambient light, sound, mechanical, and chemical contingencies. The problems presented for such a viewpoint surround the question of how, on the basis of a limited and fragmentary stimulation of isolated sensory organs, the perceiver ultimately achieves the experience of meaningfully organized objects and events. While empiricist theories have attempted to seek answers in the sources of stimulation themselves, for instance, spatial and temporal contiguities, such explanations inevitably fell short of the objects as perceived. For instance, in the case of vision, retinal images still require a perceiver who would *see* these disparate and changing impressions as unitary objects, and any postulated homunculus leads only to an infinite regress which begs the question. Modern cybernetic theory[6] attempts to solve this problem by viewing the retinal image and higher sensory neurological data (e.g., "feature detection") as input information which is actively *processed*. Phenomena ranging from perceptual illusions to the constancies of size, shape, and color "can be accounted for by a mechanism that encodes information from a stimulus into an internal representation having certain efficient characteristics from an information processing and retrieval standpoint."[7]

> Detectors are assumed to initiate neural messages in response to equally specific features of the image. Information about these features is then passed on to higher centers of the brain where it is collated and combined with previously stored information in a series of processes that eventually results in the perceptual experience.[8]

Therefore, we do not see mere retinal images, but representations of objects whose familiarity and meaningful intersensory organization is a product of internal processing. Individual differences in perception, global precepts, and the integrations of discrete data from different sensory channels with each other and with previously stored information can be explained by processing.

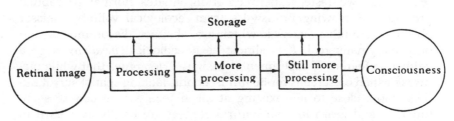

FIGURE I. The Information Processing Model (after Neisser)

Neisser's Criticism of the Cybernetic Model

Neisser's critique of the cybernetic approach is twofold, both arguments closely following the viewpoint of J. J. Gibson. The first criticism holds for any constructivist theory of perception and challenges its ability to account for verdicality. If we perceive not objects but internally constructed representations, why are they usually accurate? The only guarantee of accurate vision, Neisser reasons, must be found in the quality of the optical information available to the perceiver, and if the perceiver has any direct access to this, the notion of construction is superfluous. Indeed, Gibson begins his perceptual theory not with the retinal image but with the pattern of ambient light (called the ambient optical array) and argues that this pattern is itself highly organized so as to precisely *specify* the objects which determine its form.[9] It is then not processing but the direct *pick-up* of this information that is involved in perception, particularly the pick-up of the features of this array which remain invariant through the changes incurred in the organism's movement. "The perceiver may have to search for information but he need not process it, because it is all in the light already."[10] One does not then see images or representations but properties that specify the objects themselves. The implications of this contention are far reaching, suggesting that "students of perception should develop new and richer descriptions of stimulus information rather than ever subtler hypotheses about mental mechanisms."[11]

This brings us to Neisser's second criticism, which pertains to experimental paradigms following from the information processing model. Since sensory inputs are assumed to be isolated from each other in this model, the overwhelming majority of experiments pertain to only one sense. However, inasmuch as we do not perceive discrete bits of sensory information but "handle things we look at and feel things we taste," experimentation vitiates normal perceptual processes. Borrowing Brunswik's term "ecological validity," Neisser objects to stimulus materials which are "abstract, discontinuous, and only marginally real. It is almost as if ecological *invalidity* were a deliberate feature of experimental design".[12] He argues that while pictures flashed on screens for 50 milliseconds, lacking spatial surroundings, come close to not existing at all, objects which can be seen, touched, and heard in their natural context are hardly ever used in research. He notes that of the fifty-nine information processing experimental designs tabulated by Newell, only two – playing chess and looking at the moon — have "even a shred of ecological validity"; the rest are laboratory situations which, indifferent to time, space, and culture, miss many of the features perception manifests in ordinary life.[13] He holds the theoretical orientation of information processing theory, in particular faulty assumptions about the nature of stimuli (as discrete isolated bits), responsible for this misguided sophistication and consequent ecological invalidity of perceptual research.

Modern Controversy in Perceptual Theory

Crucial to Neisser's work is his recognition of the antinomy of information processing constructivism and the theory of J.J. Gibson, who denies the presence of any mental operations in perceptual process.[14] While Neisser borrows criticisms of the cybernetics model and the notion of the pick-up of information which directly specifies objects from Gibson, he believes Gibson's account of perception is incomplete as long as it excludes cognition. While information processing theorists tend to "glorify the perceiver, who is said to process, transform, recode, assimilate or generally give shape to what would otherwise be a meaningless chaos," Gibson's theory in which "mental events play no role at all" is inadequate because it credits the perceiver with too little.[15] Gibson's extreme view "says nothing about what is in the perceiver's head. What kinds of cognitive structure does perception require?"[16] Individual differences in perceivers, perceptual error, perceptual learning, perceptual selectivity, and all like phenomena, which involve matters beyond the given ambient array, remain unaccounted for.

Neisser's Theoretical Resolution

Neisser attempts to reconcile the antinomy of these two divergent views in his own theory of perception. In doing so he borrows the partial truths of each view and develops a conception of perception which avoids their respective pitfalls. Once defining cognition as a process "by which stimulus input is transformed, reduced, elaborated, stored, recovered, and used,"[17] Neisser now argues that perception is indeed a direct experience of objects achieved through a pick-up of the sensory information which specifies them, but that perception also depends upon preexisting cognitive structures called *schemata*, which direct this exploratory pick-up.[18] Neisser's perceptual theory readily flows into a general reconceptualization of cognition since these fundamental structures (schemata), born and modified in perception, are postulated again, as detached from the pick-up of sensory information, in memory, imagination, and other forms of cognition. Schemata are anticipatory plans that prepare the perceiver to pick up certain kinds of information and control the activity of looking by directing the exploration of objects. Perception is viewed as a cycle in which schemata, as structures making up the perceiver, direct perceptual exploration, which samples the ambient array, which in turn modifies the schemata. Perception involves an *interplay* between schemata and surroundings such that neither alone determines the course of perception. The object is also a part of the perceptual cycle, manifesting immediately meaningful "affordances" or possibilities for action and carrying implications about what has happened and will happen. These aspects of the perceptual object's meaning come first, while stimulus details are noticed later or not at all.[19]

The perceptual process is a cycle composed of the perceiver's schema and surrounding objects, and they are linked by a process of exploration. But what *are* schemata? The schema is that portion of the perceptual process that is *internal* to the perceiver. It directs movements, accepts information, and is modified in accordance with that information. Through transformation in schemata, the perceiver learns, becomes skillful, and this accounts for individual differences in perception.

> It seems necessary to credit even the youngest baby with a certain amount of perceptual equipment – not merely with sense organs but with neural schemata that control them . . . infants carry many kinds of information gathering activity. They look towards sounds, follow objects with their eyes, and reach out toward things they see.[20]

Since babies seem to recognize physiognomic traits such as smiles and frowns, soothing and harsh tones from the beginning, Neisser supposes that the schemata attuning the baby to these are innate. Ultimately, for Neisser, the schema is biologically based. "From a biological point of view, a schema is a part of the nervous system . . . an entire system that includes receptors and afferents, feed forward units and efferents . . . ." Although it is "exceedingly important," it is "excruciatingly difficult to understand these structures from a biological point of view," but they must be composed of "assemblages of neurons, functional hierarchies, fluctuating electrical potentials, and other things still unguessed."[21]

Convergences Between Neisser and Merleau-Ponty

To what extent do these developments converge with Merleau-Ponty's writings on perception? First, Merleau-Ponty rejected both empiricist and constructivist explanations of perception with reasoning similar to Neisser's. He argued that sensations, far from being original building blocks of perception, are a product of a later realistic analysis which presupposes and is founded on prior perception. Only a psychologist who has mistaken such abstractions for native perceptual experience needs to call on intellectualistic postulates to account for the meaning and unity of the phenomenal field. However, such a Cartesian formulation remains incapable of solving the problem of how such mental processes relate to physical reality inasmuch as they share no common ontological characteristics. Secondly, this critique led Merleau-Ponty, like Neisser, to abandon hypothetical postulates concerning the physical nature of sensory input as well as internal intellections which would make a meaningful organization of the former; instead, both consider a description of ordinary perception to be the proper starting point for any resolution of the difficulties these hypotheses inevitably entail. Thirdly, both distinguish their method from introspection and stress perception's reference to transcendent objects rather than internal mental representations. Fourthly, many specific findings regarding perception converge: global meaning is found to be immediately given prior to any supposed elements of the perceived object, which is apprehended as physiognomic, synaesthetic, useful, and temporal; the perceiver is found to be an active explorer rather than a merely passive spectator; though stable, perception is found to be an open, changing system in which perceiver and perceived reciprocally influence each other in a developmental process; finally, perception is found to be an original foundation on which the intellectual representations of memory, imagination and cognition in general are based.

Conceptual Divergences: Schema and Body-Subject

By contrasting Neisser's notion of schema to Merleau-Ponty's notion of the body-subject, we will find a significant divergence in their conceptualizations. This comparison shows that Neisser does not, in a radical way, hold realistic presuppositions in abeyence in the descriptive return to the phenomenal order, which he himself recognizes as a basic necessity. Merleau-Ponty, on the other hand, carried concrete description through to the heart of the perceiver.

Neisser's conceptualization of the perceiver as schemata entails three different sorts of discourse. First, on many occasions, and especially when he pushes himself to theoretical clarity, Neisser assigns schema the status of a part of the nervous system.[22] Secondly, at other times he uses the analogies of plan, notion, anticipation, or hypothesis, thereby referring to intellectually constituted entities. The schema is thus portrayed respectively as a mechanism and as an idea. When Neisser says schemata accept information, direct exploration, and are modified in turn by incoming information, their status is quite equivocal. That is, their dynamic relations with their surroundings can be viewed in either of these two ways, but here detailed specification ceases. The concept of schema, Neisser admits, is a hypothetical construct and as such is not something one might observe and describe concretely. The attempt to give this notion a biological status, as we have seen above, does not get far before its obviously conjectural character brings the discourse to a halt and leaves the task to future biologists. On the other hand, ascribing it to the realm of ideas goes little further than the mere suggestion of the above analogies, which are abandoned as soon as attempts at clarification are made. Although in his earlier writings Neisser was willing to consider the entity question to be a highly determinate hypothesis that would be tested by sensory information (much as is now done in the cognitive perceptual theories of Gregory and Bruner[23] – whose pitfalls we have exposed elsewhere[24]), he now asserts "perception is hypothesis testing in only a very general sense" since in order to be so rarely disconfirmed, schemata must be more open and less specific than a hypothesis.[25] But beyond vague analogy, what is a hypothesis, a plan, an anticipation or any idea that is "open" and "nonspecific"? Perhaps just as a continuation of the first mode of description is left to future biologists, the answer to this question must be left to future cognitivists.

Must we wait for these breakthroughs to know precisely what schemata are, let alone how they direct exploration, accept information, and become modified or more skillful? There is a third mode of discourse in Neisser's exposition, though it is quickly passed over and left unexplicated without being accorded true theoretical status. We might call this, in Neisser's most recent language, the "low road" of concrete description as opposed to the "high road" of hypothetical construction. For instance, he describes the perceiver as *looking towards* sounds, *following* objects, and *reaching to feel* things.[26] Why does Neisser resort to hypothetical thought after expressly disavowing it? Presumably, it is to explain these phenomenal data that mechanistic and intellectualistic postulates as well as their equivocations arise. Could a closer and more explicit interrogation of such phenomenal data contribute to understanding the perceiver as they have in the case of the perceived?

Merleau-Ponty sheds some light on this problem with a critique of the traditional analysis of the perceiver along the same lines as that concerning the perceived. He outlines, beyond the two kinds of being admitted by Cartesian ontology – thing and idea – a third and more primordial, however ambiguous, sort of being which is alone truly characteristic of the perceiver. Beyond biology and cognitive science, it is here that perceptual psychology finds its proper (ownmost) field. In the Cartesian tradition, "there are two senses, and only two, of the word 'exist'; one exists as a thing or one exists as a consciousness. Our experience of the body, on the other hand, reveals to us an ambiguous mode of existing . . . ."[27] Is it not the body which *looks, reaches, touches,* and lends itself to Neisser's ambivalently fluctuating interpretation of the perceiver as physical, on one hand, and mental, on the other? The body's substantiality and consequent availability (with its apparent reducibility) to the physical domain lead Neisser to biological terms while its meaningful intentions and intelligence lead him to terms of ideas, cognitions. However, in abandoning the ambiguity of concrete descriptions of the body and explaining the perceiver with Cartesian concepts, Neisser loses hold of the perceiver and is unable to faithfully conceptualize its *incarnate subjectivity,* which involves a unique kind of existence neither reducible to thing nor idea, nor even some interaction which would leave our understanding of the two unchanged (i.e., mutually exclusive).

Although Neisser gave priority to the subject matter over Cartesian presuppostions in the domain of the percept and described its original phenomenal characteristics in an unbiased way, these same notions return and eclipse an equally rigorous description when he comes to the perceiver. "The impelling intentions of the living creature were converted into objective movements – the execution of the act being entirely given over to a nervous mechanism."[28] While Neisser is optimistic that future physiologists will discover new properties of the nervous system which constitute this type of existent, he is waiting in vain; "for its part the organism presents physiochemical analysis not with the practical difficulties of a complex object but with the theoretical difficulty of a meaningful being."[29] On the other hand, any attempt to view the animation of the organism, including its perceptual explorations, as regulated by anticipations, hypotheses, plans or any mental entities whatsoever, is simply to flip the Cartesian coin, for only once the body has been assumed to be a blind, unintelligent and, moreover, mechanical entity are such *ad hoc* hypotheses required to explain or reconstitute meaningful human involvement. However, how a non-physical entity moves a physical one remains the intrinsic dilemma. This is why Merleau-Ponty would claim that in the case of the perceiver as well as the perceived, intellectualism is but a tardy and ineffective correction of realism, which has already replaced the concrete phenomenal body with abstract physicalistic principles. However, as he says, two abstractions do not add up to a concretion and will always render insoluble problems regarding the relation of the two abstract orders, due to their mutual exclusiveness. The only way to avoid the dilemmas of this approach is to do with the perceiver what has been done with the perceived: abandon naturalistic presuppositions with the intellectualistic hypotheses they support and require, return to preobjective experience, and describe it directly as it shows itself.

Let us distinguish the perceiving body, first only in a preliminary way, from the perceived (objectified) body and its supposed intellectualistic supplementations. Everyone agrees that human bodies exist in the world, may be perceived as such, and may be analyzed as an object among other objects. But such a viewpoint (intrinsically that of the other) and its analysis are not exhaustive of the body; specifically they fail to bring to light its *perceiving* character, the peculiar intentional or self-transcending aspect of the body, its first-person presence. For the latter it is necessary to recognize the body not merely as disclosed but as a *disclosive* entity. As a perceiving body, I am a viewpoint on the situation rather than merely another object in it. Even the most elementary reflexive comportments such as blinking my eyes or withdrawing my hand from a flame indicate that I am *relating to* light and heat, that they are meaningful *for me* as a bodily being. Here we are acknowledging an irreducible preobjectivity encountered in any comprehensive description of the body.

> The reflex, insofar as it opens itself to the meaning of the situation, and perception, insofar as it does not first of all posit an object of knowledge and is an intention of our whole being, are modalities of a *preobjective view* which we call being-in-the-world. . . . It is because it is a preobjective view that being-in-the-world can be distinguished from every third person process, from every modality of res extensa, as from every cogitation and can effect the union of the physiological and the psychic.[30]

As I perceive, my body has the thickness and particular positionality characteristic of a *thing* and is therefore different from cognition, which is not so limited, but it is also *sensitively aiming* at, *apprehending* its surroundings and is in this aspect different from physical things. In other words I not only *have* a body visible to myself and others, but I *am* my body. "I cannot understand the function of the living body except by enacting it myself and except insofar as I *am* a body which rises toward the world".[31] Supporting or subtending (as Husserl says "holding sway on")[32] my situation, my phenomenal body is not yet one of the objects disclosed nor a high altitude spectating cognition. My phenomenal body is an original upsurge or point of view on things and as such intrinsically eludes objectification as its hitherside, as my tacit means of communication with objects.

> I observe external objects with my body, I handle them, examine them, walk around them, but my body itself is a thing which I do not observe; in order to be able to do so, I should need the use of a second body which itself would be unobservable . . . for if I can, with my left hand, feel my right hand as it touches an object, the right hand as an object is not the right hand as it touches . . . insofar as it sees or touches the world, the body may therefore neither be seen nor touched.[33]

The perceiving body is at work in the world, and its self-effacing thrust toward its surroundings is concretely part and parcel of the accomplishment of objectivity.

It is of the very character of the phenomenal body to forget itself in its modest obsession with its surroundings. This tacit manner of being is so familiar, close at hand that it even remains on the hitherside of the body's apprehension of itself as a thing in the midst of the world. In self-perception, the body degrades itself from its primordial character as the *origin of space* into a mere object in space, and this is the basis of realistic analysis. Merleau-Ponty resists and reverses this natural direction in order to recapture concretely this hitherside of perception, the body's own perspective which, neither thing nor idea, he calls the "body-subject." In its original enactment, our visual presence is given phenomenally as a curious absence (from the order of things seen), an invisibility that allows reification only by an other, from whose perspective alone the body can be objectified.

> In the matter of living appearance, my visual body includes a large gap at the level of the head, but biology was ready to fill in that gap, to explain it through the structure of the eyes, to instruct me in what the body really is, showing that I have a retina and a brain like other men and like the corpses which I dissect, and that, in short, the surgeon's instrument could infallibly bring to light in this indeterminate zone of my head the exact replica of plates illustrating the human anatomy. . . . Now the psychologist could imitate the scientist and, for a moment at least, see his body as others saw it and conversely see the bodies of others as mechanical things with no inner life.[34]

On the other hand, inasmuch as mechanical explanations of vision do not exhaust its perceptive intelligence (precisely because they strip first-person experience away), idealism is required to further fill in this absent presence, this gap. Then it is said that controlling physical movements are ideas – plans, hypotheses, anticipations and the like. But the *origins* of such cognitions and the manners in which they would *relate* to the real world always remain obscure since cognition is by definition of an order of existence excluded from the physical domain. Merleau-Ponty leads psychology away from these ill founded alternatives: "To concern oneself with psychology is necesssarily to encounter, beneath objective thought, which moves among already constituted things, a first opening on things without which there would be no objective knowledge"[35] – whether anatomy, physiology, cognitive science and the like.

The Body-Subject of Perception

Rejecting the naiveté of realism and idealism, Merleau-Ponty attempted to return descriptively to the original situation in which "things" and "ideas" come to pass. At the heart of this situation, he finds the living body, at once ambiguously "of the stuff of the world" and an "invisible disclosure of the world." The body-subject constitutes the unitary ontological domain of the perceiver. We will briefly enumerate some of the features we have focused on more extensively elsewhere.[36]

Merleau-Ponty considers the body-subject to be a third constituent, hitherto taken for granted, in the figure-ground organization of the perceptual field. The body subtends the perceived as lifting does weight, the caress smoothness, the embrace size. This peculiar part of the background, the perceiving body, is at once both sentient and sensible, active and passive. Merleau-Ponty conceives of the "exercised" and "undergone" aspects of perception as dialectically related, i.e., internally implying each other. The lighting does not merely assail the perceiver but is taken up by vision, whose work it anticipates in the way it ranges through space and sweeps over contours much like a blind man's cane. The body's activity can mimic and follow that of things because it is one of their kin. The body aims freely and yet remains bound to its surroundings. More than a mere thing or intellectual notion, the perceiving body is a praxic power which purposefully inhabits situations. Its various "parts" each have their own unique potential for sensing and acting. These are enveloped or taken up in a unitary intention through which they are organized according to their respective functional/presentational value for the particular work being done. For distal relations, I extend my gaze and my hands fall to my sides; my visual space correlatively spreads out before me and the tactile recedes to the background. The different sensory modalities of the perceiving body access different features of the world, and these become differentiated, articulated, and coordinated by means of globally organized work. I can feel the same bristley texture of a brush with both my right and left hands, and even with my scalp, as I brush my hair. At the same time I may see the texture and hear a bristley sound as the brush glides over my hands. The "different" senses, already communing in a single bodily intention aimed at and bound to a single feature of the surroundings, therefore require no synthesis. The body-subject tacitly subtends the entire figure-ground organization of the spatio-temporal field, forming a single practical system with the surroundings it mirrors in pairing off with them.

In perception we find the body, neither a thing closed in on itself nor an unextended idea, is sensitive to things as one of their very order, that shares their very style. Things move and I move too. The cohesive unity in which the body manifests and exercises its different parts is immediately reflected in the variegated cohesion of the perceptual world, which is at once tangible, visible, sonorous, etc., and whose specific features emerge in perfect synchrony with the way the body's diacritical organization gears into it. An orchestrated intentionality toward the world it opens upon, the body skillfully comports itself through time and space, giving birth to the very order that thereby comes to pass. The body-subject I am is at once an anonymous, momentary presence and a personal, habitual and cultural-historical dilation of being-in-the-world. Spontaneously engaged in its tasks from the start, in and through the situations of which it is an intertwined part, the body originates work and, reenacting it, institutes sedimented, abiding potentialities for the perceptual disclosure of existence. Just as the perceiving body is not limited to its actual, momentary organization but "hinges on" these greater potentials, the perceptual world is given as extending beyond what is actually apprehended at the moment into hidden but virtually perceivable horizons which beckon further exploration. In this way the perceptual field is an open one with an inner depth and outer expanse; it is a *world*. A given perceptual Gestalt contains smaller Gestalten and resides in larger Gestalten thereby always intrinsically implying more to explore. One such latency of the perceptual world always present is the perceiver itself, which may be doubled back upon and made visible by self-sentience, which thereby discloses this paradoxical nexus of sensing and sensibility. Besides direct self-sentience, I am always implicitly locating myself in my apprehension of other things, which reflect my position, movement, size, substantiality etc. as much as my position, movement, size and substantiality disclose theirs. The perceiving body and its perceived surroundings are the measure of each other in their intertwinement on a single ontological plane which entails their immediate reciprocity. Perceiver and perceived at once form an inextricable proximity and an irremediable remoteness as they turn about each other reversibly, meeting but never coinciding completely. Perception is, therefore, always imperfect and incomplete, an open and only relatively stable circle of world disclosiveness.

Merleau-Ponty's Contribution

Neisser rightfully rejects the notion of information processing inasmuch as he calls our attention to a preexisting structure in the perceived world that needs no constitutive operation (and without which such operations fall into absurdity), but he does not consider the perceived world alone sufficient to account for important aspects of perception such as occasional errors, skills, individual differences, and generally the contributions of the perceiver. Merleau-Ponty is in full agreement here and his description of the perceiving body provides a key to these aspects of perception.

To understand perceptual error, we need not postulate a faulty internal representation, a mere subjectivity over and against an objective stimulus – a problem that could never be resolved! We need only recognize that perception occurs from a limited perspective which, though fully in the bodily reality of the things it attempts to perceive, does not apprehend them all at once in complete, clear, distinct truth. The brown patch in the grass that from a distance appears to be a bird is apprehended from closer bodily range as a leaf. Error is a *partial perception* that may be corrected in time through the body's skill. The *situated* body is thus the seat of perception's shortcomings but also the very (and only) means of their resolution. It is within the domain of the body's limited yet always skillfully surpassable perspective in the situation that error and veridicality are both comprehensible in dialectical relation.

One aspect of individual differences in perception has to do with the unique history of the body-subject, which rises out of relative anonymity as it develops particular habitual ways of perceiving in the course of personal, individual projects. For Merleau-Ponty, individual differences also have to do with the related fact that the perceptual world shows itself in concrete succession; as a diacritical reality, even a single property cannot be separated from the history of situations previously perceived, and that history may in some respects be unique to each person. Even on a more anonymous level, when I place my two hands in neutral water after one had been in hot and the other in cold, the water feels cool to one hand and warm to the other not only because perceived temperature of the water is a *relational* value in two different temporal melodies, but because my hands have themselves become hot and cold and are being transformed in different directions by what for objective thought can only be the same milieu. Perception's multiperspectivity rests in that of the body-subject.

Unencumbered by the biologization and cognitivization of the perceiver, Merleau-Ponty has extensively described *how* the perceiver explores the surroundings. Schemata need not be postulated to "direct" movement because the perceiver is already a moving body. With such homunculi and their infinite regressions left to those who ignore the concreteness of perception, Merleau-Ponty shows how the body itself pairs off with the world, works at accepting it, and undergoes structural modification in order to meet this other at which it aims and to which it always remains bound. The perceiver can relate to the perceived in such a reciprocal way only because, far from their being separated ontologically, they are but two mutually dependent moments of a single manner of being or flesh; and yet since they never strictly coincide, they stand in an open and potentially evolving chiasm.

Finally, with Merleau-Ponty we discover a view of the perceiver that is complimentary to the characteristics of the perceptual world which Neisser acknowledges as immediate and irreducible: its synaesthesia, physiogonomy, and affordances or demand characteristics. The perceiving body works from the whole down; its parts are not pregiven as such but develop out of a primordially syncretic unity. The singularity of the body's intention entails a transversal communion of sensory aspects to such an extent that loud colors, sharp sounds, bright tastes and synaesthesia in general are the rule rather than the exception. The functional differentiation of the senses is a developmental achievement of the body. Affordances such as "edible," "breakable," "slippery," and "sheltering," are unmediated earmarks of a field first disclosed by a praktagnostic body inhabiting it in action, whose potentials are mirrored and infused in objects. It is the whole, functional body – not neurons nor ideas – which eats and walks, and it is from this vantage point that the perceived world's form is originally apprehended. Hypotheses and plans, far from explaining these perceptual phenomena, presuppose the latter as the homeland upon which they are founded in the overall structure of existence. Merleau-Ponty allows a place for representation, decisions, and creations in dialectical relations with perception, but when one attempts to account for the origins of perception in these spheres, the order of existence is inverted in a way that precludes understanding either perception or the "higher" dialectics.

Summary and Conclusion

Although Merleau-Ponty's phenomenology of perception places him in total opposition to the cognitive psychology of perception in the narrow sense, namely cybernetic theory, the forward edge of the cognitive revolution as exemplified by Neisser opposes information processing models as Merleau-Ponty would. Neisser criticizes its atomistic, physicalistic assumptions concerning the nature of the stimulus, which alone necessitate postulations of internal processing operations to explain perception. Viewing perception not as an internal representation but a relation with surrounding objects, he calls for a *description* of the world of ordinary perception as opposed to ever more sophisticated conceptual or experimental hypotheses about the process. Beginning to carry out this directive, he finds perceptual objects immediately given as synaesthetic, physiognomic, and useful. He views perception as an open-ended process through which a historically limited person explores hitherto indeterminate but pre-structured aspects of the world beyond himself. Merleau-Ponty agrees this far. However, in conceptualizing the perceiver in terms of *preexisting schemata*, defined physiologically or intellectually, Neisser himself falls back into the Cartesian tradition, loses touch with the original phenomenal presence of the perceiver, and engages in a hypothetical constructivism which creates more problems than it solves. Namely, Neisser is unable to specify, beyond biologistic conjecture and intellectualistic analogy, just what these schemata are, how they originate, and how they relate to "outside" objects. Merleau-Ponty surpasses this forward edge of cognitive psychology by addressing everyday perception with the rigor of concrete description which leads him to the notion, still unknown to cognitive psychology, of the body-subject. In showing that the actual details of ordinary perception require this radical comprehension of incarnate subjectivity and in distinguishing it from any sort of cognition, Merleau-Ponty opposes the whole cognitive psychology of perception.

A radical revolution in psychology requires a new approach and methodology based rigorously on its subject matter rather than on a new technology that remains implicitly tied to an inadequate philosophy. From mechanical hardware to intellectual software, the computer is but a stilted metaphor for the human being. However amusing, fascinating, or even elegant such props may be, they can only detour the proper work of psychological interrogation, whose task is to understand people. The original presence of the person, already tacitly manifest and to be deduced from no other, is different from a computer; humanity remains the measuring stick against which the computer is judged as well as its judge and creator. Far from explaining existence, the computer and the Cartesian ontology to which cognitive psychology as a whole remains tied are mere cultural objects embedded within existence and supply but a meager reflection of the rest of the region in which they reside and on which they depend. Perceptual processes in particular demand that we abandon the relatively abstract concepts of mind and matter and make psychology more concrete. Although existence contains dumb mechanisms, lucid ideas, and genuinely constructive human processes, it is not exhausted in these, and it is the peculiar responsibility of psychology to address the whole life of persons. Cognition is a part of existence and cognitive psychology must be careful not to mistake that part for the whole or to uncritically impose its principles on other parts, lest it fall into the worst professional blindness. Perception is a primary and original moment of existence not resting on cognition but, on the contrary, taken up, elaborated upon, and surpassed by the latter. Only when perception, memory, language, and thought are each comprehended in their own peculiarities can their complex relations in the unity of existence be understood.

Notes

1. R.E. Mayer, *The Promise of Cognitive Psychology* (San Francisco: Freeman, 1981).

2. See J. Piaget, *The Construction of Reality in the Child*, trans. M. Cook (New York: Basic Books, 1954); N. Chomsky, *Syntactic Structures* (The Hague: Mouton, 1957); J.S. Bruner, J.J. Goodnow, and G.A. Austin, *A Study of Thinking* (New York: Wiley, 1956).

3. R.E. Mayer, *Cognitive Psychology*, p. 7.

4. G.A. Miller, E. Galanter, K.H. Pribram, *Plans and the Structure of Behavior* (New York: Holt, Rhinehart, and Winston, 1960).

5. U. Neisser, *Cognitive Psychology* (New York: Appleton-Crofts, 1967).

6. E.G., P.M. Lindsay and D.A. Norman, *Human Information Processing* (New York: Academic Press, 1972).

7. H.A. Simon, *Models of Thought* (New Haven: Yale University Press, 1979), p. 361.

8. U. Neisser, *Cognition and Reality* (San Francisco: Freeman, 1976), p. 16.

9. J.J. Gibson, *The Ecological Approach to Visual Perception (Boston: Houghton Mifflin, 1979)*.

10. U. Neisser, *Cognition and Reality*, p. 19.

11. Ibid., p. 19.

12. Ibid., p. 34.

13. Ibid., p. 7.

14. J.J. Gibson, *The Senses Considered As Perceptual Systems* (Boston: Houghton Mifflin, 1966).

15. U. Neisser, *Cognition and Reality*, p. 9.

16. Ibid., p. 19.

17. U. Neisser, *Cognitive Psychology*, p. 4.

18. U. Neisser, *Cognitive and Reality*, p. 14.

19. Ibid., p. 71.

20. Ibid, p. 63.

21. Ibid., p. 54.

22. Ibid., pp. 54, 62, 186.

23. R. L. Gregory, *The Intelligent Eye* (New York: McGraw Hill, 1970); J.S. Bruner, *Beyond the Information Given: Studies in the Psychology of Knowing* (New York: W.W. Norton, 1973).

24. F.J. Wertz, "Revolution in Perceptual Psychology: Dialogue with the New Look," in Giorgi, Barton, and Maes, eds., *Duquesne Studies in Phenomenological Psychology*, Vol. 4 (Pittsburgh: Duquesne University Press, 1983).

25. U. Neisser, *Cognition and Reality*, pp. 28, 132.

26 U. Neisser, *Memory Observed* (San Francisco: Freeman, 1982).

27. M. Merleau-Ponty, *Phenomenology of Perception*, trans. C. Smith (London: Routledge & Kegan Paul, 1962) p. 198.

28. Ibid., p. 55.

29. Ibid., p. 56.

30. Ibid., pp. 79–80.

31. Ibid., p. 75.

32. E. Husserl, *Ideas*, trans. W.R. Boyce Gibson (New York: Collier, 1962).

33. M. Merleau-Ponty, *Phenomenology of Perception*, pp. 91–92.

34. Ibid., p. 95.

35. Ibid., p. 96.

36. F.J. Wertz, "Cognitive Psychology and the Understanding of Perception," in Giorgi, ed., *The Phenomenological Critique of Cognitive Psychology* (Pittsburgh: Duquesne University Press, forthcoming).

16. The Structure of the Consciousness of the Child: Merleau-Ponty and Piaget

Richard Rojcewicz

There is a classical locus for the phenomenological critique of the cognitive approach to child psychology, taking the work of Piaget as a paradigm for the latter and the lectures of Merleau-Ponty at the Sorbonne as the most explicit attempt at the former. From 1949 to 1952, Merleau-Ponty was a professor of child psychology and pedagogy in Paris, and many of the courses he offered then dealt with Piaget. Perhaps his critique is most fully worked out in his course, "Structure and Conflicts of the Consciousness of the Child,"[1] whence the title and the themes of the present paper.

According to Merleau-Ponty, the term "structure" was specifically chosen in order to signify that the child's consciousness differs from the adult's not only by its content but also by its organization. The consciousness of the child has its own structure; the child is not an adult in miniature, with a consciousness like that of the adult only imperfect, incomplete. Instead, the child possesses an "altogether different equilibrium." The consciousness of the child must be respected as a positive phenomenon in itself and must not simply be seen as privative in relation to what it will become.

Our task then is to compare Merleau-Ponty and Piaget on this notion of structure. Specifically, just what is this structure of the child's consciousness according to Merleau-Ponty. Does Piaget also recognize it? If Piaget does not, then where does the essential difference between them lie, what does Piaget offer in its place, and what sort of critique can the phenomenologist level at him?

285

We will approach these more general questions by means of an analysis of two specific examples taken from the work of Piaget and of the criticism of it by Merleau-Ponty. The two examples concern the perception of the child and the thought of the child; or, more precisely, the child's conception of thought and the child's perceptual world.

The first question is what, according to the child, thought is.[2] Piaget uses an interrogatory method; he asks children, "With what do you think?" and then interprets their answers. To a certain extent, Piaget is aware of the dangers of questioning children so directly and making them formulate theses where perhaps they would never do so left to themselves. Piaget does not give equal weight to all responses, and is careful to distinguish between the random, the suggested, the liberated, and the spontaneous answer. He even limits himself, he says, to questions which he has found that children ask themselves on their own. Perhaps it will be shown, nevertheless, that Piaget is not sufficiently aware of the dangers of his adult interpretations.

Piaget finds that children progress through three stages in their conception of the nature of thought. In general, the progress consists in a gradual immaterializing of thought. That is, the child is first materialistic and only gradually recognizes that thought is something immaterial. Initially, children say that they think with the voice, the mouth, or even the ears. They have no notion of the psychical as distinct from the physical. There follows an intermediate stage in which we see an influence of adult notions to which the child has been exposed, but these are not fully and consistently incorporated. For example, the child now says that he thinks with the brain. But it turns out that the child is still conceiving of thought as a voice; only now it is a voice in the head which speaks to the voice in the mouth. The final, adult, stage is reached, according to Piaget, when two conditions are met: first, thought is localized in the head, and second, thought is completely immaterial.

In general, Merleau-Ponty's critique is that Piaget is translating the child's experience into his own adult categories instead of attempting to understand it as it is. These adult categories are dichotomies: physical-psychical; thing-idea; material-immaterial. For Merleau-Ponty, the child has none of these conceptions and it is wrong to call the child either a materialist or an immaterialist, in the adult sense. In fact, there is some doubt about whether these categories are spontaneously used by adults or whether instead they are merely conventional. For example, Piaget himself maintains that the adult level is reached when the child localizes thought in the brain and at the same time divorces thought from matter. As Merleau-Ponty points out,

Piaget does not seem to notice that for both these conditions to be met (immateriality and localization), the dichotomy between the material and the immaterial has to be abandoned.

According to Merleau-Ponty, when the child speaks of the body, he intends not the physical body but the phenomenal body. The child has no acquaintance with the body as science conceives it. He has only his more primordial intimate acquaintance with it as a system of means allowing him to make contact with the world. Taken on these terms, the voice, the mouth, and the ears are not material substances but are simply expressions of the phenomena of speech. The child is saying that he thinks in language. By ascribing thought to language, the child is not making it a substance; he is referring to his interior experience of those situations in which thought goes on speaking and listening.

It would appear that what Piaget finds lacking and what is at the root of his contention that young children are materialistic is their inability to conceive an alternative between opposition of the physical and the psychical. What he is ignorant of is the phenomenal body as neither the physical body nor the ideal body. On the other hand, it is just this phenomenal realm that is most evident to the child and it is what he will innocently express until influenced by adult objective notions.

For both Piaget and Merleau-Ponty, there is, of course, a progressive influence of adult ways of thinking on the child. For Piaget, this is altogether a positive influence. For Merleau-Ponty, however, something is lost in this process; the adult's viewpoint is not in every way superior to the child's. Consider, for instance, their respective views on children's drawings. A child, when shown a cube and told to draw what he sees, will invariably draw all the sides of the cube as squares simultaneously. Or, when presented with a face in profile, the child will draw it as a full face. For Piaget,[3] this is intellectual realism. The child is drawing not what he sees but what he knows. The visual realism of the adult's perspectival drawnings is superior. That is how things look in reality. For Merleau-Ponty, however, the child's drawing has a kind of priority; it is a positive mode of expression. The child is representing in his own way that to which he is present. Under the adult influence, the child will no longer draw what he sees but what he has been taught that he really sees, what he believes that he ought to see. It is the adult way of drawing, then, that manifests intellectual realism. In a way, the child's first drawings are closer to a phenomenology of perception – at least insofar as natural free perception bypasses the signs, the sensations, and the perspectives, and goes straight to the things. To concentrate on these signs and perspectives and to put them prior to the things themselves is to substitute analytic perception for free preception. It is to substitute a theory of perception for perception itself; it is to be untrue to the phenomenon of perception.

Likewise, it is in a way more adequate to lived experience to say that we think with the ears than to say that we think with the brain. The child's expression is quaint and naive. But the adult's is artificial and learned, that is, it is not from personally lived experience. Merleau-Ponty says that the material in the work of Piaget is more convincing than his interpretations, that there is often a large gap between what the child expresses and what Piaget comprehends. Perhaps we could say that it is the phenomenal, the lived, and the phenomenological, that the child is expressing if we interpret it properly and include that to which Piaget is oblivious . For Merleau-Ponty, this would be what is original to the structure of the consciousness of the child and what is not accessible to the adult. As Merleau-Ponty puts it, "That is how we need to understand the expression, 'structure of consciousness.' The child is capable of certain spontaneous kinds of conduct which have been rendered impossible to the adult because of the influence of and obedience to the ideas of his culture."[4] Yet, it is not so much that the child's consciousness is foreign to the adult's consciousness, or that the structure of his or her consciousness is irrecoverable by the adult; it is only incomprehensible to a certain kind of adult mentality.

I will turn now to our second main topic, the perception of the child. Here Piaget does not ask the child, "With what do you perceive?" Piaget would expect it to be self-evident to the child that one sees with one's eyes, and one hears with one's ears, so he feels no need to ask. Piaget gets at the child's perception in an indirect way, by observing the behavior of the child in relation to the sensory stimuli.[5]

In general, Merleau-Ponty's critique is that Piaget is giving a classical intellectualistic account of perception. He is treating perception as an incomplete act of intelligence rather than as a positive phenomenon, and so he misses that very thing he should grasp, namely, the world perceived by the child.

For Piaget, perception is to be understood in terms of what he calls sensory-motor intelligence. At first sight, this seems rather promising. To join the sensory and the motor into a unity already implies the surpassing of the traditional dichotomies between thing and idea, physical and psychical. For, following Merleau-Ponty, if the sensory-motor is a unitary phenomenon, then the sensory cannot be understood simply as an act of consciousness, the contemplation of a content, the possession of a quality; and the motor cannot be understood simply as a physical, third-person event. For understood in these traditional ways, the one is of the order of consciousness and the other is of the order of things, and there is no possible internal connection between them. Also, to speak of sensory-motor intelligence implies that there is a kind of knowledge beneath intelligence proper; this would be perceptual intelligence, a perceptual organization irreducible to ideal organization. For Merleau-Ponty, however, Piaget does not fulfill the promise contained in the notion of sensory-motor intelligence but falls back into intellectualism.

Piaget holds that perception is a special case of sensory-motor activity; it is to be understood in terms of sensory-motor structures, sensory-motor schemata. A sensory-motor schema is a schema of assimilation, and this is to be contrasted with accomodation. For Piaget, the organism does not passively relate to stimuli but elaborates them in an original fashion. (Merleau-Ponty, of course, would agree with this so far.) But how does this elaboration take place and what does it involve? This elaboration is described by Piaget as a treatment, a modification, a filtration, or an organization on the part of the subject. Or again, there is a reciprocity between stimulus and response. The stimuli are not received wholesale but are filtered through a structure; they are accepted by being fitted into or incorporated into a structure ready to receive them. Without this structure already prepared, the subject is oblivious to the corresponding connections amongst the stimuli. This internal structure is a schema. Assimilation is the organization of the stimuli to make them fit into the schema and be grasped by the subject accordingly. Accomodation is the alteration of the internal schemata to make them organize the data in more productive ways.

How do the sensory-motor schemata operate in the perception of the child? Piaget takes up this question by observing perceptual phenomena such as the constancies of size and form. What he attempts to show is that these perceptual phenomena are dependent on a prior schema which organizes the raw data in such a way as to produce the perceived constancies. The perception results from an application of a schema. These internal, prior, sensory-motor schemata are primarily the schema of the permanent object, the schema of physical causality, and the schema of space. How do these schemata arise? They are acquired by a process of decentering. For Piaget, the "universe of the young baby is a world without objects, consisting of shifting and unsubstantial tableaux."[6] There are neither single spaces, nor orderly connections, nor unitary things that are causes of the manifold appearances. This is egocentrism in the sense that there are only shifting tableaux; the child has no inkling that they come from anything outside. The child gradually decenters. In Piaget's own words: "The little child gradually ceases to relate everything to his states and his own actions and begins to substitute for a world of fluctuating tableaux without spatio-temporal consistency or external causality a universe of permanent objects structured according to an objectified and spatialized causality."[7] To take causality as an instance, at first the child knows only his own body as a cause. If pulling a string in his crib shakes a rattle and produces a pleasant noise, the child conceives his body as producing this effect in a magical manner without any intermediaries. Little by little, and mainly by experiencing disappointments, the child learns the causal connections that actually exist in the world. This is decentering, and it is by this process that the child also builds up the schemata of space and the permanent object.

For Piaget there is a difference between perception and sensory-motor schemata. Organized, meaningful perception, for example the perception of constancy, is made possible by schemata which are anterior to it, especially by the schema of the permanent object. The schema must first be acquired, then it is used to regulate the raw data. The schema has a priority which is both logical and temporal. It is logical because the schema has to organize material which is without its own synthesis. It is temporal because the schema has to antedate the perception: the schema of the permanent object is acquired at approximately six months, but the perception of the tunnel effect (perceptual constancy) is not acquired until eight months. How, then, do the schemata operate? They regulate the sensory data; they are applied whenever the subject is presented with raw data which are analogous to the data which the schema has already organized in the past. With age and practice, this process becomes automatic and scarcely noticeable.

It is now obvious why Merleau-Ponty calls this a classical intellectualistic account of perception. The regulation by the anterior schemata is a sort of projection of memories, an application of an ideal meaning onto contents which are meaningless in themselves. Piaget does speak of both sensory-motor and intellectual schemata. The schemata under discussion (the permanent object, space, causality) are called by him sensory-motor schemata, but it is clear that this is only because for him they are acquired when the child does not yet have the ability to represent things in their absence, the symbolic function proper to intelligence itself, in short, language. But, in fact, they do not at all differ in function from intellectual schemata. They are meanings or organizations which do not derive, to put it another way, from a passive synthesis (a synthesis immanent in the apprehension of the material to be synthesized), but from an active intellectual one (a synthesis posterior to the apprehension of the raw contents, which organization is subsequently imposed on them). Merleau-Ponty often criticizes the notion of perception as a projection of memories or an imposition of order onto a previously unorganized matter, and he does so again in this context. The criticism is this: in order for the imposition of meaning onto the raw data to be possible, there must be something in the present perception, in the data, that tells us that we have a case before us of a thing already encountered in the past to which the already acquired schema would be applicable. Supposedly, this something in the present perception would be its matter, since, after all, it is held to be without its own organization. But is matter indifferent to its form, such that the matter would remain constant while its form, its organization, would change? This is just what Merleau-Ponty, following Gestalt Psychology, denies. He notes, for instance, that when we reverse our perceptual figures and grounds, we do not merely obtain the same data, now synthesized in one way and previously in another way, but we are given a "whole new world."[8] That is to say, both form and content change. Merleau-Ponty's specific example is the seeing of the spaces between things as things, such as seeing the sky between the trees, or seeing land for what is meant to represent the sea on a map of a familiar shoreline. These are cases of change in organization, reversal of figures and grounds. The effect is global: it is not simply that now, for example, the sea stands out and the land recedes to the background, but rather that the very shapes change to the extent that they are no longer recognizable as familiar, and, in a way, we are confronted with a whole new world.

The phenomenon is explainable in Gestalt terms. The contour is the line which segregates the figure from the ground. But the contour does not have the same value on both of its sides: perceptually, the contour bounds only the figure. The contour belongs to the figure; it is the edge of the figure, the boundary of the figure. But the contour does not at all bound the background; the latter runs on unbroken beneath it. The contour gives shape only to the side of the figure; it gives no shape to the ground. When figures and grounds are reversed in perception, then conditions are transposed. What once had a shape is now shapeless, and vice versa. Thus, in the map example, the familiar shape of the land is lost when the sea is taken as figure, as land, for then the original land has no boundary – it has no shape at all. Shapes, then, which might seem to be a matter of mere content, indifferent to organization, are not so at all. Furthermore, Gestalt Psychology shows that even colors, perhaps the paradigm of raw data, are not unaffected by the way the perceptual field is organized.[9] Colors change when we reverse our figures and grounds. When figure becomes ground its color loses saturation and variegation. Sometimes even hue can change. Magnitudes, also depend to a certain extent on the particular figure-ground organization, that is, the same objective distance can appear greater when taken as figure rather than as ground.

The point is this: if contents (sc. shape, color, magnitude) are not indifferent to form, then it cannot be possible to impose meaning onto a previously unorganized matter as if the matter could be recognized as the same and so bear the transfer of sense. There must be something in the present perception that tells us we have a case of a thing already known in the past to which the acquired schema would be applicable. But since contents are not indifferent to form, it cannot be said that we apply the same schema whenever we recognize the same matter – for, again, the matter is the same only when the organization is the same. The present perception must already be organized like the past perception to make the application of the schema possible. But then the application of the schema also is rendered superfluous. Its work is accomplished already; the appearances already look like schematized appearances and do not need to await the imposition of a meaning from the outside, from a source beyond the faculty of grasping the contents.

Another way of looking at the issue is to say that the notion of raw data or raw contents is fundamentally unsound. A level of contents, of sensations, of meaningless sense qualities, is an abstraction. In the first place, if knowledge began with such a layer, meaning would never arise, for we would never be able to recognize in the contents any meaning which we would subsequently want to impose on it. There would be a layer of chaos and a layer of pure meaning, and the two layers would not communicate. There has to be something in the layer of contents which is the *point d'appui* for the recognition of meaning. But, then, this *point d'appui* is enough; the application of a schema is superfluous since its work is precisely to constitute a *point d'appui*. Secondly, a meaningless layer of contents is nowhere to be found in experience. If matter is not indifferent to form, if matter depends on form, then matter is never given without some form or other. The simplest and earliest perceptions have some organization and meaning, at least the rudimentary meanings contained in the figure-ground structure. A completely undifferentiated field is not visible; it is the same as keeping one's eyes closed. There must be some minimal differentiation; there must be a contour separating figure from ground, and we have seen that the two sides of a contour are filled with meaning.

For Merleau-Ponty, then, since he refuses to admit raw data or sensations, there must be an order immanent in the material, an order which arises by means of the matter's own spontaneous organization. This is what is peculiar to the phenomenon of perception and is that to which Piaget is oblivious. For Piaget, all order is in the schemata; it is intellectual. His attempt to impose order from them to the perceptual level is misbegotten. Once more, we could say, what Piaget fails to recognize in the child, in original perception, is the phenomenal realm, an organization or structure which is neither sheer chaos nor ideal meaning. For Merleau-Ponty, the child's perception, like all perception, is always organized and never consists in chaos or mere shifting tableaux. To be conscious of pure chaos is impossible in principle so long as consciousness is always consciousness of something. This does not mean that the structure of the child's perceptual world is the same as the adult's; the child's world only has global structures with little differentiation. But, right from the start, there are ensembles which deserve to be called things and which constitute a world. This would express the ultimate sense of Merleau-Ponty's statement that Piaget misses the world perceived by the child. For Piaget, the child perceives nothing like a world.

We can perhaps sum up and conclude this discussion of perception in Piaget by recounting the one instance in which Piaget does record children's own naive view of perception.[10] Children often call vision a light or say that the eyes themselves emit a little light. For Piaget, of course, this is simply more evidence of the child's substantialism. But it may be that it is again not such bad phenomenology, not a bad expression of a phenomenology of perception. It is certainly closer to lived experience to say that sight is going out towards things than to say it is a coming in of stimulation from them. This latter is the adult's learned answer; it is only true in a certain sense (the sole sense Piaget accepts as valid). The child's naive answer is also true – and in a more primordial sense; it is in this same way that the child's drawings are also true representations. The child is in touch with lived experience and that is what his statements and drawings represent. Piaget can only denigrate the child in favor of the adult, and this is because of his blindness to phenomenal or lived experience, his inability to be where the child is. Perhaps Piaget should have taken to heart a phrase he himself uses (although, of course, with his own intention, one which gives it a wholly different sense than ours): "The child explains the man as well as and often better than the man explains the child."[11]

In a final section, let us examine briefly Piaget's response to Merleau-Ponty's criticism. Piaget was certainly aware of Merleau-Ponty's courses at the Sorbonne; in fact, Piaget was his successor there. In a charming anecdote, Piaget relates that on the first set of examinations submitted to him, some of the candidates did not realize that there had been a change and wrote to the effect that "Piaget has not understood anything, as Prof. Merleau-Ponty has proved." Piaget says that he raised their grades because of it.[12]

Despite this good humor, Piaget, of course, rejects Merleau-Ponty and phenomenology. Piaget sees all phenomenology as restricted to an analysis of the individual phenomenologist's own consciousness, versus Piaget's own method which allows him to study other consciousnesses, those of children, for example, and have other people partake of his experiments and thereby verify them. This notion of verification is essentially all there is to Piaget's critique: phenomenology cannot be verified since it is simply introspection, since it remains within the phenomenologist's own consciousness. Phenomenology, therefore, is only philosophy. It is wisdom, but it is not science, not knowledge:

> What the psychologist, mindful of verification, asks is simply that the subject of the intuition should not always be the same as that which experiences it. In other words, I have confidence in what I observe in a child of 7 or 12 because, if I am unsure as to what is going on in one subject I can observe another, etc. and that, after 100, I have sufficient cases to make all the cross-checkings and tests that I need. But if I observe in myself "intuitions" that I experience, from the first I only observe the already elaborated, and then what I see is so bound up with my conception of it and so dependent on my intentions of finding this or that, that it becomes utterly impossible to trace with certainty the boundary between the intuitions of the introspector and that of the introspected.[13]

This is quite a remarkable quotation, for, among other things, we have just seen that, in substance, it is precisely the criticism that we have brought to the door of Piaget himself in view of Merleau-Ponty's phenomenology. That is, it is Piaget who has produced only the "already elaborated"; his conception of the world of the child is so bound up with his own adult interpretations and categories that he has completely missed what is original to child consciousness. Despite the 100 subjects and all the cross-checkings, etc., Piaget was still unable to "grasp what is going on," while Merleau-Ponty, supposedly contained within his own consciousness, was able to be unprejudiced about the child's consciousness. It is Piaget who has not gone beyond himself but has instead been wrapped up in his own consciousness.

Piaget's view that the phenomenologist's analyses remain confined to the philosopher's own consciousness (that is what makes him a philosopher, after all, rather than a scientist) is certainly a travesty. Phenomenology is reflective, but so is science. That fact does not make either one necessarily confined to a single consciousness; they are not introspections. Piaget tempers his remarks somewhat by noting, for example, that Buytendijk has written a phenomenology of woman, and this would seem not to be based on introspection, since Buytendijk is a man. Yet Piaget still maintains that this only seems to be so, for Buytendijk's work suffers from a "disturbing form of impressionism, as if phenomenological psychology, even when concerned with phenomena external to the ego, consisted in describing them as reflected by the ego."[14] Now, there is a sense in which there is something valid here: the phenomenology of the body, for instance, wants to deal with the lived body, the body as it is for the one whose body it is, the "subjective" body versus the "objective" one. But this in no way means that the phenomenologist is simply reflecting on the contents of his own consciousness, since, after all, the objective body, the body as science conceives it, is no different on this score. Science studies the body as it appears for the one who takes up the scientific attitude, "as reflected by the ego," then, the ego of the scientific attitude. Both the scientist and the phenomenologist observe as well as reflect. The phenomenologist does not experiment, of course, but the experimental is only one way of being empirical, and the phenomenologist is not oblivious to experimental findings. Phenomenology is empirical to such an extent that its rallying cry, "To the things themselves," can be understood as nothing but a call to observe before theorizing, to become familiar with the phenomena before holding them to be, in a radical sense, based on experience. In short, Piaget's view that phenomenology is just introspection could be called trivial in the etymological sense, except for the fact that even at the crossroads a more subtle view prevails.

Notes

1. Maurice Merleau-Ponty , "Structure et conflits de la conscience enfantine," *Bulletin de Psychologie* 18 (Nov. 1964): 171–202. Henceforth cited as "Structure et conflits."

2. Jean Piaget, *The Child's Conception of the World* (London: Routledge & Kegan Paul, 1922; reprint ed., Totowa, New Jersey: Littlefield, Adams & Co., 1975), pp. 37–60.

3. Jean Piaget and Bärbel Inhelder, *The Psychology of the Child*, trans. Helen Weaver (New York: Basic Books, 1969), pp. 63–67.

4. Merleau-Ponty, "Structure et conflits," p. 172.

5. Piaget & Inhelder, *The Psychology of the Child*, pp. 4–19.

6. Ibid., p. 14.

7. Ibid., p. 26.

8. M. Merleau-Ponty, *Phenomenology of Perception*, trans. Colin Smith (London: Routledge & Kegan Paul; Atlantic Highlands, N.J.: Humanities Press, 1962), pp. 15–16.

9. K. Koffka, "Perception: An Introduction to the Gestalt-Theorie," *The Psychology Bulletin* 19 (Oct. 1922):569.

10. Piaget, *The Child's Conception of the World*, p. 48.

11. Piaget & Inhelder, *The Psychology of the Child*, p. ix.

12. Jean Piaget, *Sagesse et illusions de la philosophie* (Paris: Presses universitaires de France, 1968), p. 37.

13. Jean Piaget, *Insights and Illusions of Philosophy* trans. Wolfe Mays (New York: World Publishing Co., 1971). p. 111.

14. Ibid., p. 142.

Contributors

CHRISTOPHER AANSTOOS is Assistant Professor of Psychology at West Georgia College. He is the editor of *Exploring the Lived World: Readings in Phenomenological Psychology* (West Georgia College, 1984).

KARL-OTTO APEL is Professor of Philosophy at the Goethe-Universität Frankfurt. His best known book is *Towards a Transformation of Philosophy* (Routledge and Kegan Paul, 1979).

PATRICK L. BOURGEOIS is Professor of Philosophy at Loyola University (New Orleans). He is the author of *Extension of Ricoeur's Hermeneutics* (Martinus Nijhoff, 1975).

THOMAS BUSCH is Professor of Philosophy at Villanova University 1975. He has written "Beyond the Cogito: The Question of the Continuity of Sartre's Thought," *The Modern Schoolman* (March 1983).

BERNARD DAUENHAUER is Professor of Philosophy at the University of Georgia. His *The Politics of Hope* is forthcoming from Routledge and Kegan Paul.

JOSEPH FLAY is Associate Professor of Philosophy at Pennsylvania State University. He is the author of *Hegel's Quest for Certainty* (SUNY Press, 1984).

DICK HOWARD is Professor of Philosophy at The State University of New York at Stony Brook. His most recent work is entitled *From Marx to Kant* (SUNY Press, 1985).

JAMES MARSH is Professor of Philosophy at Fordham University. Most recently he has written *Post-Cartesian Meditations: An Essay in Dialectical Phenomenology* (Fordham University Press, forthcoming).

HENRY PIETERSMA is Associate Professor of Philosophy at The University of Toronto. He has published articles on Brentano, Husserl, Heidegger, and Merleau-Ponty.

DAVID RASMUSSEN is Professor of Philosophy at Boston College. In addition to writing extensively in the area of Critical Theory he is the editor of the journal *Philosophy and Social Criticism*.

RICHARD ROJCEWICZ is co-director of the Simon Silverman Phenomenology Center of Duquesne University. He is the author of "Depth Perception in Merleau-Ponty: A Motivated Phenomenon," *Journal of Phenomenological Psychology* (Spring 1984).

SANDRA ROSENTHAL is Professor of Philosophy at Loyola University (New Orleans). Most recently she has written *Speculative Pragmatism* (University of Massachusetts Press, 1986).

GEORGE SCHRADER is Professor of Philosophy at Yale University, and has published on Kant and a number of Existentialist philosophers.

JACQUES TAMINIAUX is Professor of Philosophy at the Université Catholique de Louvain. His most recent work is *Dialectic and Difference* (Humanities Press, 1984).

FREDERICK WERTZ is Professor of Psychology at Fordham University. He is the editor of *Theoretical and Philosophical Psychology* (Bulletin of Division 24 of the American Psychological Association).

MEROLD WESTPHAL is Professor of Philosophy at Fordham University. He is the author of *God, Guilt, and Death: An Existential Phenomenology of Religion* (Indiana University Press, 1984).

BRUCE WILSHIRE is Professor of Philosophy at Rutgers University. His most recent book is entitled *Role Playing and Identity: The Limits of Theatre As Metaphor* (Indiana University Press, 1982).

Index of Proper Names

Adorno, T., 57-58, 61, 77, 82-83
Appel, K.-O., 56
Althusser, L., 217
Arendt, H., 90-91, 98
Aristotle, 16, 91, 99-100, 232, 237
Austin, J. L., 33-34, 42
Austin, G. A., 265

Ballard, E., 226
Bandura, A., 266
Bennett, J., 37, 48
Benveniste, E., 217
Berliner, H. J., 258
Bernstein, R., 76, 83
Bever, T. G., 253
Bosanquet, B., 190
Bradley, F. H., 190
Brentano, F., 10
Bruner, J. S., 265, 266, 272
Brunswik, E., 268
Buytendijk, F. J. J., 295
Bühler, K., 33

Carnap, R., 5-6, 8, 33
Carr, D., 116, 119, 139
Castanada, H.-N., 222
Chomsky, N., 265, 266
Cloonan, T. P., 257

de Beauvoir, S., 100
Derrida, J., 59
de Saussure, F., 43

Descartes, R., 3, 24, 48, 80, 94, 114,
   118, 140-141, 176, 182, 185, 216,
   222, 232-233, 271, 273, 274, 281
Dilthey, W., 117
Durkheim, E., 60

Einstein, A., 30

Foucault, M., 62
Feuerbach, L., 29
Frege, G., 11-12, 41
Freud, S., 64, 68, 70-71, 116, 136,
   143-144, 244

Gadamer, H.-G., 55-56, 64-66, 69-70,
   72-74, 76-78, 83-84, 136, 138-139,
   143
Galileo, G., 118, 140
Geertz, C., 217, 225
Gibson, J. J., 266, 268, 269
Giddens, A., 217, 226
Giorgi, A., 257
Goodnow, J. J., 265
Gregory, R. L., 272
Grice, P., 37, 39, 44, 48

Habermas, J., 33, 38-40, 44, 47, 54,
   57-58, 61-62, 64, 66, 68-70, 72-74,
   76, 84, 143
Hegel, G. W. F., 29, 55, 58, 74, 78, 80,
   82, 103-125, 136, 190, 204-206, 234